S0-DYA-624

All God's Creatures

DEVOTIONS *for* ANIMAL LOVERS

2024

All God's Creatures 2024

Published by Guideposts Books & Inspirational Media
100 Reserve Road, Suite E200
Danbury, CT 06810
Guideposts.org

Acknowledgments

Every attempt has been made to credit the sources of copyrighted material used in this book. If any such acknowledgment has been inadvertently omitted or miscredited, receipt of such information would be appreciated.

Scripture quotations marked (AMP) are taken from the *Amplified Bible*. Copyright © 2015 by The Lockman Foundation, La Habra, CA 90631. All rights reserved.

Scripture quotations marked (ERV) are taken from the *Holy Bible, Easy-to-Read Version*. Copyright © 2006 by Bible League international.

Scripture quotations marked (ESV) are taken from the *Holy Bible, English Standard Version*. Copyright © 2001 by Crossway Bibles, a division of Good News Publishers. Used by permission. All rights reserved.

Scripture quotations marked (GNT) are taken from the *Good News Translation*® (Today's English Version, Second Edition). Copyright © 1992 American Bible Society. All rights reserved.

Scripture quotations marked (KJV) are taken from the *King James Version of the Bible*.

Scripture quotations marked (MSG) are taken from *The Message*. Copyright © 1993, 1994, 1995, 1996, 2000, 2001, 2002 by Eugene H. Peterson.

Scripture quotations marked (NASB) are taken from the *New American Standard Bible*®. Copyright © 1960, 1971, 1977, 1995, 2020 by The Lockman Foundation. All rights reserved.

Scripture quotations marked (NIV) are taken from *The Holy Bible, New International Version*. Copyright © 1973, 1978, 1984, 2011 by Biblica, Inc. Used by permission of Zondervan. All rights reserved worldwide. zondervan.com

Scripture quotations marked (NKJV) are taken from *The Holy Bible, New King James Version*. Copyright © 1982 by Thomas Nelson.

Scripture quotations marked (NLT) are taken from the *Holy Bible New Living Translation*. Copyright © 1996, 2004, 2015 by Tyndale House Foundation. Used by permission of Tyndale House Publishers, Inc., Carol Stream, Illinois 60188. All rights reserved.

Scripture quotations marked (NRSVUE) are taken from the *Holy Bible, New Revised Standard Version Updated Edition*. Copyright © 2021 National Council of Churches of Christ in the United States of America. Used by permission. All rights reserved worldwide.

Scripture quotations marked (RSV) are taken from the *Revised Standard Version of the Bible*. Copyright © 1946, 1952, 1971 by the Division of Christian Education of the National Council of the Churches of Christ in the United States of America. Used by permission.

Scripture quotations marked (TLB) are taken from *The Living Bible*. Copyright © 1971 by Tyndale House Foundation. Used by permission of Tyndale House Publishers Inc., Carol Stream, Illinois 60188. All rights reserved.

Scripture quotations marked (TPT) are taken from *The Passion Translation*®. Copyright © 2017, 2018, 2020 by Passion & Fire Ministries, Inc. Used by permission. All rights reserved. ThePassionTranslation.com.

Cover and interior design by Müllerhaus
Cover photos by iStock
Monthly page photos by iStock
Typeset by Aptara, Inc.

ISBN 978-1-959634-03-4 (hardcover)
ISBN 978-1-959634-11-9 (epub)
ISBN 978-1-959634-10-2 (epdf)

Printed and bound in the United States of America
10 9 8 7 6 5 4 3 2 1

Introduction

My fourteen-year-old golden retriever, Ernest, padded up to me with his slow but determined gait, sat at my feet, and waited for his nightly medication. A senior dog, he gets along pretty well but still needs six pills a day and drops in both eyes to help manage various conditions. I pushed the tiny tablets into a soft, cheese-flavored pocket, which he happily consumed—he's food-motivated and not picky.

I then opened the kitchen cupboard and pulled out my own divided plastic container. "How did I become old enough for a days-of-the-week pill box?" I sighed.

"Sorry, dear," my husband, Mike, said. "It happens to the best of us."

God's Word tells us that growing old is an honor. While I don't always embrace my own mature adult status, I cherish the beautiful senior golden retrievers Mike and I have, as well as those we've rescued over the years. Each one is sweet and distinguished. I admire their snowy muzzles...yet I fuss about my own white hair. I respect the wisdom of their years, yet I disparage my own forgetfulness—will I soon be finding my eyeglasses in the refrigerator? I adapt to their mobility challenges but worry about my own. I can climb the stairs now, but eventually will I have to ride up and down in one of those chairlift contraptions my kids always tease me about?

Old age seems to present endless worries and negatives. Dogs, however, do not seem to fret about getting old, at least not in the way I do. What is it that they seem to understand about aging that I do not?

The next day I watched Ernest as we walked along the nearby towpath of the Erie Canal. He was in no hurry. His joints may be weak, but he took each step with enthusiasm. His eyes may be cloudy and his hearing muffled, but he still was aware of his surroundings, including the geese in the water beside us. His nose still works. He stopped to enjoy all the good smells. And his tail, which wagged nonstop the entire way, surely works as if it is directly attached to his big heart.

Sure, growing older can be challenging. But what if I approach it with the wisdom and grace of Ernest? What I saw on that walk was a dog who was in the moment, experiencing the great outdoors, walking beside someone he loves. Is there anything else I need to know?

Just like Ernest, all of God's creatures inspire me—to live and to write devotions to share with you. The other authors in this book are no different. They've all found spiritual insight from a pet, a bird in the sky, a wild animal they've encountered in the woods, creatures in the ocean or in their own backyard. On these pages you'll find hundreds of accounts of interactions with the critters with which we share this earth and the many ways these encounters help connect us with God. We hope they will bring you comfort, joy, and even laughter.

Of course, you don't have to be a "mature" adult, like me, to let the animal kingdom teach you some valuable lessons. God does that for us through His Scripture. Deer, for instance, are sure-footed animals able to walk gracefully and confidently through obstacles. Psalm 18:32–33 tells us that God gives us strength and feet steady as a deer. Isaiah 1:3 refers to the patient and dependable oxen, who are faithful to their master. And of course, there are the lion and the lamb, which represent Jesus's power and authority (Revelation 5:5–6), as well as His love and goodness (John 10).

Whether you are starting a family, experiencing life as an empty nester, or are now living alone, life is sure to bring changes—and sometimes challenges. The key to navigating any stage of life is to keep learning, both from God and from the animals He's created. That's what I do—thanks to my faith and a devoted animal companion by my side.

—Peggy Frezon

Guideposts contributing editor and *All God's Creatures* contributor

January

JANUARY 1

Chain of Love

If some of the branches have been broken off, and you, though a wild olive shoot, have been grafted in among the others and now share in the nourishing sap from the olive root.

—Romans 11:17 (NIV)

SOME OF THE best dogs I have ever had were never mine. They were fosters. I was just a stop on their road to a forever family that would love and care for them in the way they deserved.

"How can you fall in love with them, get them back from their hard and difficult pasts, and then just let them go?" This is a question I've been asked on more than one occasion. It's almost always asked with a measure of judgment.

But there is something special in being called to be the one who stands in the gap. As a foster family, we help the dogs work through the trauma in order to nourish and teach them that love can be more powerful than any horror. I remember Dobie, who needed someone to nurse her through heartworm treatment. When she left with her new forever person, she said goodbye in the sweetest tail wag, but she was just too happy to linger.

As I think of the many dogs who were short-timers in my life, I think of people who have been short-timers, as well. Have you ever tried to make someone a permanent fixture in your life only to realize you were really meant to be a bridge in a gap? Trauma, emotional and physical abuse, substance abuse, and heartache are really tough rivers to cross. Some of us throw out the lifeline to someone who is drowning, and someone else is called to open their arms and become that person's home. But in between those two are those of us who are called to be the bridge. We open our hearts and stand in the gap, and I find that this is when a lot of love happens.

Letting go—of both animals and humans—may not be easy, but when love no longer needs the bridge, something beautiful happens. This chain of love has many links, and I realize the strength of the chain is in knowing what link I am with each relationship that comes into my life.—Devon O'Day

God, thank You for the short-timers You've brought into my life so that I can be part of their chain of love. Amen.

JANUARY 2

Friendship Sanctuary

A friend loves at all times, and a brother is born for a time of adversity.

—PROVERBS 17:17 (NIV)

WHEN MY FRIEND Susy wrote a book with an Irishman named Patrick, she introduced me to the fascinating world of donkeys and a special one named Jacksie. Patrick grew up in a family that ran a sanctuary for injured, neglected, and abandoned donkeys. To him, donkeys are like family. Jacksie—a young donkey that had been abandoned by his mother—came into Patrick's life when he was recovering from addiction and rebuilding his life.

The first time I saw Jacksie and Patrick was in a YouTube video that highlights their unique bond. I was spellbound. Patrick is so well acquainted with donkeys that he can bray like one, and Jacksie seems to think he is a human. When Patrick brays, Jacksie runs over and puts his front hooves on Patrick's shoulders for a hug. It wasn't until I read Susy and Patrick's book, *Sanctuary*, that I learned how that bond was formed—through Patrick's long night shifts in the barn at the donkey sanctuary. He got up every three hours to feed Jacksie, create a warm nest of straw for him, and snuggle him. At the time, Patrick needed Jacksie as much as Jacksie needed him, so they grew, healed, and were strengthened together.

Patrick's friendship with Jacksie resurrected my gratitude for the relationships that God orchestrated when I needed a sanctuary of healing. These friends saw me at my worst and helped me become my best. In some cases, I found out that my gift of a friend needed me as much as I needed her.

Just as Patrick did for Jacksie and Jacksie did for Patrick and many have done for me, I pray that I will be the kind of friend others can turn to when they need a sanctuary.—Jeanette Hanscome

Walk of Faith: *Take a few minutes to thank God for the friends who became a sanctuary when you needed one. How did He use you to bless them in the process?*

JANUARY 3

Bookworm

Finally, brothers and sisters, whatever is true, whatever is noble, whatever is right, whatever is pure, whatever is lovely, whatever is admirable—if anything is excellent or praiseworthy—think about such things.

—PHILIPPIANS 4:8 (NIV)

KILLING TIME WHILE my wife and daughter went shopping for shoes—an activity I assiduously avoid—I strolled down the strip-mall sidewalk to a secondhand bookstore. For the better part of an hour, I trawled the dusty aisles, studied the titles, and thumbed through pages. In some books you could see the creases that marked the place where the reader stopped reading and dog-eared the page. I found the occasional underline and wondered what made this sentence so important to a long-ago reader.

Halfway down the Literary Classics aisle, I found a bookworm. I don't mean a person who loves books and reads a lot. I mean an actual bookworm—a worm that bores through books. A bookworm is not a true worm but the larvae of an insect—a beetle, a moth, a termite, whatever—which gnaws through the dry, starchy paper common in old volumes. There he was, a small brown worm tunneling through Tolstoy, making tiny pinholes.

When I was a boy, I was a bookworm. There was nowhere I would rather be than between the pages of a book. I would devour all sorts of books, like *Treasure Island, The Count of Monte Cristo, The Swiss Family Robinson.* Books about faith, heroism, American history. But in recent years my book reading has tapered off. It used to be, in reading books, I found myself diving deep into the important things of life. Now, too often, I just skitter along on the surface, making tiny marks like that bookworm.

There are so many good books, old and new, that would exercise my mind, enlarge my imagination, and take me places I've never been. I want to be a voracious bookworm again. Thank God for good books, and may they take us to places that God would have us go.—Louis Lotz

The more that you read, the more things you will know.
The more that you learn, the more places you'll go!
—Dr. Seuss

A Tiny Circle of Peace

He has redeemed my soul in peace from the battle that was against me.

—PSALM 55:18 (NKJV)

SHE LOOKS SO peaceful in her bed." My mom's Scottish terrier, Becky, had suffered through the flood that had caused my mom and her two dogs to be rescued by boat in the fall of 2021. A year later, I was sitting by the fireplace with my mom and her dogs, hoping they'd recover from their loss of serenity and security.

That year had caused much grief for my mom. Not only did her home get flooded, but she also lost her brother a few days after his eighty-fourth birthday and two of her four beloved dogs—one to seizures, the other to old age. The older dog, a black Shiloh shepherd named Katy, had been my mom's soul-soothing companion. Losing her hit Mom hard and still caused her sadness.

While we rocked and crocheted by the fire, we chatted about how she missed Katy and would often talk to her before realizing she wasn't there. Her current dogs helped ease the pain, but nothing seemed to fill the hole left by Katy's absence.

Seeing how peaceful Becky looked, I snapped a photo with my phone and sent it to my mom, knowing she'd like it. Then, Becky repositioned herself, looking even more at peace. I quickly snapped another photo, brought it up to see if it looked much different from the first, and beheld a surprise that sent a shiver through me.

My mom's photo in the tiny chat symbol on my phone was a picture of Katy. Because I'd already sent that first photo to her, the chat circle had appeared on my phone. When I took the second photo, Katy's picture somehow showed up on it, as though watching over Becky—and my mom. I knew that Jesus used cell-phone technology to send me and Mom a tiny circle with a guardian angel of peace.—Cathy Mayfield

Thank You, Jesus, for caring enough to use even my cell phone to bring peace to a wounded heart. Amen.

Elephant Connection

There is one body and one Spirit, just as you were called to one hope when you were called; one Lord, one faith, one baptism; one God and Father of all, who is over all and through all and in all.

—EPHESIANS 4:4–6 (NIV)

WHEN OUR FAMILY goes out of town on vacation, we do our best to visit local zoos. On our first trip to Hawaii, we were thrilled to find the Honolulu Zoo not far from our hotel. After exploring the primates, birds, reptiles, and some animals from Africa, I was eager to check out one of my favorite mammals, the elephants. When we reached the elephant habitat, I noticed from the signage that they came from India, just like me! I watched the magnificent Asian elephants with awe and fascination. They moved around lazily and appeared to be smiling as they flapped their ears and scooped chunks of hay into their large mouths with their trunks.

I wanted to learn more about these gentle giants, so I read the information available about them at the exhibit. Mari and Vaigai were given as gifts to the children of Hawaii from the children of India. Mari, who was only a few years older than me, amazingly came from my hometown in south India, Hyderabad. Like me, she was far away from her homeland. As I spent some time watching Mari in her surroundings, I felt a strange connection with her.

Believers all over the world are connected to one another because of their shared identity in Christ. We are children of God and citizens of His kingdom with the same spiritual ancestry and origins. And we, too, are far away from our permanent home in heaven. I hope when I meet believers from other parts of the world, I can look past our differences and find solidarity as spiritual siblings belonging to one family.—Mabel Ninan

Walk of Faith: *Pray for Christians all over the world by creating a yearly prayer calendar, remembering a country each day.*

JANUARY 6

A Snowy Saturday

Trust in the LORD with all your heart, and lean not on your own understanding; in all your ways acknowledge Him, and He shall direct your paths.

—PROVERBS 3:5–6 (NKJV)

THE COUNTRY ROADS leading to Foxwater Farm glistened with salt melting a fresh blanket of snow. Having grown up in Ohio, nothing about the condition of the winding pavement gave me pause. My tires held the road as I approached one of the most exciting meetings of my life. Up the final dirt lane and beyond an electronic gate, my Chevy pulled up to the heated barn.

"Here's Snowy," the breeder said as she handed me a wriggling, furry ball of energy. The white puppy snuggling in my arms became my first dog in adulthood. As I held her close, she burrowed her muzzle next to my face, indicating extreme trust and contentment.

While I signed the necessary papers one-handed, my host went over details of the purchase. She packed up a complimentary toy and a folder containing instructions and advice about feeding, veterinary care, and exercise. With my new golden retriever puppy safely in the carrier in the back of my SUV, we headed toward home. I promised the new member of my household a happy life and many fun times ahead. She listened quietly from the back of the car, only whining once as we turned onto the interstate. Perhaps she tried to ask, "Where are you taking me?"

As we arrived home, Snowy explored one room at a time. I looked on proudly as she played with a few of the toys I'd purchased ahead of time. Several potty breaks in the backyard and a mealtime behind her, she drifted off, cuddling a stuffed animal.

I learned the first spiritual lesson of pet ownership that day. In many ways, Snowy is totally dependent on me. Like me in my relationship with God, she must trust me and my understanding of the world. That night, I slept more securely, leaning on God's wisdom and love—far superior even to my boundless love for Snowy.—David L. Winters

Lord, thank You for the gift of my pet, who reminds me that I rest in Your complete care. Amen.

JANUARY 7

Feline Babysitter

Because You, Lord, have helped me and comforted me.

—Psalm 86:17 (NKJV)

LIVING ALONE SINCE my wife, Sandra, went to heaven, I face the challenge of being the single parent of two spoiled cats, Rudy and Hannah. They had initially moped around the house, missing their human mama, but eventually realized they had only me.

My days slowly filled with more time writing at my computer. The cats, though, felt they needed to assist me by sitting in front of my monitor, blocking my view. I shouted, "Sandra, can you call the cats?" With a tinge of sadness and frustration, I realized there would be no human rescue. I gave up and went to the living room to switch on the television. *What am I doing?* I thought. *I never watch during the day.*

Scrolling YouTube, I clicked on a listing for cat videos. I selected one, and images and sounds of squirrels and birds feeding and interacting flashed across the screen. "Why don't you guys watch this instead of blocking my monitor?" As if on cue, they walked toward the television screen, sat down, and stared intensely at the creatures that flitted and fluttered. Rudy decided to be more interactive, so he batted at a squirrel. As a bird flew off the screen, Hannah ran to the back of the television to chase it. Thus began their daily ritual. I was proud of myself. I had discovered *Sesame Street* for felines.

Eventually, the cats caught on to the ruse and resumed their numerous visits to my office. I must confess I was pleased I had not been replaced by a two-dimensional cat sitter. I offered a silent prayer of thanks to these two creatures who keep me company and give me comfort. By blocking my view, they helped me see what was really important.—Terry Clifton

What greater gift than the love of a cat.
—Charles Dickens

JANUARY 8

Silver Wings

You will be like the wings of a dove covered with silver, and her feathers with yellow gold.

—PSALM 68:13 (NKJV)

WHEN MY HUSBAND, Tom, retired, we moved to another town, leaving all we had known for more than forty years. We left a large home with a spacious yard and settled into a small townhome with a tiny courtyard. A window in my dining area became my "window of inspiration," where birds of various species visited the tall juniper tree behind the fence along the courtyard. There, on the other side of this glorious window, the Lord sent doves to visit me when I needed them most.

Mourning doves are native to Oregon. Their smooth fawn color is almost angelic, and their underside has a slightly pink hue. The single black spot behind and below each eye, black spots on its wings, and white edges on its long, tapered tail make this species unmistakable. Its name comes from its mournful, yet soothing, coo.

One morning last year, the sorrowful cooing I heard matched my spirit. I had just received news of the loss of a precious loved one, and I found it impossible to get a last-minute flight across the country. My broken heart stayed in prayer for my faraway family. In tears, I finally had to accept I could be with them only in spirit.

I lifted the blinds on my inspiration window, and within a few minutes, two mourning doves flew onto the fence by the bird feeder. They had often visited there, but this morning, they lingered longer than usual. I found comfort knowing the Bible reminds me what a dove represents: the Holy Spirit (Luke 3:22), and that this bird, created by God, was an emblem of peace and hope to a hurting world.

In times of sorrow, I can trust Jesus—Man of sorrows (Isaiah 53:3) and Prince of Peace (Isaiah 9:6). He understands this paradox and helps me take flight into His arms, where I find peace and rest.—Kathleen R. Ruckman

Oh, that I had wings like a dove! I would fly away and be at rest.
—Psalm 55:6 (NKJV)

JANUARY 9

A Home for Twiddle

Now to him who is able to do immeasurably more than all we ask or imagine, according to his power that is at work within us, to him be glory in the church and in Christ Jesus throughout all generations, for ever and ever! Amen.

—EPHESIANS 3:20–21 (NIV)

TWIDDLE, MY PARENTS' beloved cat, is smart and affectionate yet independent. So when they needed to move into assisted living and could no longer care for him, my sister said she and her husband would take him into their home. Though they have three dogs and knew there might be an adjustment, they wanted to help.

Once the sweet cat arrived in Nashville, he immediately took up with my brother-in-law in the "man cave." I imagine Twiddle simply wanted to avoid the dogs at first, but Twiddle and my brother-in-law grew attached. Twiddle would follow him each time he headed off to watch games on TV and would perch on the arm of his chair.

The laid-back cat didn't miss a beat. Once he adjusted to their three dogs, he settled into a routine. He has now found a spot to park himself each morning to watch my brother-in-law eat breakfast. He joins the whole family—dogs included—in the evenings, dividing his time between the back of my sister's chair and her husband's chair. Despite facing a difficult situation, Twiddle has found his place in a new, loving family.

Like Twiddle, I find myself in difficult situations and wonder how I'll manage to get through them. But then I remember—God always provides. Not only that, but He also provides in exactly the way I need, just as God provided the perfect home for Twiddle. Though we wondered if our plan to move a single cat into a family with three dogs could possibly work, it turned out better than we ever imagined. Twiddle found a loving family, and my parents knew their cat was in good hands. God generously provided.—Missy Tippens

Great is Thy faithfulness! Morning by morning new mercies I see; all I have needed Thy hand hath provided. Great is Thy faithfulness, Lord, unto me!
—Thomas O. Chisholm

JANUARY 10

Miracle Coral

Lord my God, I called to you for help, and you healed me.

—Psalm 30:2 (NIV)

I WAS SICK WHEN I stumbled upon the headline "Dolphins Line Up to Self-Medicate Skin Condition with Coral" and a picture of happy bottlenose dolphins swimming through a coral reef. Of course, I had to read the story. The article explained that zoologists from Zurich, Switzerland, had observed dolphins with a skin rash rubbing against a specific type of coral. The Indo-Pacific dolphins seemed to know exactly which coral to seek out—a variety that the zoologists eventually discovered had antibacterial and antioxidative properties.

At a time I was recovering from a virus that wasn't going away as quickly as I hoped it would, I found it fascinating that dolphins knew exactly where to go when they needed healing. They knew which piece of coral would release the restorative balm that their skin desperately needed, just as I knew the Source of strength in my weakness, the Hope in my discouragement, and my Friend in isolation. I had learned to attach myself to Jesus in moments of need, just as those dolphins literally attached themselves to what they knew would make them well again. I imagined that, like me, they had learned from experience to seek out what would help most—spending time in the miracle coral, provided by their Creator, that restored them like nothing else.

That image of the dolphins swimming through a reef of healing coral stayed with me as I recovered. It became my reminder to stay connected to Jesus, not only when I'm physically weak, but in all my moments of need, whether physical, emotional, or spiritual.—Jeanette Hanscome

Thank You, Lord, for giving me constant access to
Your healing touch and care. Help me to run to
You more often as my Source of relief in all situations. Amen.

JANUARY 11

An Opossum's Truth

But when he, the Spirit of truth, comes, he will guide you into all the truth. He will not speak on his own; he will speak only what he hears, and he will tell you what is yet to come.

—JOHN 16:13 (NIV)

PEARL THE OPOSSOM eats with the barn cats. They don't seem to mind. They don't actually seem to notice she isn't a cat. Pearl likes to keep a close check on what goodies we have each day. I really don't mind; she doesn't hurt anyone and is pretty good on the cleanup crew.

When I posted a picture of her on social media, I got a landslide of critical replies telling me she carried diseases and wondering how on earth I could allow her to eat with my other animals. Her nature is to be a predator, they said, to spread disease, and she should be out eating like the wild animals.

When God made her, as He made each and every one of us, did He instill within her a sense of right and wrong? Does she know she's eating the cats' food? Does she have a sense that it wasn't bought for her to consume? Or does she show up each night to a bowl filled with bounty and thank God by eating what has been provided?

Squirrels get tormented when they burglarize the bird feeders, but do they really know they are stealing? Or do they just think some human is trying to be nice? Blue jays are considered bullies, and starlings are thieves, but maybe they just show up at the restaurant we've provided and enjoy not having to forage quite so hard. The truth is the bounty IS for everyone. There is enough God to go around.

Whether a church or homeless camp, chicken or chimp, Christian or atheist, God doesn't limit His love and grace to those whom we feel are entitled to His supply. God fills all the feeders and all the bowls and all the churches and all the skid-row flophouses with His creation. When we realize that truth, we can truly be the hands and feet of Jesus. —Devon O'Day

God, let me walk in Your shoes and share limitlessly the open door to Your table. Amen.

JANUARY 12

The Bed Thief

To one who strikes you on the cheek, offer the other also, and from one who takes away your cloak do not withhold your tunic either.

—LUKE 6:29 (ESV)

THE SOUND OF whining alerted me to a problem in the foyer. I hurried to see why my golden retriever, Thor, was crying. A smile curved my lips at the unexpected sight.

Simon, my cat, had stolen the dog bed. Poor Thor stood off to the side, staring at Simon and whining. He glanced at me as if seeking help. But Simon looked so comfortable curled up in the middle of the paw-print bed that I hated to move him.

After whining a bit more and fidgeting around the edge of the bed, Thor decided to take matters into his own paws. As one of the sweetest dogs who ever lived, Thor wouldn't dream of being rough with Simon or making him move. Instead, he carefully stepped onto the bed and painstakingly curled his large body into a ball so he could fit next to Simon.

I laughed at the scene of the seventy-five-pound golden retriever trying so hard to avoid disturbing a sixteen-pound cat. Thor was obviously bothered by Simon being on his bed and desperately wanted it for himself. But he went out of his way to accommodate Simon and share his bed.

It wasn't until later that I saw more than humor in this comical situation. When someone uses or takes something of mine without permission, my initial response is not kindness. My response isn't self-sacrificing either. I want to take back what is mine and make the thief pay. After all, I have a right to my things, don't I? Thor's response, though, is much more Christlike than my natural tendencies. The next time I'm inconvenienced, I need to think of Thor and Simon and remember that self-sacrificing kindness is the best response.—Jerusha Agen

All who have received grace should learn to be gracious to others.
—Watchman Nee

JANUARY 13

The Gentle Shepherd

He makes me lie down in green pastures, he leads me beside quiet waters.

—PSALM 23:2 (NIV)

MY SATURDAY MORNING Bible study group has spent the last few months in a book based on Psalm 23. Thanks to this study, we've learned a lot of fascinating facts about sheep. On the morning we focused on verse two, "He makes me lie down in green pastures, he leads me beside quiet waters," I could not stop tearing up. For the first time, I heard why a good shepherd chooses quiet water for his sheep; it's because sheep are timid creatures that startle easily. A rushing stream frightens them so much that they won't drink from it. So the shepherd purposely looks for gentle waters.

Instead of forcing His sheep to toughen up by drinking from a scary rushing river, the Shepherd of Psalm 23 had compassion and brought His sheep to a calm source that felt safe. I thought about the many fears I battled as a child and even as an adult and some not-so-compassionate responses that only made me more afraid or planted worries that my fears displeased God. The image of a timid sheep being cared for by the gentle Shepherd who considered her fears, instead of shaming her or dismissing them, revealed God's compassion for me in a new way.

I thought of those He has sent to walk with me as I've overcome my fears—kind, encouraging, considerate, and nurturing people. Through that lesson about sheep, I saw God as a Father who cares for my fears instead of being displeased by them—a Shepherd who leads me like one of His most precious sheep to the quiet stream of His compassion and rest.—Jeanette Hanscome

Walk of Faith: *Read Psalm 23. Reflect on what it reveals to you about your kind, gentle Shepherd.*

JANUARY 14

Cutting Out the Cancer

And if your right hand causes you to sin, cut it off and throw it away. For it is better that you lose one of your members than that your whole body go into hell.

—MATTHEW 5:30 (ESV)

THE BIOPSY FROM the abnormal tissue on Bo's paw revealed a locally aggressive cancer. The cancer had already caused distortion and pain in the poor cat's foot to the point where he wasn't bearing weight on it. As Bo's veterinarian, I explained to his owner there was no way to treat the cancer except amputation.

"Absolutely not!" she protested.

Owners often have an initial negative reaction to the idea of amputating a beloved pet's limb, so I tried my best to convince her that this option was the only way to stop the spread of the disease and give Bo quality of life. Still, she refused.

After exhausting all my arguments, I finally said, "May I ask why you're against amputation?"

"How would you like to have your leg amputated?" she replied.

"I would be fine if I had three other good legs to walk on and my cancer was gone," I answered.

"He's walking on three legs now," she argued.

"Yes, but he's in constant pain, and the cancer is only going to get worse," I said. "It could spread to other parts of his body and kill him."

Finally, after I told Bo's owner there was nothing more I could do, she relented and allowed me to remove the diseased limb. With his cancer gone, Bo is now a happy little tripod kitty.

I couldn't help but compare the cancer in Bo's paw to the sin of envy I have struggled with in my life. Allowing that sin to fester only caused pain and bitterness. Gradually, with God's help, I learned to cut it out of my life, like a diseased tissue. Just like Bo, I became healthier and happier. I am so grateful for a loving Father who cares enough to heal me from the disease of sin.—Ellen Fannon

Father, please continue to remove sin from my heart and mind and heal me with Your loving-kindness. Amen.

JANUARY 15

High Hopes

But in keeping with his promise we are looking forward to a new heaven and a new earth, where righteousness dwells.

—2 PETER 3:13 (NIV)

OUR DOG PRINTZ loved cinnamon rolls. The first hint of that enticing aroma lured our bright-eyed Japanese spitz to the kitchen where he would settle himself patiently—at first—in front of the oven and wait with eager anticipation. As the delectable aroma grew more intense, Printz would lick his lips. His tail swished. He'd wriggle with excitement, knowing that once the goodies were out of the oven, he was in for a treat. Sometimes, I got the impression that Printz enjoyed the anticipation of the confection as much as he enjoyed the morsel itself.

Recently, I heard a radio sermon about Simeon in the New Testament. Luke records how the Holy Spirit had revealed to this righteous man that he would not die until he'd seen the Lord's Messiah with his own eyes. Surely, Simeon awoke each morning with eager anticipation, wondering, "Could this be the day?" The radio preacher went on to ask if believers today are looking forward to Christ's return with as much eagerness as Simeon looked forward to seeing Jesus when He came the first time. Christ entered the world and left it in very dramatic ways. A choir of angels announced His birth. Later, when Jesus ascended into the clouds, angels assured the awestruck disciples that He would return just as He'd departed.

The sermon made me recall Printz and his high hopes. I couldn't help pondering if I had high hopes too. Do I eagerly anticipate the Big Day? We don't know when it will be, but we do know that Jesus is coming back in clouds of glory. His return may take place years from now…or any day this week. Yes, I'm filled with anticipation. I hope you are too. Come, Lord Jesus!—Shirley Raye Redmond

I like to compare the holiday season with the way a child listens to a favorite story. The pleasure is in the familiar way the story begins, the anticipation of familiar turns it takes, the familiar moments of suspense, and the familiar climax and ending.
—Fred Rogers

JANUARY 16

Surprised by Joy

And may you have the power to understand, as all God's people should, how wide, how long, how high, and how deep his love is.

—EPHESIANS 3:18 (NLT)

CHICAGO-AREA WINTERS CAN be brutal, so when a rare warm front came through our small Christian college campus that January, *everyone* was outside enjoying it—including the squirrels. As I walked home from class, basking in the unexpected balminess, a squirrel approached me. I stopped, intrigued. The squirrel paused at my feet and then, in short and sporadic movements, climbed up my pant leg, onto my jacket, and finally, onto my shoulder. I stood like a statue, scarcely breathing, feeling like a modern-day Saint Francis of Assisi (the patron saint of animals).

I wondered what it could want. I had no food with me, and to be honest, I didn't even particularly like squirrels. I didn't try to pet it or otherwise engage it. But here, for a few moments, I had a pet squirrel who, for reasons beyond me, had chosen to befriend me. After a few breath-holding moments, I must have moved or otherwise startled my curious furry friend, because it quickly scampered down and up a tree. My reverie was broken, and the world around me reemerged as if from a strange dream.

Why had the squirrel chosen me? When I lived in the Midwest, I often experienced the doldrums of seasonal affective disorder (SAD) in the depths of the region's gloomy, frigid winters, and that year was no different. At the time, and now in hindsight decades later, I can't help thinking that God gave me a little gift that day—an unexpected, unforgettable encounter with one of His beloved creatures that, for a few moments, surprised me with great joy. But why? Because He loves me just that much.—Jon Woodhams

Joy is the serious business of heaven.
—C. S. Lewis

JANUARY 17

Oysters

Likewise, teach the older women to be reverent in the way they live, not to be slanderers or addicted to much wine, but to teach what is good. Then they can urge the younger women to love their husbands and children.

—TITUS 2:3–4 (NIV)

WALKING ALONG THE shore, I picked up an oyster shell that had numerous smaller shells piggybacked onto it. The larger shell was quite heavy, and its built-upon layers were evident. It was intriguing to see the smaller ones covering its surface.

In the wild, oyster larvae float until they are attached to sedentary older oysters. These baby oysters need the calcium from the older oysters' shells to begin their own process of shell development. Once the babies are in place, they are known as "spat."

When I first joined our church, the friendship and support of the older women carried me as a young newlywed and mother. They supported me through babysitting, meals, coffees, and walks.

One of the benefits of Christian community is that we can learn from one another. It was through the support and stories of the older women that I was encouraged to grow in my faith. When I "set" myself to them, I learned from their layers of experience. I saw how they managed their households, treated their husbands, and nurtured their children. I heard them speak of God's goodness and grace. I learned how God worked through them in good and difficult times. They provided a sheltering and nurturing environment in which I could flourish.

Now that I am one of the older ones and have many layers of life under my belt, who among the women I know is floating about and looking for a safe place to grow? Is there a younger woman within my circle of influence who might need a mentor? I pray that as an older "shell," I may be used to help a younger "spat" grow in her faith.—Virginia Ruth

Walk of Faith: *Pray that God would open your eyes to those individuals around you. Who can you invest in and build up?*

JANUARY 18

The Cygnets

O LORD, You preserve man and beast.

—PSALM 36:6 (NKJV)

I HAD MOVED FROM Oklahoma into my Indiana condo in the middle of winter, after my wife, Sandra, went to heaven. I knew the large complex encircled a pond, but the frigid weather didn't encourage me to explore the grounds. That spring, I decided to restart the daily walk Sandra and I had always taken.

Following the path around the pond, I noticed two swans gliding across the water, with a bevy of four baby cygnets paddling behind them. I had a Sherlock Holmes moment and thought, *Aha, that's why my address is on Swan Street.*

I enjoyed seeing the swan family every day. After returning from a short trip, I resumed walking but saw only one cygnet with its parents. I knew that baby swans stay with their mother for at least a year or longer, so I was worried.

I had met many of my new neighbors in passing but didn't feel comfortable asking them about the swans. One morning, the monthly newsletter from the HOA was in my mailbox. The second story was about the three missing cygnets. They had not survived, but a resident in my building named Geoff had taken them to a local university veterinary school to find out what happened.

I avoided walking around the pond for a week, worried I would find the last cygnet missing, but my curiosity won out, and I returned. Geoff was standing by the pond, face in a broad smile. I was delighted to see the one cygnet propelling itself behind his parents.

"This one's going to make it!" he declared like a proud father. "The tests showed there was nothing genetically wrong and nothing toxic in the pond."

"That's wonderful what you did," I told him.

He brushed off my compliment. "It was nothing. You would have done the same thing."

Would I have? I thought, as I walked on. I resolved to take Geoff's declaration to heart if the Lord ever presented me with the opportunity to help one of His creatures in distress.—Terry Clifton

Hear our humble prayer, O God....Make us, ourselves,
to be true friends to animals.
—Albert Schweitzer

JANUARY 19

A Doggie Named D-O-G

But now, O Jacob, listen to the LORD who created you. O Israel, the one who formed you says, "Do not be afraid, for I have ransomed you. I have called you by name; you are mine."

—ISAIAH 43:1 (NLT)

"WHAT'S YOUR FURRY friend's name?" my mom asked her neighbor. The man holding the leash smiled, then told her his dog's name.

Pronouncing it just as he had, Momma questioned, "Deogee? Hmm, that's unique. How's it spelled?"

The pup's master chuckled. "D-O-G."

It took her a moment, but soon Momma's eyes danced. "Oh, I get it." Then, turning to the prancing pooch, "D-*O*-G—what a great name!"

My mom loves to tell this story, and just as she did, her listeners often pause as the punch line settles. "Oh, 'D-O-G.' I get it." They usually reply with a chuckle, just like she did.

Having shared this story with my own daughter, Allie, recently, I watched the tween look up at me, confusion written in the wrinkles on her forehead. "I don't understand."

"The doggie's name is D-O-G," I explained.

"What? His owner didn't give him an actual name? That's mean."

My mind raced as I considered how best to clarify. "No, his name is pronounced just like the spelling of the word *dog*—with emphasis on the 'o.' D-*O*-G." I hit the middle letter with umph.

After a moment, "Ah, I get it! Like, instead of you calling me 'Allie,' you might call me 'K-*I*-D.'" She, too, emphasized the middle letter, indicating she understood. "That's funny."

And I can't help but think this makes God smile too—the One who's my Master, my Friend. After all, I'm His child, and He has a sense of humor. Though God's kind enough to call me by name, perhaps He sometimes teases me as well.

I can almost hear Him—"Come here, K-*I*-D!" —Maureen Miller

Faithful Father, thank You for knowing my name. I want to come when You call, then sit and stay awhile in Your presence. Amen.

JANUARY 20

Biting Success

He gives strength to the weary and increases the power of the weak.

—ISAIAH 40:29 (NIV)

OUR CAT, WASH, is nearly twice the size of his sister, Zoe. When he decides to eat, he positions himself so Zoe can't get near their dish. As a small, aging housecat, Zoe is not strong. Nor can she politely ask Wash to make room. But though she may be half his size, she's smart. When Wash hunkers down to eat, Zoe will get behind him and take up his tail in her teeth. Then she pulls with all her might, back legs firmly planted, front legs stiff. She can't drag him away, but her method is still effective.

"Reee-ow!" cries Wash, as he moves over. Then Zoe calmly settles in to enjoy her meal. My husband and I can't stop laughing.

Watching my little pet overcome her challenges encourages me to thank God for all the ways He helps me overcome my own. When confronted with any situation, good or bad, I have far more resources to draw upon for success than Zoe does. And yet there are still challenges that are well beyond my abilities, and I find more and more of them as I age. That's when I pray. I know God hears me and is faithful to give me the power I need to succeed. God strengthens me, especially when I'm weary.

Zoe, my weak little cat, does many things around the house as she contentedly lives out her days under my roof. My husband and I will be there for her to the end. In the same way, God, my Father in heaven, is there for me to the end. He will give me the strength I need to live out my days on earth until I join Him in heaven.—Marianne Campbell

Jesus loves me! This I know, for the Bible tells me so;
little ones to Him belong; they are weak, but He is strong.
Yes, Jesus loves me!
—Anna B. Warner

On the Fifth Day...

And God made the beast of the earth according to its kind, cattle according to its kind, and everything that creeps on the earth according to its kind. And God saw that it was good.

—GENESIS 1:25 (NKJV)

WHEN WE WERE looking for a puppy to adopt and train to become my granddaughter's emotional-support dog, we turned to my sister and her animal sanctuary, HearthFire Keep, for help in locating the perfect canine. After searching, she came back with a photo of what most certainly had to be a Chihuahua puppy, what with the apple head.

Having had many great experiences with Chihuahuas, my granddaughter excitedly agreed, and Oreo became a beloved part of our pack. Except there was a surprise in our future. Oreo was growing fast—or at least her body was. Her chest expanded, and she gained some serious weight. She doesn't necessarily look like it at first glance, but her body is rock-solid muscle. Lots of muscle. Seems that only one of Oreo's parents had been a Chihuahua.

Now that she's grown, it's quite obvious that she's half Boston terrier. That's right—she has a tiny Chihuahua head on a thick Boston terrier body. She's completely mismatched but absolutely adorable, and we all love her to pieces. Even before being trained as an official emotional-support service dog, she took to her role with gusto. Her little heart just seems to know when anyone needs special attention, from me (Granny) to the five-month-old baby.

Sometimes when I look in the mirror, I feel like Oreo. Time and a major surgery have not been kind to this body of mine. My head no longer matches my body. But God doesn't care about what I look like on the outside. He looks at my appearance on the inside. I hope He sees "the unfading beauty of a gentle and quiet spirit, which is of great worth" (1 Peter 3:4, NIV). Like Oreo, I want to be loved by others for my inner beauty and not just what people see on the outside.—Deb Kastner

Walk of Faith: *When you look in the mirror, thank God for how beautifully He created you, both inside and out.*

JANUARY 22

My Refuge

O Jerusalem, Jerusalem, the one who kills the prophets and stones those who are sent to her! How often I wanted to gather your children together, as a hen gathers her chicks under her wings, but you were not willing!

—MATTHEW 23:37 (NKJV)

MY PARROT, LORITO, climbed to the top of his cage. I watched as he stopped to chew on the wood block and then walked across the papers to perch on the other side. Unfortunately, he tramped over his own droppings. Lorito had a cut on the bottom of his left foot that had become infected, and the area needed to remain clean.

I gathered Lorito and carried him upstairs to the bathroom. After warming the water, I placed him in the bottom of the shower. The tepid liquid sprayed behind him and ran over his feet.

Once I was sure his feet were clean, I turned off the water and put my hand out for him to climb on. Lorito stepped up onto my finger, and I pulled him close.

As I held him to my chest and petted his feathers, Jesus's words resonated with my heart. *"How often I wanted to gather your children together, as a hen gathers her chicks under her wings."*

It had been years since I cuddled Lorito. He had been living with my mom to ease her loneliness and had only recently returned home when caring for him got to be too much for her.

I visited Lorito at Mom's, but it wasn't the same. I longed to hold him close and have him with me. As he snuggled next to me, I felt a prompt in my heart: this is sometimes true of me.

I can get so caught up with *doing* that I'm too busy to be with Jesus, yet He longs to hold me close. I warmed Lorito in the towel and placed him back in his cage with clean papers. Then I thanked Jesus for bringing my parrot home and for the reminder to be still and rest in His presence.—Crystal Storms

He shall cover you with His feathers, and under His wings you shall take refuge; His truth shall be your shield and buckler.
—Psalm 91:4 (NKJV)

JANUARY 23

Maya the Comforter

Then they sat on the ground with him for seven days and seven nights. No one said a word to him, because they saw how great his suffering was.

—JOB 2:13 (NIV)

MY FRIEND SUSY and her family were snowed in without power and passing around a bug when she tripped on the stairs and broke her ankle. When I called to check on her, she told me a sweet story about her newest pet—a goldendoodle named Maya.

Susy was sitting at the bottom of the stairs in agony when Maya came over and sat with her. Susy reached out and hugged Maya for support. The dog stayed with her until help arrived.

I witnessed Maya's comforting superpower a couple of months later. Susy's daughter, Teddy, was having a hard week. Susy and I went over to comfort her, and along came Maya. While I struggled to find the right words to reassure Teddy, Maya sat at her feet, just as she'd done for Susy, and let Teddy hug her.

During the next getaway to Susy's, it was my turn to benefit from Maya. I was under a lot of stress at the time, which was why Susy invited me to her home, and woke up with a crushing headache. Maya appeared in my room as if she knew I was in distress and lay beside me until I found the strength to get up to find ibuprofen. Even after I started feeling better, she was my companion. Somehow, she knew I needed a buddy.

For Susy, Teddy, and me, Maya offered an example of what a hurting person often needs most—a comforter to just sit with them. No words. No dismissive comments or promises that "You'll be fine." Just presence, touch, and ability to stay near to someone who is in pain.

Job's friends were reflections of compassion when they quietly sat with him in the ashes. My new example of how to comfort the hurting or weary is Maya, the dog who is willing to just be there.—Jeanette Hanscome

Walk of Faith: *Who has been willing to sit with you in your pain? If someone special comes to mind, send that person a note of thanks.*

JANUARY 24

Big Attitude

David said to Saul, "Let no one lose heart on account of this Philistine; your servant will go and fight him."

—1 SAMUEL 17:32 (NIV)

ONE OF THE many pets in my home is a beautiful blue beta fish named George Neptune. When we first brought George Neptune home, he was such an excitable fish. He would always swim up to the glass of his tank, puff out his flippers, and try to look big. I had heard that betas were aggressive, but this was crazy. It was like George Neptune was challenging every one of us to a fight.

Obviously, it would not have been a fair fight between a tiny fish in his fishbowl and a human. If we really fought a battle, George Neptune would not stand a chance. And yet he was so confident and self-assured. His battle prowess and oversized attitude gave me such joy. Every morning I would just look at his posturing and laugh.

Watching George Neptune has made me wonder how many times I think I am bigger and tougher than I really am. Do I look as silly as George Neptune, shaking my fist at the world?

Most of us know the story of King David and his battle with Goliath. David was so small he could not fit into Saul's armor, but still he fought Goliath. Like George Neptune, David was not afraid. We remember how the Biblical fight ends: the tiny David kills Goliath the giant. Maybe George Neptune isn't so crazy after all.

I work to find myself somewhere in the middle, not wanting to be too big for my britches but not looking for a fight around every corner either. But I also don't want to back down when I am afraid. I hope that when challenges come, I will be like David, fearless with God on my side. With George Neptune as inspiration, maybe I can get there.—Heather Jepsen

God, help me to be brave in the world, even on the days when I feel so small. Amen.

Indiscreet Appetite

What goes into someone's mouth does not defile them, but what comes out of their mouth, that is what defiles them.

—MATTHEW 15:11 (NIV)

DAISY, OUR FIFTEEN-MONTH-OLD German shepherd/English pointer mix, has an indiscreet appetite. At least that's what the doctor at the emergency veterinary clinic said. Despite regular feedings, Daisy finds far too many things to chew on and eat that she shouldn't.

Soaker hoses dug from the ground. A wading pool. Lizards, skinks, and frogs. Plastic water bottles with the water still inside them. Ink pens, metal tins, and extension cords. Wooden bookcases and table legs. House shoes. One large buckle, all the suede, leather, and cork from a sandal. Two foot massagers, along with an assortment of toys. The sandal and second foot massager are what sent her to the emergency vet to induce vomiting.

It seems Daisy can't resist putting things in her mouth. It doesn't matter if the items are meant to be eaten or not. Our veterinarian said Daisy eats all these things for several reasons. She's intelligent, inquisitive, active, easily bored, and a huntress.

It is frustrating to find Daisy eating something she shouldn't, especially the things I know can make her ill or even kill her. If I'm honest with myself, I realize that, unless I'm careful, I can take harmful things into my mind, just as Daisy takes harmful things into her mouth. When I think about Daisy's indiscreet appetite, God reminds me if I don't think on what is true, lovely, admirable, noble, and praiseworthy (Philippians 4), I'll end up with an indiscreet appetite also. To make sure that doesn't happen, I must feed on things that grow the fruit of the Spirit in me—love, joy, peace, forbearance, kindness, goodness, faithfulness, gentleness, and self-control (Galatians 5).—Sandy Kirby Quandt

Bread of Heaven, Bread of Heaven, feed me till I want no more;
feed me till I want no more.
—William Williams Pantycelyn

JANUARY 26

Brushing Benefits

Create in me a pure heart, O God, and renew a steadfast spirit within me.

—PSALM 51:10 (NIV)

BOOTS CAME TO us later in her life. This gorgeous Akita had been orphaned by the death of a friend's mother. When Boots arrived in midwinter, our school-age children took to her immediately. The kids loved her fluffy fur, and she was often patient enough for them to use her as a pillow while they watched television.

Though we'd owned an Akita before, he had been an outdoor dog. I must have forgotten just how much fur the breed puts on in winter because when March came, I thought our hardwood floors had been replaced by a tan carpet. One day, I took Boots outside for a good grooming. Brush in hand, I gently combed her coat, taking off gobs and gobs of downy white fur. My wife brought out a grocery bag to collect the produce. I brushed some more, then called for another bag. And another. Satisfied with my progress, I stopped at three bags full of dog hair.

The next day, I brushed Boots again, producing another three bags of hair. A few days after that, I collected two more. I finally lost count of the number of bags. "Where do you *get* this stuff," I wondered. Boots was not entirely happy about being groomed, but she looked like a new dog, sleek and svelte, when it was over.

The experience made me ponder my own "coat," the protective shield I sometimes put on to defend myself against the cold, hard world. Seemingly little things like sarcasm, anger, judgmentalism, and pride accrue one little strand at a time. It's possible to acquire a thick layer of these sins without noticing.

Once in a while, the Spirit sits me down to brush out the undergrowth. It's uncomfortable, having the detritus scraped from the soul. Yet it feels so good to be groomed by Him.—Lawrence W. Wilson

Search me, O God, and know my heart today; try me,
O Savior, know my thoughts, I pray. See if there be some
wicked way in me; cleanse me from ev'ry sin and set me free.
—J. Edwin Orr

JANUARY 27

Blessed or Lucky?

The prayer of a righteous person is powerful and effective.

—JAMES 5:16 (NIV)

IT HAPPENED IN a flash. I stepped from the warm white sand into the cool blue waters of the Caribbean Sea. As I did, my foot landed on something wet and supple. When it moved, I jerked my foot back. A stingray darted out of the shallow spot it had been napping in. The ray was slightly wider than a ruler, with a flat body, fins like wings, and a long tail like a whip. My heart pounding, I took another hasty step back. "Did it sting you?" asked a man hurrying toward me. I shook my head. "Wow, you're lucky. That was a stingray."

I nodded. I'd recognized the creature. But as I ventured into the water again, more watchful this time, I realized I wasn't lucky—I was blessed. Before leaving on the Caribbean cruise with my husband, I'd asked two of my close friends to pray for our safety and good health. Both women are mighty prayer warriors. They also keep their word. When they say they will pray for me or anyone else, they can be trusted to do it. I felt certain that my so-called luck was really the result of their prayerful promise.

Not long after this incident, I became the prayer chairperson of a local Bible study group for women. I took my role seriously, recalling the words of the reformation leader, Martin Luther: "To be a Christian without prayer is no more possible than to be alive without breathing." I read several books on prayer, looking for fresh insights and inspiration so that I might serve others through prayer, just as my friends had served me. The incident with the stingray could have been a painful and dangerous one but for their prayerful hedge of protection around me.—Shirley Raye Redmond

Our prayers may be awkward. Our attempts may be feeble. But since the power of prayer is in the One who hears it and not in the one who says it, our prayers do make a difference.

—Max Lucado

JANUARY 28

Adventure Awaits

And we know that in all things God works for the good of those who love him, who have been called according to his purpose.

—ROMANS 8:28 (NIV)

LUCY, MY DOG, loves to ride in the car. She'll hop in any car anytime with anyone to go anywhere. I love her sense of adventure. After a thirteen-hundred-mile road trip from Florida, where we adopted Lucy, to her new home in Minnesota, I assumed she would never want to set a paw in a car again. The next day, however, she hopped right in.

I love adventure too. I've lived in seven states, visited all seven continents, and been to more than sixty countries. But my sense of adventure disappears when an activity involves heights. When I climbed Diamond Head in Hawaii, I followed the steps of the person ahead of me. I wouldn't even peek at the magnificent view once I reached the top.

Like a good parent, God has provided me with adventures to help me grow as a Christian, even when they seemed wrong for me. I assumed He'd made a huge error when He moved me from working with elementary students to working with high schoolers labeled EBD (emotionally, behaviorally disabled). I tried to squirm out of it. Turns out it was the most satisfying job I've ever had.

Lucy's willingness to participate in any activity I provide is how I'd like to respond to God's calling. I need to remember that God always has my best interests at heart.—Linda Bartlett

Heavenly Father, help me to be open to Your leading. Let me follow You willingly, joyfully, wholeheartedly, so that I can experience the best adventure with You. Amen.

JANUARY 29

Foolish Questions

Wisdom is better than foolishness, just as light is better than darkness.

—ECCLESIASTES 2:13 (NLT)

KENAI RACED FOR the kitchen door, looked at his leash, ran to me, then about-faced back to the door. "Do you have to go out?" I asked. (Kenai's reply: *Wow, didn't I make it clear enough?*)

An hour and a half later, Kenai stared at me as I sat in my rocking chair, finishing my quiet time. A pitiful whine and a single wag of his tail alerted me. A glance at my watch showed it to be an hour past his normal breakfast. "I'm sorry! Are you hungry, Kenai?" (Kenai's reply: *Um, do you see what time it is?*)

I can almost hear our dog's thoughts when I ask these foolish questions. He knows I know the answers, and I know he knows I know the answers. Why do I even ask them?

It reminded me of a time we were visiting my mother-in-law. Our young daughter had done something she knew was wrong. I raised my eyebrows and asked her, "Do you want a time-out?" Her grandmother looked at me and asked, "Do you expect her to answer yes?" She continued, "Don't waste time asking children if they want a punishment. Choose the consequences the act deserves and follow through." Sound advice I tried to remember.

How often do I ask foolish questions of God? "Are You there, God?" "Do You even hear my prayers?" "Why did You let that happen?" Maybe it's time to rephrase those questions into statements: "Please, let me feel Your presence, God." "Thank You for hearing my prayers; let me be patient waiting for the answers." "I know You have a plan and are in control of this situation."—Cathy Mayfield

"Are You there, God?" I cried out today. "Are you breathing, My child?"
I heard Him say.

—C.M.

Road Trip Panic

When anxiety was great within me, your consolation brought me joy.

—PSALM 94:19 (NIV)

AFTER MY WIFE, Sandra, passed away, I didn't know how I would manage all alone. I sold our big house with too many memories and purchased a condominium near my sisters in Indiana.

The movers had come and gone. The reality of what came next was suddenly overwhelming. I would be traveling from Oklahoma for three days with my cats, Rudy and Hannah. We had done this before, but I had never done it alone. Sandra had always been the cat whisperer who kept them calm. How could I do this without her?

I was feeling proud of myself on the final day of the journey. I had gotten the two cat carriers in and out of the two motels without mishaps. As I approached Chicago on a congested highway, the weather got ugly—a mixture of rain, snow, and low visibility. I glanced in the rearview mirror and panicked. Hannah was out of her carrier. She had managed to unzip it and was now exploring the back seat. *What happens if she gets under my feet, and I can't control the car,* I thought, *and where do I stop?*

I had little choice but to pull over in the breakdown lane of the highway. I had the presence of mind to know that it was too risky to open a door. Hannah might bolt. I am not athletic, but somehow, I wiggled myself headfirst over the seat, miraculously grabbed Hannah, and not so gently dropped her into the unzipped crate, and closed it.

Back in the driver's seat, I heaved a sigh and thanked God for helping me along this journey. I slowly smiled, knowing whatever happened next, I wasn't alone.—Terry Clifton

Walk of Faith: *Today, recall any stressful situation or problem the Lord enabled you to accomplish beyond your natural abilities. Send up a prayer of thanks for never being alone.*

Expect Rewards

So do not throw away your confidence; it will be richly rewarded. You need to persevere so that when you have done the will of God, you will receive what he has promised.

—HEBREWS 10:35–36 (NIV)

SNOWY SHEDS VERY little but needs regular grooming so his fur does not get matted or dirty. While our Maltese mostly enjoys being brushed, he feels uncomfortable when I untangle his matted fur or comb around his mouth. But he obeys my command to stay and patiently waits for the grooming session to end because he knows what comes next. A reward. As soon as I finish cleaning Snowy's fur, I shower him with praise. He runs to the pantry and waits for me to join him, wagging his tail furiously and shuffling his paws. "Snowy deserves a treat?" I ask, as I open the cabinet to retrieve his favorite dental chew. "Sit and stay."

When he obeys my commands again, I give him the treat. He takes it to his crate to enjoy his well-earned reward. My dog also gets rewarded after I clean his eyes with water and cotton balls twice a week. He needs to stay still in the bathroom sink so I can get rid of the dirt around his eyes. Snowy doesn't like it much and has come to expect a bone or cookie after we're done.

When I obey God's commands and serve Him with my time and talents, I, too, can anticipate rewards. Jesus urges believers to expect heavenly rewards when we follow Him (Matthew 16:27). Obedience and faithfulness, even in little things, does not go unnoticed by God. God takes pleasure in rewarding us, just as I take pleasure in rewarding Snowy.—Mabel Ninan

Dear God, help me to be obedient to Your commands. Help me to set my sights on heaven and look forward to enjoying my heavenly rewards. Amen.

February

FEBRUARY 1

When Words Fail

The wolf and the lamb will live together; the leopard will lie down with the baby goat. The calf and the yearling will be safe with the lion, and a little child will lead them all.

—Isaiah 11:6 (NLT)

HAVE YOU EVER heard wolves howling in the distance and wished you could join in their haunting songs? Not to brag or anything, but I got to do just that. There I was, joining the fox, the dogs, the coyote, and the wolves, wolf-hybrids, and some other people in a good howl. It was spine-tingling and fun at the same time, and even though it was around twenty years ago, I'll never forget the transcendent moment it was.

"It" was a visit to the Colorado Wolf and Wildlife Center, a wildlife sanctuary near Divide, Colorado, just outside Colorado Springs. Having won VIP encounter passes to the center as a Christmas-party door prize, I had no idea what to expect and, honestly, wasn't that excited about it. I certainly wasn't prepared for what was about to happen that mild winter day.

As part of our tour, we were allowed to enter the enclosure with some of the canid residents, including a stunning white wolf! Atypically for me, I felt no trepidation or fear being so close to him, and that might be why what happened next happened.

This magnificent beast flopped down on his back and let me rub his belly and pet him. As I try to describe the experience for you, words fail me. While I can't remember specific details, other than the tactile sensation of his thick fur in my hands, I remember vividly how it made me *feel*. I was lifted out of the ordinary and into a realm I never knew existed. And I couldn't help thinking ahead to a time when "the wolf and the lamb will live together" in peace in the fullness of God's peaceable kingdom.—Jon Woodhams

Now to Him who is able to do far more abundantly beyond all that we ask or think, according to the power that works within us, to Him be the glory.
—Ephesians 3:20–21 (NASB)

It Only Takes a Minute

Truly I tell you, whatever you did for one of the least of these brothers and sisters of mine, you did for me.

—Matthew 25:40 (NIV)

My eleven-year-old daughter explained that she named the cat Minit because when you call her, she always comes in a minute. That turned out to be true of our little ragdoll mix. She enjoyed human affection more than most cats I've known and would happily come when called. Or when not called.

Not long after we adopted Minit, I had my second (of what would become four) joint-replacement surgery. That restricted my mobility for a few weeks. It also meant lots of physical therapy. Three times each day I would lie on the bed doing some form of knee exercise. The workouts were somewhat painful, so I tended to put them off as long as I could. One particularly disdainful exercise had me lie prone, then flex my knee as I moved my foot upward in a sort of reverse curl.

One day Minit observed this and noticed an open bit of human real estate at the small of my back. She curled up there, purring happily as I grunted and strained to finish my therapy set. It was pleasant, actually. The next day, attuned to the sound of bedsprings, Minit raced into the bedroom just as I reached the prone position. Again she nestled on my back, providing a bit of comfort while I worked the still-swollen joint. I grew to love that cat, perhaps more so because of my pain and the small bit of comfort she unknowingly provided.

So often my interactions with others have been like that. Their ordinary acts, like smiling or greeting or patting the shoulder, have had an outsized effect on my mood. Like angels unaware, they have enabled me to cope with difficult days. Hopefully, I can do the same for others.—Lawrence W. Wilson

If I can stop one heart from breaking, I shall not live in vain.
—Emily Dickinson

FEBRUARY 3

When Faith Is the Best Medicine

Now faith is the assurance of things hoped for, the conviction of things not seen.

—HEBREWS 11:1 (ESV)

A DIGESTIVE ISSUE SHOULDN'T be life-threatening. But that's what I started to fear for my eighteen-month-old Leonberger puppy. After weeks of gastrointestinal problems, Galen had become lethargic and lost over fifteen pounds from his already skinny frame.

Finally, one veterinarian found the cause and prescribed medication. I was supposed to give my pup pills for fourteen days. Though thankful for a diagnosis, despair burdened my heart. Already a picky eater, Galen had stopped eating almost completely since becoming ill, even refusing the canned food he formerly liked. How would I get him to take medicine? I couldn't force him to swallow large pills two times a day for weeks.

The next morning as I prayed for Galen's healing, God reminded me of something I'd forgotten. Our Great Pyrenees, also a finicky eater, had once needed to take pills I thought I would never get into him. But I'd ventured the impossible, and God enabled me to give him every dose of medication.

Have I been underestimating what God can do? Taking a breath, I readied Galen's canned food and pills. Silently praying, I offered Galen the food on a spoon. My heart leaped when he ate it. But would he take it again, with a pill hidden inside?

Whispering another prayer, I hid a section of pill in the next spoonful. Galen swallowed it whole. Bit by bit, he took his first dose of the medication. And the next one. He started to feel better and hungrier, which made concealing the pills in his food easier.

As I watched Galen come back to life, my soul was infused with new life too. I needed to be awakened from my spiritual lethargy, to step out in faith and trust the God of the impossible.—Jerusha Agen

Walk of Faith: *Is there a situation in your life where you're assuming the solution is impossible? Prayerfully take the first step in faith, and trust God to do the impossible.*

FEBRUARY 4

Treasures

But lay up for yourselves treasures in heaven, where neither moth nor rust destroys and where thieves do not break in and steal.

—MATTHEW 6:20 (ESV)

THE NOISE IN the backyard was so loud that we couldn't hear each other talk inside the house. What sounded like a dozen crows squawking to ward off danger caused me to stop and investigate. Surely a cat or wild animal was stirring up the neighborhood birds.

Upon walking outside and looking up in the trees, I discovered there were only two crows. They were fighting over a long strand of brightly colored plastic beads—the kind you see at Mardi Gras parties.

"Unbelievable!" I laughed. *Really guys? All this commotion for some shiny purple party favor?*

I clapped my hands to break up the fight and distract them. It worked, with one crow giving up his prize and flying away.

The crow left holding the trophy perched quietly on the pine-tree branch for a moment. Then, he must have decided the fun of the fight was over. He released the beads, letting them fall to the branches below.

I was reminded of my own quest for riches. In Matthew 6, Jesus tells me not to bother collecting treasures here on earth, for they won't last. They are frivolous because I can't take them with me after my life is done. The fortunes I must invest in are eternal in nature. Even what organizations I give money to must be weighed carefully, considering what infinite difference it will make. I looked up in the tree at those beads again, knowing I must be devoted to what is timeless, not what is temporary.—Tez Brooks

Heavenly Father, I often live my life chasing after the American dream. I'm so prone to focus on possessions this world calls valuable, striving to keep up with the Joneses. Help me concentrate on accumulating heavenly treasures. Amen.

FEBRUARY 5

As Free as a Butterfly

So if the Son sets you free, you will be free indeed.

—JOHN 8:36 (NIV)

ON A TRIP to Branson, Missouri, my husband and I planned a full weekend for our young granddaughter, Nellie—shopping at Branson Landing, eating at a restaurant with singing waiters, and going to a show. Of all the tourist attractions available, what did Nellie want to do? Visit the Butterfly Palace.

From the moment we stepped through the protective plastic curtains into the two-story exhibit, it was a magical experience. At one point, an employee pulled Nellie aside and asked if she wanted to release a newly emerged butterfly. Her eyes glistened as she turned the plastic container over to free the insect, which only hours before had been encased in a chrysalis. It paused momentarily on her dress and then flew off to join hundreds of other winged beauties from around the world.

While exploring the display, we carried tubes of nectar topped with artificial flowers that attracted gorgeous specimens for an up-close look. They landed on our clothes, our hands, and my husband's nose! From a stairway leading to the top of the aviary, we watched butterflies fluttering throughout the huge enclosure. Although they seemed to flit aimlessly about, they often homed in on orchids and other food sources.

Once freed from their chrysalises, butterflies get busy fulfilling their role in God's world by pollinating plants. Though short-lived and fragile, they go about their job with robust enthusiasm. Jesus freed me to serve Him by spreading the gospel and hopefully bringing forth fruit. Rather than flit here and there, I want to home in on His purpose for me and carry it out with the same enthusiasm. In doing so, I hope to bring God joy by staying faithful to His plans for my life, just as butterflies bring me joy by their sheer beauty.—Tracy Crump

Walk of Faith: *Take a moment to think about the unique abilities God gave you and the purpose He has in mind for you. Then get busy finding ways to fulfill that purpose.*

FEBRUARY 6

A Winter Parade

He says to the snow, "Fall on the earth,"... So that everyone he has made may know his work.

—JOB 37:6-7 (NIV)

FEBRUARY CAN FEEL quite stagnant. Trees with naked branches silently sway without leaves to carry their songs. Snow subdues nature's noises. There is no buzz of insects, and the birds' choir has bid most of its members farewell until spring. It's easy to feel that life has been sapped from the landscape. Winter's lull leaves me aching for spring's bounty. And yet, on this particular February morning, life parades right past our front door.

"Wake up! Come see!" I rouse my four children and rush them to the front windows, where we watch over one hundred elk—including cows pregnant with new calves—meandering down our street. My children are certainly awake now, their eyes wide with awe as they take in the scene. With slow, steady movements so we don't spook the elk, we move from window to window for better views. The elk stop to peruse each yard's offerings. They're searching for late-season, shriveled apples still clinging to trees. Several elk pause a few feet from our front window, nosing aside snow and nibbling at foliage buried beneath. Looking closely, they find hints of hope in hidden places. Maybe I, too, can discover life where it's least expected.

The elk parade stomps right over my winter blues. They're a welcome reminder that there is beauty to be unearthed from these slow seasons. Winter is not idle but actively waiting. Its whisper sounds like the Hebrew word *qavah*, meaning "to wait with expectation." The land is resting and restoring itself, preparing for a new season. Similarly, my soul needs these winter pauses—time to reflect, give thanks, and look forward.

Months from now, the mama elk will walk with their calves through green grass and meadows lush with wildflowers. Yet right now, in a season of waiting, they stay purposeful and focus on the new life growing inside them. They look forward to what's coming and parade on toward good things.—Eryn Lynum

You warmly in your love enfold, and keep us through life's wintry days.
—Samuel Longfellow

FEBRUARY 7

Elephants and Bees

The Lord will rescue me from every evil attack and will bring me safely to his heavenly kingdom. To him be glory for ever and ever. Amen.

—2 TIMOTHY 4:18 (NIV)

WE WERE AT Disney's Animal Kingdom in Florida for a "Caring for Giants" elephant tour. A bus took us to a back part of the savannah where our guide said the elephants "hang out," and we were able to see them from about eighty feet away, while we learned about their daily care and routine. It was especially wonderful to see a three-month-old baby elephant, who stuck tight by her mama. Then we were introduced to a cast member from Kenya, who told a remarkable story.

She said that farming is a growing part of the economy in Kenya and other parts of Africa. As farmers clear the land, they take over areas previously frequented by herds of elephants. When the elephants search for new food sources, they sometimes trample fences, venture into the fields, and partake of the farmers' crops. They can destroy an entire harvest in one day, and they may inadvertently damage homes and other buildings. To defend their crops and their families, some farmers shoot the elephants.

Fortunately, researchers have discovered that elephants are afraid of bees. They sting elephants in sensitive areas, so the elephants have learned to stay far away from the buzzing of bees. Scientists have constructed fences with beehives placed at intervals along the fence and have found that elephants will stay away. It's a clear win-win situation. The farmers save their crops and property, they no longer want to shoot the elephants, and they have an additional small source of income from the honey they can harvest.

This story made me think about how amazing our Creator is. Turmoil and strife seem inevitable in this situation. But God has provided a solution that benefits man, elephant, and bees.—Harold Nichols

Dear Lord, help me look for peaceful solutions to the turmoil of this world. Give me the creativity to find ways that I can live in harmony with all parts of Your creation. Amen.

FEBRUARY 8

A Good Greeting

Greet one another with a holy kiss.

—2 CORINTHIANS 13:12 (NIV)

IF THERE IS one thing our fluffy goldendoodle, Honey, takes seriously, it is her role as the primary greeter in our household. When the door opens, Honey first rushes to grab a toy in her mouth and then, with urgent devotion, she skids to meet us. It is with complete and total adoration and generosity of spirit that Honey prances around us and then leans heavily against our knees, tail wagging at gale-force speed. Sometimes she offers up little whimpers, and occasionally there is some uncontrollable piddling, but overall it is her eager, sincere gladness to welcome us that wins our hearts.

Honey greets us this way all throughout the day. This includes when we've just gotten up in the morning and when we come down after brushing our teeth. She will, of course, greet us with gusto when we've been gone for grocery shopping, church, or violin lessons. And most endearingly, she will greet me heartily when she's just been riding in the car with me to drop the kids off at school and we come back into the house together. She bounds in ahead of me to welcome me with all her usual affection. I never, ever doubt that Honey loves us very much. Each time we see her, we know it to be true.

This reminds me of the many letters of the New Testament and the way their authors prompt people to greet so-and-so, to greet the churches, and—my very favorite—to "greet one another with a holy kiss." A proper greeting always makes it clear to a person that they belong and they are loved. When someone enters my home, I want to be just as clear as Honey is that they are welcome and loved.—Katy W. Sundararajan

Jesus, You have always loved best. You welcome all to Your house and to life with You. Help me, at the very least, to love and welcome as well as one fluffy dog named Honey. Amen.

FEBRUARY 9

The Great Leap of Faith

He brought them out of darkness, the utter darkness, and broke away their chains.

—PSALM 107:14 (NIV)

THE PHONE CALL from our new neighbor Scott came when we were downtown that Saturday morning. Scott shared the news that our boxer dogs, McKenzie and Tyson, were running around on our street. He was concerned since he knew they were never off leash and didn't want them to be hit by a car.

We looked at each other in disbelief. This information was impossible to comprehend. We had left those two in our locked home not thirty minutes before. How could they have gotten out?

As we pulled into the driveway, everything seemed normal. Well, except for our two brown dogs streaking by us. Still not understanding how they got outside, we grabbed the treat box and split up to begin a game of capture the flag…or dog.

Oh, the joy these two were having, prancing around and teasing us while blasting through every yard in our neighborhood. Nice way to meet the neighbors! We finally snagged the pair as they tired themselves out and dragged them inside, where they immediately ran down to the basement. And that is when we realized these partners in crime had jumped three and a half feet off the ground and busted through the screen of the open window to take their joy-filled run. They were quite proud of themselves for breaking out!

I don't need to search for an open window in order to break out of any place where I'm stuck or feeling trapped. I only need to look to Jesus and ask Him to help me, forgive me my sins, and be my Savior. It is only then that I can be truly free.—Twila Bennett

So if the Son sets you free, you will be free indeed.
—John 8:36 (NIV)

FEBRUARY 10

One of a Kind

I praise you because I am fearfully and wonderfully made;
your works are wonderful, I know that full well.

—PSALM 139:14 (NIV)

I AM SO BLESSED to live in the panhandle of northwest Florida. Not only do I have the joy of watching wild dolphins frolicking in the Gulf of Mexico, but as a veterinarian, I have also had the privilege of being up close and personal with captive dolphins in our local oceanarium.

Did you know that each dolphin has its own unique sound? This high-pitched squeak produced from the blowhole is known as the dolphin's signature whistle. The signature whistle serves to identify each dolphin and to maintain group organization. Pregnant dolphins "sing" to their babies before they are born, teaching them to recognize their mother's signature whistle. Dolphins can even mimic other dolphins' whistles, which might be compared to humans calling each other by name.

As remarkable as God made dolphins—each with its individual sound of identification—He made humans in *His* image (Genesis 1:27), which makes us distinctively special. Scripture tells us that while He created people with similar characteristics, each of us is unique. We all have different passions, talents, gifts, and abilities, and these are by His will and design (Romans 12:6–8). His plans for us were laid before we were even born (Jeremiah 1:5), as were the number of our days on earth (Psalm 139:16). He even knows the number of hairs on our head (Matthew 10:30)! How incredible is the realization that the Creator of the universe knows us so intimately.

Just as dolphins feel a sense of security when they hear the signature whistles of their friends, how much more secure can I be resting in the love of the One who made me the unique individual I am?—Ellen Fannon

Father, thank You for the uniqueness and beauty of all Your creation.
Help me use my uniqueness to fulfill Your plans for my life. Amen.

FEBRUARY 11

Just Turn Toward the Light

Then Jesus spoke to them again, saying, "I am the light of the world. He who follows Me shall not walk in darkness, but have the light of life."

—JOHN 8:12 (NKJV)

SMACK! OH, NO! How well I knew that sound. I raced to the couch by the front window, hoping the bird that hit the glass had flown off and not landed on the ground.

Alas, it lay on six inches of fresh snow. I begged my husband, Kevin, to go see if it could be saved. Minutes went by as he found boots and pulled on his coat, minutes when I stayed glued to the window to make sure nothing else happened to the bird. We had several stray cats around.

When I saw Kevin cradle it in his hands, I hurried out on the porch and found a small box we could lay it in. I wanted to bring it to the warmth, feed it, and do anything to help, but Kevin insisted it would be okay outside. He positioned the box to face the wall of the house for protection from the wind.

Every few minutes, I went back out to check on it. I talked to it, urged it to get up, to get better. I prayed for God to restore it to health, as I'd been praying for my recent bout with anxiety. If that little bird could just fly, I thought, it would be okay. Many minutes went by, and although the bird eventually moved around a bit, it didn't try to fly. Maybe it was injured more than we thought.

The next time I went outside, the bird was standing in the box. I knelt close to check if I could see anything broken on its wings. To do so, I needed to turn the box toward me, so I did. And just like that, the bird flapped its wings and took off. All it needed was for me to position the box so the bird could see the light.

Maybe, if I just turn like that little bird toward the Light, my anxiety would take flight too.—Cathy Mayfield

While you have the light, believe in the light.
—John 12:36 (NKJV)

FEBRUARY 12

A Discerning Palate

The discerning heart seeks knowledge, but the mouth of a fool feeds on folly.

—PROVERBS 15:14 (NIV)

I WATCH THE PECULIAR bird outside our window. It's not his color that catches my attention—we see dark-eyed juncos, or "snowbirds," every day throughout the winter. Instead, what captivates me is what he is eating. Large flakes of snow fall in a flurry around him, quickly enveloping the landscape outside. In harsh conditions, I would think he would devour whatever food he could find. But instead, he is being picky. Selectively sorting seeds on our pedestal feeder, the junco takes his time finding the best options.

If I were a junco caught in a snowstorm, I'm afraid my lunch might resemble a more reactive palate as I gathered whatever was available. When life's conditions shift and I face uncertain scenarios, the temptation is to reach for the nearest answer or provision. And society offers a buffet of ideas to snack on and myriad solutions to try for a spin. Fearing scarcity and seeking security, I find it far easier to react and gather up whatever's in reach, swallowing an opinion or option without much thought about its value or its ability to genuinely satisfy. Instead, I want to heed a lesson from my feathered friend—to remain calm and stay choosy about what I fill my mind, heart, and body with.

Whenever I'm overwhelmed by the news or media or uncertain how to respond to society's relentless changes, I think about the junco. I engage the logical mind God has wired me with and discern what is harmful and what is healthy. I am determined to remain calm, collect my thoughts, and sort them according to God's Word and ways. Setting aside lesser attractions, I reach for God's best, filling up on His goodness, grace, and truth.—Eryn Lynum

Dear God, help me to distinguish Your truth from the falsehoods permeating the world around me. Develop a craving in my soul for everything that comes from You. When hardships hit, help me to collect myself and align my heart and mind with Yours. Amen.

FEBRUARY 13

Exercise Coach

Dear friend, I pray that you may enjoy good health and that all may go well with you, even as your soul is getting along well.

—3 JOHN 2 (NIV)

IT WAS MY first winter in northwest Indiana after moving from Tulsa. Even though I was raised in the area outside Chicago, I had forgotten how cold, snowy, and seemingly interminable the winters could be.

Housebound twenty-four hours a day with no outlet for exercise left me sluggish, crabby, and packing on the pounds. *Maybe I should join a health club,* I thought. But I knew I would find reasons not to go. I decided to buy my own exercise equipment, though I worried there would be no one to motivate me. My first choice was a treadmill, but having two cats, I was afraid they would sneak under the machine. I settled on a rowing machine and stationary bike.

My first time on the equipment was challenging, but I was determined to stick to it. On the second day of rowing, I glanced to my left. Sitting on a chair at attention, eyes focused forward, was my elderly, corpulent cat Rudy. He maintained his position throughout the entire workout. As I finished, and before he hopped down, he looked at me with a *we'll have to work on that* expression.

Thus began Rudy's role as my exercise coach. He seemed to know my start time and regimen—alternating days of rowing or biking. He was a bit more laid back on my biking days, watching from his cat tree while I pedaled away. I have no idea whether Rudy thought he was coaching me in his feline mind, but I must confess he motivated me to keep a schedule, and his constant presence kept me exercising.

Both Rudy and I can stand to lose some more weight, but I feel healthier physically, mentally, and spiritually. Funny, this elderly gent never expected to find accountability, companionship, and supervision while exercising at home with an elderly cat coach.—Terry Clifton

Walk of Faith: *Is there a goal you are struggling to reach? Whether your goal is physical or spiritual, consider reaching out to a person or animal who can provide encouragement.*

FEBRUARY 14

Mike's Language of Love

If I speak in the tongues of men or of angels, but do not have love, I am only a resounding gong or a clanging cymbal.

—1 CORINTHIANS 13:1 (NIV)

MIKE IS A medium-size brown dog whose superpower is listening. When he was just a puppy, he would greet me with excitement, tail wags, and a total face wash of licks when I arrived home. While I love him dearly, I am not a doggie-mouth-kissing human. It's just not my thing. His slobbery kisses were met with a soft correction, and that's all it ever took. Mike listened as I spoke to him in my love language—nearness. He didn't try to continue with the language of love he thought I would prefer if I just got used to it. Mike just did what I asked of him.

Have you ever been with someone who insisted on loving you their way even when you asked for what you needed? Have you ever doubted your own needs because someone you loved ignored you and insisted on giving you what they wanted? I have. I've stayed in relationships because I didn't want to hurt someone by leaving, even if it hurt me to stay.

Real love pays attention, just like Mike does. It does not ignore. Our words and requests are met with compassion. When we are connected by love to someone whose love language is so far different from our own, it just means that love takes on the form that houses both hearts.

We bless and release, remember the sweet, and move on with grace as we listen for love to come home to us in all its beautiful forms. When we meet others where they are and do our best to love them in ways that make them feel loved, we truly feel the love come back to us as Mike has shown me over and over.—Devon O'Day

God, please give me the ears to hear the needs of those I love so that I may love them better and know what type of love each brings to my door. Amen.

FEBRUARY 15

Fly

What do people gain from all their labors at which they toil under the sun?

—ECCLESIASTES 1:3 (NIV)

I SAW AN AD in a magazine for a video ($19.95 plus shipping) that purportedly shows you how to measure your dog's intelligence. "Find Out How Smart Your Dog Is!" boasted the ad. I figure it works like this: if you buy the video, your dog is smarter than you are.

I didn't make the purchase, but sometimes I think my dog really is smarter than I am. His name is Fly, and he is a Gordon setter, with silky, coal-black hair and caramel markings on his paws and muzzle. While I work in the sun, Fly naps in the shade. While my head throbs with worries, Fly—so far as I can tell—doesn't worry about a thing. I have a list of chores, and I can't get everything done, no less done well, and my frustration looms larger and more toxic every day. But Fly has no list, no frustrations, and there are more hours in a day than he really needs. Truly, he seems utterly content, wanting nothing other than to be close to his master, to love me, to walk at my side. I don't need a video to tell me which one of us is smarter.

Sometimes I feel an inner restlessness, and I try to make the feeling go away by working, accomplishing tasks, checking items off a list that somehow is always longer at dusk than it was at dawn, as though my striving made me more acceptable in the eyes of my Master. Lord, help me to set aside my list and remember that whether I come or go, pass or fail, win or lose, live or die, You are with me. Help me to realize that I will always be restless until I rest in You.—Louis Lotz

Thou hast made us for thyself, O Lord, and our heart is restless until it finds its rest in thee.

—St. Augustine

FEBRUARY 16

Buried Treasure

For where your treasure is, there your heart will be also.

—MATTHEW 6:21 (NIV)

I HEADED INTO MY daughter's bedroom to clean the hamster cage. While I adored Pumpkin the teddy bear hamster, I really hated cleaning his cage, especially the plastic tunnels. I transferred Pumpkin to his travel cage and started to disassemble the cage, starting with the tunnels. I noticed that my daughter, Julia, had placed her Bible under a section of the tunnel.

I called for her. "Why did you put your Bible there?" I asked.

"Part of the tunnel came apart," she said. "I think it's because Pumpkin is fat now. When we give him treats, he stuffs them in his cheeks and then holds out his paws for more."

"The tunnel separated, so you put your Bible there to prop it up?"

She nodded. "I saw it several days ago. It hasn't come apart since I stuck my Bible underneath it."

I had to admit it was a smart idea, even if it wasn't the ideal use for a Bible.

Julia ran off, and I continued cleaning the cage. When I reached the little house inside Pumpkin's cage, I found his buried treasure: a huge cache of treats he'd hidden for later.

I cleaned his house, replaced the cedar shavings, and then put his buried treasure back where I'd found it. When I put him back in the cage, he immediately scurried to his house. When he emerged moments later, his cheeks were puffed up, clearly filled with his most valuable possessions.

"When something is important to you, you've got to keep it close, right, Pumpkin?" I said, laughing.

My gaze landed on Julia's Bible. It sat on her nightstand because we read it at bedtime. But I'd been busy lately and hadn't even noticed that for several days now, her Bible had been holding up the hamster tunnel.

The Bible is God's love letter to us, and it's a treasure that should never be buried. Just like Pumpkin with his treats, we should consider it an item of great value.—Diane Stark

Yes, everything else is worthless when compared with the priceless gain of knowing Christ Jesus my Lord.

—Philippians 3:8 (TLB)

Scaredy Cat

He will not leave you or forsake you.

—DEUTERONOMY 31:8 (ESV)

MY FRIEND LISA recently adopted Presley, a kitty that had been found by a dumpster, abandoned along with other cats. When she brought him home from the shelter, he bolted out of the cat carrier and disappeared into the basement.

"Presley, psst. Come here." Lisa told me she used her most gentle voice, as well as treats, to coax him out of the basement. But nothing that first day tempted him to emerge.

It took Presley about eight days to come up the stairs and engage with Lisa. Each day she called him and left treats on the steps. Each day he cautiously walked up a few stairs, took the treat, and swiftly returned below, yet every day he came up a little farther. It was over that eight-day period with Lisa providing nutrients and love that Presley finally found the courage to come upstairs and stay.

Recently God has been calling me up the stairs to a new situation: my husband and I will be moving to a new location, partly for practical family reasons and partly because we heard God's "Psst, I have something for you." Some days I am ready to travel those steps, and other times I swiftly retreat back to our familiar situation. Like Presley, I have experienced an up-and-down-stairs drama: on one hand I'm scared because I do not have a clear-cut path to where we are headed, and other times, I trust God because He has gone before us.

Lisa's calling and provision of safety for Presley reminds me that the Creator of all things wants only the best for me. God promises that He will never leave nor forsake me. He is calling me to follow Him and trust His leading, knowing that stepping out in faith can lead me to a new situation that's even better than the one I left behind.—Virginia Ruth

Softly and tenderly Jesus is calling,
Calling for you and for me.
—Will Lamartine Thompson

Enough Love for More

Dear friends, let us love one another, for love comes from God.
Everyone who loves has been born of God and knows God.

—1 JOHN 4:7 (NIV)

WE RECENTLY HAD our first experience of being dog foster parents. Our daughter had seen a local animal shelter's plea for help and sent me the link. Just as I had fallen for our dog Honcho on a shelter's social media site, I fell instantly in love with Simone. But I was torn. I wanted to apply to foster as the shelter was requesting, but I also wanted to do so with the intent to adopt. I was afraid my heart could be broken if Simone went to someone else after being in our home. When I explained my concerns, they simply asked me to fill out an adoption application as well, which I happily did.

Since Honcho hadn't had a lot of socialization with other dogs, we took him with us to meet Simone. They took to each other immediately! We were able to bring our girl home. For two full days, Honcho treated Simone as if she were the best toy he'd ever been given. The two of them played constantly until they would collapse, exhausted, in the evenings. By day three, they had settled into a bit of a routine and begun to pace themselves. They're now the best of buddies.

I admit I was a bit worried to add a new member to our family. Could I possibly love Simone as much as I love Honcho? Of course I could. God's love is boundless and includes all His children, so through Him I have enough love for both dogs.

Our adoption is now final, and Simone is officially ours. She is sweet and loving and has given us more joy than we could have anticipated. Though two energetic young dogs can be a handful, we all learned we have enough love for both.—Missy Tippens

Heavenly Father, may I be as generous with my love today as
You are with Your love for me.

Lefty, the Bearded Dragon

And he was in the wilderness forty days, being tempted by Satan. He was with the wild animals, and angels attended him.

—MARK 1:13 (NIV)

MY GOOD FRIEND and neighbor Becky is a bearded-dragon lover. So far, she has welcomed twenty-six into her animal kingdom. And out of them all, only one has a defect. A baby was born with a tail that is bent to the left. There's nothing that can be done for this little guy. Because the dragons do not grow back a partial tail like a lizard does, he might not survive if the tail is removed. It's a wait-and-see situation. I've nicknamed him Lefty and keep tabs on his progress.

Becky has some theories about why this tail-twist may have happened, but her prime concern is to do her best for Lefty and all his kin, so they will be ready for homes when the time has come for them to move on. She is crazy about these little creatures, each with a personality of its own. Becky calls them magical.

Having someone like Becky to take the lead on animal kindness and care inspires me. Her desire to share these colorful little dragons with others shows me something about her sacrifice as well as her love of God's kingdom.

When Jesus was sent into the wilderness, where He was alone for forty days and nights, the animals comforted Him. Apart from Satan, there was no one else. When I think on this, I know I have long been deceived about the value of His animal kingdom. And when I see my friend Becky caring so kindly for these wee bearded dragons, proclaiming them amazing, I know God has a special purpose for even the smallest creature. Even Lefty can bring a smile.—Cathy Elliott

Every time you smile at someone, it is an action of love, a gift to that person, a beautiful thing.

—Mother Teresa

FEBRUARY 20

The Golden Hour

Holy, holy, holy is the LORD *Almighty; the whole earth is full of his glory.*

—ISAIAH 6:3 (NIV)

SNOW FALLS RIGHT along with the setting sun. Flurries of flakes create an old-time movie effect, with white static dancing across a sepia-toned world. Photographers often refer to dusk as "the golden hour," when lighting is at its finest for taking photos. Dusk also happens to be the golden hour for spotting God's creatures. As my family drives country roads solely to spot wildlife, my husband notices the silhouette of a great horned owl perched on a cottonwood branch. My eyes travel to the next tree and find a second great horned owl. A mile down the road, we discover another pair and, a bit farther, a lone fifth owl. I wonder where the owls have been all day and where they'll go tomorrow. Our golden-hour drive affords us the perfect opportunity to watch them.

I can see God orchestrating these golden-hour moments throughout my life when circumstances are perfectly aligned for me to witness His grace. Glory sightings become all the more plentiful as I learn the conditions in which they're most apt to take place and accept God's invitation to watch Him at work in the world. Just as the golden hour takes place every day, His activities in my life are regular and consistent. What's important is that I step outside my regular routine to see them. Or perhaps, even more powerful, I can make these sightings my routine—daily placing myself where I'm guaranteed to witness His beauty and wonders. I can choose to never let a glory hour go by without heeding the call to go and see all God is doing.—Eryn Lynum

Walk of Faith: *Take a walk in a natural area at dusk. Look for God's creatures and notice their many activities. Thank God for His glory, and ask Him to help you practice seeing Him at work in the world around you.*

Drawn Near

That they should seek God, in the hope that they might feel after him and find him. Yet he is not far from each one of us.

—ACTS 17:27 (RSV)

WE ADOPTED OUR Pekinese-Yorkie before my daughter entered kindergarten. She had been terrified of all dogs, so when she observed, "Mom, no one is afraid of her own dog," we knew we needed a puppy. My once-tiny daughter is now the brave young woman who has brought me along to a friend's cabin for a work weekend. Our sixteen-year-old dog has come too.

The click-clack of his toenails on the wood floor is getting on my nerves. What entices my blind, deaf dog to plod around the living room, dining room, and kitchen like a vacuum robot? What does he seek in each corner? When the vacuum robot fulfills its mission, it retreats to its place. But my dog makes no retreat. Click clack, table. Reverse. Click clack, wall. Turn right. Click clack, couch...on it goes. Maybe bringing him was a mistake.

My daughter and I have projects to do, and we had imagined a change of scenery would help us focus. But I discover emails to answer, texts to send, meals to cook. Click clack, desk. Click clack, kitchen. Much like my dog, I find it difficult to settle. What is it I am seeking, beyond the distraction of urgent tasks? Finally, my little dog comes to rest when his click-clack forays lead him to my feet under the table. I had tried to lead him to his water bowl, his food dish, even his own bed, but I think what he craves is familiar companionship.

I am like my dog. I believed I had come on this getaway to accomplish tasks, but as I drink my morning coffee waiting for my daughter to rise, I know it's her companionship that has drawn me here. I find my home with those I love at the feet of the One who loves us.—Susie Colby

I am Thine, O Lord; I have heard Thy voice,
And it told Thy love to me;
But I long to rise in the arms of faith,
And be closer drawn to Thee.
—Fanny Crosby

FEBRUARY 22

No Mavericks

Two are better than one, because they have a good reward for their toil.

—ECCLESIASTES 4:9 (ESV)

OUR MISSIONARY FRIENDS cruise the world in the *Silhouette*, a fifty-foot sailboat, serving the Lord wherever He leads. I've been a passenger on the *Silhouette* and enjoy hearing about their adventures.

One day, just off the coast of Mexico, what looked like a big wave was approaching the boat from several hundred yards away. As it neared, my friends identified it as a large pod of dolphins hunting for fish.

They grabbed their phone to video the sight. From what I observed, there must have been several hundred dolphins; their striped bodies revealed they were Pacific white-sided dolphins—a species known for their jumping and love of play.

"No wonder it looks like a wave," I marveled. They were in a straight line stretched across the horizon, probably herding their prey. When they approached the boat, the splashing got louder as they circled, split up, and headed in a different direction, obviously rounding up their dinner. A maverick mammal could never have fed himself alone. But together, they filled everyone's belly.

The teamwork they showed impressed me. Individuals united toward a common goal can always accomplish more, especially in the kingdom of God. This is why His Word so often stresses harmony. The book of Acts repeatedly models how community was necessary for the early Christians to grow and thrive. The local church is a team, as is the Church universal. Like dolphins (and me and my missionary friends), we are strongest when serving together to do God's will.—Tez Brooks

Heavenly Father, so often, the world encourages independence. Teach me Your ways and the value of community. Help me align in harmony with my fellow believers, so we may accomplish much for Your glory. Amen.

FEBRUARY 23

In Our Own Backyard

But godliness with contentment is great gain.

—1 TIMOTHY 6:6 (NIV)

SEND ME PICTURES of the deer!" I messaged my brother, begging for photos from his most recent time at the cabin where I'd spent every vacation while growing up—the place I loved more than any other, one with oodles of wildlife and beautiful scenery. I struggled with not letting my depressive feelings ruin my week. It had been four years since I'd seen the cabin, gone spotting deer, or walked the forest trails.

I put down my phone, settled on the porch swing, and opened the devotional to the day's reading. Before beginning, I heard a sound from the yard to my left. I checked to make sure the dog faced the opposite way, figuring a stray cat lurked nearby and not wanting the dog to see it and go bonkers. Looking back toward the sound, I watched a lovely doe delicately make her way down the creek bank and up the other side into our yard. She paused and gazed my way. I inched my hand toward my phone, hoping to snag her picture before the dog noticed her.

As I watched, she continued walking out of sight beside the house. I told the dog to stay and walked along the porch to the other side of the house, trying to sneak to a good vantage point for a photo. Unfortunately, the doe sensed something amiss and took off down the creek bed. I smiled as I watched her run, thanking God for letting me see the deer, along with so much wildlife on our property. Hmm...*wildlife on our property*. Could the doe have been God's reminder of how He brought us to purchase this place years before—one with "oodles of wildlife and beautiful scenery" in our own backyard? I didn't need a photo, after all. What I had right before me was picture-perfect.—Cathy Mayfield

Contentment is not the fulfillment of what you want, but the realization of how much you already have.

—Anonymous

The Nearness of a Cocker Spaniel

She had a sister called Mary, who sat at the Lord's feet listening to what he said. But Martha was distracted by all the preparations that had to be made. She came to him and asked, "Lord, don't you care that my sister has left me to do the work by myself? Tell her to help me!" "Martha, Martha," the Lord answered, "you are worried and upset about many things, but few things are needed—or indeed only one. Mary has chosen what is better, and it will not be taken away from her."

—LUKE 10:39–42 (NIV)

AFTER A BUSY week of travel, my young son, Nate, came down with a fever last weekend. As any parent knows, there are many things to be done in these situations, from monitoring a child's temperature to providing fluids and keeping an eye out for any strange symptoms that might warrant a trip to the doctor for medicine. As Nate lay on his pillow and cozy sleeping bag watching television, our senior cocker spaniel walked over and plopped down right beside him.

This dog—Schroeder—typically likes his personal space, and though he loves belly rubs, he's not one to want to cuddle up this way. He's always been very sensitive and intuitive, and I think he may have sensed Nate wasn't feeling well. Schroeder knew something I think a lot of us humans, myself included, miss—that the best thing he could offer my son was his nearness. As a result, Nate was absolutely *elated* because he knew how valuable those Schroeder cuddles were. And the dog's presence probably made him feel better than all my fussing over him did.

Often, I find myself wanting to "fix" life's challenges, whether those be my own hardships or those of the people around me. While there's nothing wrong, necessarily, with trying to help, sometimes the very best thing I can offer is my presence. Schroeder showed me the value of just being near.—Ashley Clark

Near the cross! I'll watch and wait, hoping, trusting ever, till I reach the golden strand, just beyond the river.

—Fanny Crosby

An Elephant Encounter

The whole earth is full of His glory!

—ISAIAH 6:3 (NKJV)

NEAR THE CITY of Winston, Oregon, Wildlife Safari attracts many visitors. Cars drive slowly through its 600 acres to view wild animals from various continents. There are also areas where spectators can stand behind a safe barrier, as well as a petting zoo for children.

Animals from Africa especially caught my eye, but the creature that thrilled me most was the world's largest land animal: the elephant.

Speechless, I stood behind iron bars as the enormity of an African elephant overwhelmed me. I was close enough to see its wrinkly, cracked skin. I heard its roar-like sounds and snorts. Its huge ears, as zoologists have noted, are shaped like the African continent!

I would later study this amazing animal and learn that the elephant is a great example for my daily life because it portrays important character traits from the Bible, such as temperance, power, strength, compassion, and loyalty. Despite its power, the elephant doesn't take advantage of others but exercises amazing self-control.

Scientists have proven that elephants have incredible memories and remember information for their survival and close family ties. Their remarkable recall power comes from the largest cerebral cortex of any land animal. Because they remember, they grieve when another elephant dies and often linger for long periods of time as though in remembrance. They may even hug each other with their trunks displaying emotional intelligence.

My personal encounter with an elephant was a springboard to launch me into a greater appreciation for what this animal can teach me. As a Christian, I want to strive to show self-restraint and gentleness. I want to remember what is most important in life, not the frivolous, and give a hug of hope and encouragement to those who need one.—Kathleen R. Ruckman

Dear Lord, thank You for the glory we see in all of creation—all over the world!

Living Water

He who believes in Me, as the Scripture has said, out of his heart will flow rivers of living water.

—JOHN 7:38 (NKJV)

JUST AS WE humans take marriage vows to remain faithful to our spouses until death do us part, sandgrouse are monogamous birds who form a lifelong bond with their mates. They make their nests in an indent in the ground and are usually found in treeless, dry areas, such as deserts. They are watchful parents who take excellent care of their young.

Daddy sandgrouse in particular has a tough job when his offspring are mere chicks, since the babies not only need to eat but also need a regular daily source of water. In order to provide for his young, daddy sandgrouse flies long daily treks to a water source. He then takes a long dip and wets his feathers, soaking up the water to take back home to his babies. Then he makes the difficult flight back, weighed down by that extra water. Yet no matter how demanding he may find his job, he knows how important water is to his family.

John 4 shares the story of the woman at the well who was drawing a heavy bucket of water when Jesus came around and asked her for a drink. Surprised, she asked Him why He spoke to her. He made known that He not only knew but understood her whole life and her aching heart, and He offered her Living Water so she would never thirst again. In that moment, He revealed Himself to her as her Savior.

Just like the daddy sandgrouse who brings water to his children, our Lord offers us Living Water. He knows and loves us intimately and wants us to know and love Him on the same level. In offering us the Living Water, He is offering us Himself.—Deb Kastner

Walk of Faith: *Today, as you drink a glass of water, thank God for both the natural resource that supports all human, animal, and plant life and His gift of Living Water.*

FEBRUARY 27

Deceptive Beauty

The prudent see danger and take refuge, but the simple keep going and pay the penalty.

—PROVERBS 22:3 (NIV)

FOR YEARS, MY husband and I talked about spending a whole month in Florida, but because of other responsibilities, we could never find the time. Then an opportunity opened, and we booked the month of February at our favorite vacation spot.

One chilly day, we took a walk along a secluded beach and hunted seashells. We didn't find many shells, but a variety of jellyfish covered the sand. Some were clear and as big as dinner plates, but my favorites looked like balloons with beautiful deep-blue coloring and long, nearly black tentacles. One raised its "head" and almost seemed to follow my moves as I took a video of it.

A few days after I posted my jellyfish pictures on social media, our younger son called. "Do you know what you saw? The Portuguese man-of-war!"

Research proved him right. When I posted about his revelation, a friend said her brother spent a day in the hospital and several days of painful recovery after being stung by one. Online sites said the creatures can deliver just as potent a sting after being washed ashore. Yikes! We had walked barefoot over and around them for an hour with no idea what danger we were in.

The man-of-war had no evil intentions, but I could have been harmed just the same, thanks to my ignorance. I will face many perils in this life, not the least of which are spiritual. Throughout Proverbs, God calls me to be wise—to see the danger and take refuge. The best way to foresee danger is through God's Word, and the best place to take refuge is in Him. By staying close to my Savior, I hope to step over and around the deceptive beauties of this world and avoid paying a painful penalty.—Tracy Crump

The simple believe anything, but the prudent give thought to their steps.
—Proverbs 14:15 (NIV)

FEBRUARY 28

Anticipating Needs

For your Father knows what you need before you ask him.

—MATTHEW 6:8 (ESV)

"THESE AMAZING SMALL flight machines travel over ten thousand miles on their way from their winter digs to their summer residency," explained the speaker at a lecture showcasing a bird photographer's pictures of the red knot.

"During this time they will stop at the Delaware Bay for a fuel replenishment of horseshoe crab eggs. The timing is right and crucial for the traveling birds. Many times, the birds are emaciated and will have to eat double their weight during their stopover. At the same time the birds are making their flyover, the horseshoe crabs will lay their eggs. The crabs lay an abundance—four thousand eggs in a cluster—and continue to do so, sometimes laying over twenty thousand eggs in an evening."

In the past year, our family had numerous trying situations: caring for dying loved ones, attending to their deaths and aftermath, a son dropping out of medical school and denouncing God. There were times I felt like the emaciated red knot, traveling far on life's emotional journey. I didn't have the spiritual fortitude to continue on.

Yet the words of that photographer reminded me that God put in my path the "nourishment" I needed through the encouragement of His Word and the words of dear friends. In one instance I was driving to visit my dying mother-in-law when the Christian radio announcer read a verse for the day that reminded me of God's strength lifting me during this difficult time. Another day, a dear friend called and prayed over the phone for our son.

Sitting in the lecture hall, I was in awe of how God uses His creatures to remind us how much He cares about all aspects of our lives, whether that is providing the physical food we need at just the right time, like He does for the red knot on its journey, or providing the spiritual food to nourish our spirits.—Virginia Ruth

Thank You, Creator God, that You know Your creation and its needs to survive. From the smallest of creatures to humankind, all can partake of the nourishment You provide for our journey through life. Amen.

FEBRUARY 29

Peanut Wars

For every beast of the forest is mine, and the cattle upon a thousand hills.

—PSALM 50:10 (KJV)

WHEN MY HUSBAND brought home a fifty-pound bag of unshelled peanuts from the feed store, he had no idea we'd be starting a battle in the backyard. After I filled the platform feeder with peanuts, it didn't take long before the acorn woodpeckers and scrub jays discovered the treat. That's when the peanut war began. The birds didn't want to share. They continually swooped into the feeder, flapping their wings and squawking to scare off others. If a chickadee ventured too close, a woodpecker would dive bomb the little bird until it flew away. When a Steller's jay helped itself to a peanut, the swift attack by a bolder bird prompted the timid jay to drop the peanut and flee.

Amused and exasperated, I placed my hands on my hips, declaring loudly, "There's enough for everybody. Stop fighting!" The birds couldn't possibly know I had the capacity to keep providing more peanuts, even after the first bag had been emptied. There was no reason for them to be so selfish and territorial.

The Lord used this incident to bring home a valuable spiritual lesson to my husband and me—one which we shared with our grandchildren: God is able to provide for all our needs. Jesus advised His disciples not to worry about what they would eat or drink or wear (Matthew 6:25). There is no need to worry about getting "our share." As one pastor recently quipped, "If the Lord owns cattle on a thousand hills, don't you trust Him to slip you a burger now and then?"

I'm comforted realizing that God has and will continue to bless me richly with all good things. I can be a cheerful giver and share what I have. There's no need to squabble and fuss and bicker. I trust Him. You can too.—Shirley Raye Redmond

Worry does not empty tomorrow of its sorrow; it empties today of its strength.

—Corrie ten Boom

March

MARCH 1

Dancing with Zimmi

Now you are the body of Christ, and each one of you is a part of it.

—1 CORINTHIANS 12:27 (NIV)

TECHNICALLY, ZIMMI CAN'T dance. He is a Yorkshire terrier–poodle mix, yet he attends ballet class faithfully at his flat in London. All his online classmates around the world adore him, including me. Each time I pull up a video for Ballet Based Movement or join one of their live Zoom classes, I look forward to seeing Zimmi's little hairy face. While Susan teaches the class with her mum, Elizabeth, who uses the kitchen counter or a dining room chair as a barre, the Yorkipoo watches from his basket at the back of the room, aching to participate. Sometimes he decides to join the dance by hopping up on Susan's chair/barre or strolling across the hardwood floor during our closing curtsy. Class isn't complete until Susan whisks Zimmi up to say hello (or goodbye). His picture and bio are even included on the Ballet Based Movement website.

Some ballet purists might not appreciate having a Yorkie in class, but I love seeing Zimmi as much as I enjoy stretching and dancing with Susan and Elizabeth. As a woman who has lived with a rare vision problem my entire life, fitting in has been an ongoing struggle. As a kid, I stood out as different wherever I went, including activities like dance classes. In my adult years, I felt like an oddball with other moms at church. It has taken a long time to heal the wounds that told me, You'll never really fit in.

In the process, God has helped me recognize an area of tenderness that came through this often-painful journey: I never want anyone to feel left out, unwelcome, or like they don't belong. Seeing Zimmi included in ballet class, or sometimes even treated like the star of class, reminds me that in God's kingdom, we all fit beautifully—whether we dance or not.—Jeanette Hanscome

Walk of Faith: *Do you know someone who has a hard time fitting in? Ask God to inspire you to reach out to this person and make them feel included.*

MARCH 2

Watermelon Prayers and Mango Dreams

And my God will meet all your needs according to the riches of his glory in Christ Jesus.

—PHILIPPIANS 4:19 (NIV)

BARNEY IS A happy pig. He hangs with the chickens and keeps the chicken hawks away. He also lives for his food. Barney can hear a bucket even when he's in a dead sleep and start squealing in delight. Of all the goodies he enjoys, mangoes and watermelon are by far his favorite. He literally smiles when he finds a big chunk in his trough and sits back on his rump, chomping loudly as the juice runs down his chin. His favorite hen, Rhoda, eats with him every night.

When Barney came to our rescue farm, he was running wild with a couple of other mini-pigs. The other mini-pigs settled in with the other animals quickly, but Barney didn't have a great personality, so he was stuck all by himself. The only way to catch him or to get him in a good mood was to offer him mango or watermelon. And if a pig can pray, I know Barney does—because when we are out of his favorite fruit, someone inevitably runs a sale or donates some to the farm. Barney just sits and waits as if he knows, by faith, it will show up.

Do you have faith like that? Have you ever asked God for something just because you loved it, because it was your favorite? Or do you chastise yourself for thinking you're being frivolous and so instead cheat yourself out of a blessing? God blesses us with our needs according to His supply. He has everything in His storehouse. And just imagine how it makes Him feel to bless you with something sweet and specific just because He loves you so much.

A prayer is never wasted on the God who loves you. A request is just a show of how much faith you have that He will absolutely supply your needs. Your prayers are a testimony of your faith, and trusting He will supply begins with trusting enough to ask.—Devon O'Day

Thank You, God, for loving me enough to supply my needs and also my favorite things. Amen.

MARCH 3

Doing It Scared

Have I not commanded you? Be strong and courageous. Do not be afraid; do not be discouraged, for the Lord *your God will be with you wherever you go.*

—Joshua 1:9 (NIV)

THIS WEEK, I feared a meeting with a difficult person. But then I remembered what I learned from my granddaughter Temperance and the borrowed horse she's been riding, Shiloh.

At ten years old, Tempe desperately wanted to ride as tall and strong as her mom, our daughter Rebekah, did. But every time Tempe went to her 4-H horse meeting, she felt afraid and cried. The smallest in her class, Tempe was a wisp compared to the fifteen-hands-tall, red dun quarter horse with the dark line down her back. Even though Shiloh had a calm, sweet temperament, Tempe had learned to ride on a stubborn Shetland pony that always bucked her off. "He ruined horses for me," she told me. She knew that falling from a horse twice as big could really hurt.

Nonetheless, Tempe put a foot in the stirrup, swung her leg over the saddle, and got up on Shiloh, scared. And despite the fact that she screamed so all the neighbors could hear when the horse clipped into a lope, she wouldn't give up learning how to ride. In fact, this week Tempe and her mom will pick up Daisy, a golden palomino quarter horse with white tail and mane. Happily, Tempe won't have to borrow a ride anymore. She's excited that Daisy is "kind of lazy" and that when she's squeezed into a trot, it's a slow pace around the practice ring.

Tempe says she's still kind of scared when she gets up on Shiloh, who will be her horse this coming weekend for 4-H horse mastership, the culminating competition for young people pursuing a horse project for the year. But Tempe said, "I'll just do it scared."

Tempe's story about Shiloh taught me that the only way I can conquer my fears is to step into the stirrups of that apprehension and trot right through it. My fears do not disappear if I continue to avoid them. They will still be waiting for me if I choose to do only that which is comfortable in my life. Facing my fears and doing them scared makes me stronger and less fearful on this ride of life.—Janet Holm McHenry

Walk of Faith: *Think of an activity, meeting, or conversation you might be avoiding because you are fearful. Pray for strength, knowing God is with you, and do it scared.*

MARCH 4

Spring Peepers

The least of you will become a thousand, the smallest a mighty nation. I am the LORD; in its time I will do this swiftly.

—ISAIAH 60:22 (NIV)

FOR AN ANIMAL so small, they make a powerful noise. Not only are peepers loud, but their chorus is almost always a welcome one. Their song announces the coming of spring.

The snow had barely melted late last March when my husband, Mike, and I went out to walk the dogs. It was one of those nights when the air smelled green and wet, and I had a bounce in my step, knowing that spring was just around the corner. Then I heard it—the high-pitched chorus of PEEP PEEP PEEP. Among the tiny frogs, the males make the loud high-pitched noise to attract mates. There must have been dozens of them peeping. Together, they sounded like the jingle of sleigh bells.

"Oh, don't you just love peepers?" I said.

"We used to hear them every spring when my family went to the lake," Mike answered.

Although they're easy to miss, I remember finding one and picking it up when I was a child. The little peeper was brown, less than an inch long, with sticky toe pads, and it surely weighed less than an ounce. It had a dark cross pattern on its back. Their scientific name is *Pseudacris crucifer,* the latter word meaning "cross-bearing." At the time I didn't think anything spiritual of it, but now I do. All God's creatures have the potential to teach me something spiritual.

Peepers are barely noticeable during the day. But when they sing, one can't miss them. There are times when I feel insignificant and powerless. When I do, I remember the peepers. God made them small but mighty.—Peggy Frezon

From a small seed a mighty trunk may grow.
—Aeschylus

MARCH 5

Finding Beauty in the Commonplace

So God created…every winged bird according to its kind. And God saw that it was good.

GENESIS 1:21 (NKJV)

SIX TINY BEAKS aim straight toward the sky like stunt jets in formation. When mama bird returns, I realize the nest on our trellis belongs to a family of common grackles. It's my last choice of bird species for avian neighbors. I was hoping for a more colorful variety, like our red-winged blackbirds, or perhaps a phenomenal vocalist like our finches.

The common grackle seems a bit, well, *common*. The adults frequently monopolize the aspen trees in our front yard and scare off our migrating songbirds. And yet, as common as their name suggests they should be, these six chicks are pretty extraordinary. A week ago, a late-winter storm dumped snow across town. Wind and sleet whipped at our trees for days. Branches hung heavy in a wet blanket of snow. Yet, amid the chaos, the chicks managed to make their way into the world outside their eggs. It was an exceptional feat.

One hundred years ago, another seemingly ordinary bird overwhelmed the skies. As innumerable flocks of passenger pigeons flew overhead, no one thought something so common could go extinct. I watch mama grackle return to the nest with another meal for her young. In a few weeks, they will fledge and merge with the countless adult grackles adorning the trees of our neighborhood. But if the extinction of passenger pigeons taught us anything, it's that what is common is not invincible. What seems plentiful today may one day be gone. So this morning, I take extra time from a respectful distance to watch the chicks and find beauty in the commonplace.—Eryn Lynum

Walk of Faith: *Enjoy a walk today, and take time to appreciate commonplace things. Is there a bird, tree, or flower you normally walk right by? Stop to appreciate its beauty.*

MARCH 6

The Great Protector

He will cover you with his feathers. He will shelter you with his wings. His faithful promises are your armor and protection.

—PSALM 91:4 (NLT)

STORM WAS A white spitz. He was great on a leash and fun to walk around our new neighborhood at his side. Because of his wolf-like appearance, I was asked more than once if he was indeed a wolf. But his real domain was our fenced backyard. There he reigned supreme. He was generally quiet, but when an occasional meter reader decided it was easier to scale the fence than knock on the front door, Storm's barking and growling quickly sent the intruder back in the direction from whence he came.

Then one night a violent storm arrived. The thunder rolled and the lightning flashed, and we assumed Storm was safe in his doghouse until, shortly after midnight, he started barking. A look out the window revealed a large shape in the back of the yard, probably a fallen tree branch, but as violent as the weather was, it was not the time to venture out to look. Storm posted himself by the back door and stared fixedly at the back of the yard. He refused to come into the house, and even when the weather passed, he continued barking. At first light the source of Storm's exhausting protective display became clear. A full-grown poplar tree had been uprooted at the back of the yard and lay on the ground by the back fence. Storm had been protecting us from this unwelcome menace.

Storm's protection called to mind our heavenly Father. He has promised to protect me from all harm if I have faith and trust in His plans. It's difficult to keep faith when the terrors of this world buffet me, but the Lord is indeed my Great Protector, and He will be fiercer in His protection than Storm was on that dark, rainy night.—Harold Nichols

The LORD says, "I will rescue those who love me. I will protect those who trust in my name. When they call me, I will answer; I will be with them in trouble. I will rescue and honor them."

—Psalm 91:14–15 (NLT)

MARCH 7

My Owl Companion

I am like a desert owl, like an owl among the ruins. I lie awake; I have become like a bird alone on a roof.

PSALM 102: 6–7 (NIV)

IN THE LAST days of his life, my husband enjoyed birdsong. I was thinking of him when I joined a bird walk at a local garden. Our guide taught us to distinguish ravens from crows and identified songbirds and waterfowl, but his passion was the bird we didn't see: the owl. He knew the owl's favorite haunt, so we left the path to bushwhack through woods to a far corner where the tallest trees grow. No owl. We backtracked along the forest's edge, but still no owl.

I, too, had discovered a love of owls after my husband died. At home in silence and solitude, I felt consoled by images of these creatures. I hoped I would spy real owls in the nearby woods and enjoyed thinking about their presence even if I didn't see them.

Several weeks later I returned to the garden at midday, a terrible time to look for owls. My friend and I were there to enjoy the spring bloom, not birds. On a hunch, however, I led my friend into the pine grove the owls purportedly favor, and there, above us, perched an owl. I stared upward, and soon my friend and I were joined by others, curious to discover what we were watching. Silently the owl rotated his head, seemingly oblivious to his audience. But then he tilted toward me and winked, a silent greeting.

Some claim owls signify sorrow. Others fear owls as harbingers of doom. But to me, an owl is a companion who silently validates my experience of loss. When we found the owl so unexpectedly, I, too, felt found, seen by a welcome witness.—Susie Colby

A wise old owl lived in an oak
The more he saw the less he spoke
The less he spoke the more he heard.
Why can't we all be like that wise old bird?
—Nursery rhyme

MARCH 8

A Warm Rain at Night

You send the darkness, and it becomes night, when all the forest animals prowl about.

—PSALM 104:20 (NLT)

ACCESS TO A vernal pool—check. Rain gear—check. Flashlight covered with red tissue paper—check. I've wanted to witness this event for years, and I was ready.

It's nighttime in the early days of March. A warm, gentle rain is falling. My husband, Jeff, and I are primed to observe spotted salamanders on their trek from sheltered forest burrows to water. The window of activity is brief. In just one night, hundreds to thousands of salamanders throughout our area make the trip to vernal pools for mating.

Males generally are first to migrate, placing a sperm packet on the ground enroute. The females pick it up later. Each female will then lay approximately one hundred eggs, which form into an egg mass, clinging to underwater plants. Within days, adults leave the pool to return to their ground habitats. Once the eggs hatch and the young develop lungs, they leave the vernal pool and join the adults.

The salamander migration occurs under the cover of darkness and often goes unnoticed by other living things. It's a small, fleeting detail among uncountable details in creation. Yet, I know that our God sees to all the details in His creation. From salamanders to me and you, the Lord is on the day-and-night watch. How comforting it is that no darkness in our life is so deep, no detail is so trivial, no event is so fleeting that it remains outside the watch of our Father. "He will not let your foot slip—he who watches over you will not slumber" (Psalm 121:3, NIV).

Jeff and I peer one last time into the pool where salamanders enjoy their warm evening pool party. We steal away, careful where we step in case there are late arrivals, and return home thankful to share in God's grace and care.—Darlene Kerr

For God is in the darkness, His presence in the shadows, unseen,
He is there, His guiding hand leading in the night.
—Patrick Sookhdeo

MARCH 9

Amara, the Brave Chicken

Be sure you know the condition of your flocks,
give careful attention to your herds.

—PROVERBS 27:23 (NIV)

AMARA IS A Silkie chicken, jet black with black skin. After being mauled by dogs, she was brought to Shasta Wildlife Refuge, where Amara met her future owner, Hollianne, a wildlife volunteer. It was after hours, and although the Silkie had a hole on her back the size of a half dollar, she couldn't be taken in for treatment because she was a domestic animal. Hollianne would have to foot a very high bill if she took the chicken to a vet for an after-hours emergency. It was expensive, and the chicken's prognosis was poor. Besides, the animal wasn't even Hollianne's.

In an effort to save Amara, Hollianne took her home and tried a treatment she knew from her many years of experience with wildlife—an antiseptic flush of the wound three times a day, vitamin E oil, and an oral medication to fight infection. She'd already prepared a fancy carrying bag for baby raccoons that were rehabbed at Shasta Wildlife Refuge. She'd keep Amara safe in that bag for now.

For two days, Amara didn't move, though she let Hollianne tend to her wound. Hollianne asked her boys to pray, and they made a faithful team.

When Hollianne finally took Amara out to feed her, she discovered the chicken had a bad limp. Could this sweet girl get no break? Hollianne decided to continue the treatment for the weekend. About three days later, Amara emerged from her raccoon carrier, walking around with barely any lameness. The boys thought a miracle had occurred.

Amara recovered with time, care, and prayer. She still loves the raccoon carrier. In fact, she lays her eggs in it. Now a beloved pet, Amara was pronounced quirky enough to fit in perfectly with Hollianne's family. —Cathy Elliott

Father, thank You for showing me how to be loving not only to people but also to animals. Help me to be more caring to all who abide in Your kingdom. Amen.

MARCH 10

Loving Ginger

Love is patient, love is kind.

—1 CORINTHIANS 13:4 (NIV)

WHEN I WAS in college in India, I volunteered with an animal rescue organization. They had freed more than a hundred beagles and similar dogs from a pharmaceutical company that had been performing illegal testing on them. I helped with the adoption program, assisting families who wanted to welcome these canines into their homes. Before I knew it, I fell in love with the dogs and wanted one myself.

A gentle and sweet-tempered American foxhound chose me to be her human mom. I named her Ginger and took her home. It was clear from day one that my new friend had never lived in a house before. She was afraid of everything—stairs, people, and sudden noises. Ginger sat in a corner of my room all day, frightened and refusing to socialize with my parents or me. She also took much longer to housebreak. Even though I was disappointed because I had thought I'd found a perfect pet, I couldn't abandon Ginger.

Our new pet needed some time and a lot of patience on our part. It took almost a year for Ginger to enjoy human company and learn the ways of our home. Because my family loved her, we were willing to overlook her accidents and gently train her.

Ginger lived a long, healthy life, passing away at almost thirteen years of age. I think of her every time I find it difficult to get along with someone. My instinct is to give up. But God reminds me to be loving and patient, just like He is patient with me and just like I was to Ginger. I ask God to fill my heart with His love so I can persevere and give relationships time to evolve into beautiful friendships.—Mabel Ninan

It does not dishonor others, it is not self-seeking, it is not easily angered, it keeps no record of wrongs. Love does not delight in evil but rejoices with the truth. It always protects, always trusts, always hopes, always perseveres.

—1 Corinthians 13:5–7 (NIV)

MARCH 11

Alike, Yet Different

Now to each one the manifestation of the Spirit is given for the common good.

—1 CORINTHIANS 12:7 (NIV)

I'VE ALWAYS WANTED an orange cat. So when my two ancient felines died within months of each other, I found myself at the animal shelter, hoping the orange kitten advertised on its website was still available. To my surprise, *two* orange kittens, obviously littermates, were up for adoption. They looked exactly alike. Which one should I take? I sat on the floor to see which kitten would choose *me*. But that didn't work either. Both kittens climbed all over me, begging to be "the chosen one."

Finally, I told the attendant, "Just give me one. I can't tell them apart, anyway."

She replied, "If you take one, the second is free."

Free? Who could pass up a "buy one, get one" bargain like that?

So I ended up with two identical kittens, Tom and Jerry, that I could tell apart only by their different-colored collars. As time went on, their individual personalities emerged, making it easier to identify them. Tom is the cuddler, Jerry the adventurer. Tom is quiet, content to nap his days away, while Jerry is constantly looking for mischief. Although they look alike, they are unique with their own traits.

Christians also have unique traits. While we share many common attributes with fellow believers, we have individual gifts bestowed upon us by the Holy Spirit to be used for the good of the church. Some gifts are more obvious, such as teaching, whereas others may be less noticeable, such as serving in the background. Each believer has an important function in the work of God's kingdom. Together, we use our various gifts to build up the church and serve each other in order to live in purr-fect harmony.—Ellen Fannon

Father, help me use the gifts You have given me for Your glory. Amen.

MARCH 12

Pesky Perseverance

I see what you've done, your hard, hard work, your refusal to quit.

—REVELATION 2:2 (MSG)

THEY WERE BUILDING under the cover of darkness.

How else could it be? We'd gone to bed only to awaken the next day to discover their abode above the hot tub once again. Hadn't we done everything in our power to deter them, even knocking down their hard-earned work from the year prior upon the barn swallows' return?

"Not this year," my kind husband said, sweeping away the remains of their nest. "They're so messy. Why don't they build in our barn?"

I'll admit I've wondered the same, even asking them, "Don't you see that big, red building?"

Unwavering, the swallows swooped, making me dodge; the territorial creatures were clearly annoyed with my inquiry.

Holding my ground, I considered my next move. I wedged a shoe in the cranny where they'd insisted on constructing their stucco sanctuary. But their plan would not be thwarted. The birds simply built around the sneaker. In retaliation, I flipped on the outdoor ceiling fans on the porch, hoping that would discourage their efforts. Imagine my surprise when we woke to find the nest almost complete.

Alas, they've succeeded and have taken up residence in their new home above the hot tub. They'll make a mess, and I'll grumble, then I'll devise a new strategy for next spring when the couple returns. Until then, the lesson of the tenacious barn swallows? Perseverance pays off.

I can almost see our Creator smiling, having witnessed our struggle from heaven's perch. Perhaps He's whispering, *Good and faithful swallows, I've seen your hard work. Now, enter your nest.*—Maureen Miller

Success is the sum of small efforts, repeated day in and day out.

—Robert Collier

MARCH 13

Sticking Close

I have set the Lord always before me; Because He is at my right hand I shall not be moved.

—Psalm 16:8 (NKJV)

THE POND AT Wall Springs in Palm Harbor, Florida, has a special allure in the spring—ducklings. For weeks, I made my weekly fifteen-minute walk along the Pinellas Trail to the state park and scanned the water to no avail.

Finally, when the once bare trees overflowed with verdant leaves, my search yielded the desired results. I stood in the middle of the bridge overlooking the east side of the pond and observed yellow and brown bundles surrounding a female mallard. I counted twelve babies.

As the weeks went by and the birds grew, so did their playfulness. I couldn't help but smile as I observed their antics. They dove into the water, flapped their wings, and swam after their mother. Their frolicking brought such joy to my heart. I was determined to return as often as I could.

On one visit I found the small group by the edge of the pond. A few sat with their mother in the dirt. The father mallard stood on the wood border and overlooked the water as the others swam around. Their fuzzy down covering had transformed into sleek feathers.

Every time I saw them, I counted fewer ducklings—a duck or two less each week. In the end only two remained. It breaks my heart to think of what happened to the ones who didn't make it. I considered what allowed the two ducks to survive when their siblings did not—they were probably the ones who swam close to their mother.

I felt God remind me that I am like the ducklings: when I follow shiny objects and distractions, I become easy prey for the enemy of my soul. But when I stick close to my Savior, I'm not lost to discouragement or despair. Christ carries my burdens and sustains me.—Crystal Storms

Father, help me to keep my eyes on You and stay by Your side. Guard me from distractions and temptations that can pull me from my purpose. Thank You for holding me steady. Amen.

MARCH 14

Petey's Purple Boot

But let all who take refuge in you be glad; let them ever sing for joy. Spread your protection over them, that those who love your name may rejoice in you.

—PSALM 5:11 (NIV)

IT WAS PURPLE and tight, made of stretchy material, and my golden retriever, Petey, hated it. The rubber boot was supposed to slide over and protect his injured foot. That is, if I could wrestle it on him.

A few days earlier, Petey had been outside and ripped his toenail. The injury was deep enough to require antibiotics and painkillers. Without his protective boot, the wound would get dirty and possibly infected. The covering allowed the injury time to heal.

As I tried to pull the boot over his wound, I thought about how I sometimes resisted things that were good for me. A healthy diet. Physical exercise. Enough sleep. And sometimes, God's direction. Just recently I felt Him encouraging me to forgive someone who had hurt me deeply. I didn't want to do it. I resisted His nudging and pulled away. Forgiving this person would be uncomfortable, just like Petey's purple boot.

But at the post office a few days later, I encountered the woman who had hurt me. I wanted to avoid her. But when I looked at the package she was holding, all I could see was the big, bright purple shipping label. Yup, as purple as Petey's boot. I paused, then stepped next to her and smiled. "Nice to see you," I said. She looked surprised and relieved. "You too!" she said. Speaking to her was the first step toward healing our relationship.

When I got home, I helped Petey into his purple boot. "C'mon, it's good for you," I said. This time, he seemed to relax. Maybe he understood. I know I did.—Peggy Frezon

Dear God, treating a spiritual wound is as important as treating a physical wound. Thank You for covering me and protecting me until I am ready to take the steps to heal. Amen.

Just Dance

Wearing a linen ephod, David was dancing before the LORD with all his might, while he and all Israel were bringing up the ark of the LORD with shouts and the sound of trumpets.

—2 SAMUEL 6:14–15 (NIV)

ONE OF THE most amazing privileges of my life was going on safari in Africa. As part of a mission trip to the southern part of the continent, my team and I visited the South Luangwa National Park in Zambia. I loved observing all the animals in their natural wild homes, but one of my favorites was the elephant.

In the zoo, we often see elephants sway back and forth, which can be a sign of distress. In Africa, their behavior was completely different. These elephants seemed to stroll the countryside, enjoying it at their own pace. Watching them was as peaceful as they seemed to be.

One evening while on safari, we came to a group of elephants at sunset. A young male was apart from the group, flapping his ears and moving back and forth a bit. Our guide stated that the elephant was just testing his strength, but it sure looked to me like he was dancing. Here was this magnificent creature, dancing away, as the sun set behind him. It was a powerful moment.

Thinking about it now reminds me of David dancing before the ark. Where I come from, we usually don't dance in worship. In fact, we have a hard time even letting loose to clap our hands! But sometimes I long to dance, showing others that I celebrate the love and goodness of God through the movement of my body.

If that dancing elephant can create a powerful moment, I know I can too. But I don't need to dance for that to happen. I can use my body to praise the Lord by hugging a friend in need, reaching out to stroke my beloved pets, and welcoming neighbors with a wave. The power of the moment comes from celebrating God—no matter how I move my body.—Heather Jepsen

Thank You, God, for placing a song in my heart. Please show me what "dance" I can do in praise of You this day. Amen.

MARCH 16

Dogged Obedience

Because you have obeyed me.

—GENESIS 22:18 (NIV)

"MARLEY. MILLIE. COME." I was standing by our back door calling our two terriers to come into the house. They can be so frustrating because they only listen when it is convenient for them. If they would come in when they are called, they would receive treats or be protected from imminent danger. Most of the time they move by their own agenda and at their own time.

Their attitude reminds me of myself. Most of the time I want to behave according to my own agenda and time, not God's. I do not want to listen and follow the guidelines God gives me through His Word. I go about what I want to do, unaware that God is looking out for my welfare.

As I read the story of Abraham's obedience to offer up Isaac (Genesis 22), I am reminded that I need to obey God regardless of the perceived outcome. My ways and understanding are not God's ways and understanding. Left to my own devices and thoughts, I would never have imagined God's rescue plan and future. Yet because Abraham obeyed God, he was blessed beyond measure. Not only was his son rescued by God, but Isaac became the first generation in a long line of God's people.

When our terriers listen, I am so joyful. I want to bestow treats and favor on them. I want to give them much more than they deserve. When I listen and obey God, I imagine He is joyful. Yet even when I'm not obedient, He blesses me beyond measure. Thanks to Him, Marley and Millie are reminders to me that by listening to God and following His Word, I, too, am rescued by Him.—Virginia Ruth

Thank You, God, for the examples You have shown me through our dogs' behavior. May I learn to obey You in all circumstances. Amen.

MARCH 17

A Tail to Wag

But may the righteous be glad and rejoice before God; may they be happy and joyful.

—PSALM 68:3 (NIV)

I NEED TO CONFESS my guilty pleasure, if you will. I love golden retrievers, especially puppies. Goldens make wonderful pets for families with children. Little Boy Raleigh, our current golden, exhibits all the typical breed characteristics. He is intelligent, playful, and loyal; he chews everything and wags his tail a lot. If he is around his humans, his tail is usually wagging.

When a dog wags his tail, it is another way of communicating. Among other things, like nervousness, it can express a state of energetic enthusiasm, relaxation, or happiness, letting his human know all is right in his world. Most of the time dogs are not aware that their tail is wagging. It is an instinctive reaction that shows how they are feeling emotionally. Dogs have tails and aren't ashamed to use them.

Children usually are good at displaying emotions, whether happiness or excitement. In some ways they are unashamed and react more like a dog wagging his tail. It just comes naturally for them.

Sometimes I wish humans had an external, instinctive way to show how things are going for them. Sure, a smile tells someone I am happy, just as a wave of my hand signals openness, but I don't consider those instinctive ways to share my feelings. If I had a tail, I would want it to be wagging as a signal of my true happiness—a blessed life because I seek God. Even without a tail, I am not ashamed to share this emotion. —Ben Cooper

Lord, because of You, all is right in my world. Let my contentment be as evident to others as it would if I had my own tail to happily wag. Amen.

MARCH 18

Claiming What's Mine

We are heirs—heirs of God and co-heirs with Christ, if indeed we share in his sufferings in order that we may also share in his glory.

—ROMANS 8:17 (NIV)

THE TREES LINING the lake's perimeter are alive with the movement and colors of great blue herons. Months ago, when we moved in, neighbors told us about the heronry on the lake, a small island with skeletal cottonwood trees. The branches will fill out, they promised, and come spring, the herons will return. Sure enough, in the middle of March, we began noticing the tall, stilt-legged birds with windswept mohawks intently watching the island from peripheral trees.

While they were away, a resident eagle had moved in. Osprey hawks circle nearby. Red-winged blackbirds swoop and squawk and sing their many songs. Yet every bird knows to whom this island belongs. Now the herons band together to take back what is rightfully theirs—the trees and nests in which they've raised their young for countless seasons.

I'm reminded of the daughters of Zelophehad in Numbers 27:1–11 and Joshua 17:3–6. When the five sisters lost their father and had no brother to receive an inheritance, they faced the prospect of their family's legacy being handed away. Instead, they stood boldly before Moses, Eleazer the priest, and the chiefs and congregation. They asked for what rightfully belonged to them. Moses sought wisdom from God and received this response in Numbers 27:7 (NIV): "What Zelophehad's daughters are saying is right. You must certainly give them property as an inheritance among their father's relatives and give their father's inheritance to them."

Whenever Satan tries to claim the ground beneath my feet, I can stand firm on God's promises. Like the herons raising their next generation of fledglings, I can take back what is rightfully mine. Mine is an inheritance rich in freedom, righteousness, purpose, and delight!—Eryn Lynum

That you may know what is the hope of His calling, what are the riches of the glory of His inheritance in the saints, and what is the exceeding greatness of His power toward us who believe, according to the working of His mighty power.

—Ephesians 1:18–19 (NKJV)

The Smaller Picture

Open my eyes that I may see wonderful things in your law.

—PSALM 119:18 (NIV)

JUST AFTER CRAIG and I arrived at the Kaloko-Honokōhau National Historical Park on the Big Island of Hawaii, I spotted a shady, inviting inlet perfect for wading. A couple of others were standing in the water, sheltered from the pounding Pacific just beyond.

I kicked off my sandals and headed into the water only to hear, "Ma'am."

And then I noticed. Right at my feet was a honu—a giant green sea turtle. And those other couple folks in the inlet? They were uniformed park rangers protecting the turtles from those unaware. Apologizing, I hurried back to the sand and admired the honu from the beach.

As I sat on the shore, I saw why these turtles are easy to miss: their greenish-brown shells look similar to smooth algae-covered rocks in texture and color. And when the turtles are in the water, their heads are typically submerged. The longer I sat, the better I trained my eyes to notice the details—the pattern of the turtle's back, the green fat layer underneath, its curious black eyes.

That near mishap of a morning meetup with a honu sparked a sense that God wanted me to notice the details of our trip to the Big Island. We'd just been through a painful injustice and were fearful for our future. With this experience, I felt as though God said, *I've got this, down to the last nitty-gritty point.*

The big-picture shoreline of Hawaii is magnificent, but in the days afterward, I began to notice the smaller things. Granules of black sand. Small pools with sea creatures along the shore. An endless number of tropical flowers in all colors of the rainbow. And the rainbows themselves after misty sprinkles.

Sometimes life is big-picture heavy. But I worship and serve a God, my Rock, who thankfully is in the endless details—many I am unaware of, like that honu sea turtle disguised as a rock.—Janet Holm McHenry

Walk of Faith: *The architect Ludwig Mies van der Rohe said, "God is in the details." Look around today to notice what God is doing in the details of your life.*

MARCH 20

Close Encounter

The wind blows wherever it pleases. You hear its sound, but you cannot tell where it comes from or where it is going. So it is with everyone born of the Spirit.

—JOHN 3:8 (NIV)

MY WIFE AND I have enjoyed hosting a variety of birds on our four-acre property. Some, like finches and hummingbirds, we attracted with feeders. Most of them showed up on their own, though, like the starlings, turkey vultures, and Cooper's hawk.

Woodpeckers were among the party crashers. Drawn by the soft wood in several dead trees, these hammering birds were frequent backyard guests. I got used to seeing them, especially the more common downy woodpeckers, and took a certain comfort in the tapping sound of their hunt for food.

One day, rounding the corner into our wooded backyard, I caught a flash of red. I froze. There on a stump before me was none other than Woody Woodpecker. Three times the size of his downy cousins, with a flaming-red crest atop his head, this pileated woodpecker calmly worked the stump for a beetle or some insect larvae. Awed by its size and beauty, I made a furtive move for my smartphone in hopes of snagging a photo.

It was not to be. Woody took flight into a tree. Though I cautiously pursued, he was nowhere to be found. I never saw him again. I've often related that story to friends. Some appear skeptical. Others nod and say, "Great. Now how about those Cubs!" It seems the importance of the encounter is mine and mine alone.

My encounters with the Holy Spirit are exactly the same. Unexpected. Brief. Powerful. They leave me deeply awed. Yet few others care or comprehend the reality I've experienced. These treasures are mine alone. —Lawrence W. Wilson

Walk of Faith: *Quiet yourself and seek the Spirit. Don't worry about how to relate your experience to others.*

MARCH 21

Sowing Seeds

Then He spoke many things to them in parables, saying: "Behold, a sower went out to sow.... But others fell on good ground and yielded a crop: some a hundredfold, some sixty, some thirty.

—MATTHEW 13:3, 8 (NKJV)

IN THE RAIN forest of Chile lives a fascinating marsupial, native only to southwestern South America, called the *monito del monte* or "monkey of the mountain." Though perhaps this species isn't aware of how important their actions are, they contribute to the regrowth of the rain forest through snacking. That's right—when they chow down on fruit the trees produce, they spit the pits onto the fertile rain forest floor where other trees can then grow. As they move from place to place, foraging for the best eats, they are unwittingly spreading the seed as they go.

As I learned about these monkeys of the mountain, the parable of the sower (Matthew 13:3–9) immediately came to mind. Jesus tells the story of farmers tossing their seeds out. Some fell on the path, and the birds ate them. Others ended up in the stones, where they quickly grew but withered away, or into the thorns, which choked them out.

But the seed that fell on good ground—my heart, willing and open to hearing and responding to God's Word—yielded a massive crop.

I think about the monkeys of the mountain who unknowingly spread seed to grow the rain forest. I pray to become more conscientious about how I absorb the Word into my own heart and spread it to others. It's the good news!—Deb Kastner

How beautiful upon the mountains are the feet of him who brings good news, who proclaims peace, who brings glad tidings of good things, who proclaims salvation, who says to Zion, "Your God reigns!"

—Isaiah 52:7 (NKJV)

MARCH 22

Chicklet's Little Life

In him was life, and that life was the light of all mankind.

—JOHN 1:4 (NIV)

WHEN BABY CHICKS are hatched on a farm, everything is their predator. Other animals, the cold, the damp, sickness, even a bad chicken mama can be a detriment to a new hatchling. One morning I saw Demetria, one of my beautiful ebony-green hens, sporting a flock of new babies. Five fuzzy chick babies were peeping all around their mama.

That same day, Niblet, another hen, was clucking loudly in the backyard with three new little hatchlings of her own. When I left for work, I said goodbye to eight new chicken babies. I returned home to find one baby chick weak and wet in a puddle. After a complete count, I saw there were only two chicks left—one little chick with a mama and the weak little chick I rescued.

I raised "Chicklet," as I called her, in a cage inside. She feathered out, ate with an uncontrollable urge, and seemed happy to rejoin her mama after a month of being inside. She was so joyous as she followed the older hens around, pecking at the ground and grass. I tried to confine her to a safe place outside, but she would have none of it. Freedom was the only thing she was having that day!

And at the end of that day, she was gone. Maybe she joined my neighbor's coop. Maybe a cat found her. Maybe an owl took her to her nest for her babies. But she, in her sweet short life, had taught me a lesson. It is not the number of days we have but how we spend our days that brings quality to our life. Chicklet was happier in her one day of sunshine than in all her "safe" days locked away in her cage. She had survived, if only for her one perfect day. It made me want to relish the sunshine more on this day and every day, knowing each one was perfect and made just for me.
—Devon O'Day

Thank You, God, for this beautiful day of freedom in the sunshine.
Let me live it fully with joy. Amen.

MARCH 23

Morning Meet and Greet

You will show me the way of life, granting me the joy of your presence and the pleasures of living with you forever.

—PSALM 16:11 (NLT)

SOMEDAY I'LL LEARN not to turn my phone on before I begin my devotions. More often than not, comments from family or friends on somebody's Facebook post cause a sense of loneliness or a feeling of being left out.

Today, I'd almost skipped going out on the porch for my morning devotions. I remembered the days our home was filled with our daughters' friends, homeschool clubs, and nearby cousins. I missed the laughter and music and girlish giggles. I shook the melancholy away and tied the dog to the porch swing.

No sooner had I opened my Bible than a deer came out of the woods and into our yard. She didn't stay long, just enough to say, "Hello!" She walked off, and I returned to reading, smiling at the special treat. Then, a flash of pink flew by. Pink? I knew we had red cardinals, but pink? I looked the way it had flown and saw a pair of strawberry finches sitting on the corner of the roof overhang. I'd noticed the finches at our feeder over the winter months, an unusual occurrence for us. These two seemed to be conversing about the weather or some such triviality. They'd been there only a few moments when a Carolina wren perched on the tippy-top of a dead branch in our oak tree and began a concert loud enough for our neighbors down the road to hear. The pair of finches stayed to enjoy the chorus.

In a few moments, God's pleasures had changed my morning mood. A deer saying "Hello." Finches having a "meet and greet." A wren's melodic song. Our dog stretched out at my feet. And the Word Incarnate on my lap. Lonely? Nope, not me.—Cathy Mayfield

Walk of Faith: *Are you feeling lonely today? Open your Bible, and invite God to fill your day with His Word and His creation.*

Caring for Cats

Let each of you look not only to his own interests,
but also to the interests of others.

—PHILIPPIANS 2:4 (RSV)

I WAS IN BULGARIA with a group of American students shortly after the revolution that overthrew Bulgarian dictator Todor Zhivkov in 1989. In the early days after the fall of Communism, this first cultural exchange between American and Bulgarian students at Sofia's premier university garnered local attention. Our worlds, recently so different, were beginning to merge as we shared ideas about culture and faith.

Older Bulgarians remembered this wasn't the first new government to promise prosperity. Some of them, especially the grandmothers (fondly known as *babas*), had held on to faith in God despite the state declaring itself officially atheist. The babas had continued to pray for their grandchildren, some of whom were now part of our exchange.

Our group was honored with abundant meals, emblems of anticipated prosperity. Few students, Bulgarian or American, could finish these lunches. Embarrassed by the waste, I collected leftovers. I secreted my "doggy bag" to the park bench where a baba neighbor fed the local cats. As the cats thronged about her expectantly, the undeterred hope in their eager cat eyes reminded me of the glimmer I saw in Bulgarian students' faces. Giggling and gesturing in wordless conspiratorial conversation, this baba and I fed her cats, who responded by purring and complaining in language she and I both understood.

My new companion and I were bonded not by the thrilling exchange of new ideas but by love and care for cats and a friendship that crossed generational, cultural, and political divides. The cats accomplished for us what was intended in our exchange program. Our shared empathy for kitties and caring for them together blessed us in ways we couldn't articulate to one another. Sometimes love requires no words.—Susie Colby

Nobody cares how much you know, until they know how much you care.
—Theodore Roosevelt

MARCH 25

Voices

Evening, and morning, and at noon, will I pray, and cry aloud: and he shall hear my voice.

—PSALM 55:17 (KJV)

OUR CHILDREN'S 4-H activities often turned into family projects, and none more so than when our older son participated in an amphibian monitoring program. As a family, we listened over and over to audiotapes of twenty-one frogs and toads native to our state and learned to identify their individual voices. Then, with flashlights in hand, we made nighttime trips to a nature center pond. There we spotlighted the little hoppers to get a head count.

Many years later, I still enjoy identifying several species that call to one another around our home on spring and summer evenings. The upland chorus frog vibrates like a finger running over the teeth of a comb. I love hearing the southern leopard frog that sounds as though he is rubbing an inflated balloon and then chuckling—ha-ha-ha. The Fowler's toad often startles me on walks with his nasal "waaaaah" that mimics a baby's cry. And then there is the strumming bass serenade of the American bullfrog or its frightened scream when it jumps into the water after I've startled it.

Though I can differentiate these amphibian species and a few others by their collective calls, I can't tell them apart as individuals. Yet God knows me. Out of the eight billion or so people on the planet, He can pick out my voice when I call on Him.

How amazing is that?

Whether I am distressed or in trouble or just need a listening ear, God hears my cry. Any time of day, I can share my joys and my sorrows with Him. From my first plea for salvation to my last whispered word, God knows me for who I am—not just one of His children but *me*.—Tracy Crump

Walk of Faith: *Go to the Lord today with a pressing concern and pray with assurance and conviction that He hears your voice, knows you, and loves you.*

MARCH 26

Patience of an Owl

But let patience have its perfect work, that you may be perfect and complete, lacking nothing.

—JAMES 1:4 (NKJV)

MY FAMILY AND I thoroughly enjoyed our tour of a nearby bird sanctuary. As we walked through the exhibits, employees and volunteers provided short talks about the birds and their habitats. Nothing spurred my imagination more than the lecture about, and demonstration with, the wise owls.

A young woman dressed in camouflage held a barn owl, using her gloved hand. She explained owls can rotate their necks 270 degrees, enabling them to silently search the landscape. Piercing eyes provide binocular vision, allowing extreme focus on objects great distances away. For example, a northern hawk owl can spot a vole from a half mile away.

I couldn't get over the asymmetrical ears located at slightly different heights on their heads. The unusual placement of the ears allows owls to hear in multiple dimensions so they can pinpoint the location of their target. Each anatomical feature gives them another tool for hunting. God thought of everything.

The lecturer shifted positions for effect. Then she asked the children to stand still for five minutes. Within thirty seconds, most of the children had moved, leading to giggles and other reactions. Our teacher used this illustration to talk about the owl's most valuable tool: patience. An owl might wait motionless for hours to locate a target.

This sent my mind spinning back to a recent contentious conversation with a friend. Where was my patience as I bluntly corrected an error of fact? Without waiting to hear my buddy's entire point, I quickly offered an alternative view.

As a Christian, my first priority should be the gospel. Truly caring about my friend should have led me to practice patience: listening and hearing him out. Through patience and restraining my tongue, perhaps I could become wise like the owl and a better friend.—David L. Winters

Lord, help me to exercise patience when talking with others. Teach me to wait for the right time to speak. Please fill my words with grace. Amen.

MARCH 27

The Path of Leash Resistance

Truly my soul finds rest in God; my salvation comes from him.

—PSALM 62:1 (NIV)

EVEN THOUGH I felt overwhelmed by my schedule—fulfilling a writing deadline, organizing a progressive dinner, and rehearsing a presentation—I agreed to meet my friend Geneva at the community park for an afternoon hike with her two adorable beagles, three-year-old Misty and her pup Mickey, who sported long droopy brown ears. Despite wanting to focus on the early spring sensations around me, my mind shifted back to all that needed to be done at home.

At first the four of us were walking in silence and perfectly in synch along the paved trail. Misty followed Geneva a leash length away, staying on the pathway, calmly sniffing items close by. But then Mickey charged ahead into the uncut grass, straining on the leash, lunging at something far from us. The energetic beagle returned to his mother several times, nipping at her ears. After fifteen minutes of this running back and forth, Geneva commented, "That pup is going to sleep good when we get home!"

When I returned home, all my chores were still in front of me. I thought about how Mickey used all his energy chasing after any distraction and tugging at the leash. I took a deep breath and prayed over my to-do list, just like I should have done at the beginning of the day. I prayed that I would stay close to God and stop pulling at my spiritual leash. From now on, I will let Him set my pace and focus on His guidance. At the end of the day, I'll be able to say that I used all my spiritual energy in following God's plan. Only then will I learn the lesson of resting easy.—Glenda Ferguson

Walk of Faith: *Before you physically start your day, quiet your mind. Inhale, exhale slowly, and pray over your to-do list.*

MARCH 28

Awe-Inspiring Closeness

Yours, Lord, is the greatness and the power and the glory and the majesty and the splendor, for everything in heaven and earth is yours.

—1 CHRONICLES 29:11 (NIV)

I'VE ALWAYS THOUGHT pelicans, with their large throat pouches, were rather funny-looking birds. I have sometimes seen them from a distance while visiting the Florida coast. Recently, while staying at a condominium on the bay side of Okaloosa Island, Florida, I spent a good bit of time on the balcony watching the pelicans from our sixth-floor view.

The birds would float in the water, then sometimes take off and fly around looking for a fish. The water was very shallow and perfectly clear, so they had a great setup for scoping out something to eat. They looked rather small from where I sat. And I had never been close enough to one to get a feeling for their size.

Then one day at the condo while I was working on my computer out on the deck, a noise drew my attention. One of the pelicans, its wings spread wide, its throat pouch extended, soared so close to our balcony I felt as if I could reach out and touch it! It was huge. I was stunned, because from six floors up, I'd had no idea how large they really were.

As it flew away, my heart was pounding. It was a magnificent creature. Immediately, I realized how I had misinterpreted its size from my vantage point. Then it hit me how I sometimes do that with God. When I worry or am fearful, I am not trusting His provision. Anytime I think of my close encounter with the soaring pelican, I'm reminded that God is bigger than I sometimes give Him credit for being. I need to remember that God is all-knowing, all-powerful, and ever present. He loves me. I am in good hands.—Missy Tippens

O Lord, our God, the majesty and glory of Your name transcends the earth and fills the heavens. O Lord, our God, little children praise You perfectly, and so would we. And so would we. Hallelujah! Hallelujah!

—Linda Lee Johnson

MARCH 29

Flights of Angels

For he will command his angels concerning you to guard you in all your ways.

—PSALM 91:11 (NIV)

SPRINGTIME IN SOUTH Louisiana is marked by the return of cardinals in their red glory to city yards. These birds do not migrate but in winter may move from the city to more heavily wooded areas. People announce their presence on social media with photos and captions: "Look what I saw in my yard." Their beautiful song tells of their presence, even when they are not visible.

Once cardinals have picked out a spot, they can be very devoted to it. Our daughter-in-law has a cardinal who visits her car every day to deposit a "love note," and one day he flew into the car when the door was open. The females are harder to spot since they lack the bright coloring, but where there is a male, there will be a female close by, as cardinals usually stay with the same mate for their entire life. And the loving pair can often be seen beak to beak, with the male feeding the female.

The word *cardinal* is derived from the Latin noun *cardo*, meaning "hinge." My wife and I believe that cardinals are a hinge between heaven and earth, being the spirit of loved ones sent by God to watch over us. We know that God's angels are always around us, and male cardinals are one of their most visible forms. The harder-to-spot female is simply a reminder that we need to be vigilant for angels who are present but a bit more difficult to spot.

In *Hamlet,* Shakespeare has Horatio say to the dying Hamlet, "Good night, sweet prince, and flights of angels sing thee to thy rest." I like to think of cardinals and their songs as a reminder of the flights of angels who are here for me on a daily basis.—Harold Nichols

Dear Lord, thank You for sending Your angels to watch over me. Help me to be aware of their presence and to respond to their gentle guidance. Amen.

MARCH 30

Puddles or Ponds?

"For I know the plans I have for you," declares the Lord, "plans to prosper you and not to harm you, plans to give you hope and a future."

—Jeremiah 29:11 (NIV)

I PULLED INTO THE grocery store parking lot just as the downpour started. It had been raining almost nonstop for days, and the crummy weather matched my mood. Our middle son was moving into his first home, which was great, but it pushed my husband, Eric, and me one step closer to being empty nesters. Although we still had our youngest son at home, I was already dreading this new stage of life. I've always hated change.

I was preparing for a mad dash into the store when I spotted a mother duck waddling across the busy lot, her three babies following behind. Normally, the sight would've made me smile, but today, I just felt concerned for the ducks' safety.

My mood didn't improve as I shopped. How will I learn to cook dinner for just three people? And in a few short years, I'd be cooking for only two. Would I feel lonely as an empty nester? Would my life lack purpose without my kids at home?

After paying, I headed outside into the rain. As I loaded the groceries into my car, I spotted the mother duck and her babies, now swimming in a giant puddle on the far side of the parking lot. I couldn't help smiling as I paused and gazed at them.

An older gentleman walked by and said, "The rain doesn't bother them a bit. We see a puddle, but they see another pond to swim in."

I realized that I could see the changes in our family the same way. Instead of fearing the change, I could remember that this new stage was a part of God's plan and He would be there with me.

My new chapter wasn't a puddle. It was a pond, and it was time for me to go swimming.—Diane Stark

It is comforting to know that the God who guides us
sees tomorrow more clearly than we see yesterday.
—Author Unknown

MARCH 31

Bunny Blessings

When he saw the crowds, he had compassion on them.

—MATTHEW 9:36 (NIV)

MY FIVE-YEAR-OLD GRANDDAUGHTER, Lily, and I waited in a long line at the garden center. "I can't wait to see the bunny!" she said. Rabbits were her favorite animal. She'd befriended a wild one in the yard and named it Salad. She drew pictures of bunnies and asked for rabbit stories at bedtime. But it seemed like every other parent, grandparent, and child in the county was there at the garden center at the same time, waiting. At Easter, every child wanted to meet a bunny.

When we finally got to the front of the line, Lily plopped down on the hay bale, grinning. The attendant put the large gray rabbit in her arms. Lily brushed her cheek against its velvety fur. The rabbit wiggled its nose and burrowed up against Lily's chest. It was so gentle and calm. Lily looked at it lovingly. I felt as if something special passed between the two of them. But then abruptly, Lily handed the rabbit back to the attendant and stood up.

"Wait! You have more time," the attendant said.

"There are lots of kids waiting," Lily said, looking at the line. "I want them to get a turn too."

I couldn't believe that my granddaughter had patiently endured an incredibly long wait and then willingly gave up her time so that other children would be sure to have their special moment. But that rabbit had clearly touched her, almost as if it had whispered a special secret in her ear. I know that Easter isn't about the bunny, but that day, in that moment, I felt that Easter was all about the bunny.—Peggy Frezon

Walk of Faith: *As you move through the Easter season, be sure to include an unselfish, Christlike act of service.*

April

Better Safe than Sorry

The prudent see danger and take refuge.

—PROVERBS 22:3 (NIV)

WHEN MY THIRD mystery novel was published, a book club in Albuquerque asked me to speak at their monthly meeting. I arrived at the designated location twenty minutes early, so I sat quietly in my car going over my notes. At one point, the scurrying of several small creatures in the empty field across the street caught my eye. Prairie dogs! Intrigued, I stepped out of my vehicle and meandered across the street for a closer look. One of the prairie dog sentries, keeping a watchful eye for hawks, snakes, and other predators, caught sight of me. He gave a sharp warning whistle. Suddenly, all the scurrying little creatures disappeared into their burrows.

I meant them no harm, but the little sentry didn't know that. He'd done his duty, alerting his fellow prairie dogs to possible danger, and every one of them had heeded the warning. Better safe than sorry, I guess.

Maybe I should be more like a prairie dog, heeding the warnings around me. Besides labels on everything from medicine bottles to household cleaners, there are many scripture verses that provide warnings too. It would be to my advantage to pay attention to them.

Over and over again, the Lord warned the Hebrews not to worship idols—or there would be consequences. The Old Testament book of Proverbs is filled with cautionary words about everything from drunkenness to sexual immorality, lying, and foolhardy pursuits. Jesus taught people not to build their house upon the sand (Matthew 7:26), and God Himself warned the visiting Magi in a dream not to return to Herod's palace after they'd worshipped the Christ Child (Matthew 2:12). They wisely heeded the warning, returning to their own land by another route.

Have you ever had an occasion when God nudged you *not* to do something? I have, and I'm thankful I listened. Like the prairie dogs, I'm better safe than sorry!—Shirley Raye Redmond

Dear Lord, help me to be obedient to Your words and heed Your warnings. It truly is better to be safe than sorry. Amen.

APRIL 2

Sharing a Smile

A cheerful look brings joy to the heart.

—PROVERBS 15:30 (NLT)

MY GRANDDOG, HALSEY, is a black brindle "Frenchie"—a French bulldog—with huge bat-like ears. Because he belongs to my naval officer son-in-law and oldest daughter, he's appropriately named for one of the navy's five-star fleet admirals.

Halsey has quite a fan base in the neighborhood where they live. On walks, my daughter says, they seldom go more than a block without someone commenting, "Oh my gosh! He's so CUTE."

Like many dogs, Halsey hates the rain. Sometimes my daughter and son-in-law find it challenging to coax him outdoors for a potty break.

This is why, when I spotted a display of doggie raincoats in a store, I knew I had to buy one for Halsey. But which one? I finally chose a ladybug-red one with black spots. The color would complement his black fur. And the ladybug spots? A bonus. I couldn't wait to hear how Halsey liked his new outerwear.

My daughter called a few days later with a report. "Halsey's not real crazy about wearing it," she said, "but oh, my gosh, the reactions we get when people see him are worth it. Everyone smiles."

I don't have a cute Frenchie with a ladybug raincoat, but I, too, have the power to make people smile. Recently, I prayed with an anxious dental patient at the office where I work. I mailed a cheerful card to a sick friend. I texted a hope-filled Bible verse to a neighbor who's going through a challenging season. Something as simple as smiling at a stranger as we pass in the store can infuse a little sunshine into someone's rainy day—even if I don't have an adorable Frenchie with a red raincoat walking beside me.—Lori Hatcher

Walk of Faith: *Today, make it your goal to see how many people you can share a smile with.*

APRIL 3

A Husband's Love

Husbands, love your wives, just as Christ loved the church and gave himself up for her.

—EPHESIANS 5:25 (NIV)

OF ALL THE different birds that come to the feeders in our backyard, Mr. and Mrs. Cardinal are the ones I enjoy watching most. It isn't because they are prettier than the others. The reason I enjoy watching them is the love between them.

The chirps are the first thing that tells me the cardinals are near. Following that, I see a flutter among the leaves. Mr. Cardinal arrives first. He surveys the surroundings. After he decides it is safe, he chirps for his wife to join him. Another flutter in the leaves, and Mrs. Cardinal arrives. When he sees her, he flies to the feeder.

Instead of eating, like I would expect him to do, he picks up a seed. With the seed in his beak, Mr. Cardinal flies to his wife. He tips his head. She tips hers. When their beaks meet, he gently drops a seed into her waiting mouth. This routine is repeated several times before Mr. Cardinal stops at the feeder to eat.

I never tire of watching these lovebirds. Their routine is always the same. Mr. Cardinal arrives and makes sure it is safe before beckoning his mate to join him. He puts her needs before his own. Only after he is sure his wife has eaten all she wants does he eat.

As I watch this pair, I see love and devotion. I see care and selflessness. I see the act of putting another first. In watching, I see the type of sacrificial love a husband and wife are to share. While I watch, God brings to mind the love, care, and selflessness my husband shows me. Through these cardinals, God reminds me of all the times my husband puts me first, and I offer a prayer of thanks.—Sandy Kirby Quandt

You can give without loving, but you can never love without giving.

—Robert Louis Stevenson

Lucy Lessons

Weeping may stay for the night, but rejoicing comes in the morning.

—PSALM 30:5 (NIV)

THE NEWS WAS bad. So, I did what I always do with bad news—I took a walk with my dog, Lucy. My great-grandson had been born with many defects and was now in cardiac arrest after surgery. Lucy knows nothing of the sadness in the human world, so she is wonderful company when I am sad.

The day was full of hopefulness even though I was not. As we traveled the road, Lucy met her first turtle, fresh from hibernation. Lucy has learned to be gentle with our cat, so she applied her kitty wisdom to this new life form. She lightly pawed the shell, which sent the turtle into retreat. As the turtle once again showed signs of life, Lucy went into full play mode. She wiggled, spun, and jumped. The turtle was not amused and sank farther into its shell.

With the concern over my great-grandson, I felt like that turtle. I was glad when friends reached out to ask how my great-grandbaby was doing, but sometimes I needed to pull my head into a shell and just meditate on God's overall goodness. God has always been constant and would carry our family through. But it would not be easy. Psalm 23 does not say *we* will walk through the valley of the shadow of death; it says *I* will. I felt like I was in that shadow at present. Though friends meant well, I knew the walk was mine. God in His graciousness sent Lucy to be with me to remind me that joy will come again.

A few hours later, my sadness turned to joy. A change in medication helped my great-grandson get his heart rhythm under control. Recovery would not be easy or swift, but he was on his way.—Linda Bartlett

Have I not commanded you? Be strong and courageous. Do not be afraid; do not be discouraged, for the LORD your God will be with you wherever you go.
—Joshua 1:9 (NIV)

APRIL 5

Swartz Come Home

See, I am doing a new thing! Now it springs up; do you not perceive it?

—ISAIAH 43:19 (NIV)

I MOVED TO INDIANA after my wife's passing. I was lonely without Sandra, and it was comforting to be near my sisters. Colleen invited me to dinner one night. I enjoyed her and my brother-in-law Jim's hospitality, good food, and seeing their two black cats, Swartz and Eggers. Their fur color seemed to be the only thing they had in common. Swartz was a crowd pleaser and cuddler. Eggers, a former street cat, was a loner, aloof and wary. And don't even try to pick up Eggers. He would have none of that. The cats had set boundaries with each other and their owners.

When I arrived, I noticed a change in Swartz and Eggers. They seemed more at ease.

"What happened to those two?" I asked Jim.

Jim laughed, "Eggers played 'Lassie' the other morning."

In response to my puzzled look, Jim explained. The previous morning, he had gone to the kitchen to announce it was feeding time. Only Eggers came running, but he ignored his food and made a beeline for Jim. Eggers looked up at Jim and ran to the sliding glass doors, agitated and whining.

"I didn't know if it was my lack of coffee, but Eggers appeared to repeatedly jerk his head toward the door," Jim said, laughing.

Could Swartz have gotten out? Colleen and Jim had gotten home from a trip the night before. Did the cat sitter forget to let him back in? Eggers's whining and head gestures continued, so Jim stepped outside. *If I was Swartz, where would I go?* he wondered. Jim felt led to the storage shed. Swartz was curled inside an old tire.

I was in awe that the Lord had used Eggers and his owner to bring Swartz to safety. I realized the Lord was also concerned for my safety and comfort, leading me back to Indiana and family.—Terry Clifton

Walk of Faith: *If you know someone who has experienced a loss, contact them. Share a meal or, if possible, arrange to visit. Most importantly, let them know you will be there if they need anything.*

April Morn

And God said, "Let the waters bring forth swarms of living creatures, and let birds fly above the earth across the firmament of the heavens."

—GENESIS 1:20 (RSV)

THE WOODSTOVE IS hungry, and logs don't chop themselves, so out to the woodpile I go. It is April, a slushy little month that can't seem to make up its mind—winter one day, spring the next. It might snow tomorrow, but today feels like spring. The air is moist and warm, the rhubarb is up, and my maple trees are festooned with swollen green buds.

On my way to the woodpile, I hear something that stops me in my tracks—a melodious, flute-like trill. It sounds like *ee-oh-lay.* It's a thrush, the first one of the season. I lift up my eyes, moving my vision from tree to tree, trying to find her. *Ee-oh-lay.* Finally, there she is, a medium-sized bird just a tad smaller than a robin, reddish brown on top, the breast white with dark spots. The thrush can actually sing duets with itself, singing pairs of notes simultaneously. The result is an eerie, liquid song, and according to Henry David Thoreau, "Whenever a man hears [the song of the thrush], he is young again, and Nature is in her spring."

Two hours later, the firewood is chopped and stacked. I lost sight of the thrush, but I can still hear her. My back is sore from the splitting, but it is a good soreness, and my mind is clear, and my heart feels light and right. I thank the thrush, wherever she is, for keeping me company. As I walk back to the house, I realize that Thoreau was right—I feel young again, and Nature is in her spring. God is good, life is good, and there is a rhubarb pie in my future.—Louis Lotz

This is my Father's world, and to my listening ears all nature sings, and round me rings the music of the spheres.

—Maltbie D. Babcock

APRIL 7

If It Quacks Like a Duck

Walk with the wise and become wise, for a companion of fools suffers harm.
—PROVERBS 13:20 (NIV)

DURING ONE OF our visits, my sister Kristy and I reminisced about the quirky pets we'd had in the past. The memory we laughed over the hardest was of a cat Kristy got during college. Her name was Zoey, but to us, she will always be known as "the cat that quacked like a duck."

When Kristy and her husband got married, Zoey went with them to their first apartment, which had a pond that attracted ducks. Zoey's favorite spot was by a window in the kitchen overlooking the duck pond. One day, Kristy heard quacking coming from the kitchen. When she walked to the window, she discovered the quacks weren't coming from the ducks. It was Zoey. She'd spent so much time watching and listening to ducks that she started mimicking them.

After that trip down Pet Memory Lane with Kristy, I decided to do an internet search for quacking cats. Though I didn't find an official answer for why Zoey quacked, I read stories and fun facts about cats chirping, quacking, and making other sounds that seemed to mimic the animals they watched while sitting by a window or on the deck.

Zoey the quacking cat is my favorite illustration of my tendency to start behaving like those I spend time with. When I hang around a friend who has a propensity for focusing on the negative, I can find plenty of things and people to complain about too. On days spent with sisters in Christ who see the good in others, share what God is teaching them, and enjoy themselves even when things don't go their way, I do the same. If I am going to mimic my companions like Zoey mimicked the ducks, I want to sound like those who reflect Christ.—Jeanette Hanscome

Blessed is the one who does not walk in step with the wicked or stand in the way that sinners take or sit in the company of mockers.
—Psalm 1:1 (NIV)

APRIL 8

No Words Needed

Just ask the animals, and they will teach you.

—JOB 12:7 (NLT)

THE BURBLE OF our creek and the porch swing lulled me as I turned to the day's devotional reading. A hectic week with my uncle's progressing dementia exhausted me and gave me constant anxiety. What if he had needs I couldn't meet? Would I have the time, patience, and energy to keep helping him? I prayed today's devotions would hold some uplifting words.

Before I began reading, my dog jumped up from his place on the porch beside me, ears alert, and looked toward the trees along the creek. A slight rustling came from one of the trees. *Just a squirrel gathering nuts*, I thought. I went back to my devotions.

But Kenai whimpered and strained the leash to get a closer look. Something larger than a squirrel was coming down a wide hemlock branch like a kid on a slide—an opossum! The bulk of the grayish critter seemed too heavy to balance on the wiggling branch, but on he went, sliding, then grasping with his paws. I thought he'd fall into the creek any second.

As I watched, he wrapped his thin, muscular tail around the limb and dropped, hanging upside down over the creek, his hand-like front paws stretched toward the ground. Then, he let go, and I heard a splash. A moment later, he popped up in our yard from the creek bed and moseyed his way to wherever he was headed.

Not needing written words, God had shown me in the opossum's forward-moving perseverance while tottering on a flimsy hemlock over rushing water how I could go on—slide through when I can, grasp at the True Vine when needed, hold on with all my might, and drop into the Living Water of Christ when I can't hold on any longer. Like the opossum, I'll pop up on the other side and keep on keeping on.—Cathy Mayfield

Father, thank You for how often Your critters show me how to get through this life. Amen.

APRIL 9

Better Together

And let us consider how we may spur one another on toward love and good deeds.

—HEBREWS 10:24 (NIV)

I'D NEVER WANTED to play pickleball, but while visiting friends in France, I was eager to participate in their new routine. They'd moved there to care for parents who could no longer care for themselves. Nurses and therapists attended to their parents daily, so once each week my friends drove an hour away to play pickleball.

New to the game, I found tossing the ball and stretching to serve an awkward sort of pirouette. Lunging to scoop the ball was a stiff-legged lurch. My friends couldn't help but giggle. Graceful, I was not.

The route from the pickleball courts crosses the Camargue Natural Park, where thousands of pairs of wild flamingos breed. Forty years before, I'd seen flamingos in Kenya. From a red clay road above the Rift Valley, I watched a flock of flamingos below, a pink shroud resting on Lake Nakuru. Now, I looked forward to seeing the birds close up.

The first bird came into view like a small orange buoy on the water. It wasn't graceful at all. Flamingos' beaks are crooked, like outsized broken noses. Picking their way in the shallows, flamingos walk like preteens on stilts, bending stiff legs both forward and back at the joints. But suddenly a cloud of pink tutus is born upward, graceful as a ballet troupe, the pink shades varied as shades of a sunset.

Grace was evident not in movements of single birds but in the movement of the flock. Individual flamingos are odd, awkward creatures but together they are graceful as dancers. I wonder if the same might be true of us. My own individual efforts are often awkward, but grace is stirred when I act in concert with others. Grace that transforms gawky birds, transforms my poor pickleball skills into laughter, and turns my friends into compassionate caregivers.—Susie Colby

Lord, may we find our flock and discover grace in caring for one another. Amen.

APRIL 10

Have Hope

May the God of hope fill you with all joy and peace as you trust in him, so that you may overflow with hope by the power of the Holy Spirit.

—ROMANS 15:13 (NIV)

I WANTED TO SEE deer, so my husband, Tim, and I made the twenty-minute drive to John Chesnut Sr. Park in Palm Harbor, Florida. It's one of my favorite parks because every time I've gone there, I've seen deer.

It was the first warm weekend of the year. We coasted through the park with the windows rolled down, hoping to spot deer in the grassy areas by the road. Everywhere we looked there were people. People playing football, having picnics, grilling hot dogs, walking the trails.

Finally, we parked at the south end of the park. Tim led the way as we navigated along the dirt trail and past the boat dock to the boardwalk that runs along Lake Tarpon. Water lay to the west and dense woods to the east.

"See any alligators?" a man asked as he passed us.

"No. See any deer?" I responded, hopeful.

He confirmed my fears. "Too many people out today."

A few minutes later Tim stopped, held one finger to his lips, and with his other hand pointed toward the trees.

I turned and observed two deer standing ten feet past the elevated fenced path. One stood in front of the other as they nibbled leaves and grass from the base of the forest. The doe to the left perked up her ears, lifted her head, and looked at me. Then she went back to enjoying her afternoon snack. The one to the right remained partway hidden by a tree.

I watched the deer as my heart praised the Lord. I had given up hope of seeing any and would have missed them because I was looking the other way. But He surprised me with a deer encounter. This sweet experience reminded me of God's love and how He delights in me.—Crystal Storms

Walk of Faith: *Consider a time you'd given up hope and God surprised you. Write it down where you can look back on it to encourage you that you are His beloved child in whom He delights.*

APRIL 11

Pinpricks of Heaven

When Jesus spoke again to the people, he said, "I am the light of the world. Whoever follows me will never walk in darkness, but will have the light of life."

—JOHN 8:12 (NIV)

WITH NO STREETLIGHTS for miles, our yard is cast in inky darkness. One warm spring evening my husband, Mike, and I sat on the front steps, winding down after a hectic day. Nothing but a sliver of moonlight cast a soft glow in the night. I let out a deep breath, trying to exhale away the business of work, family stress, and what seemed like endless bad news on the television. I knew God was there, but was He really paying attention to my worries and challenges? Was He working in the greater problems that unsettled the world around me?

I cast my gaze to the field across the street. At first, I saw nothing but more darkness. But then I noticed a pinprick of light—and then another. One faded just as another appeared. "Fireflies," I said, as my husband smiled and nodded. As a child, I remembered catching fireflies in a jar and watching them glow before releasing them. The twinkling lights gave me comfort in the darkness.

As I looked closer, I saw that the entire field was twinkling, little bits of light shining here and there, high and low. And all at once the night didn't seem so dark. I felt an overwhelming feeling of hope wrap around me. "I wish there was a way I could capture this," I said, nodding toward the lights. Mike squeezed my hand and raised his eyes up to the heavens. My gaze followed, and I knew I was indeed surrounded by the greatest Hope of all. I didn't need to keep fireflies in a jar like I did as a girl. The light of Jesus shone all around me.—Peggy Frezon

I have come into the world as a light, so that no one who believes in me should stay in darkness.
—John 12:46 (NIV)

APRIL 12

Lessons in Gentleness

For everything there is a season, a time for every activity under heaven.

—Ecclesiastes 3:1 (NLT)

UGH! COCKROACHES! I hate 'em. Why did God create bugs in the first place?" exclaimed my mother as we talked on the phone. Mom had just hunted down a particularly nasty palmetto bug, and she was not happy. "No matter how much I spend on exterminators and sprays, they still get in and terrorize me."

I know the facts about how important bugs are to our world's ecosystem, how they help break down leaf debris, release nitrogen into the atmosphere, and serve as a food source for other creatures, but this didn't seem like the right time to share that information.

Later that day, with Mom's "Why did God create bugs?" question still ringing in my ears, my two-year-old grandson, Collin, and I puttered around my backyard.

"Find me a worm or a gwub, Gigi," he said. I grabbed my shovel, and we headed to the garden. As I turned over dirt, grass clippings, and decaying leaf matter, he watched intently for movement. Sure enough, something wiggled. "A worm!" he squealed, reaching to pluck it from the soil.

"Be gentle," I reminded him. "It's one of God's creatures. You can play with it, but you don't want to hurt it." He nodded, then gently lifted the wiggly creature from the soil. "I be gentle, Gigi."

Why did God make bugs? I know He made them to break down leaf debris, release nitrogen to the soil, provide food for other creatures, and occasionally terrorize my mother. But I couldn't help but wonder, that day, if God created a worm and buried it in my backyard so I could teach a little boy how to value nature and be gentle.—Lori Hatcher

Let your gentleness be evident to all. The Lord is near.

—Philippians 4:5 (NIV)

APRIL 13

The Never Empty Nest

And I am sure of this, that he who began a good work in you will bring it to completion at the day of Jesus Christ.

—PHILIPPIANS 1:6 (ESV)

I PAUSED TO WATCH the scene unfolding outside the window. Was that the baby robin, now nearly grown up? Sure enough, the remnant of mottled coloring matched the fledgling I'd watched leave the nest weeks before.

One of the parents stood on the grass with the adolescent. The adult bird dug up a worm with lightning speed, then tossed it to the adolescent. The youngster fumbled with the long worm and dropped it. The parent picked up the worm again, split it into smaller pieces, then flung the smaller section to the youngster. The adolescent gobbled that down and waited for more.

I smiled as I watched them repeat the sequence several times. The adult continued to give the young robin a full-sized worm; the young robin continued to struggle to swallow it. The parent would then patiently chop the worm into smaller sections and pass those to the youngster. Eventually, the adolescent perched on the low limb of a nearby pine as the parent flew up to the nest where it had new eggs to tend.

I hadn't known that robins continue to parent so long after their young leave the nest, even when they have new babies on the way. This adolescent, who in some species would have to fend for itself, continued to go to its parent for help, and the parent continued to instruct its older offspring in becoming an adult robin.

My heart swelled as I realized I was like that adolescent bird. I've been a Christian for years and perhaps should be more spiritually mature. But thankfully, God doesn't leave me to manage life on my own. When I stumble or can't handle the hard things, He swoops down, protecting me and instructing me so I can grow into the person He created me to be.—Jerusha Agen

God loves us too much to leave us the way we are.
—Jonathan and Jennifer Campbell

APRIL 14

Birding Paradise

Now go out to the street corners and invite everyone you see.

—MATTHEW 22:9 (NLT)

TUCSON AUDUBON'S PATON Center for Hummingbirds was a recommended location for birding. That morning, I saw various types of buntings, orioles, hummingbirds, warblers, goldfinches, thrashers, and woodpeckers. Feeders of all kinds lined the property, with delectable offerings of seeds, suet, sugar water, and fruit.

All this was made possible because of one couple's vision to transform a barren piece of land into a beautiful garden. What they created was a desirable stopover for migrating birds.

Gardening enthusiasts Wally and Marion Paton bought the derelict property in Patagonia, Arizona, in the early 1970s. They found while refurbishing the landscape that the more they planted, the more hummingbirds visited. Soon, migrating birds of all kinds showed up.

Long before social media, news of the birders' garden spread by word of mouth. Visitors came from all corners of the country and every walk of life to sit under a shade canopy, watch, and be delighted.

According to their daughter, while others were erecting fences and hedges to afford their space privacy, her parents were opening their gate and welcoming anyone to sit in their backyard for as long as they wanted. The couple's hospitality drew thousands of birders annually.

How like this scenario is to the broad invitation and winsome hospitality of God. He does not build fences to keep people out of His kingdom. He invites and welcomes all. In Luke 14, the Father urges everyone to come so the house can be full. In John 14, Jesus assures us that there is more than enough room in His Father's house.

The invitation is given. The kingdom of God is open. In it all races, sexes, and ages are welcome.—Darlene Kerr

And on this road, with every step we take, Your faithfulness is our portion;
You've prepared a city bright and fair whose gates forever stay open.
—Sam Yoder

APRIL 15

Things Unseen

For we do not wrestle against flesh and blood, but against the rulers, against the authorities, against the cosmic powers over this present darkness, against the spiritual forces of evil in the heavenly places.

—EPHESIANS 6:12 (ESV)

I GRABBED THE SHOULDER of my daughter, Anicah, and pointed urgently into the reef. We were snorkeling off the coast of the Florida Keys, and a jellyfish was closing in. Transparent, it allowed the current to carry it, unseen by me until now. It was quite by accident that I noticed the water had turned blurry for a brief moment.

I blinked. Had I encountered a discarded zip-top sandwich bag in these emerald seas? I looked closer. It was a jellyfish—beautiful and delicate. I stared, marveling at God's creativity. Then glancing around, I snapped out of my admiration.

An entire smack of jellyfish surrounded us!

I knew that just one touch could result in a painful and possibly life-threatening sting, so I decided to treat them respectfully and got Anicah's attention. We backed up, kicking frantically with our fins. Reaching the boat's ladder, we safely boarded.

"That was close. It almost got us," she said, pulling off her mask.

I smiled. "You mean 'they.' There were two dozen or more."

I never told Anicah how many jellies were really there. She would have never snorkeled again. But as we sailed back to Marathon, I pondered our experience. How often do I swim along in life, blindly unaware of the good and evil unseen forces all around me?

Whether I have angels fighting for me or demons reaching out their tentacles to sting me, God's Word teaches of the invisible armies waging war over my well-being. I must keep up my guard and stay close to Jesus to ward off potential attacks.—Tez Brooks

We face dangers every day of which we are not even aware.
Often God intervenes on our behalf through the use of His angels.
—Billy Graham

APRIL 16

Kindness Counts

For nothing will be impossible with God.

—LUKE 1:37 (ESV)

COLLEGE TUITION CAN be a beast. That's what my sixteen-year-old grandson Josiah is learning from his show steer of the same name, because black Angus steers are not known for their sweet temperaments. College Tuition, Josiah's Future Farmers of America project, stubbornly resists a show halter and often rams him against a fence. Sometimes the steer will jerk, pulling the halter out of Josiah's grip before putting his head down in charge mode.

But that's not been my experience with College Tuition. I take prayer walks throughout my community, often strolling along the perimeter of our small high school campus in the Sierra Valley. In the back of the school by the FFA barn and facilities, I often greet Josiah's steer, as well as two others. I'll stop, say hello, and rub College Tuition's belly with my walking pole. Soon his tail will start swishing in contentment.

Now, would I get into that pen with College Tuition or another steer? Not a chance! I'll leave the task of showing a thirteen-hundred-pound steer to someone stronger, younger, and braver—someone who needs a way to raise college tuition. But perhaps a softer approach toward the tough ones of our lives works better.

Recently, I attended an event where I had a face-to-face meeting with someone who wasn't a beast but who had said unkind words about me. Remembering that a softer approach is more effective, I said, "So nice to see you. I hope you are doing well."

The woman said she was going through a hard time, having just suffered a great loss.

So I said, "Let me pray for you." And I did.

Not all people will be receptive to kind words, but I'm trusting God to protect me from the beasts of life and remind me to treat others with kindness and a soft touch.—Janet Holm McHenry

Do things for people not because of who they are or what they do in return, but because of who you are.

—Rabbi Harold S. Kushner

APRIL 17

Who Walks with You?

Do you not know? Have you not heard? The LORD is the everlasting God, the Creator of the ends of the earth. He will not grow tired or weary, and his understanding no one can fathom.

—ISAIAH 40:28 (NIV)

MY FATHER HAD a long and good life, but that didn't mean I wasn't overcome with grief when he passed. The evening after his funeral, my daughter Sallie and I went out to walk Ruby, our year-old black Lab. There is nothing like an active dog to remind you that life goes on after loss. Because she's so energetic, I usually take her to run in the park. But this evening, the three of us stayed close to home, just circling the block.

As the spring twilight fell, the birds sang their goodnight songs, and the frogs began to croak. Nature seemed particularly busy in the neighborhood. Passing under a large oak branch, we heard a persistent high trill. As we stopped to identify the source, a feathery force swept over our heads. Startled, Ruby pulled us into the next yard.

"What was that?" I asked, as my daughter and I caught our breath. Peering up into the tree, I looked hard. *Was it the spirit of my father?* There, tucked up in the branches of a large oak, was a feathery gray screech owl, perched back on the branch, blinking its big golden eyes down at us. I took a deep breath, and something inside my soul knew. The bird wasn't a spirit, but it was a sign. My father, with all his wisdom and knowledge of the natural world, was gone. Yet he was still here: still in our hearts, still part of the miracle of creation, still a child of God. This little owl was a sign of connection, filling me with a sense of belonging. God was present, especially in the saddest of times.—Lucy H. Chambers

Praise to the Lord, who hath fearfully, wondrously, made thee! Health hath vouchsafed and, when heedlessly falling, hath stayed thee. What need or grief ever hath failed of relief? Wings of His mercy did shade thee.

—Joachim Neander

APRIL 18

Flying Side by Side

It's better to have a partner than go it alone.

—ECCLESIASTES 4:9 (MSG)

EACH SPRING, LIKE clockwork, they return.

A committed couple, the Canada geese resume swimming in our pond and ambling through the pasture. When the season changes and the time comes, they'll fly away—side by side.

Though I can't wander too close, they never turn down a handful of seeds tossed in their direction. Honking, they then waddle about, pecking the ground with what I like to imagine is gratitude.

Each year, I wait for goslings, but—despite an egg or two deposited in their nest under the willow tree—I've yet to witness offspring. Perhaps because eggs are snatched by predators prior to hatching, no babies ever join the duo for a swim, which makes me wonder, *How must they feel? Do they cast blame in an instinctual bird-like manner? Mourn their loss?*

I, too, have experienced loss and, out of hurt, hurled stones of condemnation, namely at my husband, Bill.

Still, this feathered couple never appears at odds. Rather, they seem unified, singular in heart and mind.

The other evening as Bill and I drove home from town, we spied a pair of Canada geese flying above us in the opposite direction. "Could that be them?" I inquired, though I knew there was no way to confirm.

"Maybe it's date night," my better half replied. Then, with his best gander impersonation, "Honk! Which sounds best, darlin'? Fancy Italian food or casual American fare? Honk! Honk!"

I couldn't help but laugh. Despite loss and blame, our relationship has flourished with Christ as our commitment. He makes the bad times tolerable, eases my sadness when it comes, and helps me to find forgiveness and refrain from throwing stones.

With grateful hearts, we're free to fly together—much like our Canadian couple.—Maureen Miller

Let us prize these moments and care for one another deeply—for each of us, and our relationships to one another, are precious and fleeting.... Amen.

—Douglas Kaine McKelvey

APRIL 19

Beware of Dogs

Beware of the dogs, beware of the evil workers,
beware of the false circumcision.

—PHILIPPIANS 3:2 (NASB)

THE GATE LEADING to our backyard has a large metal sign that reads, "Beware of dogs." We didn't hang the sign—it was there when we bought the house. Nevertheless, we left it in place for our two Chihuahuas. Franny and Fritz, weighing five and nine pounds respectively and unable to hold their "lickers," need all the doggy ego boost they can get.

When the apostle Paul wrote "beware of dogs" to the Philippians, he wasn't referring to ferocious canines. Rather, he was warning them about those who lead people astray with incorrect doctrine. In Biblical times, dogs were considered unclean animals, and the Jews often applied this word to describe Gentiles. Paul used the word *dog* to describe the Jewish leaders trying to corrupt new believers.

Scripture is full of warnings to be on the lookout for false teachers. In the Sermon on the Mount, Jesus said, "Beware of the false prophets, who come to you in sheep's clothing, but inwardly are ravenous wolves" (Matthew 7:15, NASB). If there are so many admonitions to be on our guard against deceptive teachers, God must have felt we needed repeated warnings.

It is easy to be misled by charismatic teachers who preach messages that sound good—messages I want to hear—particularly if I don't know the Bible. "For the time will come when they will not tolerate sound doctrine; but wanting to have their ears tickled, they will accumulate for themselves teachers in accordance with their own desires" (2 Timothy 4:3, NASB).

Sometimes falsehoods are so subtle, they are easy to sneak in along with sound theology. I need to know the Scripture and to pray for the Holy Spirit to give me discernment in its interpretation. Then I can be on guard against unbiblical doctrine and speak up if preachers or teachers are presenting something other than the Truth—just like the sign in my backyard does.—Ellen Fannon

Lord, open my eyes to Your Truth and give me Your wisdom
and discernment. Amen.

APRIL 20

My Shield of Protection

God's your Guardian, right at your side to protect you.

—PSALM 121:5 (MSG)

IF YOU LIVE in Minnesota, it's not uncommon to hear the solitary call of a loon at dusk while canoeing around one of our ten thousand lakes. It's a treat to experience their high-pitched wail, which is one of the ways they express concern over an intruder. That would be me...in the canoe, getting too close for comfort. If I'm lucky, I may see two loons on the lake, but never more than that at one time.

That changed during a recent visit to the home of some friends who live on a lake just outside Elk River. It was still a chilly thirty-degree day at the end of April, and we stood in their kitchen chatting. I looked out the window to see ten to twelve loons of various sizes cavorting right near the shoreline. It was too early for any newly hatched chicks to be present, but some of them were younger adolescents. The outer circle seemed to stand guard while the inner group flipped up their tails and dove straight down to capture a delicious fishy snack.

It was hard to tell exactly how many there were, as they can stay underwater for up to five minutes. After the insiders had their treat, they switched places with the others. There was an element of care and caution on the part of the watchers. They were all, however, oblivious to the presence of humans not twenty-five feet from where they swam.

As I reflect on this delightful experience, it occurs to me that the Lord looks out for us in a similar way. He does not stand watch from a distance, but is right in our midst. He enjoys being present in our fun and oversees our safety, even when we are not aware that danger may be lurking. He is always nearby as our Friend, our Guardian, our Father, and our Lord.—Liz Kimmel

Thank You, precious Protector, that You are all-seeing and all-loving. Thank You for the relationships You have blessed me with. Help me to sense Your nearness. Amen.

APRIL 21

Birdsong at Dawn

Let everything that breathes sing praises to the LORD! Praise the LORD!

—PSALM 150:6 (NLT)

I'VE STARTED SOMETHING new this spring. I sleep with the bedroom window cracked open at night.

An unexpected delight to this new routine is waking to birdsong. Right before dawn's first light, the tweeting, whistling, and chirping begins. The concert lasts for approximately twenty minutes. Individual birdsongs often become indistinguishable as voices overlap and merge into one unique morning melody.

I lie in bed listening as daylight slowly lightens our room. It seems as if birds are taking the lead in the wee morning hours to praise their Creator. I can't help but forget my initial grogginess and join the chorus, not tweeting, but thanking God for the beauty of the world He has given to me, the birds, and all creation.

I don't know how long an early morning awakening will last for me—I've been known to say early mornings are overrated (being more of the night owl's persuasion). Perhaps it's just for a season that I'll enjoy this daily delight. Then when the air conditioner ramps up in response to hot, muggy nights and the windows are closed tight, the predawn performances will end for me. I'm saddened at the thought. Yet, I'm reassured that the birds will continue with or without my listening ears.

For now, I enjoy the avian symphony. The psalmist wrote in Psalm 98:4 (NIV): "Shout for joy to the LORD, all the earth, burst into jubilant song with music," and I eagerly join in and rejoice as creation sings. Praise is on my lips. I thank Him for a new day of life. I pause to count my blessings. There's so much to sing about! It's a beautiful beginning to the day.—Darlene Kerr

Walk of Faith: *Catch a predawn praise session of your own. Set your alarm for daybreak or crack open your window before you go to bed so you can hear the dawn chorus. As you listen to the birds, sing praises to God and rejoice.*

APRIL 22

No Looking Back

Forgetting what is behind and straining toward what is ahead, I press on toward the goal to win the prize for which God has called me heavenward in Christ Jesus.

—PHILIPPIANS 3:13–14 (NIV)

MY FAMILY AND I were walking through the Kangaroo Walkabout at the Columbus Zoo when an employee warned us that kangaroos roam freely and we might encounter one up close. While this was an exciting thought, I was distracted by the family drama unfolding. We were visiting the zoo with extended family, and someone had made a comment that hurt my daughter's feelings. "I'm never going to forget that they said that," Julia said. "I'll never forgive them either."

While I didn't want her to hold a grudge, I, too, was upset about the comment. I wondered how it would impact our relationship with this person going forward. I was trying to think of something helpful to say when a kangaroo hopped across the path right in front of us. Julia looked at me with wide eyes. "That was so cool," she said.

We watched as the kangaroo hopped around the enclosure and eventually stopped in front of a group of trees. It just stood there as though it was frozen.

"He's acting like he's stuck," Julia said. "Why doesn't he just back up and go another way?"

A little boy standing nearby answered. "Kangaroos can't jump backward because their feet and tails are too big. It's physically impossible for them to go backward."

A zoo employee nodded. "He's right. Kangaroos can only hop forward and side to side."

We watched as the kangaroo took a few side hops to get around the trees before hopping away at full speed.

Suddenly, I knew what to say to Julia. "Families can't move backward either. We have to forgive one another so we can move forward."

Julia and I found a quiet corner to pray and ask God to help us forgive the one who'd hurt us because we didn't want to get stuck in the past.—Diane Stark

Be kind and compassionate to one another, forgiving each other, just as in Christ God forgave you.

—Ephesians 4:32 (NIV)

APRIL 23

Patient in Suffering

Be joyful in hope, patient in affliction, faithful in prayer.

—ROMANS 12:12 (NIV)

BUCKSHOT, OUR BEAGLE/LAB mix, was a gentle, sweet, tolerant dog. You could even say he was patient in suffering. Bucky had many health concerns throughout his years. From the time he was two years old until he died, he needed daily insulin shots to help control his diabetes. When he was five, he needed surgery to remove his left eye, the result of a different disease. But Bucky never allowed all his health concerns to make him grouchy.

It wasn't until Bucky went to the animal hospital, had an ultrasound, was diagnosed with pancreatitis, and needed to stay several days for observation that I realized I wasn't the only person who thought Bucky was an exceptional dog.

The afternoon I picked him up from the hospital, I was surprised when Bucky was brought out to me. It wasn't the doctor or vet tech who brought Bucky out. It was the veterinarian's preschool daughter who had the honor.

I couldn't help but smile when this small child led Bucky out on his leash. She stopped in front of me, and as she patted Bucky, she said, "I like him. I want to take him home with me." I assured her I liked Bucky, too, and would take extra special care of him when I took him home. But it wasn't until her mother told her to tell Bucky goodbye that the little girl relinquished his leash to me.

Through Bucky's illnesses I learned several things, and the biggest is this: discomfort does not have to make you disagreeable. Bucky never let his pain and discomfort cause him to be grouchy or anything other than loving and friendly. Likewise, my physical discomfort does not need to make me disagreeable or grouchy. Perhaps it is a loving spirit in the midst of pain that people notice, reminding us all to be patient in suffering. It's a lesson I learned well from Bucky.—Sandy Kirby Quandt

Father, thank You for placing Bucky in our home and using him as an example of patient suffering throughout all his many illnesses. Teach me to be as patient in my suffering. Amen.

APRIL 24

Mobbing

Though one may be overpowered, two can defend themselves.
A cord of three strands is not quickly broken.

—ECCLESIASTES 4:12 (NIV)

IT IS CALLED "mobbing," and I'm watching it happen right now, this minute. Three smaller birds—red-winged blackbirds, I think—are swooping and dashing at a hawk. The hawk is circling lazily over my field, head down, looking for breakfast. Ordinarily, blackbirds stay far away from big predators like hawks. I mean, bantamweight boxers do not ordinarily climb into the ring to battle a heavyweight. But it is springtime, when blackbirds are feeling a surge of hormones, and they become very territorial.

Any apex predator—hawks, owls, even the occasional eagle—that crosses into the blackbirds' airspace risks getting mobbed. Mobbing doesn't actually harm the larger bird, although now and then you'll see a feather fly loose. The object is to pester the predator and drive him away.

And the tactic works today. Tired of being harassed, the hawk catches an updraft and goes elsewhere to hunt, flapping her wings and soaring off into the distance until she is just a speck in the sky, and then the speck is gone. The blackbirds follow her for a while, then—mission accomplished—they turn around and return to base.

Sometimes I am the hawk, getting pestered by small problems that keep coming at me. I'm talking about those pebble-in-your-shoe problems that keep you from moving in the direction of your dreams—recalcitrant coworkers, family flare-ups, health issues—minor difficulties that come pecking at you one after the other. It's no fun to be the hawk.

But more often I am the feisty little blackbird. An obstacle may seem insurmountable, but I find that when I prayerfully join together with like-minded family and friends—fellow blackbirds—we accomplish big things. So bring on the hungry hawks and the ornery owls—I am not afraid. There is strength in numbers. It's fun to be the blackbird. —Louis Lotz

But their strength is the strength of numbers and of stubbornness and persistence; do not underestimate it.

—Robin McKinley

APRIL 25

Tracing My Faith Steps

I am reminded of your sincere faith, which first lived in your grandmother Lois and in your mother Eunice and, I am persuaded, now lives in you also.

—2 TIMOTHY 1:5 (NIV)

SINCE AN EARLY age, I have been fascinated by the North American buffalo and where they roamed. My childhood nature books contained photos of bison grazing on the wide-open prairie. So when I moved to southern Indiana with its steep hills, woodlands, and river obstacles, I was intrigued to learn that the area was known as the Buffalo Trace Trail.

Centuries ago, thousands of bison created the pathway by migrating east and west, year after year, across my county. My friend guided me to a location where a deep and wide remnant from the trail had been trodden down by the massive beasts. She described how long-ago travelers through the dense Hoosier National Forest took advantage of the migrating mammals' beaten path. Those hoofprints and footprints laid the foundation for some of the first roads.

During a Bible study recently, I was asked to trace the names of those who laid the faith foundation for me. I knew exactly who they were. My great-grandmother Birda set the example for my walk of faith. Every Sunday, she strapped on her sensible shoes and donned her flowery hat for the quarter-mile pilgrimage to church. My grandma Cora followed her example. For almost a century, she performed volunteer work for the parishioners and participated faithfully in Bible study.

At times, I strayed from my faith. I became disappointed when my life did not follow an uncomplicated pathway, especially when I was fired from a job I thought was perfect for me. After that, I experienced periods of not living according to God's plan. My mom directed my footsteps around the challenges I faced and guided me to the correct path of a better profession. Following the faith steps of those godly women, I am now laying the foundation for others to follow.—Glenda Ferguson

Walk of Faith: *Trace your faith walk, then read 2 Timothy 1:5 and insert the names of the people who guided you to God.*

APRIL 26

Miracle of the Sandhills

The locusts have no king to lead them, yet they cooperate as they move forward by bands.

—PROVERBS 30:27 (TPT)

WE WERE PRIVILEGED to live in Kearney, Nebraska, for four years and witness one of God's great seasonal miracles. Each year from early March through early April, approximately six hundred thousand sandhill cranes descend upon the area as they pause in their five-thousand-mile migration to gather fuel for the next stage of their journey. The birds come from Mexico, New Mexico, Texas, and California and pause here before heading to breeding grounds in Siberia, Alaska, and Canada. At night they roost on the islands in the river, and by day they feed on snails and corn in the surrounding fields.

These are magnificent birds, as tall as four and a half feet with a wingspan of up to ninety inches. It's amazing to see them covering a field or filling the air in flight.

Migration is truly one of God's great miracles. Whether it is these birds, wildebeests in Africa, whales along the Pacific coast, or monarch butterflies, these creatures put aside their tendency to compete and dominate and move forward to preserve their lives and their species.

We viewed this behavior again when we lived along a hummingbird migratory path in Mississippi. Almost overnight, the birds moved from competing for food at our feeders to waiting patiently for a spot to open so they could take their turn to drink.

There is much I can learn from these migrants' behavior. I am competitive by nature and fiercely cheer for my favorite sports teams, but I can too easily carry that competitive spirit into the workplace, my neighborhood, even my family. Thinking of the enormous cooperation required by cranes, wildebeests, whales, butterflies, hummingbirds, and others in their migration makes me consider what I might accomplish by prioritizing a spirit of cooperation each and every day in my life.—Harold Nichols

Dear Lord, please help me to keep my competitive spirit reserved for appropriate situations and to be more cooperative with others in all aspects of my life. Amen.

APRIL 27

Abide in Me

Remain in me, as I also remain in you. No branch can bear fruit by itself; it must remain in the vine. Neither can you bear fruit unless you remain in me.

—JOHN 15:4 (NIV)

WE HAD JUST moved into a new house. One early spring day I sat on the deck and thanked God for how He had blessed us with a wonderful, safe, and beautiful place in which to live.

Abide in me. I felt the words.

Our deck overlooked a stately maple tree that had grown in that spot for decades, maybe centuries. As I sat there, I watched a squirrel scurrying around the tree trunk. It took a few steps, then glanced back as if beckoning me to watch. First, it dug up some seeds around the trunk and sat back on its haunches to nibble. Then, as a loud crow cawed from above, it scampered partway up the tree, where it took refuge behind a limb. After a while, the squirrel continued up to a crook in the branches. There, it gave me one more look before diving into a large hole. The last thing I saw was its bushy tail disappearing.

The words came to me again. *Abide in me.*

I marveled—how well the word *abide* captured the essence of this beautiful maple. The squirrel lived there among its leaves, hidden from predators. That great old tree provided the squirrel shelter, a source of food, protection from rain and snow, security against predators, and a place to sleep and raise its young. Everything it needed. I, too, had a wonderful home with a roof over my head and all I needed. But the squirrel helped direct my thoughts to something greater. I raised my eyes higher, higher even than where my new friend lay tucked among the sturdy branches of the maple, to my Shelter, my Source of Nourishment, my Protection, my Place of Rest.

And the words filled me with peace and comfort. *Abide in me.* —Peggy Frezon

Abiding is a journey of growing spiritual roots down deep so that you can do more than just survive, you can thrive.
—Elisa Pulliam

APRIL 28

Saving Light

The people walking in darkness have seen a great light; on those living in the land of deep darkness a light has dawned.

—Isaiah 9:2 (NIV)

WHEN I ENTERED the small antique shop, I immediately noticed the salesclerk looking upward, very concerned. A hummingbird was zipping around near the ceiling, sometimes battering itself against light fixtures and windows. The doors were open, but the hummer couldn't distinguish between the light of an open door and the lights in the room. I was concerned it would burn up all its strength before it could find its way out.

"If I may make a suggestion," I said quietly. "Maybe we could turn out all the lights so the hummingbird can clearly see the door."

The clerk nodded, and we went throughout the store, turning off every lamp, display, and lighted gadget. But the hummingbird was still confused. We waved fans and books and tried to guide it to safety. By now several other customers were helping too. At last, the tiny bird found the door and flitted to freedom and safety outdoors.

Watching the frantic hummingbird struggle to escape the shop, I recalled times in my life when I've felt confused and lost, trapped and scared. In the same way that turning out all the other distracting lights helped the hummingbird find its way to the saving light of the doorway, turning to God through prayer or reading His Word gives me relief from distracting thoughts and negative feelings and helps me to focus on what needs to be done. When I *start* with prayer, asking for help from God, the one true Light, and patiently wait for an answer, help comes. From there, under His guidance, I can find a way to the best outcome. I no longer feel confused, lost, trapped, or scared. God lights my way into His marvelous light.—Marianne Campbell

But you are a chosen generation, a royal priesthood, a holy nation, His own special people, that you may proclaim the praises of Him who called you out of darkness into His marvelous light.

—1 Peter 2:9 (NKJV)

APRIL 29

Caterpillar Playground

Command those...to put their hope in God, who richly provides us with everything for our enjoyment.

—1 TIMOTHY 6:17 (NIV)

MY HUSBAND, DAVID, and I were visiting my parents when I realized our granddaughters, Lauren, eight, and Caroline, six, had been playing outside for quite a while. Mom and Dad live in the country on eight acres, and David and I often bring a grandchild or two (or four!) along on our weekly visits. On this practically perfect April evening, the girls had quickly busied themselves with the make-believe games that wooded settings and nature inspire.

Scanning the backyard, I spotted them, crouched with their heads together, fully engaged in something. As I drew near, I caught snippets of their conversation.

"No, Blueberry," Caroline said, "you can't go on to the next station until you've finished this one."

"Let him try the stick course," Lauren said, "he seems to like climbing better than walking."

When she spotted me, Lauren launched into an animated description. "First I found a caterpillar, then Caroline found one." She held up the fuzzy insect for my inspection. "This is Blueberry. We made a playground for them. It has a climbing station made out of sticks, a grassy area, and a section with seashells and pine cones." She pointed to a pile of leaves. "There's even a snack spot in case they get hungry."

Watching the pleasure they received from those two little caterpillars reminded me of the truth of 1 Timothy 6:17—that God creates all things for our enjoyment.

That beautiful sunset? God painted it with you in mind. The wide ocean? He knew you'd enjoy watching the waves.

And two fuzzy caterpillars in a patch of woods exactly where two little girls would play? Created just for them.

As I listened to the girls describe their caterpillar adventure on the drive home, I smiled.

I suspect God did too.—Lori Hatcher

They speak of the glorious splendor of your majesty—
and I will meditate on your wonderful works.

—Psalm 145:5 (NIV)

The Healing Power of God's Creations

Heal me, O Lord, and I shall be healed; save me,
and I shall be saved, for you are my praise.

—JEREMIAH 17:14 (ESV)

MY HUSBAND AND I feel especially close to God in nature. God's beautiful creations never cease to amaze us, and His creativity is evident with every blossom and leaf shape and in the intricate detail of the tiniest critters and magnificence of His larger mammals.

Not only is my husband a biologist by trade, but he also is a very outdoorsy kind of person. Getting outside soothes and refreshes him. It's something he needs every day. So when David contracted pneumonia, he found it very difficult to stay inside and rest as the physician instructed.

When the fever finally broke, he couldn't stand being cooped up inside any longer. "Let's go for a short walk around the house," I suggested.

As we strolled, David spotted large birds flying overhead and thought they were hawks that frequented our property. But as they continued to circle and flew closer, he realized they were Mississippi kites. Stunned, we welcomed the sighting. We've seen them occasionally in Georgia but never before in our yard.

Later that day when we took another lap around the house, we saw them again, circling and eventually landing in a pine tree in our backyard.

"It's too late for them to be nesting," said David.

Each day as we took our walks to build David's strength, we saw the beautiful birds soaring in the air currents and often landing in the same pine tree. A pair of them.

The very day the doctor cleared David to return to work, the kites disappeared. It's as if God sent them to give David the encouragement he needed each day. We've always appreciated the beauty of God's creations and how close they make us feel to our Lord. But it was during the time of David's recuperation that we felt the healing nature of God's creations too.—Julie Lavender

Walk of Faith: *Reach out to someone who is ill or recovering. Ask if they might like to sit outside, take a short walk, or go for a drive.*

May

MAY 1

Lost

You, Lord, are my lamp; the Lord turns my darkness into light.

—2 Samuel 22:29 (NIV)

WHEN I CALL my dogs inside, our younger golden retriever, Petey, comes running. But Ernest often remains ambling somewhere along our acre-plus fenced yard. This is because at fourteen years old, Ernest is partially blind and mostly deaf.

One inky-dark night, I stepped onto our back deck and was soon joined by Petey. I scanned the yard. "Ernest! Come here!" I called loudly. We employ several techniques to try to get his attention. I flicked the outside lights. I waved my arms over my head. I tried sending Petey back to find him. But Ernest was nowhere to be seen. In the darkest corners, he will often just stand there, unsure of where to go.

I don't like the dark either. When I get stuck in one of life's dark corners, I'm often unsure how to get out. I may try to feel my way around, or like Ernest, I may just stand there. On my own, I feel lost and afraid. I imagine that's how Ernest feels too.

As often is the case, I walked out to help him. When I reached the very back, I saw Ernest standing by the fence. He didn't know I was near until I was right upon him. When he finally saw me, he bounded toward me, uncharacteristically agile for his age, his tail wagging and his ears flopping. Because he knew I was there, he found his direction.

This is how I am with God. When I am lost, I search for Him. He is often closer than I know. And when I find Him, I go to Him with my whole heart.

I gave Ernest a pat on the head, and the two of us walked back home.—Peggy Frezon

Hope is being able to see that there is light despite all the darkness.
—Desmond Tutu

MAY 2

The Firefly Surprise

"Unless you people see signs and wonders," Jesus told him, "you will never believe."

—JOHN 4:48 (NIV)

AT FIRST, IT seemed like a normal summer night. The air was humid, and the temperatures were warm despite the twilight. May in Florida is a beautiful time. Then my young son, Nate, came running into the house from the backyard. With excitement in his voice, he told me he'd just seen fireflies! My husband and I, along with our dog, followed Nate into the yard—I could not believe my eyes. While I expected to see a few fireflies, instead I saw dozens of them fluttering through our yard. I felt like I was in a magical movie scene.

I know to some this may be a regular occurrence, but where we live, fireflies are not common, especially in residential areas. It truly was a treat to watch them light up the evening sky, their little lights glowing like tiny stars that had fallen from space into our yard.

To me, the image is a great reminder that in the dark and difficult seasons of life, when God's presence perhaps feels very far away and sadness drowns out His gentle whisper within our hearts, something is about to rise up from the ground to light our way once more. How amazing to think that firefly larvae are essentially worms living in the soil long before they grow their wings! Even when all seems dark and still in the yard, hope and light are transforming from the ground. The same is true for my life—and yours as well. If you're in a difficult season, I pray you're encouraged to remember that fireflies are best seen in the darkness.—Ashley Clark

Here come real stars to fill the upper skies, and here on earth come emulating flies, that though they never equal stars in size, (and they were never really stars at heart) achieve at times a very star-like start.

—Robert Frost

MAY 3

No Matter How Small

Whatever you do, work at it with all your heart, as working for the Lord, not for human masters, since you know that you will receive an inheritance from the Lord as a reward. It is the Lord Christ you are serving.

—COLOSSIANS 3:23–24 (NIV)

MY FRIEND CRYSTAL and I sat on her back porch, drinking coffee and talking about parenting. "Some days, I don't feel like I do anything that matters," I said. "I love my kids and I'm doing my best, but most of the time, I don't think they even notice what I do for them."

Crystal nodded. "When kids are young, it's easy to wonder if the little things we do every day will amount to anything."

"Reading the same books, singing the same songs. Will it make any difference?" I squinted into the wooded area in their backyard. "What is that?"

"That's our beaver. Isn't he cute?"

He was walking slowly, dragging a small branch behind him.

"There's a decent-sized creek back there. That little beaver has been dragging pieces of bark, twigs, and whatever else he can find into the creek so he can build a dam."

"How long has he been working on it?" I asked Crystal.

"Quite a while now. I see him working almost every day."

"Poor guy. I bet he wishes he could find some big logs. He'll probably never finish if all he has to use are twigs."

Crystal handed me her phone. "I've been taking pictures of his progress." I scrolled through the photos, amazed at how those twigs and leaves—such small, seemingly insignificant items—had been combined to create the beaver's dam. It looked like his work was almost complete.

We sat in silence, and a knowing crept over me. "I do think our parenting efforts count," I said. "Every meal cooked, book read, and act of love—no matter how small—will add up and matter in the long run. We just can't see it now because we're still in the middle of the work, just like the beaver." —Diane Stark

Walk of Faith: *What small actions can you take today that will have a big impact over time?*

MAY 4

She Didn't Know Any Better

Teach them his decrees and instructions, and show them the way they are to live and how they are to behave.

—Exodus 18:20 (NIV)

LIFE ON A farm invites all manner of wildlife, intentionally or not. Feral cats, abandoned or simply wanderers, end up at our farm on regular occasions. We have warm places for cats to cuddle up in winter, plenty of water in the summer, and medication for ills and wounds for those that need care.

Every spring, stray pregnant mother cats seem to show up just in time to bring their litters into the world in a safe place. Then after the kittens are weaned, the untouchable mothers often disappear only to return again in spring pregnant again.

Some of those mother cats know how to train their offspring, while others seem clueless, their babies barely fed enough to survive. Some mamas will even dispose of offspring rather than care for them. Even in the wild it is apparent that motherhood is not something born in all. Parenting is not automatic. More often than not, motherhood is taught by another mother or someone in the community who steps in. On many occasions, I've even acted as mama to cats and other animals on my farm.

I met a young woman who started a pregnancy clinic called Open Door that took young parents with broken places, bruised pasts from their own bad parenting, and substance abuse issues and brought them into a place of love and education. The staff taught the young parents how to care for these new lives without judgment, only love.

Teaching through love has been saving babies, reuniting families, and creating families of all kinds, both furry and human. My feral cat mamas always remind me that love is the best teacher of all. And one of these days that love might even let me get close enough to catch them!—Devon O'Day

God, teach me to teach in such a way that Your plan of love can take root and ripple through the lives born through the generations. Amen.

MAY 5

Goldfinch Rest Stop

Not abandoning our own meeting together, as is the habit of some people, but encouraging one another; and all the more as you see the day drawing near.

—HEBREWS 10:25 (NASB)

RETIREMENT HAS MANY benefits. I find the small, unexpected moments most pleasing. In years past, I missed out on many of them because of work's beckoning call. Now, occasional glimpses materialize as my mornings take on a less hectic pace.

Over the past three years, I have been blessed to witness a goldfinch event that happens only one day each May. A flock of American goldfinches stops over just as the apple blossoms are at their peak. My backyard is filled with roughly thirty migrating goldfinches. Bright yellow and black males are accompanied by their less colorful females.

The event lasts less than a day, and I have been given the honor of seeing them come through each consecutive year. They fly in, spend a few hours feeding, and move north toward their destination.

Curiosity had me wondering what drew them to my backyard each year. Were they after my honeybees collecting the nectar? After doing a little research, I found finches are vegetarians and their diet consists mostly of seeds, but they can get some needed energy from the sugary nectar to help sustain them on their migration journey. I like the idea of my orchard serving as nature's rest stop.

The goldfinches I see each May travel in a group. As I travel my own path, I wonder where my rest stops are. Each Sunday, I gather with my church flock and find energy for the new week. I am nourished and encouraged by feeding with them on the Word of God. He established the church to energize all who attend, but I also need daily nourishment, which I get from personal devotion time, a daily rest stop with Him.—Ben Cooper

Thank You, Lord, for the rest stops You provide me through my church and personal devotions. They fuel me so I can keep moving forward. Making use of these rest stops You have established keeps me flying toward You. Amen.

MAY 6

Foolish Fear

I sought the LORD, and he answered me; he delivered me from all my fears.

—PSALM 34:4 (NIV)

THERE WAS A ruckus going on outside. My dogs were barking as if their lives were on the line. I rushed out to face the problem—hopefully before there was bloodshed. I checked their fenced area and saw nothing at first, but then I looked in the direction of their yips. A small fawn was caught in the bushes next door, too frightened by the dogs' barking to join its mother at the top of the hill. The doe had become used to our dogs' noise and knew that she was not in harm's way because of the fence. But the fawn, with no worldly experience, was petrified and stayed hidden in the bushes.

After sizing up the situation for a few minutes, I decided the fawn wasn't going to leave the safety of the bushes on its own. The family needed my help. I went out the gate and approached the bushes from the side opposite where the doe waited. After a few shouts of "shoo, shoo," the frightened fawn scampered up to its mother atop the hill. They both pranced off to the woods behind our house out of sight. All barking ceased.

Later that afternoon the doe returned alone. I watched her from my backyard. She seemed to lock eyes with me as if to say *thank you* for helping scoot her baby back to her.

There have been times in my life when I've reacted like that fawn, too paralyzed by fear to follow God's leading as He beckoned me up a new hill. I need to remember that Jesus is as protective as a fence, keeping me safe against harm.—Linda Bartlett

But whoever listens to me will live in safety and be at ease,
without fear of harm.
—Proverbs 1:33 (NIV)

MAY 7

The Whip-poor-will's Return

The heavens declare the glory of God; the skies proclaim the work of his hands. Day after day they pour forth speech; night after night they reveal knowledge.

—PSALM 19:1–2 (NIV)

WHEN I HEAR a whip-poor-will's distinctive call, I will always think of my Grandpaw Jim, who used to go outside his house and call to them in hopes they'd return the message. Sometimes it worked, and other times it didn't. I live on the Gulf Coast of Florida, so whip-poor-wills spend their summers in our area. I can remember my grandfather always asking, "Have your whip-poor-wills returned yet?" and wanting to compare notes about the timing.

To me, there is something comforting and exciting about the first time I hear the whip-poor-wills in the spring—knowing they survived another winter and knowing they returned. There is such hope and security to be found in the predictability of nature's rhythms. I believe these patterns are one way that creation "declares the glory of God." Just as I know the sun will rise and set each day, I can count on the return of the birds through the seasons.

What a reminder that God is with us and His plans and provision are greater than our own. When I'm tempted to see myself as too powerful—those times I begin to believe that my own efforts or strength or striving can sustain my world—I'm reminded of the whip-poor-will's return. I know not where the birds go or how they find their way home. But God does. He guides their way, and He guides mine too.—Ashley Clark

Father, thank You for the rhythms of life and for always guiding me. Amen.

MAY 8

Do the Bunny Hop

Six days you shall labor, but on the seventh day you shall rest; even during the plowing season and harvest you must rest.

—EXODUS 34:21 (NIV)

MY DAUGHTER AND I were just returning from an evening walk with the dog, enjoying the mild early summer stroll. The sun always glints through our neighbor's gigantic maple tree at this time of day, and as I squinted, I was quite sure I saw a rabbit hop vertically up into the air under that tree.

Looking more closely, my daughter and I saw that there were actually four rabbits under the tree, and they were playing together. The neighborhood in which we live is fairly overrun by rabbits during this season. We see them nibbling in our garden beds and racing away from the dogs. They hide under bushes and do what they can to startle us when we drive down the streets.

But I rarely see rabbits playing, and I had never seen them play like this. They were essentially playing leapfrog, taking turns hopping—yes, vertically—high into the air and then over another rabbit. They frolicked like this in the yellow evening sunlight for a handful of minutes and then sped off to the backyard.

The playfulness of those bunnies stayed with me as summer began in earnest. I had never imagined a rabbit's life to necessitate play, but they sure seemed delighted in playing. Those moments of gladness and fun that I witnessed were a demonstration of one of the ways God created them to live and be.

Summer is ticking on, and my family and I are taking some time to play together. It can be hard to let go of all the work that life entails, but I am trusting that God created us also for the restfulness and play that summer includes. —Katy W. Sundararajan

Thank You, Lord, that all of creation knows the rhythms of rest and play. Please remind my heart of my own created nature, and point me toward play. Help me to be like the bunnies. Amen.

MAY 9

The Persistence of Ants

See, I am doing a new thing! Now it springs up; do you not perceive it? I am making a way in the wilderness and streams in the wasteland.

—ISAIAH 43:19 (NIV)

LATELY, WE'VE HAD a lot of rain as well as warm temperatures, so I should've known the inevitable was coming, yet it always catches me by surprise. I was leisurely making a cup of tea when I spotted them. Ants. Marching their little bodies all over my counters and around my oven. The scene reminded me of a children's book I loved when I was younger, in which the character destroys her house in pursuit of an ant.

In my case, nothing in the kitchen was destroyed—*this* time, at least. I found the trail of ants pretty quickly, and my husband was able to knock out the problem with a few borax traps. But the whole endeavor got me thinking about the persistence of ants. Just when you think you've taken care of them, they find a new way inside your house. While this can be comical as well as frustrating, it's also rather admirable. At the slightest opportunity, ants are ready to mobilize to gather food for their colony. I wonder, *Am I living with such expectancy and willingness in my own life? Am I ready to simply go, moving behind life's "walls" to pursue the provision God has offered?*

Sometimes in my own life, I find myself expecting spiritual provision to come in the form of a delivery rather than requiring any action on my part. But the ants are a great reminder that walking with the Lord in steadfastness requires intentionality and persistence. Some days, provision might come easily, but other days I may have to explore and stir up new spaces to discover what God has for me. Like ants, I must be persistent to see He is always doing a new thing.—Ashley Clark

Father, give me eyes to see Your provision in my life and a heart to pursue the path You've laid out for me. Amen.

MAY 10

Ambassadors of Unity

Finally, all of you, have unity of mind, sympathy, brotherly love, a tender heart, and a humble mind.

—1 PETER 3:8 (ESV)

THE NEIGHBORS ACROSS the street from us have chickens in their backyard. This practice is becoming more common in our inner-city community because people are looking for creative ways to afford their morning omelets. Dockery, the oldest son, tells me their four chickens provide them with at least a dozen eggs each week.

I knew the chickens were there, but I'd never seen them out of their cages until one day they were on my side of the street. I was very worried for them. Would they get lost? Would they get run over by the cars on our moderately busy street? Did the family know their charges had escaped? Dockery took it all in stride when I knocked on their back door to inform them that the hens were loose. Edie, the next oldest child, assured me that the chickens always come home at night. But for my peace of mind, the kids went out to round them up.

When the family went on a trip recently, they asked some friends to tend the chickens in their absence. While they were away, my neighbors saw a Facebook post with a photo of their chickens. "Does anyone know whose chickens these are?" read the post. Turns out, the adventuresome fowl had roamed several blocks away! After a few hurried phone calls from the neighbors to their friends, the inattentive caretakers were directed to the address where they could retrieve the missing ladies.

The unexpected doesn't give us much warning. And as it turns out, chickens on the loose in the neighborhood make excellent icebreakers. People interact with one another when something unusual draws them out of their homes. We are able to overcome things like inconvenience and embarrassment, and we get to become part of each other's lives.—Liz Kimmel

Thank You, dear Shepherd, for the ways that You direct our paths every day. Help us to seek unity as we intersect with those we meet. Amen.

MAY 11

Perfect Peace

Peace I leave with you; my peace I give you. I do not give to you as the world gives. Do not let your hearts be troubled and do not be afraid.

—JOHN 14:27 (NIV)

NATURE IS MY sanctuary go-to when the world crumbles. It's where I go to meet God. So, on a day when countries were bombing each other into oblivion, when my great-grandson awaited surgery that would either end or extend his life, when my cousin was again struggling to overcome addiction, I took a walk.

It was a particularly harsh spring day. The temperature was below normal, and the day was as gray as an old, overused dishcloth. I didn't want to take a walk, but I needed to. I needed to know God was still there.

I strolled down the dirt road with my dog, Lucy, to the place where cattails were numerous and the trees provided some shelter from the wind. Chickadees chittered above while red-winged blackbirds sang to each other on the reeds. A pair of geese swam close by, seemingly unbothered by the raw cold.

I hoped to see a beaver or a muskrat emerge from its winter quarters, but it must have been too cold yet. I did, however, see a familiar van amble down the path. It was Diane, who had been on a nine-month mission trip and was home. She stopped and we hugged. What a blessed moment.

I walked home with more pep in my step. After seeing all the two-footed friends (birds and human), I felt reassured that God was still in His place, watching over all of us. Back home I settled myself in my lounge chair and continued to see nature send messages of peace to me. A cardinal and a chickadee shared the bird feeder while a squirrel picked at seeds below.

While the world as a whole had not improved in the last half hour, I felt perfect peace knowing God is still in control.—Linda Bartlett

Be a rainbow in someone's cloud.
—Maya Angelou

MAY 12

Tiny Toad

For who has despised the day of small things?...They are the eyes of the LORD, which scan to and fro throughout the whole earth.

—ZECHARIAH 4:10 (NKJV)

LOOK WHAT I found!" my four-year-old grandson said, as he opened his hand but cupped it enough to keep his little treasure from escaping. It was the tiniest baby toad I'd ever seen, smaller than a dime.

This sweet boy had found the miniscule toad in my courtyard. He placed it on the concrete patio and watched it hop. He giggled, caught it, put it down, and watched it jump again. At one point, the wee critter landed in the dirt around a fern and mushroom, and its brown color made it almost impossible to see. But it was scooped up again by a squatting, curious boy, whose eyes were fixed on it.

I ran inside for an empty container and placed some grass on the bottom so the toad could go home with my grandson.

"We'll poke holes in the lid so it can breathe," I said.

My daughter-in-law watched.

"Oh, but the teeny toad has a mommy," she said with a kind smile. "Do you think its mother might be looking for her baby?"

Immediately, I knew the value of what she said and looked into the eyes of my grandson.

"Your mama is right. Let's put the baby toad back where you found him."

My grandson's bright smile let me know what he was thinking too. He bent down and placed the itsy-bitsy critter in the dirt, and then we asked Jesus to help the toad find its mommy.

I learned that day that to hold God's tiniest creation in human hands is a precious thing but to let it go is sacred.—Kathleen R. Ruckman

Lord, I place all things great and small into Your hands and under Your watchful eyes—for You know best and are Creator of all. Amen.

Stepping into the Unfamiliar

But blessed is the one who trusts in the Lord, whose confidence is in him.

—Jeremiah 17:7 (NIV)

I WATCH AT THE kitchen window, but there's no movement except raindrops pelting the glass. I've observed baby cottontail rabbits curiously emerging from beneath our shed for three weeks. They cautiously wander farther each day. But this morning is different. We've had a dry month; this is their first encounter with rain. I wonder if they hesitate to come out into a wet world. They cannot remain in that burrow forever. Just as they've learned to avoid neighborhood cats and watch for shadows of overflying hawks, they'll learn to navigate this new challenge.

I find the same is true when I encounter new and unfamiliar conditions. The temptation is to burrow into what I know is safe—but what might I miss? In the unknowns of life, God coaxes me toward new confidence. I practice discernment and develop an awareness of my surroundings. He has far too much in store for my life for me to be held back by apprehensions and anxiety. He rescues me from fear paralysis and beckons me into His wild and wonderful world.

Buds on the trees and flower blossoms below unfurl as the rain relents. The landscape enlivens with colors and aroma. I can smell the wet earth and the fragrance of things growing. The rabbits emerge, their noses following the scents of green grass and delicate flower petals. Perhaps during our next rain, they'll remember this tasty aftereffect. Maybe they'll fear less and focus on what they know is true: the flowers won't bloom unless the rain falls. Sometimes it's these unfamiliar places that lead to great things. In the midst of ambiguity, I can step out into uncharted territory knowing that God is bringing about His good plans in my life.—Eryn Lynum

Dear God, I trust You in the unknown. As I step into new circumstances, fill me with confidence rooted in Your faithfulness. Turn my attention to the good things You are bringing forth. Amen.

Nuthatch Finds a Home

Take delight in the Lord, and he will give you the desires of your heart.

—Psalm 37:4 (NIV)

A SPRY GRAY NUTHATCH inspected the small, peaked birdhouse nestled in our willow tree. I held my breath and even crossed my fingers. Would the bird make her home here and raise her young?

My husband and I had searched for our own new house late last summer. We didn't need much room for just the two of us and the dogs. But the desire of my heart was a house with a small office with a window where I could watch the birds as I worked. It wasn't a necessity, but still I wished for it. At last, God led us to a cute little cottage, which had the office of my dreams! Now as I sat at my computer and looked out my writing window, as I've come to call it, I wondered if the nuthatch I spied would be my new neighbor.

I watched the bird flutter from the feeder filled with sunflower seeds to the birdbath with cool, fresh water. She poked in the shrubs and evergreens before returning to peek inside the birdhouse. Then she flew away. I went back to work, disappointed.

But soon after, the nuthatch returned with a sprig of straw held fast in her beak. She rested on the perch and gazed back at me as I watched from the window. Then she slipped into the birdhouse. Was the food, water, and shelter I'd provided right for the desires of her heart? I hoped so. I prayed that a little bird would find the blessing of home in the place that had become my blessing—the special, long-dreamt-of place God had graciously provided for me, because He cares about the desires of my heart.—Peggy Frezon

God knows the dreams and desires in your heart; in fact, He gave them to you. He will order your steps and take you where you need to be.

—Joel Osteen

MAY 15

Slipping Out

If I say, "My foot slips," Your mercy, O Lord, will hold me up.

—Psalm 94:18 (NKJV)

WHILE OUR FAMILY has always had dogs, it's only been about two years since we adopted our first cats. Yes, you read that right—cats, plural. We'd actually asked for only a single cat, but these two males were bonded black-and-white tuxedo brothers. How could we say no when the shelter asked if we could take two?

Not surprisingly, I've discovered being a cat mama is a lot different from being a dog mama. When a dog does something wrong and I catch her, she looks guilty and pitiful. When one of my cats knocks something breakable from the bureau, he looks me straight in the eye with a very clear message—*I meant to do that.*

Recently I've had a new issue with the boys. When I let our dogs out back to do their business, the cats have been sneaking out right under my feet. These guys are indoor-only cats, and every time they get out, I experience a moment of panic. Most of the time they instantly realize they're not where they are supposed to be and slip back in as if that was what they meant to do all along. The one time they found the nerve to go down the deck steps, they immediately returned and stood at the sliding glass door, waiting to come back inside. I couldn't help but roll my eyes.

I have to admit I've done the same thing in my own life, slipping out where I'm not supposed to be, realizing I've made a mistake, and then running back to where I was in the first place. I wonder if Jesus is rolling His eyes as He opens the door and lets me back in.—Deb Kastner

Ask and it will be given to you; seek and you will find; knock and the door will be opened to you. For everyone who asks receives; the one who seeks finds; and to the one who knocks, the door will be opened.

—Matthew 7:7–8 (NIV)

MAY 16

Resting Place

I will both lie down in peace, and sleep; for You alone, O Lord, make me dwell in safety.

—Psalm 4:8 (NKJV)

I TOOK OUR YORKIE, Minnie, out for her final opportunity of the night. The porch light illuminated the area by the front door as I climbed down the steps and turned right toward the grass out back. A dark spot amid the seashell border along our home drew my attention. Was it a leaf or piece of bark? I peered closer. No. A bird rested atop the seashells, of all places.

At the base of our roses, small white seashells cover the ground. The mourning dove remained still with her dark gray feathers fluffed out and her body low to the ground. I spoke sweetly to her and promised not to disturb her as we passed.

Minnie and I continued out to the grass with the aid of a flashlight until we completed our purpose. We returned a few minutes later. My winged friend continued in her fixed position. I told her she was safe as I crept past her. Minnie hadn't noticed the resting bird. I kept her leash taut in case she caught sight of the feathered bundle and attempted to disturb her resting place.

The mourning dove trusted me. She trusted me to keep Minnie away from her. She trusted me not to disrupt her peace. She trusted me when danger surrounded her.

Her trust challenged me. Do I trust God enough to rest in the shadows when problems are coming? Am I at peace when chaos surrounds me? Do I remain steadfast when threats abound in the dark?

God is worthy of my trust. His presence is my resting place, a sweet refuge from the cares of this world. No matter what I face, I can trust Him.—Crystal Storms

I will say of the Lord, "He is my refuge and my fortress;
My God, in Him I will trust."
—Psalm 91:2 (NKJV)

MAY 17

A Miniature Marvel

Everything was created through him; nothing—not one thing!—came into being without him.

—JOHN 1:3 (MSG)

I LOVE FARM-SUPPLY STORES, especially in the spring, when I watch newly hatched chicks flutter and chirp under warm lights in tin watering troughs that have been converted into incubators. Everything about them is tiny—from their bright eyes and pointy beaks to their fuzzy bodies and orange feet. Yet their brains, as small as they are, have been programmed to keep all the newly formed organs working properly.

Our Creator even designed a special tool for the baby chick that disappears soon after it is born. Called the egg tooth, it is a sharp projection on the end of the beak that has a special purpose. A developing chick gets its air from thousands of air holes in the shell of the egg. When the chick is ready to hatch, it needs more air than the holes in the eggshell can supply. The chick uses its egg tooth to poke a hole in a large bubble of air at the big end of the egg. This sack will supply the chick with air while it uses the egg tooth to break free from the shell.

As I watched the feathery chicks pecking for food, I marveled at this brilliant tool. How does the chick know to start pecking at the part of the shell that holds the air supply? The great Designer planned it that way!

If God took so much care in creating the chick, I can't imagine how He feels about me! God has planned every day of our lives and given us everything we need.—Randy Benedetto

Body and soul, I am marvelously made! I worship in adoration—what a creation! You know me inside and out.
—Psalm 139:14–15 (MSG)

MAY 18

Chewing Cud

Bear with each other and forgive one another if any of you has a grievance against someone. Forgive as the Lord forgave you.

—COLOSSIANS 3:13 (NIV)

DURING COVID-19 LOCKDOWN, I made a thirty-minute drive every week to deliver groceries to my disabled sister. I often started out the trip thinking about a million other things that needed doing, but the beautiful countryside soon quieted my mind and turned my thoughts toward God. In the spring, I passed fields carpeted with yellow wildflowers and more than once stopped to take pictures.

On one drive, cows caught my attention. I turned up a short side road and got out of my car. The biggest bull I'd ever seen assumed an intimidating stance, making me grateful for strong fences. As I snapped photos, the cows wandered over but seemed mostly curious. They soon lay down and went back to chewing their cud. I've read how dairy cows spend almost eight hours a day chewing their cud, which makes them healthier and helps them produce more milk. Maybe so, but it doesn't seem like the most appetizing way to enjoy a meal.

Watching these ladies, I wondered how often I bring old grievances back up and chew on them awhile. Unlike the natural digestive processes of the cows, rehashing my anger only produces bitterness. Focusing on "who was right, who was wrong?" sours my thinking and makes me ready to lower my horns and go after the first red flag I see, a decidedly unhealthy situation.

I've learned to stop the process before getting to that point by turning my thoughts back to God. Only He can help me produce the product He wants—forgiveness. I've discovered through trial and error that I can't do it on my own. By ruminating on grievances, I grow more bitter. By ruminating on God, I grow more like Christ, the One who forgave me.—Tracy Crump

Never does the human soul appear so strong as when it foregoes revenge and dares to forgive an injury.
—Edwin Hubbell Chapin

The God Who Sees Me

O LORD, you have examined my heart and know everything about me. You know when I sit down or stand up. You know my thoughts even when I'm far away. You see me when I travel and when I rest at home. You know everything I do.

—PSALM 139:1–3 (NLT)

AS A FREQUENT visitor to a local garden, I witness the subtle changes from week to week and sometimes day to day. One event that I particularly look forward to is the emergence of miner bees in spring. They emerge from holes in the ground when the early wildflower spring beauty blooms.

Hundreds of miner bees feed on the flowers. Small in size, they would go unnoticed if not for the sheer volume of black-bodied bees buzzing in an area bursting with white and light-purple blooms.

In a few short weeks, the bees and flowers are gone, causing me to consider my own transitory sojourn on the earth. King David wrote in Psalm 39:5 (NLT), "You have made my life no longer than the width of my hand. My entire lifetime is just a moment to you." Nevertheless, God, the creator of miner bees, sees us all.

One of my favorite Hebrew names for God is *El Roi*, which is commonly translated as "the God who sees me." Genesis 16 recounts the story of the runaway servant girl Hagar, who in the midst of despair and perceived insignificance, has an encounter with almighty God. El Roi is the name that Hagar gives God after He assures her of life and a future for her son.

Sometimes it feels like my unanswered prayers indicate I am unseen by God. Where is my deliverance from chronic insomnia? Then I remember Hagar and David who testified that God saw them in their dire circumstances. Their encounters with God give me confidence that while I wait, He is working out His plan for my life and future, as well. I grab onto the truth of El Roi. I find solace in knowing that God sees me. I am never alone.—Darlene Kerr

No matter what may be the test, God will take care of you; lean, weary one, upon His breast, God will take care of you.

—Civilla D. Martin

MAY 20

Happy Memories

You make known to me the path of life; you will fill me with joy in your presence, with eternal pleasures at your right hand.

—PSALM 16:11 (NIV)

CHECK OUT THESE dogs!" I typed onto my Facebook post. It was National Rescue Dog Day, and I was sharing a message about some homeless dogs at our local shelter. My hope was that I could bring awareness to the joys of rescuing dogs. At the same time, I couldn't help thinking of the dogs I had rescued over the years. In particular, a dog named Happy.

Happy was a skinny beagle-Lab mix who had been abandoned in the woods, hungry and scared. When we couldn't find his owners, my family took him in. I was just five years old at the time, yet I knew instantly that God had sent Happy to be my best friend.

I fed him, he licked my face, we played together…but what I remember most is just his presence. He was always there. Whether I was playing with friends in the yard, alone in my room, or asleep at night, Happy was always beside me. It was the best feeling, to be so loved.

Did God bring Happy into my life because the dog needed me, or did He bring the dog into my life because I needed him? As often is the case, I think it was a little bit of both. And not long afterward, God came into my life too. I remember the feeling of learning He was there beside me and that He loved me very, very much.

Now, with more maturity, I continue my walk with God. I strive to show Him the same unswerving love and devotion that Happy had always shown me. And it starts by just spending time in His presence. —Peggy Frezon

Dear God, just as my dogs enjoy time spent with me, I'm grateful for my time with You. May Your presence wrap around me and allow me to know You more. Amen.

MAY 21

Made for Praise

The people whom I formed for myself that they might declare my praise.

—ISAIAH 43:21 (ESV)

THERE WERE DOZENS of birds flitting around and singing in the rafters of the rustic outdoor music hall where my family had gathered to listen to a night of string performances. We kick off summer here every year with four nights of family violin camp. We felt as glad as the birds sounded to be outdoors, taking in the music. Spring had been chilly, and the dusty, cobwebby dregs of winter had been ours to discharge at the start of camp two days ago.

I settled back in my seat as the first piece began. I breathed a sigh of happy relief, enjoying the lively, opening quartet. And then, after a moment, I heard them above the violins—the birds. Oh, the wild ruckus! Those birds had not learned their concert etiquette; that was clear. They had not stilled their wings, they were not quiet at all, and, in fact, they were making their own music.

I tilted my head back for a second time that night to gaze up at the birds. The smile returned to my face. There was no mean intention, no cruel attempt at actual distraction. The birds were living their best life and singing their best song. Song upon song upon song trilled throughout the high, open ceilings during the concert—sometimes mingling with the strings, sometimes standing out on their own. The birdsong was their inherent gift to share, and no other concert could cause them to stop.

I often marvel at the birds and the constancy of their song. Beauty and praise, every day, in every place, and all because they can. My beautiful song of praise is planted in me from creation's beginning. I could learn from the birds to let my praise daily rise up, above and within the songs of those around me.—Katy W. Sundararajan

How can I keep from singing Your praise
How can I ever say enough
How amazing is Your love
—Chris Tomlin

Amazingly Made

Let the morning bring me word of your unfailing love, for I have put my trust in you. Show me the way I should go, for to you I entrust my life.

—PSALM 143:8 (NIV)

WE BROUGHT TWO baby rabbits home from the feed store, and I read everything I could about how to care for them. Sadly, I learned rabbits are frequently abandoned because they are quite different from what people imagine. The image of a bunny is a soft lovey that only needs a few carrots to be content, but in reality, rabbits are strong-minded, quirky, and independent. Like humans, some are cuddly and some are standoffish. I also learned that rabbits chew electrical cords as happily as hay, carrots are not very good for them, and they require a large space to be happy and healthy. We all vowed enthusiastically to provide the best life possible for our new friends.

When the honeymoon ended, we realized that this relationship, like any, required considerable effort. We passed the baton of responsibility around, until we settled into a routine that worked for everyone in the family. I soon noticed that, rather than complaining, we were waking earlier to take care of them. "I've got the buns in the morning," I would say, and someone else would answer, "No, don't worry; it's my turn."

Morning with the buns has proven to be sacred time. The sun streams in the big windows, and the bunnies binky (jump in the air, twisting in delight), flop, and touch noses with me when I put my face close to them. Hutch chores are a hay-scented reminder of simpler times. As I sit on the floor observing their strength, beauty, and distinct personalities, I feel directly connected to the wholeness and wonder of creation. As I leave the hutch and enter the world, the vision of God they provide stays with me, providing perspective on the other responsibilities I will face in the coming day.—Lucy H. Chambers

Be Thou my Vision, O Lord of my heart; naught be all else to me, save that Thou art; Thou my best thought, in the day or the night, waking or sleeping, Thy presence my light.

—Dallán Forgaill

MAY 23

Beware: Danger on the Loose

The prudent sees danger and hides himself, but the simple go on and suffer for it.

—PROVERBS 22:3 (ESV)

I PARKED IN MY neighbors' driveway and exited the car. The yard was eerily quiet. The neighbors' two dogs usually barked constantly when their owners were gone. But today, I'd seen from my backyard an acre away that both dogs had escaped their kennel.

Afraid the dogs might venture to the front and cross the busy road, I had to try to return the dogs to their kennel. The trouble was I'd never met them and didn't know what kind of welcome I'd receive.

Armed with treats I brought to entice the dogs, I approached the side of the house, thinking they could still be in the backyard and hadn't heard me arrive. Knowing I shouldn't sneak up on dogs that might be inhospitable, I called out in my best canine-friendly tone.

Nothing. I tried a whistle instead.

Barks and growls launched from the backyard. Instinct kicked in, and I fled to the safety of my car. I opened the door and ducked inside just as the two dogs flew around the house, snarling and barking.

I tossed them treats from behind my car-door shield, but the dogs stayed close to the car and wouldn't stop growling and barking. They were in danger but wanted to chase away the person who could help them.

I called the owners, and they returned home in time to prevent disaster. But the experience lingered in my mind. How many times have I been in spiritual danger and tried to chase away God or helping friends? Sin I refuse to acknowledge or a poor decision can lead me astray. But pride convinces me I don't need God's help. Yet I'll only be safe if I run to the Savior who has come not to threaten me but to offer me safety in His arms.—Jerusha Agen

Lord, help me to recognize when I'm in danger, even of my own making, and to welcome aid from You and the people You send my way. Amen.

MAY 24

We Can Trust the Mover

"For I know the plans I have for you," declares the Lord, "plans to prosper you and not to harm you, plans to give you hope and a future."

—Jeremiah 29:11 (NIV)

I WAS SITTING ON our screened porch when a movement caught my eye. A bright-eyed anole lizard stared at me from atop a bistro chair. I see anoles all the time, but few make it into my screened porch.

"Uh-oh, little guy," I said as we eyed each other. "You can't stay in here. I don't want you climbing up my leg or jumping on me. And besides, you'll starve. Or dehydrate. Or both."

If my granddaughter Lauren had been there, she'd have scooped it up and carried it outside. Not me. Ain't no way.

Moving slowly so I wouldn't startle it, I gently lifted the chair with the lizard on it. Mercifully, the creature stayed frozen in place. I held my breath as I carried the chair and its passenger out the door. Scurrying back into the screened porch, I breathed a sigh of relief and latched the door behind me as I watched the lizard sprint down the chair leg and into the bushes.

My experience with the lizard reminded me of the summer of 1979. In my opinion, my parents had made the worst decision of their lives—to move our family one thousand miles south to Dad's hometown of Columbia, South Carolina. I was heartsick. Leave the safety of our sweet little town? Move away from my friends, family, and beloved grandmother? What were they thinking?

I know now that God, not my parents, orchestrated our move. He lifted me from the rocky shores of Rhode Island and settled me in the Sandhills of South Carolina to bless me, not harm me. In my new location, I met my future husband, made lifelong friends, and most important, attended a church where I heard the gospel and accepted Jesus. Like my lizard friend, I didn't understand the purpose of our relocation, but now I am infinitely grateful. Someone wiser than I knew what was best.—Lori Hatcher

Father, even when You move me where I don't want to go,
help me trust that You know best. Amen.

Under His Wings

Jerusalem, Jerusalem, you who kill the prophets and stone those sent to you, how often I have longed to gather your children together, as a hen gathers her chicks under her wings, and you were not willing.

—LUKE 13:34 (NIV)

I HAVE SEVERAL OUTBUILDINGS that offered perfect places for birds to build nests. A nervous little phoebe thought she had found one when she decided to construct her nest and eventually hatch her brood right inside the doorway of our chicken house. For several weeks, each time I opened the door to feed the chickens or ventured in to gather eggs, momma would frantically fly out and voice her outrage at her privacy being invaded. Eventually, she'd had enough and abandoned her nest and hatchlings altogether.

With their protector gone, two of the young chicks jumped out of the nest onto the floor and cried out for their mother. As I entered the chicken house at the end of the day to close the door, I found a hen who was not on the roost like the others. She was on the floor with her wings puffed out. I picked her up to place her on the roost where she belonged and was amazed to find the two phoebe chicks under her. That hen responded to their cries, showed compassion, and became a surrogate mom to them.

What an amazing example from nature of how God hears my cries and steps in to rescue me, protect me, and accept me into His family. Sheltered under His wings, I feel secure and safe. What a comfort knowing this compassionate God has adopted me for evermore.—Ben Cooper

Under His wings—oh, what precious enjoyment! There will I hide till life's trials are o'er; sheltered, protected, no evil can harm me; resting in Jesus I'm safe evermore.

—William Orcutt Cushing

MAY 26

Ready to Run?

Therefore, my beloved brethren, be steadfast, immovable, always abounding in the work of the Lord, knowing that your labor is not in vain in the Lord.

—1 CORINTHIANS 15:58 (NKJV)

WHEN I TOOK Minnie out to go potty at the end of the evening, I noticed a bunny munching on grass behind our home. As we turned the corner to head his way, he tensed his body like a runner at the start of a race, ready to bolt. I talked sweetly to the bunny, assuring him he was safe. Neither Minnie nor I would bring him harm. He relaxed his body and returned to eating.

I didn't want to break his trust, so I led Minnie to the patch of grass in the front of our home by the road. As my Yorkie sniffed around, I considered how running is often my first response when a difficulty arises.

When things get hard, I sometimes look for a way out, an easier path. Instead of confronting a friend, I avoid the subject or limit my contact. If the words don't come when I sit down to write, I work on another project or delete emails. I sometimes say "no" to opportunities with too great a responsibility.

But God has shown me how to stand firm and remain steadfast when I'd rather run. He promises in Isaiah 26:3 (NKJV), "You will keep him in perfect peace, whose mind is stayed on You, because he trusts in You."

With my eyes on Jesus, I can remain steady in the face of adversity. With Christ as my goal, I can remain faithful in the middle of trials. With God by my side, I can accomplish difficult tasks.

Minnie took care of her business, and we headed back inside. I peeked around the corner to see if the bunny was still there. He looked at me but remained dedicated to eating his dinner, no longer ready to run. Neither was I.—Crystal Storms

To me, it has been a source of great comfort and strength in the day of battle, just to remember that the secret of steadfastness, and indeed, of victory, is the recognition that "the Lord is at hand."

—Duncan Campbell

MAY 27

It Takes a Village

The earth is the LORD's, and everything in it, the world, and all who live in it.

—PSALM 24:1 (NIV)

I'VE OFTEN HEARD the phrase "it takes a village," but I didn't really know how true that was until our family participated in the launch of a nest of baby cardinals. We could see the nest in the bush through the window outside our dining area. While sitting at our table, we'd watch from about four feet away, but when we stood at the window, our bird's-eye view was only two feet away. It was so exciting to see the mother and daddy cardinals bring food to their babies, whose open mouths peeked up over the top of the nest expectantly.

During the weeks we watched the developing birds, we had to protect them from our dogs when we let them out in the backyard. We also had to watch for the neighbors' cats. As the hatchlings became fledglings, we had a bit of a scare. My husband was eating breakfast when he noticed a sudden burst of bird activity and squawking. He went outside to check for cats. Instead, he found the cardinal parents, as well as several robins, towhees, and wrens, flapping around the yard, sounding an alarm at the presence of a barred owl. The owl was getting too close to the baby cardinals that were now on the ground. My husband helped shoo the owl away, and we kept watch the rest of the day. Thankfully, "our" fledglings made it.

It really does take a village to raise a child, and this time it felt as if we, and the birds that gather in our yard to eat out of our feeders, were instrumental in helping a clutch of cardinals safely leave the nest. What a joy to witness!—Missy Tippens

For the beauty of the earth, for the glory of the skies, for the love which from our birth over and around us lies; Lord of all, to thee we raise this our hymn of grateful praise.

—Folliot S. Pierpoint

MAY 28

The Duck Wrangler

Answer me speedily, O LORD; My spirit fails! Do not hide Your face from me, lest I be like those who go down into the pit.

—PSALM 143:7 (NKJV)

WHEN MY SON'S neighbor heard faint quacking from a drainpipe in front of their houses, she called animal control and alerted Jeremy. Overnight downpours had washed ten newly hatched ducklings into the storm system. After Jeremy helped the control officer remove grating that covered the sewer, they spied the ducklings huddled at the bottom. The hatchlings were too far away to reach, and neither of the adults could fit into the drain.

Our nine-year-old granddaughter saved the day. Nellie donned her rain boots and climbed down a ladder into the dark, narrow sewer. She wrestled the ducklings one by one into a laundry basket and handed them up to her dad. Together, they took the fluffy brown-and-yellow babies back to the lake behind their house. When they couldn't find the mother duck, who often fed in Jeremy's backyard, another female mallard showed interest. Soon the ducklings swam off with their adopted mom, obviously happy to be free again.

What a nail-biter rescue! I'm not sure anyone could have convinced me to squeeze into a dark pit the way Nellie did. But then, how many times do I stumble into pits, sometimes of my own making? I think about years of barely keeping up with credit-card payments when I unwisely overcharged. Seeing interest pile on every month helped me understand the psalmist's cry, "My spirit fails!" Fortunately, God kept me from sliding any deeper into debt. He put my feet on firm ground, and I was grateful, just as the ducklings were, to escape that pit.

Nellie's mom dubbed her the duck wrangler. I'm so glad she showed up to help the ducklings just as God showed up for me. As Nellie said, it was a pro-DUCK-tive day.—Tracy Crump

No matter how dark and hopeless a situation might seem, never stop praying.
—Billy Graham

MAY 29

Calling Crows

In everything set them an example by doing what is good.

—TITUS 2:7 (NIV)

MY HUSBAND, THE biologist, is a crow-whisperer. Well, to be more accurate, I guess I should say he's a crow *caw*ller. You see, David has an uncanny ability to place his hand over his mouth, *caw* with a loud and gravelly voice, and sound just like a crow. At least, that's what other crows seem to think.

For as long as I can remember, David has amazed our kids and me by calling crows when he hears one or two in the distance; soon, the black birds are circling closer overhead. One time he performed his trick expecting a couple of birds to fly nearby, and before we knew it, more than a dozen crows were circling overhead.

Once while we visited our grandson and his parents, the adults sat on lawn furniture while two-year-old Benaiah played on the swing set. David heard a crow in the distance and *cawed* for it to come closer. We had no idea the little one was watching until we saw him place his chubby little hand over his mouth and attempt to squeal into his hand like his granddaddy.

Months later when Benaiah visited our house, he and I played in the sandbox on our front porch. Suddenly, he put his hand to his ear and said, "Do you hear that?"

When I listened, I could hear the faint call of a crow. Benaiah walked to the edge of the porch, placed his hand over his mouth, and *cawed,* just like his granddaddy. My grandson's actions reminded me that his little eyes—as well as those of others around me—are always watching. I made a mental note to set good examples for him in everything I do, because I would never want to lead anyone astray.—Julie Lavender

Dear God, please help me to remember that others are watching me, whether it's a little one who might be influenced by my actions, a family member who loves and trusts me, friends and acquaintances, or even strangers. Let my life reflect You always. Amen.

MAY 30

The Hidden Spider

And we know that in all things God works for the good of those who love him, who have been called according to his purpose.

—ROMANS 8:28 (NIV)

WHEN MY THIRD novel released, my mom gave me a very special gift: an heirloom rose *just* like the one featured in the story. As I waited in indecision to plant it—unsure exactly where it should live in my yard—I noticed the rosebush wasn't thriving as it should, and I noticed something else too. A tiny green spider. My, was it cute! I'll admit, I may've even given it a friendly "hello" or two. But soon I began to realize that the spider's habitat was not sustainable. The rosebush needed to grow deeper roots.

I was in a quandary. Should I move the spider to another bush? Capture it until I was done planting, then release it back on the roses? Ultimately, I decided that the least intrusive option was to keep my little green spider friend right where it was and simply use care with planting. I am happy to say the spider survived the transplant just fine, and now its habitat is thriving! I imagine in a few more weeks, it will be very happy having so many more rose stalks to choose from.

In my own life, I often resist a habitat change—whether it's a circumstance, an opportunity, or any kind of change, really. I like to stay put right where I am and tend to get content there. But sometimes what I don't see is that my own "rosebush" is going to wither if God does not place me in deeper ground. If you're going through something similar today, I pray God encourages your heart with the reminder that even in the midst of all life's transplants, God is with you, for you, and working for your good.—Ashley Clark

High King of heaven, my victory won, may I reach heaven's joys,
O bright Heaven's Sun! Heart of my own heart, whatever befall,
still be my vision, O Ruler of all.
—translated by Mary Byrne and Eleanor Hull

MAY 31

Finding Rest

The Lord replied, "My Presence will go with you, and I will give you rest."

—Exodus 33:14 (NIV)

I SAT AT THE computer in my home office, feeling overwhelmed by the amount of work I needed to complete. My husband, Eric, said, "I'm heading to the kitchen for a snack. Do you want to come?"

I shook my head. "I've got too much to do to take a break. Thank you, though."

Eric left and I tried to focus, but something outside caught my eye. A hummingbird was flying in front of my window. I smiled as the tiny bird flapped its wings, hovering in the air as if it was effortless. *I'll have to move as fast as that hummingbird to get through my to-do list today,* I thought. *And I still won't finish everything.*

Eric returned with a bowl of pretzels. "You can eat them while you work," he said.

I pointed at the hummingbird. "I'm going to imitate that little guy today. Hummingbirds never stop moving."

"That's not true," he said. "They can't move that fast indefinitely. They get tired and rest, just like other birds." He looked at me pointedly. "All God's creatures, including humans, need to rest."

"I don't have time today."

"Hummingbirds refuel almost constantly by eating nectar from the flowers. Humans need rest and food to keep moving, and I don't mean just pretzels."

I knew he meant spiritual food. I'd skipped my devotional reading that morning so I could start working a few minutes sooner. But I realized now that the strategy had backfired. I felt exhausted and cranky because I was working in my own strength. I hadn't asked God for His help.

I reached for my Bible just as the hummingbird flew away, probably to rest in a tree or enjoy some nectar from the lilies in my flower bed.

That tiny bird reminded me that no matter how busy I am, I still need to invite God into my day, to ask for His help with my daily tasks, and to find rest in Him.—Diane Stark

Lord, help me to remember that Your presence is just a prayer away. Amen.

June

JUNE 1

Tiny Foghorn

Therefore I tell you, whatever you ask for in prayer, believe that you have received it, and it will be yours.

—MARK 11:24 (NIV)

THE MEMPHIS JUNE day promised to be a hot one, but the early-morning air was still cool as I walked at a nearby city park, where a figure-eight walkway wound around two ponds.

As is most often the case when I walk, I was praying. As I've aged and faced some health issues, my anxiety level has increased accordingly, and I was pouring out my anxieties and trying to come to terms with the things that gnawed at me. Was God hearing my desperate pleas or was I just talking to myself?

I occasionally see a turtle near the edge of the water, but that morning, only ducks and geese (along with their offspring) swam the pond and dotted the sidewalks. Other than an occasional goose honk, the steady *whoosh* of nearby commuter traffic, and the splashing of the fountains that aerated the ponds, it was quiet.

Where are the frogs? I wondered. I had never seen one there before. The words were a slight detour but part of my stream-of-consciousness prayer nonetheless. Had the pesticides used to keep the lawn mosquito- and weed-free taken away their sustenance, or had something worse befallen them? I continued on my way, still praying, when a sound froze me midstep. *Croooooak! Croooak!* A frog! And not just any old frog, but a bullfrog, sounding very much like a tiny foghorn. I scanned the water for a moment, and then *splash!* Not far from where I stood, the top of a dark-green head and two eyes emerged from the water, surrounded by concentric ripples.

Thank You, Lord!

I can't always pinpoint the moment when God answers one of my prayers, but that day I could. A casual mention of frogs, inserted into my rambling prayers, had been answered swiftly and decisively by a heavenly Father who wanted me to know He was listening.—Jon Woodhams

Cast all your anxiety on him because he cares for you.
—1 Peter 5:7 (NIV)

JUNE 2

The Street Kitten

Love does no harm to a neighbor. Therefore love is the fulfillment of the law.

—ROMANS 13:10 (NIV)

MY FRIEND HAS a heart for cats. She spends late nights trapping feral cats and pays to have them spayed and neutered. She fosters kittens and socializes them. We call her the "Felinethropist."

Recently, the Felinethropist came to the downtown bookstore where I work. We mentioned that a lady who receives services from the homeless center next door had just come in with a tiny kitten. My friend headed to her car to get food for the little cat. When she returned, she told us that the social worker at the homeless center explained that it would be in the best interest of her client to not separate her from the kitten now, because it had become a comfort item. The social worker promised to contact the Felinethropist as soon as she could come for the kitten.

That evening, the social worker called my friend and said her client wanted the kitten to get help. My friend rushed downtown and took her immediately to the vet. The kitten, only 1.2 pounds, was flea-bitten and weak. They cleaned her up, gave her antibiotics, and fed her baby food and electrolytes. Within hours, she was purring and content. They texted me a video of little Tinkerbell sleeping soundly, the most precious cream-and-gray cat imaginable. Tink currently lives with ten calico kittens my friend is fostering. When she is old enough, she and a calico friend will go to a couple who are excited to give them a good home.

The world can be so hard and can make us feel powerless to help, but that day I watched my friend, the vet, and the social worker use their talents to be the hands of God, loving their neighbor's one kitten, one thoughtful gesture and one connection at a time.—Lucy H. Chambers

Breathe, O breathe thy loving Spirit into ev'ry troubled breast.
Let us all in thee inherit, let us find the promised rest.
—Charles Wesley

JUNE 3

Thankful for Spiders

The word of the Lord came to me: "Son of man, you are living among a rebellious people. They have eyes to see but do not see and ears to hear but do not hear, for they are a rebellious people."

—Ezekiel 12:1–2 (NIV)

IN THE MORNINGS I like to take my dogs for a walk on a trail near my house. This trail is just a paved path next to the road, but it also borders a wild area of woods and grasses. In the spring, my walk is graced with the most beautiful sight—spider webs touched by dew.

On cool spring mornings, the sun comes in low on the horizon, lighting up the tiny spider webs in the grass and on the plants. I know God made all the good creatures of earth, and I know spiders have their place in His created order, but I don't really like spiders. I've never had a bad run-in with one—I just find them creepy, especially when they're in my house. That makes me appreciate the beauty of their homes even more.

As I walk along the trail in the morning, cars stream by. People are heading off to work or getting kids to school, focusing on where they are going rather than what's in front of them—spring beauty on display. It reminds me of the message from the prophet Ezekiel, that people have eyes but cannot see God's beauty. They have ears, but they cannot hear the message of God.

I often get distracted by the hustle-bustle pace of life and forget to look and listen. But the dewy glistening spider webs remind me that beauty and wonder are all around me right before my eyes if I remember to stop and look.—Heather Jepsen

Thank You, God, for all the beauty of the earth, even spiders. Help me to see and appreciate all Your gifts this day. Amen.

JUNE 4

Lucky Nugget

The Lord is good to all; he has compassion on all he has made.

—Psalm 145:9 (NIV)

When a week-old fluffy black chick was dropped off at Shasta Wildlife Rescue in Anderson, California, they couldn't house her. The organization only offered homes for wildlife, not domestic animals. Holli, my friend who works there, had longed to acquire chickens for some time, so she grabbed the opportunity to care for the chick at home, naming her Lucky Nugget. The chick was Holli's constant companion for weeks, even sitting on Holli's arm when she crocheted. Nugget hung on as if she were on a fast Ferris wheel. Always up to something silly, Nugget kept Holli and her family entertained.

One morning, Holli heard a "cock-a-doodle-doo" from inside the bathroom, where Nugget's brooder-box was stored at night. The truth was revealed. Holli didn't have a chicken after all, but a rooster.

Since it was illegal to keep roosters in a residential area, Holli wasn't sure what to do. Nugget had already been dumped in a parking lot and left to his fate. Now, she couldn't part with him. So she contacted all her neighbors, asking them to allow her to house him. The neighbors rewarded Holli's love for critters by putting up with his crowing for a few months. In fact, they said they loved hearing him. But eventually, as it sometimes happens, Lucky Nugget turned mean and defensive. His luck had run out. Holli had to make a tough decision and rehomed Nugget.

When I look at my own nest and behaviors, I recognize that sometimes I'm also hard to love, even by those closest to me. But even if I turn a little mean toward others and a bit sure of myself, my Home—my Father—is secure because my Father loves me unconditionally. —Cathy Elliott

Father, how well and kindly You love me and all Your creatures.
It is good to belong to You, for I am always loved. Amen.

JUNE 5

Identifying Counterfeits

Beloved, do not believe every spirit, but test the spirits, whether they are of God; because many false prophets have gone out into the world.

—1 JOHN 4:1 (NKJV)

THE LILAC HEDGE lining our backyard is a flurry of activity. My husband and I sit on the deck watching the sunset, which seems to cue an opening act for the sphinx moths. As our eyes adjust, we realize dozens of these massive, plump moths are filling up on evening nectar. It would be easy to mistake their rapid wing beats, hovering acrobatics, and nectar-gathering antics for that of hummingbirds. They so resemble a hummingbird that I'm sure they're more often identified as a bird than an insect. However, as we watch them in the backyard, actual hummingbirds whizz above our heads as they visit each flowering bush. Next to the hummingbirds, the moths reveal their true identity.

I wonder how many times I mistake something for something it's not. How many false ideas or replicas of reality do I entertain simply because I'm not in close proximity to the truth? Just as I watch the hummingbirds collecting nectar before nightfall, I want to remain near to God's Word so that I can quickly identify counterfeit "truths." I want to measure every idea and opportunity against what He says and practice my ability to distinguish imitations. Then, as I study Scripture's details, counterfeits will look drastically different from God's nature. Familiarizing myself with every facet of His goodness, I can, as Romans 12:2 says, renew and transform my thinking and "discern what is the will of God, what is good and acceptable and perfect" (ESV).

With His promises fresh in my mind, every lesser thing will be exposed for its falsehood. Scripture brings into focus differences that were previously blurred. Just as the hummingbirds' and moths' discrepancies become evident when they are side by side, I can place everything next to God's living and active Word and choose what is noble, worthwhile, and holy.—Eryn Lynum

Dear God, hide Your Word in my heart and teach me to identify counterfeits. Be near to me so that anything false or futile will stand in stark contrast to the good plans You have for my life. Amen.

JUNE 6

We Are Family

Yours, Lord, is the greatness and the power and the glory and the majesty and the splendor, for everything in heaven and earth is yours. Yours, Lord, is the kingdom; you are exalted as head over all.

—1 CHRONICLES 29:11 (NIV)

WE WERE HEADED to the mountains for a family trip. We wanted to be close to nature, watch birds, maybe even see a bear or two. I couldn't wait! As the alarm went off at 4:00 a.m., I heard a banging outside. It was too early for work to start on the oversized house being built behind us, so my mind went immediately to robbers.

I jumped out of bed and flipped on the outside lights. Obviously, the thieves had been surprised by the lights and were trying to make a getaway. Grabbing a flashlight, I ran to the window. A fat raccoon blinked in the beam, holding her little paws up to shield her masked eyes.

Here was my robber, popping the bubble of my overactive imagination. The raccoon ran from the trash cans toward the cover of a big oak-leaf hydrangea. Three smaller coons scurried behind her, indignant that their moonlight feast had been interrupted.

Hurrying to dress for our trip, I thought about the raccoons. As big, new houses went up in the neighborhood, there was less room for the wildlife that had always lived near us. But here were four raccoons, using their nimble hands and clever instincts to survive in a quickly changing environment. We would need to help the raccoons find a new home—safer for them and for us—but seeing their dexterous hands and shiny fur up close reminded me how wonderfully made each member of God's family is. This unexpected vision of a family of beautiful, intelligent animals so close to home was a message that I need to care for God's creation in the city and not just be a nature lover when I'm on vacation.—Lucy H. Chambers

God gave us eyes to see them, and lips that we might tell how great is God Almighty who has made all things well.
—Cecil Frances Alexander

JUNE 7

What's in a Name?

"You did not choose me, but I chose you."

—JOHN 15:16 (NIV)

WHAT DO YOU think about 'Scuppers'?" I asked my family as we discussed names for our yet to be adopted dog. *Scuppers, the Sailor Dog* had been a favorite book when the children were young, and since we loved being on the water, I thought it would be an appropriate name.

"Cute name," came the consensus. So Scuppers came into our lives. When the time came for a boat ride, we put a life jacket on him and tried to ease him into being on the water. He first took a canoe ride on our little pond, and while he didn't get panicky or upset, we could tell he was simply enduring the trip rather than enjoying it. We were disappointed but saw his potential to be on the water with us. We knew that the more experiences he had on the water, the more comfortable he would be.

Even though Scuppers isn't yet a true water dog, he may yet live up to his name. He now anticipates jumping into the bottom of the canoe as we prepare to launch it. Our next plan is to have him aboard a sailboat with us.

Living according to one's name makes me think of being called a child of God—one who represents the family of God. There are times I am not living up to that responsibility: I am selfish, cruel, hateful, and mean-spirited. I may do as God asks, but I am not cheerful or happy about it. Like Scuppers on his first boat ride, I am enduring the situation.

Fortunately, God is the patient and loving Parent who sees what I will become in addition to where I am now. The more I experience life with Him, the more I become accustomed to His plan for my life. Just as we provide Scuppers with opportunities to be a sailor dog, God provides me with opportunities to live up to being called His child.—Virginia Ruth

Heavenly Parent, thank You for calling me Your child even when I do not act like it. May I become the child You envision. Amen.

JUNE 8

Building a New Nest

Train up a child in the way he should go: and when he is old, he will not depart from it.

—PROVERBS 22:6 (KJV)

A SMALL HERD OF squirrels inhabits our yard. At least that's what it feels like when they seem to constantly empty our bird feeders and scamper across the lawn. I love the little rodents and enjoy watching them leap from branch to branch in the tops of trees like acrobats. Some of their antics remind me of my daughter's ballet leaps and turns.

Those reminders are bittersweet, however, because her college graduation and recent marriage changed her zip code, taking her two states away and ending her time as a dancer and instructor—and with me. I'm having a hard time with the baby of the family moving that far away and starting a new home.

With fewer kids coming and going now, I seem to notice the squirrels even more. One in particular has decided to sneak onto my porch and gnaw through the fabric of an outdoor glider swing we've had for years. Bit by bit, the squirrel carries chunks of stuffing from the swing to a nest in the top of the oak tree out back.

It's always fascinated me how animals learn to take care of their young. A combination of God-given instinct and training from their parents, I presume.

Watching that squirrel, I couldn't help but think about my daughter building her own nest in a new location. I had the blessing of homeschooling her for a dozen or more years and watching her obtain a college degree. I've taught her and nurtured her, and now it's time to let her go. With God's help, I'm sure she'll continue to thrive and build a life of her own, even though I miss her greatly in my nest.—Julie Lavender

Dear God, please bless those who are leaving home to build a new nest elsewhere. And especially bless the family members who'll miss them greatly when they move away. Amen.

JUNE 9

Finding the Path

Your word is a lamp for my feet, a light on my path.

—PSALM 119:105 (NIV)

SPRING IN MISSOURI is turtle season. Once the weather warms up, it doesn't take long before we see turtles out in the yard and near the streams. We also see them in the road.

My family is a turtle-helping family. If we see one in the road and it is safe to stop, we pull over and put on our flashers. Then one of us jumps out and carries the turtle the rest of the way across the road. Often the little box turtles we find are too small to climb up a curb, so we are happy to give them a lift.

Turtles travel in spring to mate or to find a place to lay their eggs. They are determined reptiles, focused on going to a certain place, even when it looks like they are simply meandering along.

Since we see so many turtles, I've tried to learn more about them. Did you know that turtles have an internal compass and a "mental map" of their home area? This is part of what helps them navigate to where they are going.

A turtle's ability to stay the course and focus on where it's going reminds me of the path I follow in my own life. Each morning I wake up and seek God. I read my Bible, offer a prayer, and listen for God's word to me. Like the turtle's mental map, the Word of God is my compass for life.

Sometimes I might wander off the path, but God often sends a friend, family member, or kind stranger to help me stay the course. Just like the turtle knows where he is going, I also know where I am going with God as my compass. Sometimes I just need a helping hand to get there.
—Heather Jepsen

Walk of Faith: *Make a list of things that will help you stay on the path God has prepared for you. What habits might help you seek God in your life?*

The Voice of a Rooster

Jesus said to him, "Assuredly, I say to you that this night, before the rooster crows, you will deny Me three times."

—MATTHEW 26:34 (NKJV)

WHEN I WAS growing up in Ohio, Mother made sure each of us children received regular doses of Scripture. In addition to church attendance, she read Bible stories to us from the time we were very young. The lessons about Bible heroes and heroines continue to pay dividends in our lives today.

The town of my upbringing sat squarely in the middle of farm country. It wasn't unusual to see and hear farm animals, including chickens and roosters.

If you've ever met a rooster, chances are he proved quite territorial. Most roosters make one thing clear to paperboys and postal carriers alike: I am the rooster around here, and I rule the roost. Even riding my bicycle along country lanes could bring an occasional rooster out of nowhere, quickening my heartbeat and urging me to peddle on past. *Get away from here!* the rooster seemed to be trumpeting.

Encounters with roosters have always reminded me of the story of Peter in the Bible. Jesus warned him that before the rooster crowed, Peter would deny his Savior three times. Although this sincere disciple refused to accept the words of Jesus, he soon found himself doing just what Christ had predicted. The sound of a rooster crowing reminded Peter of his sin. It drove him to repentance. Roosters speak to my conscience as well. The last thing I want to do is fall short of the high calling of salvation. Even so, I miss the mark sometimes.

Providentially, God knew that His followers would mess up. I require confession and repentance when confronted by the Holy Spirit. When I turn from wrongdoing, Jesus is eager to forgive and gather me into His arms. What a Savior who places roosters in my life to wake me up to His love.—David L. Winters

The eternal God is your dwelling place, and underneath are the everlasting arms.

—Deuteronomy 33:27 (ESV)

JUNE 11

Searching for Bald Eagles

Respect everyone, and love the family of believers. Fear God, and respect the king.

—1 PETER 2:17 (NLT)

WE DONNED OUR hiking gear and set out with a group of strangers on a guided walk to reach the optimal viewing site of nesting bald eagles. With life spans of between twenty and thirty years, bald eagles typically mate for life and return to the same nest every year to raise their young. This couple has been under observation for several years.

Once we arrived at the viewing platform, the ranger set up a scope for a closer look. Both eagles are aware of the platform and of the humans who stare in their direction. We were told that the male often accommodates human interest by performing spectacular flyovers, making dramatic use of his massive eight-foot wingspan. He plays to his audience.

The ranger explained that the female exercises studied indifference to human observers. "She's actually built up one side of the nest from last year, obscuring the interior that faces the platform. She ignores everyone, most often turning her back to us as she sits on her nest or goes about her business," she said. "She's sassy."

Sassy. I looked up the definition. I assume the ranger meant "lively and spirited." Or did she perhaps mean "rude"? Was this eagle sassy or was she merely shy, reclusive, or protective? Regardless, she now has a label that follows her year after year.

This gave me pause, and I reflected on how quickly I jump to judgments, assigning motivations and misreading behavior. Only this week, I labeled a stranger as a "jerk," based on his reckless driving. I find myself calling a political leader an "idiot" because I don't agree with his policies. Some labels through frequent use have become permanently linked to the person's name, like "Drama Queen [name]." I asked the Holy Spirit to remind me of the momma eagle whenever I'm tempted to label someone. God, You alone see people with clarity and know their hearts.—Darlene Kerr

Walk of Faith: *Take a moment to reflect on a label you've given to someone. Ask for God's forgiveness, and then challenge yourself to accept "labels" only on packaging.*

JUNE 12

A Hidden Fawn

I do not hide your righteousness in my heart; I speak of your faithfulness and your saving help. I do not conceal your love and your faithfulness from the great assembly.

—PSALM 40:10 (NIV)

THREE MORE STEPS and we would have tripped over it. My wife and I were taking a morning walk through our meadow, wading through the tall bluestem grass, when a fawn popped out of hiding and trotted away on wobbly, stick-skinny legs. "He was right there in front of me," my wife said, laughing, "and I never saw him."

That's the idea. Fawns know how to hide. Their coat, reddish-brown and freckled with white spots, offers excellent camouflage. And a fawn's scent glands are not yet fully developed, so he has almost no odor. Predators can't see the fawn, hunkered down in the tall grass, and they can't smell it. No wonder there are so many deer around here. Fawns are good at hiding.

I keep my faith hidden deep in my heart. But sometimes I wonder if it is a little too well hidden, if you know what I mean. If a neighbor was hungry and I had food, I'd share some. But recently, when a neighbor was going through a hard time and clearly needed the Lord, my faith stayed hidden, deep in my heart. Sharing my political views comes easy to me. What my favorite sports team *should* do to have that winning season—I'll talk about that at the drop of a hat. But my relationship with Christ, the most crucial and controlling factor in my life—too often that stays hidden. Maybe I'm afraid I will say something wrong. Maybe I worry that my life doesn't match my witness and my testimony will come off as hypocritical.

A fawn needs to hide, but my faith needs expression. No more reticence about sharing my faith with friends and neighbors. No more hiding God's faithfulness to me.—Louis Lotz

For the Spirit God gave us does not make us timid,
but gives us power, love and self-discipline.
—2 Timothy 1:7 (NIV)

JUNE 13

God's Timing

For he says, "In the time of my favor I heard you, and in the day of salvation I helped you." I tell you, now is the time of God's favor, now is the day of salvation.

—2 CORINTHIANS 6:2 (NIV)

LUCY CAME TO us in God's timing. We had tried two different dogs from local shelters, but they weren't the right fit. One had too much energy for a couple of old fogies and a mature cat. The other couldn't warm up to my husband, even after spending a month with us. Thankfully, both of these pups found the right home. But there were no other adoptable dogs that met our qualifications nearby.

We still felt our family was not complete, but I hoped that when we traveled to Florida as snowbirds my friends there could help us out. We had lived in Florida before moving to Minnesota, and I had spent time volunteering at a dog shelter, so I had friends still active in dog circles. But none of my Florida friends had any leads. While I was thrilled that most available dogs had been adopted during the pandemic, we still longed for a four-footed fur baby of our own.

A chance conversation solved the problem. Joe, our neighbor in the condo building, knew a couple two blocks away that, because of health issues, needed to surrender their three-year-old pup. Lucy had been well loved and took to my husband right away. She slept all night without a peep and rode happily in the car. She checked all the boxes. Even after a thirteen-hundred-mile car ride to Minnesota, she still hops into any car ready to go anywhere.

Only God in His infinite wisdom and timing could have brought together the perfect match at the perfect time.—Linda Bartlett

Heavenly Father, thank You for the gift of Lucy. She was worth waiting for and continues to be a blessing. Even in the small details of life, You give us the best. Amen.

JUNE 14

Cautious Cottontails

Be very careful, then, how you live—not as unwise but as wise.

—EPHESIANS 5:15 (NIV)

WHILE HIKING ONE morning at Sugarloaf Ridge State Park in California, I spotted a cottontail rabbit. It was foraging on the side of the trail, its eponymous white tail barely visible beneath its hindquarters. I expected the bunny to frighten easily and dash away as soon as I came into view, but it let me get within fifteen feet—although it remained alert and seemingly unafraid. I slowly pulled out my camera and snapped a few photos. But as soon as I moved closer, the composed cottontail hopped into the blackberry vines, where I could not follow.

Maybe its retreat to safety was due to instinct, or perhaps it was a result of experience with a human; whether instinct or experience motivated it, the rabbit wisely followed the tried-and-true path to keep safe.

Like the rabbit, experience has taught me many useful lessons in life. I don't have to rely on my faulty human instincts, which are far less fine-tuned than those of a rabbit. Instead, God instilled within me the ability to learn, remember, and reason so I may carefully make wise decisions to ensure I'm kept safe both physically and spiritually. Careful decision-making applies to everything from safely driving my car to discerning whether an online sale is a scam or not.

The rabbit didn't dash away from me in a panic. It calmly assessed the situation and acted accordingly. Likewise, I don't have to panic when faced with potentially harmful situations. God has given me everything I need to make wise decisions. Both the cottontail and I benefit from being careful in how we live. As I open my Bible and mindfully put what I read there into daily practice, I can grow in wisdom and discernment, keeping myself spiritually safe in a world that too often can lure me toward danger and away from the safe path with God.—Marianne Campbell

Every experience God gives us, every person He puts in our lives is the perfect preparation of the future that only He can see.

—Corrie ten Boom

JUNE 15

Prodigal Macon

He was lost and is found.

—LUKE 15:24 (NKJV)

MY SISTER, KAY, was dog-sitting for my nephew's black Labrador, Macon. He was a lovable old gentleman with woeful eyes. He wasn't sad at all, but he had a condition called ectropion, where the lower eyelids droop away from the eye. No one could prove it, but we suspected he used that eye condition to get anything he wanted.

Kay said Macon was a sweetheart, except for one problem, and she could not figure out how to handle it: Macon commandeered her bathtub when he was inside. All day, except for brief breaks to eat. He even slept in the tub. At night, an occasional belch or another socially frowned-upon sound from the tub awakened Kay.

"I would be fine with that, but he won't budge when I try to take a shower. He loves water, even if it comes from a showerhead," Kay explained, laughing. "Have you ever tried to drag an eighty-pound wet Labrador out of a tub?"

She eventually pulled him out, but Macon drenched the bathroom walls as he "shake-dried" himself. She was now forced to time her showers to sync with Macon's feeding times.

When I called Kay a few days later, I inquired about how her bathtub guest was doing. Macon had gone missing the previous morning after a delivery man had left the back door open. Kay had been frantic, running down the alley behind her house, calling for Macon. She eventually found him a few homes down, having a great time romping and playing with a toy poodle in her neighbor's sprinkler.

"As I walked him home, he tried the 'I'm sorry' look with his eyes," she said, "but it wasn't compelling. It didn't matter. I was thrilled to have found him."

Kay's story reminded me of the Bible's account of the return of the prodigal son, whose father rejoiced when his reckless son returned home. Macon was a canine prodigal whose caregiver was delighted to have him back where he belonged, even in her bathtub.—Terry Clifton

A dog is one of the few things in life that is exactly what it seems.
—Anonymous

JUNE 16

You Are What You Eat

You will always harvest what you plant...But those who live to please the Spirit will harvest everlasting life from the Spirit.

—GALATIONS 6:7–8 (NLT)

MY FRIEND CAROL has lived in several different homes since I've known her. She has an affinity for places that are also attractive to the avian communities that intersect with her human neighborhoods. For a season she lived close to me, on the bluffs overlooking the Mississippi River, just south of downtown St. Paul. Her house at that time was a townhome, and she thought it only fitting that she should put up a birdhouse fashioned like a row of townhomes. It was a beautiful abode for her feathered friends.

After a while, Carol noticed weeds kept growing inside the birdhouses. She cleaned them out several times before getting impatient and disassembling them altogether. It was only after she threw them away that she realized what had caused the problem.

The food she provided for the birds was an inexpensive seed, and as the birds were not the neatest of eaters, some of their cast-off dinner ended up getting wedged inside the houses and sprouting. It didn't take very long for the sprouts to become visible as they worked their way through gaps in the wood.

I'm pretty sure that my life has sometimes looked like that bird condominium, with weeds poking their way out in the oddest of places and in the most unattractive ways. Like low-quality bird feed, some things I allow into my soul and spirit are not always good for me. If what I ingest spiritually is not pure and healthy, the byproduct could look like selfishness, anger, or greed. I don't need to rid myself of the birdhouse; rather I need to improve my "birdseed" according to God's will.—Liz Kimmel

Help me, Holy Spirit, to be discerning about the things that my spirit, soul, and body feast upon. Amen.

JUNE 17

A Narrow Escape

Surely he will save you from the fowler's snare and from the deadly pestilence.

—PSALM 91:3 (NIV)

WHEN I FINISHED my yard work and came into the house, my wife said, "Who were you talking to out there? I was at the window, and I saw you talking to the ground, gesturing, pointing, waving your arms. It looked like you were having an animated conversation with the lawn."

I had no idea someone was watching. "I was talking to a toad," I said, embarrassed.

"Well, that explains everything," she deadpanned.

I had been using the Weedwacker, trimming the grass by the barn, and I came within a half second of Weedwacking Mr. Toad. I saw him move—it was just a slight motion—and I swung the Weedwacker away at the last second. Then I proceeded to tell him that he'd had a narrow escape and ought to be more careful about where he walks. He blinked and hopped away on his fat little legs, not knowing how close he'd come to getting scalped. "You're welcome," I called after him.

It is scary—when I stop and think about it—how many narrow escapes I've had. That time when my car hit an ice patch and went sailing right through a red light, and no vehicles were coming the other way. The time I was trimming that old maple tree, standing at the top of the ladder when it began to slide sideways; at the last second it caught on a branch and stopped. When I was out on the lake with a dead motor and a storm rising and I heard a voice on a loud hailer, "Sir, do you need a tow?" It was the coast guard.

Narrow escapes. White-knuckle squeakers where things could have gone badly for me, but they didn't. And sometimes I can almost hear a voice from heaven whispering, *You're welcome.*—Louis Lotz

The angel of the LORD encamps around those who fear him,
and he delivers them.
—Psalm 34:7 (NIV)

JUNE 18

Monkey See

Let no corrupt word proceed out of your mouth, but what is good for necessary edification, that it may impart grace to the hearers.

—EPHESIANS 4:29 (NKJV)

A DAY AT THE zoo ranks among our family's favorite outings. When the weather is mild and many of the animals come out to play in the sun, we relish the fellowship with each other and the opportunity to view God's creatures up close and personal.

Among my personal favorites is the monkey exhibit. Dozens of playful primate poses spur me into action, mimicking their facial expressions and body language. Nieces and nephews giggle as I get more and more into character as a monkey, flailing my arms about wildly.

One particular monkey focused on me. She moved as close as she could to the barrier separating us. Bouncing up and down, my new friend seemed to dare me to imitate her moves. Of course, I quickly obliged, bouncing up and down in time with her movements. She raised her left arm, and I did the same. My simian friend eventually won the contest by dropping to the dirt and doing a somersault. This coup de grâce went to a place where I couldn't follow, unwilling as I was to roll around on the concrete.

As I walked away, the Holy Spirit whispered a word of truth. How often do I mimic the bad behavior of others on social media? While a spirited debate can be enjoyable and considering various sides of an issue can be profitable, my conduct has not always reflected Christ or represented what it means to be His follower.

Deciding I would not just mimic the bad behavior of others, I walked out of the zoo determined to mirror God and let Him have control of my thoughts and my voice on social media. After all, I didn't want to make a monkey out of myself.—David L. Winters

Dear God, let my speech represent You well. Amen.

Something Amazing

You shall teach them diligently to your children, and shall talk of them when you sit in your house, and when you walk by the way, and when you lie down, and when you rise.

—DEUTERONOMY 6:7 (ESV)

DID YOU HEAR that?" my mother asked, emerging from our guest room. "It was a bobwhite." I shook my head. As far as I knew, our home in the foothills of the Rockies was out of range for the chunky little quail. "There it goes again," she said.

This time, I heard it too—the distinct call of the bobwhite. We quickly made our way to the backyard where I noticed my neighbor Becky leaning over the fence that separates our properties. "I thought I heard a bobwhite," she explained excitedly. The three of us watched and listened. We were soon rewarded with the sight of the plump bird waddling through the sweet peas, gleaning seeds and insects. Amazed, we wondered how the bird got here. Where had it come from? These birds don't fly very far. Had it blown in from the plains? There was no explaining it. It was a puzzle we contemplated the rest of the summer, long after the little bird disappeared from the neighborhood.

To be honest, I loved the idea that the bobwhite was not confined to the region highlighted in the birder's guide, just as I'm always slightly tickled when it rains even though no rain was predicted in the day's forecast or when someone is healed from cancer when the doctors have given the patient no hope.

God is awesome. He can part the sea. He can walk on water. Our God is always doing something amazing—many things we can't even explain or fully understand. Such marvels can bolster our faith as we ponder the wonders He's performed in our lives and the lives of others—wonders far more amazing than the unexpected appearance of a bobwhite. —Shirley Raye Redmond

Walk of Faith: *Think of one amazing thing God has done for you and share the story with someone else.*

JUNE 20

Casting Out for God

A new command I give you: Love one another. As I have loved you, so you must love one another. By this everyone will know that you are my disciples, if you love one another.

—John 13:34–35 (NIV)

THE ARTICLE ABOUT three thousand largemouth bass being released into nearby Patoka Lake had me hooked. After all, my husband preferred bass fishing because largemouth bass strike on almost any shiny lure. Then occurs the thrilling part of the sport for him—reeling them in as they twist and pull on the line. I discovered from the article that a local fish farm raised and supplied the largemouth bass. The fishy part, though, was the microchipping process. I was familiar with using the implanted devices to identify and reunite lost pets with owners, but using those in fish?

Fish biologists inserted the numbered devices into the fry (baby bass) with the date, place of release, and the fish farm as the place of origin. Recreational fishermen, like my husband, who catch the largemouth bass will allow biologists to scan the chip, thus contributing data about the maturing population in the lake.

As I thought about how the chip identifies the fish, I realized that God has His own way of identifying me in the world. My microchip is how I love others. How could someone identify me as a Christian? If I were sitting in my church that might be a clue, but if I were out in public, would my love shine? As I cast out my line, I promise to do my best to show not just my love but also God's love to everyone. I want to go all in for Him—hook, line, and sinker.—Glenda Ferguson

But you are a chosen people, a royal priesthood,
a holy nation, God's special possession.
—1 Peter 2:9 (NIV)

JUNE 21

Tiny Creations of Hope

After the earthquake a fire, but the LORD was not in the fire; and after the fire a still small voice.

—1 KINGS 19:12 (NKJV)

SOME DAYS IT feels like the sun doesn't shine, yet it's not raining or even cloudy. I try to fend off those feelings, especially first thing in the morning.

Today began that way. However, I took our dog and my devotionals out to the porch swing. Remembering the doe that had graced our yard with a visit the morning before encouraged me to look for another such happening to remind me of God's presence in my day. Maybe even a return of the doe or possibly a fawn. What a delight that would be!

Keeping watch for whatever God would send, I read through several devotions. I paused in the middle of the next reading to peer into the woods. Surely something would show up, even a cardinal singing would perk me up. When I saw only trees swayed in the wind, I sighed and went inside for another cup of coffee.

Back on the porch, I set down my cup and glanced into the woods again. I always enjoyed the way the sun dappled the ground. Today, only a single ray made it through, lighting a thin sliver of bark on one tree, radiant in the dark forest, pointing straight to the heavens. Then I noticed movement in the air to my left. Another sunray shone on the porch beside the swing. A tiny speck of an insect flitted in the beam, as though mesmerized by floating puffs and swirls of steam from my coffee. The miniscule insect and the swirling puffs dawdled to dance to a silent melody, happy and carefree on this lovely blue morning. I smiled.

Yes, sometimes God sends me big things—a doe, a fawn, a cardinal's song. And sometimes, just tiny creations of dancing hope.—Cathy Mayfield

The little things? The little moments? They aren't little.

—Jon Kabat-Zinn

JUNE 22

The Border Patrol

Start children off on the way they should go, and even when they are old they will not turn from it.

—PROVERBS 22:6 (NIV)

RECENTLY, I SAW a meme online that showed a herd of white sheep. They all seemed to watch four border collies approach from the side, every eye open, every head turned toward the sight. And no wonder. The dogs were very notable—all dressed in the same black-and-white uniform. They marched in single file. Mother first, followed by three pups. Like troops. They meant business, and the sheep knew it.

I sent the meme to Alan, a friend from church. I knew he'd gotten a border collie pup from his sister, who breeds them. He messaged back that his Maggie, now six months old, was doing well. In fact, he'd turned around the other day to find that while he'd been dealing with his chickens, the pup had worked some sheep into Alan's sorting/holding pens all by herself. He remarked that because of her strong instincts, she would likely do the right thing without any formal training.

Even if we have good instincts, I think we all need some guidance in this world. I did and still do. Whether from a parent or other trusted leader, I'm learning to embrace those directions until they become like an instinct. But when I'm counseled by God and His example, I automatically move forward to do the right thing. Without question. The example He sets is the one I trust.—Cathy Elliott

There are two ways of spreading light: to be the candle or the mirror that reflects it.
—Edith Wharton

JUNE 23

Showing Our True Colors

Do not conform to the pattern of this world, but be transformed by the renewing of your mind. Then you will be able to test and approve what God's will is—his good, pleasing and perfect will.

—ROMANS 12:2 (NIV)

AS A CHILD, I was fascinated by chameleons' ability to change color. I even had a few chameleons as pets, and I loved placing them against different backgrounds to watch the color of their skin change. It seemed like magic.

Here in Florida, small green lizards, called anoles, are plentiful. It is rare to step outside on a warm day and not see several of these delightful creatures scurrying from one area to another. Although technically not chameleons, the green anoles are sometimes called American chameleons because they can change color from green to brown and back to green. The color changes, which are caused by hormones, can be used as camouflage to help them blend in with their surroundings. Factors such as temperature and mood can also affect their skin color. A number of other animals besides chameleons use camouflage to protect themselves against predators.

As a Christian, however, I am not called to blend in with my surroundings. On the contrary, my true colors should stand out as a witness to those around me. Separating myself from the crowd, away from the background of the world, can be challenging, especially when all around me, the world is doing its best to make me conform to standards that go against what Scripture teaches. Nevertheless, my true colors should not change based on my environment or my mood. I want my stand for Christ to be noticeable.—Ellen Fannon

Father, forgive me when I try to fit in with the world. Help me be bold and willing to stand out for You. Amen.

JUNE 24

The Blessed Boundary

I run the way of your commandments, for you enlarge my understanding.

—PSALM 119:32 (NRSVUE)

THESE PAST THREE weeks, we've been dog-sitting for Sunny, who is an adventurer and is curious. Plus, she is still a little bit of a puppy. We have found that Sunny likes to push her boundaries more than our own older, calmer, and very familiar dog does and has even escaped twice, causing a few anxious minutes.

While Sunny loves being with us and is happy in our home, she also seems to think there is more out there for her to partake of, participate in, and enjoy. We don't have a fenced backyard, so Sunny's owners sent her with an extralong tether to keep her close enough while still allowing her a small sense of freedom and flexibility.

We were all surprised when, tethered to the patio table at dinner one night, Sunny took off after a bunny and broke the line, racing first into the neighbor's yard and then beyond. I was so worried that she would run into the street. I raced after her, shouting for the kids to help. But we struggled to catch up with her as she scampered through one yard and then the next.

As I collected my thoughts, I saw the way Sunny kept her eye on us. Now she had made it a game of chase. She wanted her taste of freedom, but she wanted us to come get her too. She likes to be with us; she likes to be near.

I heartily dislike the idea of a tight tether cutting into my neck, my space, my ability to be free and be "me." Yet, even as I roam, I know I want to be near Jesus, to live a life within that blessed boundary. —Katy W. Sundararajan

Let thy goodness, like a fetter,
bind my wandering heart to thee.
—Robert Robinson

JUNE 25

Asking for Help

If either of them falls down, one can help the other up. But pity anyone who falls and has no one to help them up.

—ECCLESIASTES 4:10 (NIV)

AS I WAS putting finishing touches on a writing project, I heard a *thunk* on my front porch. *Oh good. A delivery. Maybe Craig's tractor parts had arrived.*

But it was no delivery man. It was a thief instead: a mama doe, who had tipped over one of the eight flowerpots on my front steps. Not only that, but she'd also chomped the tops off my petunias.

I grabbed my walking pole by the front door, ran out the door, and chased her across my front lawn. "Go away! Eat someone else's petunias!" That might sound unkind, but it's tough growing flowers at five thousand feet in the northern Sierra Nevada mountains...and petunias in pots were the only flowers I could grow. Now I had nothing but stubs.

At that moment, I noticed another new addition to the front yard: the tiniest of fawns lying in the pine needles underneath the front-yard trees. Soon it jumped up and headed toward its mama, who skittered to the neighbor's yard.

A half hour later, I thought to check if my uninvited guests had returned. Sure enough, the little one was at the fence that separates our front and back yards. Peering over the fence from the backyard was mama. There was no way the little one could leap over the fence as its mother had. So after I opened the gate and pointed mama in the right direction, she and her fawn reunited in the front yard...headed, I assumed, for other flowerpots in the neighborhood.

Sometimes, I, too, get stuck on the wrong side of the fence and find myself up against a barrier of impossibility. Such was the case, for example, when my daughter had a heart attack, and I was more than four hours away. I called my friend, who happens to be my pastor. He was there in minutes praying with my daughter and her husband.

The next time I'm desperate for help, I'll remember the deer family and look for someone, or Someone, who can help me get over or through that impossible barrier of circumstances.—Janet Holm McHenry

When I see fences that separate, Lord, I'm grateful that You see passageways. When I fall down, thank You for always providing me a way up. Amen.

JUNE 26

A Close Encounter and a Call to Action

Then the LORD God took the man and put him in the garden of Eden to tend and keep it.

—GENESIS 2:15 (NKJV)

THERE ARE MOOSE in the lake!"

Our son's voice jolts my husband and me from sleep. Dizzy from leaping out of bed, I run out the front door, through our neighbor's yard, and to the lake. Two beautiful moose stand in the water a hundred yards offshore. Neighbors are already gathered at the water's edge, watching the magnificent creatures. One neighbor, who has lived here for forty-seven years, says he has never seen moose in this area.

When we moved to the neighborhood six months ago, we knew we were setting up home in the wildland urban interface, where suburbia presses into the wilderness. Wildlife frequents our lake and backyard—but moose are visitors we never expected!

These close encounters with animals always make me think about Adam and Eve in the garden of Eden. It must have been a gift to observe up close so many of God's wonderful creations! What colors did they glimpse amid a flurry of birds flitting from tree to tree? What scents did their noses gather from a garden rich in blooms and nectar? I imagine their proximity to God's creatures fueled the call to stewardship in their hearts.

Observing our moose visitors, I feel a deep sense of awe and an urgency to protect and preserve the wonders of God's world. Moments like these challenge me to steward all God has made so that others may also enjoy and see the goodness of the Lord in creation. Today this stewardship takes the form of giving space and respectfully watching the moose from a distance. Other days it looks like planting milkweed for monarch butterflies or cleaning up trash along the river. Whatever it looks like, I determine to enter into creation often, steward it well, and share its wonders with others.—Eryn Lynum

Walk of Faith: *What is one way you can encounter and protect God's creation this week? Choose to plant native flowers, hang a birdhouse, and invite a friend to join your efforts!*

JUNE 27

Harder than It Looks

The Israelites sampled their provisions but did not inquire of the Lord.

—Joshua 9:14 (NIV)

LAST SPRING, I decided to take up the hobby of bird feeding. After five minutes of internet research, I set out for Walmart and returned an hour later with all manner of feeders, seed, suet syrup, and even a lovely earthen birdbath.

Sure enough, within a day or two the birds began to frequent my little oasis. Bird book in hand, I kept watch for each new species that arrived. I especially enjoyed watching hummingbirds visit their feeder, suspended from the eave outside the living room. It was a delight to see them flit by each morning and evening. Then I noticed the army of ants making its way down the line between the eave and the sugary water. *Buzzards,* I thought. *Thieves. What a nuisance.*

And I'll never forget the day the first goldfinch appeared. My finch feeder was well stocked with thistle seed. "Eat up, my little friend," I said. "That's all for you." The next day the little bugger came back with an entire flock of his closest friends. The rascals cleaned me out in less than an hour.

Between the ants, squirrels, moles, starlings, chipmunks, and squawking blue jays, my backyard was more nuthouse than aviary. Who knew feeding birds was so hard? By midsummer I was more than tired of the work but remained committed to finishing what I'd started. "Never again," I muttered, putting the feeders away in the fall.

Often, I've rushed into other, more serious, pursuits with too little thought and preparation. Like Joshua and the Israelites, I've leapt to action without inquiring of the Lord. The results are predictable: poor decisions, unintended consequences, and loss of opportunity, money, or reputation. Over the years, I've learned this lesson: think before you speak, think twice before taking action, and first of all, pray!—Lawrence W. Wilson

Walk of Faith: *Even if you think your plan is simple, pray about it. Allow one day to speak with the Lord and for Him to speak with you.*

JUNE 28

A Chorus of Praise

Speaking to one another with psalms, hymns, and songs from the Spirit. Sing and make music from your heart to the Lord.

—EPHESIANS 5:19 (NIV)

MY HUSBAND AND I, along with our son, squeezed in an early summer's evening walk just after a refreshing rain shower. The road, still damp from the moisture, glistened in the sunshine. Droplets sat atop the green grass on the side of the road.

When our conversations about weather and coworkers and upcoming plans ceased, we noticed the chorus of amphibians that surrounded us.

"It's like they're praising the Lord for the rain," I commented. "Croaking songs of praise."

My biologist husband, David, began pointing out the variety of frogs calling into the evening.

"Those are spring peepers," he said. "They sound a lot like sleigh bells when they peep in chorus. Hear that low-pitched 'waaah, waaah' call? That's the sound spadefoot toads make."

We took a few more steps, and David pointed out the sound of a green tree frog.

"They sound almost like small dogs barking," I said.

To my untrained ear, all those peeping, croaking, barking amphibians sounded like a noisy bunch of frogs, and it was difficult for me to distinguish each particular species. But my husband the biologist recognized each individual sound.

I couldn't help but compare the chorus of frogs singing praises for the rain to a world with many people praising God at the same time. A "chorus of praise," so to speak, across the globe. Each of us with different voices, different languages, and different methods of worship. And yet, our Creator God knows and recognizes each individual voice. I feel certain that God is pleased with our prayers and praises, songs and hymns, just like I believe it makes Him smile to hear a chorus of frogs and toads on an early summer's evening.—Julie Lavender

Walk of Faith: *Spend some time listening to different frog and toad calls online. Look at pictures and admire God's creativity with the different characteristics of each species. Take a walk one evening after a refreshing rain shower and identify the sounds you hear.*

Hang Ten

And the Spirit and the bride say, "Come!" And let him who hears say, "Come!" And let him who thirsts come. Whoever desires, let him take the water of life freely.

—REVELATION 22:17 (NKJV)

SINCE I LIVE in landlocked Colorado, having the opportunity to experience the magnitude of the Atlantic Ocean when I visited St. Pete, Florida, was a real treasure. I was amazed watching the surfers who manage not only to stand up on their boards but also to confidently ride the waves. But after watching an amazing animal documentary on Africa, I realized that's nothing compared to the amazing sight of the surfing hippos living in Loango National Park in Gabon, Africa.

These hippos, who are usually found bobbing up and down in cool lakes, make their way one by one to the ocean and waddle in until they can catch the surf early in the day in Gabon. The saltwater buoys them up so they can ride the waves despite their girth, and they use the surf to make short work of moving up and down the coast.

Watching these amazing animals doing what at first appears impossible made me think about the many ways God lifts me up in my life, buoying me so I, too, can do what at times may seem impossible. He gives me a moment of peace in a house overfilled with noisy grandchildren. A neighbor offers to blow the snow from our sidewalks during Colorado blizzards. No matter how small the impossible might appear, the God who is the Living Water constantly amazes me with the many ways He works in my life.—Deb Kastner

Dear Jesus, thank You for being the Living Water in my life and for making the impossible possible. Amen.

The Sound of Spring

Praise him with the sounding of the trumpet, praise him with the harp and lyre.... Let everything that has breath praise the LORD. Praise the LORD.

—PSALM 150:3, 6 (NIV)

WHERE I LIVE in Missouri, we have lots of frogs. Lucky for me I really enjoy them. There is something about the way frogs jump that seems so carefree and happy. Whenever I see a frog or a toad, I am like a kid again. I can't help but try to catch it and hold it in my hand for a little while. As if I've captured something magical, a frog in my hand feels like a little blessing from God.

Did you know that frogs hibernate during the winter to survive the cold? Water-based frogs will stay in the shallows of a pond. But toads and tree frogs will actually dig a little hole in the dirt and sleep below the frost-line. Just like other hibernating creatures, when the spring thaw comes, frogs and toads wake up. Toward the end of winter, I long to hear their calls in the night sky. The arrival of the frogs' song is one of the first signs of spring, and every time I hear them, my heart sings. The song of the frog is a resurrection moment and an announcement of joyful new life.

Psalm 150, the final psalm in our Bible, tells us to praise the Lord. The writer asks us to play all sorts of instruments to announce and praise God. With a harp or flute, cymbals or trumpet, all are called to praise. Even dancing is encouraged!

When I hear the frogs singing each spring, they remind me of this scripture. Their calls are like tiny trumpets, and their leaps are like the joy of spirited dancing. Frogs call me to praise the Lord as spring awakes from its winter slumber.

The spring season is a busy time for me as a pastor and a mom, but whenever the frogs call, I pause and listen. "Praise the Lord!" I cry out with them. "Let all that have breath praise the Lord!" What a joy and a blessing.—Heather Jepsen

Walk of Faith: *Listen for the sounds of nature, then pause and say a prayer of thanks and praise to God.*

July

We All Belong

Now you are the body of Christ, and each one of you is a part of it.

—1 CORINTHIANS 12:27 (NIV)

MOVING TO A country home, I looked forward to enjoying wildlife in my own backyard. There were squirrels, of course, but also chipmunks, rabbits, moles, woodchucks, deer, burrowing crayfish, opossums, raccoons, a fox, and a coyote, as well as all manner of birds, including a Cooper's hawk. This was in addition to the chickens, parrot, Great Dane, and two Chihuahuas kept by our neighbors. I had my eye out for a unicorn! Other than that, I thought I'd pretty much seen it all.

One summer evening, the neighbors popped over for a visit. Their teenage daughter, Hannah, an animal lover in her own right, eagerly watched the sky as we grown-ups chatted. "What are you looking for?" someone asked.

"Bats!" she said eagerly. "They should be here any minute."

Looking up, we could see their wispy wings flitting around, not in circles but with the jagged changes of direction more typical of a running back or rabbit.

"I'm out!" my wife called, diving for the cover of the garage. It was hard to blame her. Bats are, well, creepy. Reclusive, nocturnal, screechy, erratic—they're easy to vilify.

"But they're so cool," Hannah said. "And they're eating your mosquitos!"

Hmm, I thought. It's true that we don't have many mosquitos. I guess a dozen bats eating up a thousand mosquitos an hour beats the smell of citronella. I wasn't thrilled about the bats at first, or the coyote or the woodchuck or the burrowing crayfish. But I discovered that each of them had its place in our little ecosystem.

God's family is a bit like that. Some brothers and sisters in Christ I would choose to associate with. Others, perhaps not. But they all belong. And I need each one, whether I like them or not.—Lawrence W. Wilson

Walk of Faith: *Pray for the church member who gets on your last nerve, and ask God to reveal what you can learn from that person.*

JULY 2

The Prairie Dog Alarm

Therefore, dear friends, since you have been forewarned, be on your guard so that you may not be carried away by the error of the lawless and fall from your secure position.

—2 PETER 3:17 (NIV)

MY HUSBAND AND I were driving through Wind Cave National Park in South Dakota, which is surrounded by miles of barren landscapes. We stopped and got out of the car to watch several prairie dogs. Each one would stop every few feet to sit on its hind legs and sniff the air, then go back to scurrying.

Suddenly, one prairie dog stopped, threw his head backward, and made a terrible screech. Multiple times, he screamed with his mouth wide open, facing the sky, his tiny arms stuck out to the side.

We realized we must have been too close for comfort. While we laughed at this director of security, his buddies did not. Every prairie dog disappeared into the nearest hole, and the dust bowl they had previously been making cleared in an instant.

This prairie dog's warning came from the depth of his soul. That sound meant business, and everyone obeyed.

I think about the multiple warnings in Scripture and how I nonchalantly read them. "Do not boast." "Do not conform to this world." I believe that God's warnings were meant to be like the raucous call of the prairie dog. *Look out! This is dangerous! I know that this could hurt you, so you better run!*

Can you imagine what would happen if I read these words of warning out loud and with intensity? I might realize more often that my Father is always standing guard and protecting me so I don't get into trouble.—Twila Bennett

Walk of Faith: *The next time you are reading a passage from the Bible that contains a warning, change the tone of your voice. Loudly read as if God were saying it out loud to you. Then try to listen to that warning as you go about your day.*

JULY 3

The Trumpet Call of God

For the Lord himself will come down from heaven, with a loud command, with the voice of the archangel and with the trumpet call of God, and the dead in Christ will rise first.

—1 THESSALONIANS 4:16 (NIV)

THE FIRST TIME I saw elk was while camping in Rocky Mountain National Park. Surrounded by snowcapped peaks, glistening alpine lakes, and flickering aspen leaves turned gold by the fall frost, these large animals were surprisingly elegant.

That night, I was awakened when a male bugled beside our tent. It was a bit startling to say the least—especially since I was sleeping! This awe-inspiring, unmistakable elk call didn't sound anything like my usual alarm clock.

The next day, the large herd came down out of the mountains to graze on the lush, green lawns at the base of the mountain. Several coyotes stalked the herd, but the herd was strong and chased them away when they ventured too close.

Later that winter I spotted hundreds of elk grazing in a pasture. I don't know what startled or signaled them, but they jumped a barbed wire fence in groups of twos and threes, flowing like waves in the ocean. What I would have given for a telescopic lens with a good camera attached to it. Not one hoof hit the fence! Those beautiful antlers can weigh as much as forty pounds, but the elk carried them as gracefully and proudly as a king with his crown.

When the elk bugled in my ear, I was reminded of God's promise that Jesus will return when we least expect it, with a loud trumpet that will be heard to the ends of the earth. I hope I'm alive for that event, but if not, I sure know what it feels like to rise up out of a "dead" sleep! —Randy Benedetto

When the trumpet of the Lord shall sound, and time shall be no more, and the morning breaks, eternal, bright and fair; when the saved of earth shall gather over on the other shore, and the roll is called up yonder, I'll be there.

—James M. Black

JULY 4

Beauty in the Mud

He brought me up out of the pit of destruction, out of the mud;
And He set my feet on a rock, making my footsteps firm.

—PSALM 40:2 (NASB)

SOMETIMES A FLEETING glance can affect your whole day. I was driving recently on a steamy Southern summer morning and saw two different versions of the same thing. A recent rainstorm had left patches of mud at the edge of the street that I travel to leave my subdivision. As I drove slowly by, I saw a gorgeous black-and-blue butterfly (one of the swallowtails) resting on the mud, then lifting up, and then settling back down. I was struck by the juxtaposition, but there it was, bringing a shining splash of beauty to the wet dirt. I noted it and went on, my mind quickly flitting, like a butterfly, to the next thing on my agenda.

Later that day I saw another beautiful butterfly, a tiger swallowtail, in a patch of muddy ground. This time, because of the repetition, I took further notice. As my thoughts lingered on the sight, the verse from Psalm 40 came to mind, and I tried to remember the melody from the hymn "He Brought Me Out," based on the verse.

I live a good life, blessed beyond any expectations or hopes I might have had when I was younger. I am happy and fulfilled. I can hardly make the leap to say I am in miry clay. But I wrestle with depression and anxiety, stemming from a medical test a few years ago that left me with a form of PTSD and a newfound sense of my own mortality. Medication helps, but I find myself sometimes looking for reminders that God is with me. Seeing those butterflies in the mud that day reminded me that God, like the butterflies, is with me. He cares enough about me to bring beauty to my life, even in the dust and mud of uncertain, difficult times.
—Jon Woodhams

He brought me out of the miry clay, He set my feet on the Rock to stay;
He puts a song in my soul today, a song of praise, hallelujah!
—Henry L. Gilmour

JULY 5

God's Creative Gifting

Now there are varieties of gifts, but the same Spirit.

—1 CORINTHIANS 12:4 (ESV)

WHAT IN THE world is that bird doing?" I said to my husband. Our kitchen window overlooks the wooded edge of our backyard, where birds, cats, and other suburban creatures often entertain me as I wash dishes.

David came close and looked over my shoulder. "Beats me," he said. "That's kinda weird." A chestnut-colored bird with a long tail hopped around in the underbrush. Every so often, he'd flick his feet, scattering leaves and pine straw.

I grabbed my field guide and flipped the pages. "The brown thrasher is known for foraging among the undergrowth for insects," I read. "It often uses its feet to kick up leaf litter and then sweep the area for tasty bugs."

The brown thrasher's method of foraging was different from any other bird I'd seen, but it was efficient. And dramatic, with its hops, sidesteps, and flourishes. The bird's unique approach reminded me that there are many ways to get the job done. I often see this within the body of Christ.

One Bible study teacher loves to share facts and history. Another prefers story-driven lessons. Yet another uses video and audio clips to drive his point home. In our caregiving ministry, Sally shows her love to hurting people by fixing homemade meals and desserts. Pete reads Scripture and prays. Sarah sends greeting cards with handwritten notes inside.

Our goal is the same—to minister to each other in Jesus's name, but our approach differs. I'd never expect a brown thrasher to suck nectar from a morning glory like a hummingbird, nor should I expect one believer to minister like another. The diversity within the animal kingdom and within the body of Christ stands as testimony of God's creative gifting.—Lori Hatcher

Father, thank You for reminding me that You created each of us with different gifts, talents, and approaches for our good and Your pleasure. Amen.

JULY 6

The Bison Train

The one who calls you is faithful, and he will do it.

—1 THESSALONIANS 5:24 (NIV)

WHEN MY HUSBAND and I visited a bison ranch in Wyoming, we took a small train out into the pasture so we could feed the bison. The train followed a track through the many acres of land where the bison lived, rattling the whole way. As soon as the bison heard the train, they came running from all directions.

The driver gave us handfuls of food pellets. We stuck our arms out the windows, and the bison eagerly ate the food from our palms. As exciting as that was, my attention eventually went to the bison at the front of the train. He had stuck his head into the train and was eating from the driver's hand. It was obvious these two had a relationship and a history together. The bison even nuzzled the driver, and the driver scratched the big fella's enormous head, talking to him the whole time.

This particular bison did not approach us for food. He stayed with the driver. In fact, he never left the driver's side. This bison knew to run toward the sound of the approaching train and the driver who would provide food for his needs. Based on their interaction, it seemed the bison knew the driver was faithful and would not disappoint.

Looking at the bison, head and shoulders squeezed through the open door at the front of the train and large slobbery tongue flinging saliva all over the driver as it ate food pellets, I realized I also have Someone who is faithful, who will not disappoint. I have God. Because of my relationship and history with Him, I know I can depend on my faithful God to provide for all my needs.—Sandy Kirby Quandt

O God, our help in ages past, our hope for years to come,
our shelter from the stormy blast, and our eternal home.
—Isaac Watts

JULY 7

Be Still Like a Bunny

Be still, and know that I am God.

—PSALM 46:10 (NKJV)

MY HUSBAND AND I had just moved into our new house, and I was up to my elbows with boxes that needed to be unpacked. After tackling the chore for several days, I was exhausted. *Lord, there's so much to do,* I thought as I gazed out my window. Just then I noticed a tiny creature, a pygmy rabbit, resting in the yard. This adorable, brownish-gray bunny sat perfectly still while the wind blew its soft fur. I could see its ears perk up at times, aware of the quietest sounds. I couldn't take my eyes off him. Being new to central Oregon, I felt truly blessed that this miniature cottontail chose my yard to pause in.

I think what touched me most was the rabbit's serenity in contrast to my fatigue and striving for perfection, trying to empty out thirty more boxes and get it all done quickly.

As I continued to watch, the bunny stayed in one spot, enjoying the cool grass, bordered by the high desert in my backyard. A light rain fell, but the bunny kept still. There he was—a small creature in this big world, poised in confidence and tranquility. He won my heart.

Later that evening, I opened my front door and saw the bunny, or one like it, sitting near the porch facing me, then it hopped away. I believe the Lord was trying to teach me something before the day's end—and before I became overwhelmed again with unpacking and my mile-long move-in list. God whispered to my heart through this little creature*: Be still, and know that I am God.* Everything would get done, in His time. —Kathleen R. Ruckman

Thank You, Lord, for teaching me through what You have created. May I, too, be still in Your presence and bask in Your care and everlasting love.

A Fish Story

I came that they may have life, and have it abundantly.

—JOHN 10:10 (RSV)

CHILDHOOD VACATIONS MEANT two weeks in the mountains at our family cabin, where plumbing had only recently been added and a potbellied stove was our sole means of cooking or warming the kitchen-bedroom-living room. The six-hour drive often took twelve: flat tire, overheated radiator, and comfort stops. Once the drive was extended by an hour's return to the picnic table where I had left my stuffed kitty. I don't remember my parents' patience wearing thin, but it must have been stretched on those road trips. Dad worked long hours, so vacations were special times under bird-speckled skies, by tadpole creeks and fish-filled lakes. We hiked, swam, and fished.

On days when the sun set late, Dad tried to recapture the special vacation magic by taking my brother and me to our suburban park after work. One evening, my brother caught a fish from the pond. We plopped it in a paper bag and headed home. When we opened the bag over a cutting board, the fish was still alive! Astounded, my eight-year-old brother was convinced God must have intended the fish to live. My parents filled the bathtub, and the fish leapt into the water, circling like a goldfish in a bowl. Later, the fish was returned and released in the pond to live its best life.

That one ordinary day became as memorable as my summer vacations. In that doomed fish, my brother saw the promise of abundant life, and in my brother's earnest faith, my parents recognized an opportunity to illustrate Jesus's promise. I can only imagine what tales the fish told his fish family, but in my family, that fish story reminds us that life is precious and there's joy in celebrating it, even on an ordinary day.—Susie Colby

Glory be to God for dappled things—
For skies of couple-colour as a brinded cow;
For rose-moles all in stipple upon trout that swim
All things counter, original, spare, strange…
He fathers-forth whose beauty is past change:
Praise Him.
—Gerard Manley Hopkins

JULY 9

By My Side

Surely your goodness and love will follow me all the days of my life, and I will dwell in the house of the LORD forever.

—PSALM 23:6 (NIV)

WHEN WE ADOPTED Snowy, I thought the white Maltese would make a great companion for our only son, who was about seven years old at that time. While Snowy loved playing with Ryan and enjoyed the attention he showered upon him, the dog stayed close to me for most of the day. Maybe because I worked from home, fed Snowy his meals, and groomed him. Maybe he shadowed me due to the fact his previous owner had abandoned him and he had grown insecure. Snowy followed me everywhere I went, waiting for me patiently outside the bathroom when I took a shower. He seated himself on the floor only a few inches away from me when I worked in the study or watched TV from my couch. At first, Snowy's clinginess annoyed me, but eventually, I got accustomed to it.

Recently, when I was bedridden for a few days due to fever and headaches, Snowy stayed curled up in his bed, which is located next to mine. He went to the kitchen only when my husband served him his twice-daily meals. He made quick trips to the backyard to relieve himself. I didn't have the energy to pet the pooch or speak to him, but my Maltese never left my side.

Snowy is a tangible reminder of God's presence in my life. God never abandons me, and is close to me always, even during difficult or trying times. His constant presence guides, strengthens, and encourages me. When I was sick and my headaches seemed unbearable, I experienced His inexplicable comfort and unconditional faithfulness. Snowy left me alone for brief periods, but God never did. He promises to remain close to me at all times, and I can count on Him to keep His promise.—Mabel Ninan

And surely I am with you always, to the very end of the age.
—Matthew 28:20 (NIV)

JULY 10

Feathers of an Angel

As for God, His way is perfect; The word of the Lord *is proven; He is a shield to all who trust in Him.*

—Psalm 18:30 (NKJV)

NAPPING ON THE sunporch is a favorite activity. I can fall asleep looking out over the back garden, which represents hours of hard work. My nap partner is a cockatoo named Bruno.

A fluffy, salmon-colored bird, my companion likes nothing more than to spend time with me. She snuggles close to my face and brushes her soft feathers across my chin. If she rubs me the wrong way, it tickles, and I start to laugh. She mimics my chuckles, which makes me laugh all the more.

As I drift off to sleep, she stands guard balancing with one leg on my chest and the other tucked up against her own torso. A gentle breeze wafts through the sunroom and a delicious sleep envelops me.

All too soon, I awake to the sound of Bruno talking to someone outside. Parrots mimic familiar phrases, but some experts doubt they understand the context and meaning of language. As a longtime bird owner, I beg to differ. Bruno often uses phrases to send me messages. If she needs to return to her cage for a bathroom break, she says, "Got to go bye-bye." But this lazy afternoon, she wanted me to know we had a visitor. She repeated her typical greeting, "Are you my honey, honey?"

I slowly rose while giving Bruno a helping hand back into her house. My neighbor's visit included borrowing a couple of eggs and a brief chat about the unseasonable weather.

As my neighbor left, my thoughts turned to the Lord. Both my pet and my Savior like to warn me about unfolding events. Bruno provides a gentle word now and then, but God teaches me something new every time I open the Scripture. His instruction gives flight to my thoughts and life. Both God and Bruno surround me with wings of love.—David L. Winters

As an eagle stirs up its nest, hovers over its young, spreading out its wings, taking them up, carrying them on its wings.

—Deuteronomy 32:11 (NKJV)

The Lessons of the Firefly

In the same way, let your light shine before others, that they may see your good deeds and glorify your Father in heaven.

—MATTHEW 5:16 (NIV)

OOOH! LIGHTNING BUGS!" I exclaimed, as my husband and I sat in the gazebo on the edge of a lake where we were camping in northern Alabama.

We don't often see the light-emitting beetles in the Florida panhandle where we live. The unexpected appearance of the magical insects in the dusky sky transported me back to my childhood in Ohio, when I'd run barefoot through the soft grass capturing as many of the creatures as possible and placing them in a jar with holes in the lid. At the end of the evening, the jar would be lit up with dozens of fireflies emitting their golden glow before I released them. No matter how dark it got, I could always find my way back to the light.

"Go catch them," my husband dared.

"Okay, I will," I said. Despite the fact I am now in my sixth decade of life, I felt like a kid again as I attempted to chase down the elusive bugs. But I found I wasn't as proficient at catching fireflies as I had been as a child. Each time I saw a flash of light and started toward it, it would disappear before I caught it. Eventually I gave up, having procured no lightning bugs. But I still enjoyed the game and the memories evoked by the experience.

As Christians, we are supposed to let our light shine for Jesus, but sometimes I tend to be like a firefly, letting my light flicker on and off. It's difficult to lead people to Jesus if my light goes out and leaves them stumbling in the dark. I'm glad Jesus is faithful and His light is constant. Jesus is the Light that guides me home.—Ellen Fannon

This little light of mine, I'm gonna let it shine.
—Harry Dixon Loes

JULY 12

Take Time to Rest

Now, because of you, Lord, I will lie down in peace and sleep comes at once, for no matter what happens, I will live unafraid!

—PSALM 4:8 (TPT)

NESTLED CLOSE TO the busy sights and sounds of Interstate 35 was a sheltered glen that served as the perfect nursery for a flock of wild turkeys. It was almost completely surrounded by leafy trees that hid it from view of most nearby houses and shopping malls. My friend was delighted to find that the height of her home gave her a perfect vantage point to observe without disturbing.

In the early summer, babies hatched—dozens of them. Each turkey hen can lay up to seventeen eggs. When the wild turkey chicks exit their shells, they are not blind and helpless like their chicken cousins. Rather, their eyes are open, and their legs are ready to run. Wild turkeys are quite active, but the brand-new babies need a period of rest during the daytime hours. For the first few weeks, they are not able to fly up to the tree branches to roost like their older family members.

In this particular glen, my friend watched the mothers settle their youngsters into a hollowed-out circle for their afternoon naps. They came every day without fail for a period of several weeks. Sometimes the moms gently covered the babies with their wings while they slept. At other times the hens stood guard for the duration of the nap until the kids had regained their strength and were ready for more exploration.

God is just like this in His care for me. Life is so busy. I often feel like I never stop running. But He prepares the perfect place of rest ahead of time. He gently leads me to that place. And He guards and protects me while I am being refreshed.—Liz Kimmel

What a great protector You are, Lord. Thank You that I have no need to worry about anything when I submit to Your watchful care. Amen.

JULY 13

The Joyful Poodle

May the God of hope fill you with all joy and peace as you trust in him, so that you may overflow with hope by the power of the Holy Spirit.

—ROMANS 15:13 (NIV)

LAST NIGHT, I sneaked outside for a few moments in hopes of catching some holiday fireworks. My sweet son was sick with a fever bug, so we'd had to cancel our plans. As I spied the tips of the fireworks going off behind the trees, I had the most welcome surprise! A woman came by on the sidewalk, walking her enthusiastic little poodle named Sadie. As a dog lover, I immediately crouched down to give the poodle a few pets, and my gesture was happily welcomed by her.

In Sadie's mind, we were now best friends. She jumped on me, gave me tiny dog licks, and even tried to come inside my home with me. What an unexpected joy she brought to my evening, especially on a night when other plans had been canceled.

As I walked away from that interaction, I was reminded of the power a joyful heart can bring. I don't know about you, but I sometimes approach walking out my faith as a discipline—don't do this or that in the pursuit of righteousness. But isn't my faith so much more? When I trust in God and experience the fullness of His presence, my joy should be overflowing onto others. Being joyful isn't selfish. In fact, it's one of the greatest forms of our witness!

None of us knows what another person is going through at any particular time, so I want to be prepared for all my daily interactions with others to be a gift and a blessing.—Ashley Clark

Walk of Faith: *Do something today that will stir God's joy in your heart and watch it spill over onto others.*

Butting Heads

So the last will be first, and the first will be last.

—MATTHEW 20:16 (NIV)

I'D HEARD CHICKENS have a pecking order, but I hadn't realized that cows do too. I noticed it on our cattle ranch one day when two mama cows were butting heads.

"What are they doing?" I asked my husband, Craig.

He explained they were determining dominance of the cow herd. He had just brought a couple dozen cows from leased pasture back to the ranch. Like teenage girls in a made-for-television movie, the cows were challenging each other to create a pecking order in the herd.

"There will be several fights as they butt heads and push one another around," he said. "One by one they'll give up until there's a leader." That leader—sometimes called the "boss cow"—is the one the others follow. Usually stronger and bigger, that queen of the cows often pushes her way into the feeding area, nudging out the lesser ones.

Watching the two cows butt each other around made me wonder, *Do I do that?* Do I interrupt conversations to put in my two cents? Do I try to impress others with my latest résumé entries? Do I put myself first in line instead of helping someone else?

I'd never considered the probable origin of the expression *butting heads*. I had thought if I butted heads with someone, they were frustrating me and my best attempts. Now, with a picture of two mama cows ramming each other, I wondered if that was how others see me when I am only looking out for myself.

Jesus said, "The first shall be last and the last shall be first." Truly, I now know that I don't need to be first or the best of this human herd in life. Instead of butting heads, this queen cow will defer to the Prince of Peace.—Janet Holm McHenry

Walk of Faith: *Think of a situation in which you've butted heads with someone. What could you have done differently to find a peaceful resolution? If appropriate now, make amends.*

When Doves Cry

And the voice of the turtledove is heard in our land.

—SONG OF SONGS 2:12 (ESV)

I LOVE THE SOUND of a mourning dove. Its voice whisks me back to early childhood on my family's small Michigan farm. It's always summer in my memory. I am seven or eight, standing in our backyard, the fields behind the house rippling in amber waves. The July-bright sun is climbing in the cloudless sky, the air is hot and still, and the quiet trill of insects hints at life all around me. Then I hear a mourning dove's cry as my mother and grandmother toil in the sweltering kitchen to "put up" vegetables from my mother's bountiful garden. The day stretches before me, unconstrained by deadlines or to-dos. I am safe and loved—cousins and grandparents live just down the road that was named after my maternal ancestors.

Until recently, I thought I'd never seen a mourning dove. They were always within earshot yet out of sight. Then I discovered that the mourning dove is also called a turtledove. Of course I've seen mourning doves—innumerable times! I'd dismissed them as pigeons. Now I know that this gray-brown bird is my lifelong unseen friend.

My father has been gone for four decades. My mom passed away a few years ago. As the youngest in my family, I'm watching as my siblings and I get older. I have a wonderful, fulfilling life, but sometimes the relentless, accelerating march of age and time, as well as my own mortality, overwhelm me.

The mourning dove's melancholy cry recalls a carefree time when mortality was the furthest thing from my mind. In those moments, through the elegiac "voice of the turtledove," I hear God whisper to me, *I was with you then. I'm with you still.* —Jon Woodhams

Walk of Faith: *What sounds remind you of God's abiding love? Listen for them throughout your day.*

JULY 16

A New Song

Sing to the LORD a new song; sing to the LORD, all the earth. Sing to the LORD, praise his name; proclaim his salvation day after day. Declare his glory among the nations, his marvelous deeds among all peoples.

—PSALM 96:1–3 (NIV)

I FEEL BLESSED TO be able to experience the wonders of nature. Recently, I was working with my honeybees, when I heard a virgin queen bee piping. Very few beekeepers find themselves in the right place at the right time to hear this. A normal hive has tens of thousands of bees all buzzing in a colony. The shrill cry of a newly hatched queen is distinct and can be heard above the humming of the hive.

Queen piping sounds like a new song for the bees in Morse code with buzzing dots and dashes. The purpose of her song is to announce to the colony her arrival as the new queen. Since she is still developing, her pheromones are not strong enough to fill the hive. Piping calms the colony and assures them the future is going to be okay.

I wonder what it would have been like witnessing the Israelites miraculously crossing the sea on dry ground as they escaped Egyptian captivity. Then imagine seeing Pharaoh's pursuing army drowning as the water closed in on them. Exodus 15 tells us a new song was sung throughout the camp, a song that told of how God had saved them. A song, much like queen piping, to calm the thousands hearing it and reassure them that the future is going to be okay.

May I always be ready to sing a new song that encourages others and reassures them that no matter how difficult things appear, God is in control and the future is going to be okay.—Ben Cooper

O for a thousand tongues to sing my great Redeemer's praise,
the glories of my God and King, the triumphs of his grace!
—Charles Wesley

Fighting with Fools

If it is possible, as far as it depends on you, live at peace with everyone.

—Romans 12:18 (NIV)

MY FRIEND DAVE is a serious birdwatcher. His backyard abuts a golf course, making it a lovely habitat for winged visitors. On a recent visit, Dave gave me a tour. The pièce de résistance was a bluebird house. After a couple of years trying, he'd been able to attract a pair of the lovely little creatures. Though not exactly rare, bluebirds are none too common in these parts. I was happy to see them flitting back and forth between the fifth fairway and their tiny home.

"One thing puzzles me," Dave said. "Last year they nested in that house." He pointed to a smart-looking birdhouse just off the south corner of the yard. "This year they moved over there." He indicated a somewhat dilapidated birdhouse on the opposite side of the lot. "I just can't figure it out." Me neither.

A couple of weeks later, I saw Dave again. "I solved the mystery," he said, then went on to tell me about the house sparrows that had moved onto his property. This aggressive species is known to compete with bluebirds for space. Apparently, the sparrows had taken over the nicer digs, forcing a fight-or-flight response from the bluebirds. The tamer bluebirds chose to fly the coop.

Over many years, I've learned the wisdom of the bluebird. As a younger man, I saw every challenge as an opportunity to fight. I labored to win every argument, prove every point, and be the victor of any conflict, real or imagined. I was also about as likable as a house sparrow.

Time and the counsel of the Holy Spirit have shown me that peace is often of greater value than victory. The bluebirds found they could be content without winning every fight. I can too.—Lawrence W. Wilson

If a wise person goes to court with a fool, the fool rages and scoffs, and there is no peace.

—Proverbs 29:9 (NIV)

JULY 18

The Sleep of the Righteous

In peace I will lie down and sleep, for you alone,
Lord, make me dwell in safety.

—Psalm 4:8 (NIV)

RUBY, OUR ONE-YEAR-OLD black Labrador, awakens with the first song of the birds and is ready to take on the day. She and I walk before breakfast, we'll head to the park after, and she will often take a dip in the pool when we return. She's a busy girl, and being busy keeps her from eating shoes and chairs and other delicious, but sometimes dangerous, things around the house.

As the summer got hotter and we could only walk her in the early morning or the evening, we realized she needed more activity to keep her out of trouble. We set up a baby pool in the yard and put in the hose, her favorite orange squeaky pig, and a plush Frisbee that looked like a donut with sprinkles.

Delighted, Ruby hopped in and out of the baby pool, throwing the pig and donut into the big pool, retrieving them, and putting them back into the baby pool. She wrestled the hose with her snout and paws, watering the plants, spraying us, and making us laugh with her antics. All afternoon she made up games, keeping us amused.

When she had worn herself out, I toweled her off, and we went inside. After dinner, Ruby lay belly up, snoring on her striped bed, the picture of complete peace. We had created an environment that brought out the best in her, and it kept her out of trouble. I realized that God has created a world for me that contains equal delight, along with some tempting dangers. The more I focus on the good God has created, the more joy I am able to discover. And like Ruby, when I am engaging fully, living as I am intended to live, I sleep in tired contentment at the end of the day.—Lucy H. Chambers

True religion is real living; living with all one's soul,
with all one's goodness and righteousness.
—Albert Einstein

JULY 19

A Fair Friend

But we all, with open face beholding as in a glass the glory of the Lord, are changed into the same image from glory to glory, even as by the Spirit of the Lord.

—2 CORINTHIANS 3:18 (KJV)

MOMMA, KNOW WHAT I have?"

Our nine-year-old daughter, having returned from the community carnival, held her hands behind her back, but I knew.

"A fish?"

Thrusting the plastic bag forward, she confirmed my guess.

"And I didn't even have to play the goldfish game. Someone just gave him to me, for free! Wasn't that nice?"

Cynicism crept in. *Nice? Forced to again try to keep an aquatic creature alive, only to watch your child grieve days later?* Still, I heard myself say, "Yes, dear. What's his name?"

Without hesitation, her smile broadened. "Buddy," she said.

I couldn't help but smile too. My daughter's joy caused me to go the extra mile and provide a proper home for her friend. Unlike the other two or three fair fish, this one received a filtered tank and some colorful glass stones. Twice a day, he was fed a pinch of food. Once a month, we changed his water.

And guess what? One year turned into two. Two to three.

Soon we'll celebrate our fourth year with Buddy the Goldfish. Though his color has turned from bright orange to iridescent white—due to the lack of natural sunlight, we're told—and he's tripled in size, he seems healthy and happy.

While our teenage daughter has taken interest in other things, like horses and hanging with human friends, her goldfish greets me each morning, then watches me from his tank as I move about the kitchen.

Indeed, Buddy is now my pal, and every day he reminds me that when I go the extra mile for others, I'm adding life—vitality and vigor—to their days. Just as we transformed the life of our free-to-a-good-home friend, I, too, am being transformed to better reflect the image of Christ.—Maureen Miller

All things bright and beautiful, all creatures great and small,
all things wise and wonderful, the Lord God made them all.
—Cecil F. Alexander

The Song of the Voles

A cheerful heart is good medicine.

—PROVERBS 17:22 (NIV)

I KNEW THE BOY had been sick, with hospitalizations, blood transfusions, and doctor visits one after another. That's a lot of weight for four-year-old shoulders. He called to me across the fence: "I caught something!" He had pounced on the little critter, trapping it beneath an upside-down bucket. I lifted the bucket and found myself staring at a tiny, brownish rodent. Small ears, small eyes, a short hairy tail. It was a vole.

"What do voles do?" he asked. I said that, so far as I knew, they spent most of their time digging tunnels. The boy said that he dug tunnels in his sandbox and that he liked to sing as he worked away. Then he got a thoughtful look on his little face, and he asked, "Do you think voles sing when they dig?"

I spent the evening writing the lyrics to the "Song of the Voles." The next morning, I announced to the boy that I'd put my ear to the ground and heard the sound of tunneling and singing. And the song went like this:

Tunneling, chunneling, up hills and knolls,
Out of our way! We are the voles!
No stones, no boulders, no rigmaroles,
Will stand in our way. We are the voles!

No rocks can stop us, no animals top us,
No storms can dampen these bold, hearty souls.
We thunk on the chipmunks, we roll o'er the moles,
We roust all the rabbits for their rabbit holes.
Out of our way! We are the voles!

The "Song of the Voles" isn't going to make anyone forget Rodgers and Hammerstein or Stephen Sondheim, but the boy liked it, and he threw back his head and laughed out loud. And any day you can make a child laugh is a good day.—Louis Lotz

As You have filled me with gladness, oh God, let me share my gladness with others. Amen.

Crabby Prayers

The prayer of a righteous person is powerful and effective.

—JAMES 5:16 (NIV)

NOOOOOOOOO!" MY GRANDDAUGHTER Lauren's deep-green eyes scrunched in distress. "You can't eat them. They're alive!"

Lauren and her younger siblings had been splashing happily in a tidal pool, scooping up hermit crabs, and chasing minnows when their dad approached.

"Hey, kids, look what I caught." He flopped his net over the tidal pool, and a blue crab tumbled out. We gathered around, keeping a respectful distance from the red and blue snapping claws.

Lauren was particularly enamored. "Look at his colors, Gigi," she said. "I've never seen such a beautiful crab. What are you going to do with it, Daddy?"

"Eat it," he said, in a matter-of-fact way. "Blue crabs are good eatin'."

That's when Lauren began to wail. She begged. She pleaded. She listed compelling reasons why he should let the crab go free.

"I'll tell you what," he said. "If I don't catch enough for everyone to have one, I'll let 'em go."

Lauren looked up at him with big, sad eyes. He walked back to the shoreline and soon returned with another crab. And another. And another. If he found three more, we'd be eating crab for dinner.

Josiah continued to walk the shoreline for an hour, but every swish of his net came up empty. True to his word, as the family headed in for lunch, he released the four crabs to the ocean.

"What was the saddest day of my life is now the happiest day," Lauren exclaimed, hugging her daddy and skipping off to join her siblings. As she passed me, she leaned in and whispered, "I prayed, Gigi."

"I did too," I said as we exchanged happy grins.

I shared the confession with Josiah later. "I knew something was up," he said with a laugh. "All of a sudden the water got murky, and I couldn't see a thing."

For the rest of the week, despite his best efforts, he didn't catch another crab. And we all know why.—Lori Hatcher

Prayer is the greatest of all forces, because it honors
God and brings Him into active aid.
—E. M. Bounds

A Watchful Eye

Start children off on the way they should go, and even when they are old they will not turn from it.

—PROVERBS 22:6 (NIV)

THE LAKE WAS directly behind our spot at the campground, providing a welcome bit of calm after a busy week. Young boys fished from the shore. Kayakers glided by. But it was a mother mallard duck and her six ducklings that captured my attention. These weren't downy babies. They were perhaps one to two months old. They did not form a tight line behind their mother as younger ducklings do. Instead, these six swam near her side yet still under her watchful eye.

Her ducklings were growing up. She had protected them well. Soon they would no longer need her supervision. They would leave and be on their own. It wouldn't be long before they established their own home apart from her. Had she trained them well? I wondered. Would she miss them when they left?

I noticed one duck in particular. He appeared more independent than his siblings. When he swam away from his mother, she turned her head toward him. Although her five other children surrounded her, it was the one who swam away she paid attention to. Before long, he returned. His was merely a brief exploration. He wasn't ready to leave quite yet. Someday he'd be ready, as would the others. Today was not that day, however.

As I watched this mallard with her ducklings, I realized she and I are not that different. It would not matter if I had five other children around me—my attention would turn toward the one who swam away. As I watched the duck swim from his mother, I thought about my only child. I thought about his difficulties. Difficulties he couldn't fix. Difficulties I couldn't fix. Difficulties only God can fix. I also realized that no matter how far away my son might swim, he will never swim beyond God's reach.—Sandy Kirby Quandt

Father, even though I don't have as much influence over my son as I once did, he remains my child. I pray the training he received when he was young keeps him close to You. Amen.

JULY 23

The Stowaway Spider's Silk

The heart of man plans his way, but the LORD establishes his steps.

—PROVERBS 16:9 (ESV)

IT ALL STARTED innocently enough.

I opened the porch screen door to let our senior cocker spaniel out into the yard, then spent a few moments checking my plants and flowers. I added some birdseed to the feeder, then brought our dog back inside. The entire event took less than five minutes, so imagine my surprise when I washed my hands, looked into the mirror, and saw *a spider* had been hitchhiking in my hair! Looking back now, I have to laugh because my first reaction was to make sure the spider wouldn't get hurt when I removed it. I gently got it out, only to find it climbing into the sink—a rascally little thing.

Finally, I used some tissue to move the small spider to a better location outdoors. I'm happy to report no spiders or humans were injured in the process. What amazed me the most was the way the spider released a thread of silk so it wouldn't fall. When spiders do this, I always watch in awe as they seem to float through the air. Spiders use these silk lines to protect themselves and to shimmy their way back where they belong.

Faith can be a lot like the spider's silk. We use it in our day-to-day work of weaving webs, but we can also trust the Lord will suspend us by His invisible thread above the dangers lurking below. I may not see the spider's silk, and likewise, I may not always see the ways God is working in my life, but I can trust the Holy Spirit will anchor me and never let me fall.—Ashley Clark

The LORD watches over you—the LORD is your shade at your right hand; the sun will not harm you by day, nor the moon by night. The LORD will keep you from all harm—he will watch over your life; the LORD will watch over your coming and going both now and forevermore.

—Psalm 121:5–8 (NIV)

JULY 24

More Teddy than Bear

"No weapon forged against you will prevail, and you will refute every tongue that accuses you. This is the heritage of the servants of the Lord, *and this is their vindication from me," declares the* Lord.

—Isaiah 54:17 (NIV)

OUR 130-POUND AKITA, appropriately named Bear, stood nearly thirty inches high at the shoulder. Having the massive head and shoulders characteristic of the breed, he was an intimidating presence. Visitors often cowered at the sight of Bear, though he was more teddy bear than grizzly. We knew him to be harmless—a big baby in disguise.

Not everyone was frightened of Bear though. One day, I heard him barking and snarling in the backyard, uncharacteristic behavior for our gentle giant. Rushing outside I saw him run to the end of his zip line and extend the lead all the way to the end, then lunge with all his might against it. *What's out there? What could have this normally placid animal so upset?*

It took a moment, but I finally spotted the mallard hen and her brood of ducklings calmly paddling back and forth in the stream bordering our property. I couldn't help but chuckle. Bear looked at me, then back at the ducks, and back to me again as if to say, *Don't you see that? The ducks! They're in our yard. Do something!*

I wasn't so much laughing at Bear as laughing with him. The ducklings seemed to enjoy the joke too. For all his bluster, the massive canine posed no threat to them whatsoever. The zip line gave him some freedom, but the steel cable easily kept his massive power in check.

I try to remember Bear, the helpless giant, when I encounter spiritual obstacles that seem formidable, even frightening. When I am tempted, seemingly beyond what I can bear, I know that no scheme of Satan is stronger than the Spirit within me. When threatened by evil people with ill intent, I'm as safe as the ducklings paddling in the creek. The Lord is my defender.—Lawrence W. Wilson

Heavenly Father, You are powerful and good. I take refuge in Your protection and peace. Guide my steps today. Amen.

Singing over Me

For the LORD your God is living among you. He is a mighty savior. He will take delight in you with gladness. With his love, he will calm all your fears. He will rejoice over you with joyful songs.

—ZEPHANIAH 3:17 (NLT)

A FELLOW HOMESCHOOL MOM asked if I wanted to teach at an upcoming homeschooling convention. I certainly had the experience: I've spent more than twenty-seven years of my life homeschooling my four, now-adult kiddos. And I continue to stay in touch with the homeschool world through various friends and organizations.

However, the more I thought about teaching four workshops at the convention, the more I began to panic. What if I don't do a good job? What if I get nervous and stammer over my words? What if I don't say the right things? I worried about letting the audience and God down.

I retreated to my front porch to sit in the swing and pray. It's my favorite place to talk to God—in good times and in challenging ones too. I prayed out loud about my decision and debated calling my friend to tell her I didn't think I could do it.

Movement caught my attention, and I saw a small wren fly to the birdbath. Tentative at first, it eventually stepped into the water and splashed joyously. Droplets of rain went everywhere!

When it finished the dance, the wren flew to the tree right next to my porch swing and began to sing. The trills of melodious notes filled the air. I closed my eyes and swung back and forth, listening. It felt like the Creator was singing over me, notes of beautiful harmony.

I knew it was an answer from the Lord. I felt like God said to me, "You got this. And I'll be with you." With a new sense of peace about teaching at the convention, I slipped back inside and sat down at the computer to start preparing for my workshops.—Julie Lavender

God speaks to us in bird and song, in winds that drift the clouds along, above the din and toil of wrong, a melody of love.

—Joseph Johnson

Majestic Crowns

Honor and majesty are before Him; strength and gladness are in His place.

—1 CHRONICLES 16:27 (NKJV)

MY FATHER, HUSBAND, and I visited Crater Lake, one of the seven wonders of Oregon. The crater was formed thousands of years ago when Mount Mazama erupted, one of the earth's largest eruptions in the past 12,000 years. The water in the crater is as blue as sapphire, with an unusual stillness due to its depth.

That day, we drove slowly around the caldera rim, which ranges from 7,000 to 8,000 feet in elevation. Looking down into a meadow, Dad was the first to see a large herd of elk. Male and female elk were equally stunning, but the amazing antlers of the males gave them an appearance of majesty. The animals grazed on the fringes of a captivating natural wonder, but they, too, were a wonder and touched our hearts with awe.

Weighing up to 700 pounds, North American elk are one of the largest deer species on earth. They are social animals, and it is not uncommon for two hundred or more to gather. The call of a male is described as an "otherworld," bugle-like sound. When on alert, the males lift their heads with antlers tipped upward, eyes widened, and ears rotated. Perhaps the elk were on alert that day, as we watched them from a distance.

My father lived to be almost ninety-one, and in his last days, there were tender moments when we spoke of Crater Lake and the beauty there. Through my experience of seeing the elk, almost hidden in the periphery of a spectacular natural wonder, I have been inspired to take notice of *all* the blessings around me, whether a butterfly, a bird, a baby in a stroller—or creatures with majestic crowns tucked in an obscure meadow.

There are miracles in nature that can make a lifelong memory, created by the God of wonders. Although these are just shadows of the glory to come in heaven, I don't want to miss them!—Kathleen R. Ruckman

Lord, thank You for revealing who You are through nature,
where the invisible becomes visible. Thank You for preparing
an eternal place where Your glory and majesty will remain forever.

JULY 27

My Good Shepherd

He shall feed his flock like a shepherd: he shall gather the lambs with his arm, and carry them in his bosom, and shall gently lead those that are with young.

—Isaiah 40:11 (KJV)

EVER SINCE MY mother placed a stuffed toy lamb in my crib, I've had an affinity for these cuddly creatures. That threadbare toy comforted me for many years, and I still have it today.

One of the things I love about lambs is their joyful playfulness and the way they spin in circles, jump in the air, and run around crazily. They are truly darling! Sheep are also fearful creatures who need constant protection because they're utterly defenseless against predators. The whole herd becomes dangerously stressed when one of them is endangered. Because sheep are prone to wander off when they get bored or if something interesting catches their attention, they must be kept in a well-fenced pasture.

Better yet, a shepherd watching over them will pursue wandering sheep and bring them back to safety. A shepherd must be alert to spot sheep who stray from the safety of his care, and he must be strong enough to carry sheep that can weigh hundreds of pounds. A shepherd is careful and calm in a crisis. Even when sheep repeatedly need to be rescued, the shepherd will save them every time.

It's no wonder that in the Bible people are often compared to sheep. I don't spin in circles, and it's been a long time since anyone described me as truly darling, but I have a lot of other sheep-like characteristics. I wander. I get bored, fearful, and stressed. And I am defenseless without Jesus. Jesus, my Shepherd, protects me, searches for me when I get lost, and keeps me safe. He will save me every time.—Randy Benedetto

My Good Shepherd, Overseer of my soul, I'm as helpless as a lamb.
Protect me and make me whole. Amen.

JULY 28

Soaring High Above

But those who wait on the L*ORD* *shall renew their strength; they shall mount up with wings like eagles, they shall run and not be weary, they shall walk and not faint.*

—ISAIAH 40:31 (NKJV)

WE LIVE IN a small town with rural fields surrounding the area. Between our house and the houses to the rear of us is a seldomly used (thankfully) train track and a field with a small stream. This brings us occasional wildlife sightings, everything from foxes to rabbits and the occasional (presumably lost) pelican.

All the small wildlife draws stunning red-tailed hawks into the area. I love sitting out on my back porch and watching them catch the wind and soar, often in twos or threes. They're so majestic my breath catches. I often notice them perching magnificently on top of fence posts, on traffic lights when I'm stopped for a red light, or on streetlights in the dusk of evening. Their dark eyes miss nothing as they turn their heads to display their hooked beaks and ruffle their fine feathers. If God made these fine birds with their massive wingspans, what must the angels look like?

I don't know when I first started doing this, but now every time I see a hawk, whether white-tailed or red-tailed, I say a small prayer of thanksgiving. And since I've started praying, I've started seeing hawks more often, everywhere from a mountain drive to a trip to the local grocery store. I believe it's God's way of reminding me to keep my focus set on Him.

To God be the glory!—Deb Kastner

Walk of Faith: *Choose an animal you often see around you, and use it to remind you to say a prayer of gratitude to God for watching over you.*

JULY 29

Doing Our Part

Do everything you possibly can for those who need help.

—PROVERBS 3:27 (ERV)

ONE EVENING LAST summer, my twelve-year-old son, Nathan, and I went for a walk. He was talking about his new video game, but my thoughts kept wandering to a friend who was going through a painful divorce. We'd been meeting for lunch to talk about her situation, but she'd texted that afternoon to tell me she was moving to a different state for her job. I wasn't sure how I could help her if she lived far away.

As we walked closer to the small pond by our house, we heard the frogs croaking. "Every time I hear that sound, I wonder about the tadpoles we helped," he said.

In May, Nathan saw that a puddle in our driveway was full of tadpoles. He watched them for days, fascinated. When the water started to dry up and there was no rain in the forecast, he used a plastic cup to transfer the tadpoles to the pond. "I tried so hard to save them," he said. "I just wish I knew for sure how many survived."

"I understand how you feel, but sometimes when we help someone, we don't know how their situation turns out," I said. "I think it's only natural to wonder about it, but that part isn't our responsibility. The Bible says to help others when we can. That's our job. We do the best we can, and the results are up to God."

Nathan smiled. "Then I'm sure the tadpoles made it."

"I bet you're right, Bud."

As we walked away from the pond, I thought again about my friend. Just as Nathan had done his part with the tadpoles and trusted God with the results, I would do what I could to help her and then remember that her fate was in God's hands.—Diane Stark

Do your best and let God do the rest.

—Ben Carson, MD

JULY 30

Persistence

And I tell you, ask, and it will be given to you; seek, and you will find; knock, and it will be opened to you. For everyone who asks receives, and the one who seeks finds, and to the one who knocks it will be opened.

—LUKE 11:9–10 (ESV)

DONKEYS," MY WIFE, Christine, said. "Must be two dozen."

We were driving through Lake George, Colorado, known for having a herd of wild asses—rumored to be descendants of animals that miners released after the gold rush.

I stopped the car. The road was covered with Eeyores of various colors. White, black, gray, tan, even spotted. I rolled down my window, and immediately a jack walked over and stuck in his head.

I pushed his nose away, but he forced his head forward. Again, I shoved his muzzle, but he wouldn't budge, thrusting in farther. I tried to ignore him, but his lips flapped at my face as if trying to communicate.

"You want a scratch?" I rubbed his ears, and he leaned his head against my chest. Mud flaked onto my shirt. I didn't care. I had a wild donkey in my arms, and I couldn't let go!

He stilled, enjoying the attention—or maybe the cold air blowing from the dash vent.

My heart was full—I kissed him right on the nose.

I'll call you Nicholass.

After a few more seconds, Nick gave a gentle snort and sauntered away. He'd gotten what he came for; his tenacity had paid off.

That brazen donkey reminded me of the widow in Luke 18:1–8 who finally got what she wanted from a judge because of her persistence. Much like Nicholass, she, too, knew the value of stubbornness. I drove away with a better appreciation for the benefit of being steadfast in my prayers. I know the Lord desires to meet my every need and even my wants. I just have to be stubborn as a donkey when it comes to petitioning the Lord.—Tez Brooks

Dear God, I know You never ignore me. Help me remember that, instead, You prompt me to spend more time with You in prayer when You delay Your answers. Teach me to trust Your timing and never give up. Amen.

"Flutter, Flutter, Little Butterfly"

The LORD your God in your midst, the Mighty One, will save;
He will rejoice over you with gladness, He will quiet you
with His love, He will rejoice over you with singing.

—ZEPHANIAH 3:17 (NKJV)

SEE THE BUTTERFLY?" I asked our infant granddaughter. I knew she didn't know what a butterfly was, but the fluttering wings caught her eye.

I'd taken our granddaughter outside to wait for my daughter to get home from work. Sometimes, I'd put her in the stroller and travel the sidewalk back and forth while waiting for her mama's car. This day, however, I chose to sit on the concrete steps leading down the hillside.

While bouncing her on my knee, I sang my favorite childhood songs, including one I'd made up for her mother when she was a toddler. Then I noticed the butterflies. I first learned about cabbage butterflies when I was young. These small yellow or white butterflies would flit about our area in large numbers all through the spring and summer.

At this point in her growth, our granddaughter had begun to detect moving objects, so it didn't surprise me that she saw the butterfly. However, when she began following it with her eyes, then swiveling her head to see it, I marveled at the curiosity she must be feeling. I decided to make up a song for her, as I had done for her mama all those years before, to suit this moment's importance.

For the next several years, every time my granddaughter saw a butterfly, she'd ask for her song. Any time we did a video chat, she wanted to hear that song. I even made a tiny board book with the song written in it and pictures of butterflies, and she made me read it a dozen times in a row each time I visited. One might say I rejoiced over her with singing—just as God does with me!—Cathy Mayfield

Flutter your wings in the sun, butterfly. God rejoices over us as time goes by.
—C.M.

August

AUGUST 1

Bumblebee Neighbor

A soft answer turns away wrath, but a harsh word stirs up anger.

—PROVERBS 15:1 (NKJV)

ALL THE CHILDREN on our block knew to steer clear of our neighbor Mr. Johnson. An older man and avid turf-management specialist, he spent considerable time tending to his yard. This made him protective and grumpy when neighborhood kids carelessly walked on his lawn. Katy bar the door if a baseball or disc flew into his backyard.

Most of us kids focused on his faded yellow overalls and black T-shirt. His signature lawn-care outfit earned him the title of Mr. Bumblebee. It fit well with his stinging tongue. Although too young to appreciate all his hard work, I mainly wished he would act a bit friendlier.

One particularly warm afternoon, I found my mother watering her flower beds. As we talked about the flowers and my day, Mr. Johnson looked over at her.

"Hi, Mr. Johnson," my mother said pleasantly.

He responded with a polite hello and continued on with his business. I thought about how nicely he acted toward her but how surly he seemed to us kids. As I thought about bringing it up to my mother, I noticed that she carefully watered her hollyhocks, avoiding a large bee.

"Mom, why don't you spray that bee and knock him into next Tuesday? He might sting us."

"Bees are good for the garden," she said. "Like our neighbor, the bees treat us well if we treat them the same way."

Her words resonated as I returned to the house. In a God moment, I quickly saw the parallel between the bumblebee in the garden and Mr. Bumblebee's warm response to her. My friends and I were often being scolded for riding our bicycles on his lawn or sailing a Wiffle Ball into his yard. Perhaps he reserved his stinger for those of us who posed a threat. I realized that if I began to treat Mr. Johnson with respect, maybe he would become as harmless as a content bumblebee.—David L. Winters

Lord, help me to treat everyone with kindness and respect today. Amen.

AUGUST 2

Teeming with Tadpoles

When anxiety was great within me, your consolation brought me joy.

—PSALM 94:19 (NIV)

I USUALLY READ THE newspaper while I eat breakfast. The news had been bad recently, and it seemed to be getting worse. Even the weather forecast was ominous: heat, drought, no relief in sight. I felt so agitated, I couldn't read anymore. Folding the newspaper, I decided to do something productive instead and take my dog, Ruby, for a walk.

As the paper had warned, it was hot, even so early in the morning. We walked along, and I noticed the puddles on the sides of the street were drying up. Then one big puddle caught my eye. It seemed to be electrified. The surface pulsed, reflecting the sunlight in every direction, like a cat's paw on a cool mountain lake. Ruby and I walked over to investigate.

The puddle teemed with tadpoles. There must have been thousands of them. They had recently hatched—they had no legs yet; they were just little black buds of life with tiny tails whipping back and forth. They were magnificent, and they held the promise of so many frogs to come. I paused in wonder at the sight.

Here I am, God seemed to say as I looked at this lowly puddle filled with vigorous life. *I have been making frogs since long before newspapers were ever invented. As long as there have been people to make news, there has been strife and worry, yet life goes on. I have faithfully continued to make frogs, and I will continue to walk with you, even when you are afraid.*

I finished my walk in a completely different mood, focusing on the miracle of tadpoles, the graceful limbs of the old trees, and the puffy clouds that were building up in the sky, promising some welcome rain.
—Lucy H. Chambers

The goal of life is to make your heartbeat match the beat of the universe, to match your nature with Nature.
—Joseph Campbell

AUGUST 3

Damaging Words

A perverse person stirs up conflict, and a gossip separates close friends.

—PROVERBS 16:28 (NIV)

MANY CREATURES TAKE shelter in Camp Roger's protected woods in Rockford, Michigan. One of my favorites is the pileated woodpecker. They are huge birds, often growing to be sixteen to nineteen inches in length, with brilliant red heads, coal-colored feathers, and white stripes on the face and neck.

While I was eating outside one day with coworkers, I caught sight of a pileated flying to a tall pine tree. With the speed of a jackhammer, the bird pounded the wood with his beak. The flip of his neck was so fast that my eyes could hardly register each hit. He hopped around the entire trunk of the tree, going up and down the bark to discover the insects he knew were there. Around camp, we have seen a single woodpecker destroy a wooden wall with its constant pecking.

Gossip can be as destructive as that bird's beak.

After listening to a friend tell me about an important event in her life, I ended up sharing pieces of the story with a few people. Later, I overheard one of those people retell what I had told her, but she had completely turned the situation upside down and embellished it in an ugly way. I jumped in to clarify, but it was too late. The gossip had turned into a damaging and mostly untrue rumor about a dear friend who had trusted me with her personal information. My heart sank.

Plain and simple, words have the power to destroy a relationship more quickly than the beat of that woodpecker's beak can demolish wood. I learned an important lesson that day—that keeping my mouth shut and being a trustworthy friend is more important than sharing a story. —Twila Bennett

Dear Lord, the next time I'm tempted to share a story that isn't mine to tell, remind me of that pileated woodpecker, and instill in me the power to be quiet. Amen.

Bully of the Barnyard

There is no fear in love. But perfect love drives out fear, because fear has to do with punishment.

—1 JOHN 4:18 (NIV)

FIONA IS A rooster named by a little boy who loved watching Shrek movies. A mixed breed of beautiful birds, his yellow mane, orange eyes, and deep red-and-green plumage was stunning as he strutted around the barnyard.

Full of personality, Fiona knew his name and would run at rooster-breakneck speed across the pasture when he heard it. He was aggressive with the hens, and we had a coop full of "little Fionas" just weeks after his arrival. He was aggressive with humans too. He was an "attack chicken" when I collected eggs, pecking at me viciously. Sometimes just to be mean, I think, he would run across the yard to where I was sitting at the picnic table and just flog the daylights out of my leg. Simply put, Fiona was the bully of the barnyard.

I have known people like Fiona, ones who used a bad attitude to cover up a lack of belief in themselves. There's the ornery person at the office who can throw you off the scent of their fear by an attack to your spirit. A "friend" on social media, who will toss out a hurtful comment to a post you made in order to hide their lack of confidence or fear of not being accepted. These "bullies of the barnyard" strut away and leave us in shambles, never seeing their display for what it really is—a decoy.

Perhaps I'm putting too much stock in a rooster's bad attitude being more than just that, but when I've approached Fiona quickly and picked him up, he would coo like a pigeon and lay his head on my shoulder. To me, that says his fear was making him puff up and cause a ruckus, because being vulnerable was just too darn scary.

I know the only way to stop a bully is to see them—really see them. I don't like to think of myself as a bully, but I do like knowing that God sees me—really sees me—through both the hurt thrown my way and the hurt I might cause and loves me anyway. And that's something to crow about.—Devon O'Day

God, let me see past the hurt being thrown at me to hide the fearful, needy soul You have put in my path to love.

AUGUST 5

His Healing Hand

Are not two sparrows sold for a penny? Yet not one of them will fall to the ground outside your Father's care.

—MATTHEW 10:29 (NIV)

I CAME BACK FROM lunch one day to find a small cardboard box sitting in the treatment area of the veterinary clinic where I work. We have a number of "good Samaritans" who bring in sick or injured wildlife, and a closed cardboard box is a good indication that the creature inside is not a house pet. Upon opening the top, I found a tiny hummingbird huddled in the corner of the box, one of its wings drooping pathetically. I gently lifted the fragile bird and examined the abnormal wing. As I suspected, the wing was broken. Fortunately, however, it was a closed fracture, meaning the bones had not poked through the skin.

Now what could I do? Although I treat a lot of birds in my vet practice, this hummingbird was a first. There was no way I could devise a tiny splint or even wrap the injured wing to the patient's body. I knew I could use some help in healing this hummer, so I sent up a quick prayer. I decided to provide supportive care and let God take care of the rest. I took the bird home and kept it confined for three weeks while I syringe-fed it nectar several times a day. I never tired of watching the little creature's excitement as it poked its long, thin tongue through the end of the syringe to lap up the nectar. After three weeks the bones healed, and after ascertaining the bird could fly, I released it back into the wild.

Once again, I was amazed at the intricate detail with which God designs and cares for a multitude of creatures. Not only did He create such a beautiful and unique animal as the hummingbird, but He also provided perfect healing in this seemingly insignificant little creature. Scripture tells us that if He cares this much for the birds of the air, how much more does He care for us. What a comforting thought that we have a heavenly Father who knows and cares about the tiniest details of our lives.—Ellen Fannon

Cast your cares on the LORD and he will sustain you;
he will never let the righteous be shaken.
—Psalm 55:22 (NIV)

AUGUST 6

Below the Surface

Search me, God, and know my heart; test me and know my anxious thoughts. See if there is any offensive way in me, and lead me in the way everlasting.

—PSALM 139:23–24 (NIV)

WHILE WE WERE visiting Hawaii, my family went snorkeling at Hanauma Bay Nature Preserve on the southeast coast of Oahu. Thankfully, one doesn't need to be an experienced swimmer or snorkeler to enjoy the myriad marine life beneath the pristine waters in this calm and lovely bay. It was an unforgettable experience. The colorful fish were beautiful and abundant—parrotfish, butterfly fish, sunny yellow tangs, and even slithering eels.

I felt a tingle of delight when a green sea turtle leisurely swam past right in front of me. I rejoiced in seeing a part of God's creation that I'd never experienced before. While standing on the beach staring out over the water, I had no hint of the splendors below the calm surface. I had to plunge into the sea to enjoy the beauty concealed there.

The experience made me realize that Christ can easily see below the surface of my being—deep into my heart and mind. He understands my motives, my hopes and dreams. Yes, He can also see my inner rebellion, even when I may appear smilingly compliant to others. He knows when I embrace a modern idolatry, harbor bitter feelings toward someone who has wronged me, or hold a grievance against someone I love. Nothing escapes His notice.

On the other hand, it's a great comfort to know that Jesus can also see the goodness below the surface as I patiently endure a snub when I've been wrongly misjudged or received an undeserved rebuke. He sees it all. He knows and cares. And best of all—as I experience the wonder of nature, Jesus is always beside me, whether on land or in the sea. —Shirley Raye Redmond

Even Death and Destruction hold no secrets from the LORD.
How much more does he know the human heart!
—Proverbs 15:11 (NLT)

AUGUST 7

Warning Swarm

Ears that hear and eyes that see—the LORD *has made them both.*

—PROVERBS 20:12 (NIV)

PAM, VAL, AND I were hiking one day when we heard a sound like none we'd ever heard before: a low drone that grew louder and louder the closer it came, as if something was overtaking us on the path. We looked overhead, but it wasn't an aircraft; it was an enormous swarm of honeybees!

"Uh, I'm allergic to bee stings," said Val, with some trepidation.

"Let's stop here then," I said, "and let them pass."

It was truly a remarkable spectacle, a dark, undulating cloud of bees passing over the trail and up the mountain, coupled with the sound of thousands of tiny wings beating the air. The swarm even cast a visible shadow—there were so many of them. But it was a fearsome sight too. We worried they might turn and surround us. We said a quick prayer for safety and watched in awe as the bees went on their way. Our path was safe and clear. Thankfully, we had heeded the warning sound.

This is just one example of a potential danger that has come my way and the warnings I've had to avoid it. I'm grateful my Father in heaven has given me "ears that hear and eyes that see." With these tools I can discern nearly everything the world can throw at me. Swarms of bees, people who seek to do me harm, temptations of all kinds that would lead me away from God—there are warning signs for all of them. Some of the warnings are more subtle than others; even the buzz of the honeybees wasn't clear at first. But using my eyes and ears soon told me all I needed to know, and my friends and I were kept safe.—Marianne Campbell

Dear Lord, thank You for my vision and hearing. Please help me to use the eyes and ears You've given me in ways that are pleasing to You. Amen.

AUGUST 8

Sentry Duty

Lord Almighty, the God of Israel, enthroned between the cherubim, you alone are God over all the kingdoms of the earth. You have made heaven and earth.

—Isaiah 37:16 (NIV)

ONE HOT SUMMER afternoon, I took a much-needed day off to visit the zoo with my son. I'd been working a lot and had constant anxiety about launching a book I'd recently finished. I knew I needed a break.

After we spent some time admiring the fennec fox and watching the lemurs swing in their enclosure, we arrived at the meerkats. I noticed quite a few burrow openings scattered across the exhibit. Native to southern Africa, these small mammals are experts in living underground, and their burrows contain multiple rooms and entrances. They are also extremely social, taking turns hunting for food and babysitting newborn pups. As prey animals, one of their important duties is to keep guard against predators.

A meerkat lay on the ground against the glass of the exhibit with his hind legs sprawled out. He did not mind that I stood so close to him on the other side of the window. I could tell he was relaxing but not sleeping. And he could rest because another meerkat had taken up the duty of sentry. Perched on his hind legs on the highest mound, the watchman looked for danger. In the wild, he would alert the mob with a high-pitched call if he saw a large animal or raptor so the others could scatter or hide.

As I looked intently at the cute animal stretched out and breathing deeply, I realized that I, too, could relax. The stress of launching a book had caused me to toss and turn in my bed at night. Worry plagued me during the day. But I could trust in the wisdom and sovereignty of God and rest in the knowledge that He was my Sentry, watching over all the details of my writing ministry as well as my life. —Mabel Ninan

Dear God, You are sovereign over my life. I surrender all my concerns and cares to You, and I receive Your peace and joy. Amen.

AUGUST 9

Pinkie the Opossum

For who makes you different from anyone else?
What do you have that you did not receive?

—1 CORINTHIANS 4:7 (NIV)

MOM OFTEN TELLS me about the animal adventures she experiences living on eight acres of land in the country. Abandoned cats and dogs sometimes wander up to her doorway. She feeds them and does her best to find them good homes. For a while, a feral cat family lived in her backyard.

One day I visited her at dinnertime. As night fell, her kitty friends gathered for their evening meal. I watched them slink around the edges of the darkness meowing softly at each other. A second glance revealed a strange-looking cat waddling up to the food bowl.

"I call him Pinkie," Mom said, with a twinkle in her eye, "because he has a pink nose."

"What's wrong with his tail?" I said, squinting into the ever-growing darkness. "And it has no fur." At Mom's chuckle, I flipped on the porch light for a better look. There, sitting shoulder to shoulder with the feral cats and munching from the food bowl, was an opossum.

"That's an opossum!" I said. "Why don't the cats chase him away? Or why hasn't he chased them away?"

"I think they're thankful they get to eat," Mom said. "They're not about to squabble over who has a right to be there and who doesn't. Maybe they realize none of them is entitled to eat. They're all here by my good graces."

I never expected a pack of feral cats and an opossum to teach me a lesson in generosity and gratitude, but there it was, playing out in front of my eyes. *How often are you reluctant to share what God has freely given you,* the Spirit whispered to my heart. *And how quickly do you forget that everything you have comes from God's generous hand?* When Jesus sent out His disciples to minister in His name, He reminded them to give to others as generously as He had given to them. If Pinkie the Opossum and his kitty friends learned to share what they'd been given with grateful hearts, I think I can too.—Lori Hatcher

Freely you have received; freely give.
—Matthew 10:8 (NIV)

AUGUST 10

Never Alone

For He Himself has said, "I will never leave you nor forsake you."

—HEBREWS 13:5 (NKJV)

SOME OF MY family's favorite animals to visit at the Denver Zoo are the sea lions. We always grab the zoo's daily schedule, so we'll know what time they'll be fed, then we find a table and a snack while we watch a couple of trainers offer interesting information as the sea lions swim and jump and bark for their fish.

Being kept in captivity means these sea lions are safe from the apex predators common to their natural homes. One of the most difficult parts of being a baby sea lion, I would think, is that after Mama and her baby bond for a couple of weeks, she must go out and fish to keep both her and her pup alive. Unlike other species, sea lions don't enlist aunties or other family members to watch over the pups when Mama has gone. No—they are left all on their own until the mother returns.

There have been times in my life when I've felt completely abandoned and all alone, yet I know God promises He is always with me and will never forsake me. In those moments when I feel as if everyone I know has deserted me, it helps me to remember Jesus, who Himself felt forsaken by the Father on the cross (Mark 15:34).

When I pray and reach for God's presence, I know I am safe from apex predators as long as I'm in His arms. There I will find rest.—Deb Kastner

And He said to them, "Come aside by yourselves to a deserted place and rest a while."
—Mark 6:31 (NKJV)

AUGUST 11

Those Pesky Mosquitoes

But if serving the LORD seems undesirable to you, then choose for yourselves this day whom you will serve, whether the gods your ancestors served beyond the Euphrates, or the gods of the Amorites, in whose land you are living. But as for me and my household, we will serve the LORD.

—JOSHUA 24:15 (NIV)

MOSQUITOES ARE OFTEN jokingly called the Minnesota state bird. In other words, they are quite plentiful in our state. I know they are food for pond creatures, but other than that, they are just pests to me. What was God thinking?

I decided to look on the internet to find out if mosquitoes had any useful qualities besides being food for toads and frogs. Under the question, "What good do mosquitoes do in the world?" nothing was listed. In fact, some mosquitoes can be quite deadly! I don't want to meet up with the ones in the west Nile, nor do I want to mess with the tsetse flies. My Minnesota mosquitoes are pesky, but not that dangerous.

Searching the web for a positive contribution of mosquitoes made me wonder about my legacy. What good do I do? God made us to be servants to help others, care for His creation, and spread His love. Is this what I am doing on a daily basis? Or am I just a pest?

I enjoy reading, watching TV, and socializing, but frankly that's not what I want written on my tombstone. I would hope there might be a few words about service to others. I need to do more foot washing and less grandstanding. I decided to get in my car, drive to the local food bank, and offer my services. I knew they were searching for volunteers, and I had some extra time to give.—Linda Bartlett

Volunteers don't get paid, not because they're worthless,
but because they're priceless.
—Sherry Anderson

Mission Impossible

The thief comes only to steal and kill and destroy; I have come that they may have life, and have it to the full.

—JOHN 10:10 (NIV)

A SMALL NOISE DISTURBED the silence. I looked up from my reading, but the sound had stopped. I went back to my book, but there it was again, this time louder. Out of the corner of my eye, I saw the tail of a red squirrel hanging down from above the window.

Confused, I watched the tiniest hands and face peek through the glass. The squirrel began rattling the screen. He reappeared and then dropped his entire body to the middle of the window. With arms and legs spread, he crawled back to the corner of the screen, grabbed it with both hands, and violently shook it. Thankfully the window was closed, as he was on a mission to get inside.

I slowly moved over to the window to take a video. No one would ever believe this. The squirrel scurried back and forth on the window, trying to find a way in and desperately attacking that screen with every bit of strength he had. Can you imagine the destruction a red squirrel could do inside my home? He might be small, but he'd be a mighty intruder in a place where he did not belong.

Our Lord is the opposite. He brings peace, love, joy, growth, and life. He does not have a mission of destruction; He only wants the best for me in absolute abundance. Similar to a river overflowing the bank, the life Christ gives has no boundaries and cannot be held back. This gift of life is free for the asking and given with incredible love.—Twila Bennett

Lord, thank You for the way You see me. I am blessed for the life You have given me through Your Son. I am in awe that You only want what is best for me. Amen.

AUGUST 13

The Toad in the Road

For the Spirit God gave us does not make us timid,
but gives us power, love and self-discipline.

—2 TIMOTHY 1:7 (NIV)

LET ME START by saying, I love toads.

My affinity for them probably goes all the way back to my mom reading the Frog and Toad book series to me when I was a child. I've always found toads to be whimsical and cute. Not to mention, I truly appreciate their excellent bug control.

Yesterday after some rain cleared, I noticed one of the smaller toads that lives in our yard had jumped into the road. Toads love sidewalks and roads because it's easy for them to catch food there. The dips in the streets also provide little puddles that form breeding sites. Concerned for the toad's safety, I gently nudged it out of the road. After it hopped back into the yard, it became too afraid and wouldn't move any farther. I was satisfied the toad was back in the grass, but before going inside I waited to make sure it eventually jumped into the grass and away from danger.

Just like that toad, when I am faced with an unexpected detour, my natural instinct is to freeze. I allow confusion and overthinking to affect my vision of where I should go next. All the while, I don't realize God is directing me away from danger, toward green pastures. Second Timothy 1:7 is very clear that the Holy Spirit's work in our hearts does not produce the fruit of confusion or timidity. Rather, God offers us power, love, and self-discipline when we allow the fullness of His presence to shape our minds and hearts. I just have to trust him, even if He's nudging me away from the road before me.—Ashley Clark

The LORD is my shepherd, I lack nothing. He makes me lie down in green pastures, he leads me beside quiet waters, he refreshes my soul. He guides me along the right paths for his name's sake.

—Psalm 23:1–3 (NIV)

AUGUST 14

So That's the Reason!

Every good gift and every perfect gift is from above, and comes down from the Father of lights, with whom there is no variation or shadow of turning.

—JAMES 1:17 (NKJV)

THE FLASH OF blue beckoned me to the window to see if the indigo bunting had returned to our bird feeder. But my attention was drawn instead by something else—weeds. They had been growing outside our window for weeks now. Multiple excuses kept my husband from hitting them with the Weedwacker. I almost went out and yanked them out of the ground, but back trouble kept me from doing that again. The last time I tried pulling those tall weeds out, I ended up on the concrete carport, unable to stand. I had to crawl inside, since no one could hear my cry for help.

With a deep sigh, I tried to look past the weeds and find the bunting. But then, something else caught my eye. The morning dew sparkled on a horizontal weed frond…no, wait! That was not a slim leaf but a spider's web connecting two of the plants. A black-and-yellow garden spider hung from the horizontal anchor. As I watched, he swung to the right and grabbed another stem. After attaching his web, he dropped down again and swung to the left. Up and down, across and through, round and round, he designed a predator's masterpiece. Later in the day, I returned to find the spider winding web strands around a small insect stuck to the web.

If those weeds hadn't been there, I wouldn't have had the joy of watching so closely while the spider did his thing to procure his lunch. I guess God had a reason for the weeds—a gift for the spider and for me. I just needed to look closer. —Cathy Mayfield

Walk of Faith: *When things seem out of place or a cause for chaos, look closely to see God's fingerprints in the midst.*

AUGUST 15

Whose Garden Is It Anyway?

For in him all things were created: things in heaven and on earth, visible and invisible, whether thrones or powers or rulers or authorities; all things have been created through him and for him.

—Colossians 1:16 (NIV)

WE HAVE YUMMY conifers in our yard (yes, some conifers can be eaten). Delectable daylily buds. Fragrant ripening tomatoes and other vegetables. A cherry tree. Birdseed galore. And all the critters that are attracted to these food sources in our yard and garden.

My husband, Jeff, takes a defensive posture. Despite his efforts, sometimes we are thwarted. We must replace trees and plants. We lose crops. Our sod is torn up. Carpenter bees make perfectly round holes in our wood decking. Some flowers never bloom because the buds were eaten.

One particular day was especially discouraging. We had huge, ripe, ready-to-pick-tomorrow tomatoes bursting on our vines. We got up that morning to disaster. All the ripe tomatoes had a bite taken out of them by groundhogs on their early morning foraging.

"I don't mind sharing, but must they ruin every tomato?" I felt aggrieved at their destruction. After all, it's our garden. *Or is it?*

I recently read Mary Ann Hoberman's picture book *Whose Garden Is It?* in which a woman stops to admire a beautiful garden. "Whose garden is it?" she inquires. The gardener says, "It's clear as can be! This garden you see belongs only to me!"

No sooner has he said this than up pops a rabbit, then a woodchuck, a bird, a bee, a butterfly, a snake, a squash bug, a mole, a squirrel, and others that disagree with the gardener's statement. They make their claim on the garden as well.

So, whose garden is it? My husband and I are mere caretakers. Birds, animals, and insects live and thrive within the space, extracting sustenance from the items that grow in our soil. But the owner? Scripture repeatedly reminds that it's God who owns our little garden and indeed all of creation—including those juicy tomatoes with one little bite out of each of them.—Darlene Kerr

All things bright and beautiful, all creatures great and small,
all things wise and wonderful, the Lord God made them all.
—Cecil F. Alexander

He Is My Lion

The lion, king of animals, who won't turn aside for anything.

—PROVERBS 30:30 (NLT)

IN THE DARKNESS, the loud roar of a lion hushed the crowd, and an air of excitement filled the room. This was our signal that the movie was about to begin! Leo the Lion was a famous mascot for the Hollywood film studio Metro-Goldwyn-Mayer, and he was my first introduction to the "king of the jungle." In the early 1950s, that magnificent lion with its bellowing roar was a wonderment to my young ears.

Once I visited a wildlife sanctuary where lions roamed in their natural habitat. The male in the pride had paws as big as my head! I was grateful to be safely in the safari bus, but I would have loved to pet him and get an up-close look at him. The vibration of his roar made the hair stand up on my arms.

While the male was clearly the leader of the pack, the mamas were the mentors, teaching the young lions how to stalk, play hide-and-seek, and wrestle, all without getting hurt. When I was raising my son, I would wrestle with him, rolling and romping in the living room—we called it "wooly-boogering." I was careful to make sure my young son never got hurt—and now he is careful not to hurt me when we do a little (mock) wrestling.

My heavenly Father is both leader of the pack and mentor. He is mighty and strong but always considers my weakness. He teaches me about love and forgiveness. He will never hurt me.—Randy Benedetto

Heavenly Father, Your Son is called the Lion of Judah, representing Your courage, might, power, strength, and majesty! I am awed by You! Thank You for being kind and gentle with me. In Jesus's name. Amen.

AUGUST 17

Twinkling Memories

Now faith is confidence in what we hope for and assurance about what we do not see.

—HEBREWS 11:1 (NIV)

GROWING UP, I spent part of every summer in the Smoky Mountains. Blue-green ridges rolled in every direction, the cool air smelled like magnolias and peaches, and every night the garden lit up with thousands of twinkling fireflies that spangled the darkness with a beauty so magical I couldn't believe they were real. My grandmother showed me how to cup them gently in my hands and watch their light shine through my fingers.

Back in the Smokies with my family this summer, I pulled a shawl around my shoulders and sat on the porch looking out at the sunset. The mountains were undisturbed by time. I thought of happy times shared with my parents and grandparents and stories of their experiences in this same place before I was born.

Then I remembered the fireflies. *Where were they?* The garden should have been filled with their twinkling, but I saw nothing. Deflated, I went inside. My daughter suggested there were too many houses now for fireflies. My husband said perhaps my memory was exaggerated. I thought back. Sometimes my grandmother and I had to look hard to find them. One place we could count on was under the big hemlock tree.

I went back out and crossed the yard to a large tree whose limbs swooped gracefully to the ground. I pushed into the little space inside the branches. There were the fireflies, lighting up the shadows, as incredible as ever.

I fell asleep that night with cool mountain air coming through the screens and my mind filled with beautiful memories of silent firefly fireworks shows. I thought how often the world tries to downplay God's presence in our lives. But just like those fireflies, God is always present—I sometimes just need to look in the right places to see Him light up the darkness as He has done for generations before me.—Lucy H. Chambers

God gave us memory so that we might have roses in December.
—J. M. Barrie

AUGUST 18

Beware the Thieves!

Further, my brothers and sisters, rejoice in the Lord…it is a safeguard for you. Watch out for those dogs, those evildoers.

—PHILIPPIANS 3:1–2 (NIV)

MY HUSBAND PLACED our picnic hamper on the wooden table, and I anticipated a leisurely lunch in the mountains beside a gurgling stream. It was a perfect summer day in New Mexico with deep blue skies, sun-dappled trees, and a cool breeze. As we began to unpack our sandwiches and chips, a scrub jay flew boldly into our secluded nook. It was soon followed by a second jay and then a third. Jokingly, Bill declared, "Bandits, twelve o'clock high."

The jays squawked noisily as though demanding a snack. The birds didn't seem afraid of us at all, and I suspected they intended to steal our food the first chance they got. I was right. As I leaned forward to retrieve a can of soda from the hamper—*whoosh*—a fourth jay swooped down from a nearby tree and flew off with half my ham sandwich.

"You little thief!" I exclaimed.

When one of the jays boldly fluttered up onto the far end of the table, we realized that we wouldn't be able to eat in peace. We reluctantly packed up and retreated to our vehicle. Frankly, I felt robbed. I didn't resent losing half a sandwich, but the birds had also stolen the joy of our planned picnic.

I sometimes let people rob me of anticipated joys too. There's a name for a person like that: *killjoy*. Paul's letter to the Philippians cautions believers about allowing others to steal our joy in the Lord. I know, too, that Satan is always looking for opportunities to upset my peace of mind, to fill my heart with doubt and despair. I stay alert. I'm watchful. If they have a chance, the killjoys will steal so much more than my sandwich.—Shirley Raye Redmond

Joy is strength.
—Mother Teresa

AUGUST 19

When Dusty Didn't Trust Me

The fear of man lays a snare, but whoever trusts in the LORD is safe.

—PROVERBS 29:25 (ESV)

THIS IS DUSTY." The zookeeper training me to volunteer at the children's petting zoo unlatched the cage door. Inside sat the fluffiest rabbit I'd ever seen. Cloud-like ivory-colored fur puffed around his body and upright ears.

"He's an Angora rabbit and very easygoing." She reached inside and pulled him out. She gently transferred him to his back, his fluffy feet sticking into the air. "See? Most rabbits won't let you do this."

From the moment I met him and felt his unbelievably soft fur, Dusty was my favorite animal at the petting zoo. He seemed to like me, too, trusting me enough to let me hold him on his back.

But one day, when I picked him up and shifted him to his back, he flailed and kicked. I held on to him tightly so he wouldn't fall and returned him to his cage. My arm throbbed from the scratches he'd given me as I tried to figure out what had happened to make him react like that. Perhaps I hadn't supported him in the same way I usually did. Whatever I'd unintentionally done differently, Dusty no longer felt safe. He didn't trust me anymore. Thanks to the painful scratches, I didn't trust him as much either.

Not wanting a repeat of that incident, I never held Dusty on his back again. I still brushed him, petted him, and carried him upright to meet visitors, but we never regained the trust we'd once had.

My experience with Dusty makes me recognize how fragile trust is in all relationships. Time and again, someone close to me has betrayed my trust. After trust is broken enough times, I wonder if I can really trust anyone. But then the glorious answer comes—I can trust God. He will never betray my trust. He is faithful to me even when I am faithless.—Jerusha Agen

If we are faithless, he remains faithful—for he cannot deny himself.

—2 Timothy 2:13 (ESV)

AUGUST 20

Never Too Busy

But encourage one another daily, as long as it is called "Today," so that none of you may be hardened by sin's deceitfulness.

—HEBREWS 3:13 (NIV)

I BABYSAT MY FRIEND'S son for a couple of hours one summer afternoon. When she came to pick him up, she lingered at my door and fidgeted with her purse. She talked about her husband's recent health diagnosis and expressed her concern for his well-being, fearing the worst for their future. I took her shaky hand in mine and started praying as tears rolled down her cheeks. We hugged goodbye, and she left with her son.

Later that day, when my son and I came home from an errand, we saw a black cat wandering outside our door. As dog owners, we craved the company of cats and welcomed any opportunity to pet them. We called and signaled for the feline to come to us, but she was shy. We decided to sit on the steps outside our door to see if she would warm up and approach us. After a few minutes, the cat meowed and walked toward us in slow motion, her tail held high. She allowed us to rub her back and stroke her head. Soon, she lay down near our feet, feeling content.

As I reminisced on the events that transpired near my door that day, God impressed upon me that I can only love others when I make myself available to them. That stray cat came around when I waited for her. When my friends know I'm willing to spend time listening to them, they can open up to me, giving me opportunities to pray with or help them.

I was motivated to declutter my calendar and create more white space in my daily schedule. I don't want to be so busy that I miss opportunities for God to use me as His instrument of blessing to others.—Mabel Ninan

He who is too busy doing good finds no time to be good.
—Rabindranath Tagore

AUGUST 21

Solid

Everyone then who hears these words of mine and does them will be like a wise man who built his house on the rock. And the rain fell, and the floods came, and the winds blew and beat on that house, but it did not fall, because it had been founded on the rock.

—MATTHEW 7:24–25 (ESV)

A RECENT TRIP TO Spain provided an opportunity to explore the countryside, where I noted that the chimney on some of the houses sported giant nests. White storks sat atop the nests, feeding their young. I watched them for a few minutes, observing the care they took in tending their babies.

One particular bird flew down to a field, grabbed a mouse, and brought it back to her fledglings. She perched on the rim of the nest. As heavy as she was, her homemade structure never budged or tipped. It was supported well.

I later learned storks build nests that can weigh up to half a ton. Tree branches can break under their weight and are too risky for rearing their young. So, to avoid a collapse, they look for sturdy foundations like electrical poles or brick chimneys. Homeowners are careful not to use their fireplaces until the hatchlings have abandoned the habitat.

It's important to choose a firm foundation spiritually, as well. In the seventh chapter of Matthew, Jesus shares a parable of the wise man and the foolish man who each built their dwellings on very different foundations. The passage explains the value of wisely positioning my heart, mind, values, beliefs—my entire world—on Christ. He is my only reliable foundation. When I place my trust in people, plans, or pursuits, I'm like the foolish man substituting sand for bricks and asking for disaster.

Just like those stork parents, I, too, want to choose a sturdy, unshakable footing for my life by following the Lord's precepts. Only then can I rest, knowing whatever comes, winds of change or storms of life, I am securely grounded in Him.—Tez Brooks

Let each one take care how he builds.... For no one can lay a foundation other than that which is laid, which is Jesus Christ.

—1 Corinthians 3:10–11 (ESV)

AUGUST 22

Guarding My Boundaries

It was you who set all the boundaries of the earth; you made both summer and winter.

—PSALM 74:17 (NIV)

SUMMERTIME MEANS RESTFUL evening walks. Once the sun dips toward the horizon, my husband, Stan, and I follow the lakeside road that winds through our neighborhood, deep in conversation about our day. Until we reach a certain stretch of woods, that is. Then Stan grows quiet, and I can feel him tense. He takes off his hat as he scans the trees, on the lookout for his adversary.

It doesn't take long. A large bumblebee look-alike zooms over and hovers in front of Stan's nose, keeping pace with us no matter how fast we walk. Swatting at it with his hat does no good, though Stan can't help but try. It often zips around and taps him on the back of the leg, which results in my husband executing perfect ballet twirls. While the bee has never stung him, Stan finds the whole experience unnerving.

Research leads me to believe our challenger is a carpenter bee. The male protects his nest from all intruders, which apparently include innocent walkers. The good news is that male carpenter bees don't have stingers.

This territorial insect caused me to wonder how well I protect my boundaries. So many things—and people—can encroach on my time with God. I sit down to read my Bible, and a text comes through or the dryer buzzes or I remember I need to take food out of the freezer for dinner. Sometimes the day passes, and I don't get back to that precious time with the Lord.

Short of getting in people's faces, I plan to institute tactics to defend my worship that include turning off the phone, closing my door, and tuning out distractions. I just hope I can do as good a job of guarding boundaries as that carpenter bee.—Tracy Crump

Try prioritizing God in your life by putting Him into your schedule and working everything else around Him.

—Joyce Meyer

AUGUST 23

Give Yourself Time

Wait for the LORD; be strong and take heart and wait for the LORD.

—PSALM 27:14 (NIV)

WE THINK OF August as a summer month, but nature knows better. The signs of autumn are everywhere. Blackberries are ripe, and the goldenrod is in full bloom. The first leaves on my black gum trees are turning red, and the ivy clinging to my farmer neighbor's silo is flowering. Ivy is one of the few plants that flower in autumn, making it an important food source for my honeybees. August seems like summer, but nature knows that a change is coming.

One sign of autumn I've been studying for the past week is a monarch butterfly chrysalis suspended beneath a hanging basket. Monarch caterpillars may spend their lives munching in the milkweed, but they seldom pupate there. They prefer to form their chrysalis in more protected places—beneath picnic tables or patio furniture, on climbing vines, or under sunflower leaves. Anywhere sheltered. This particular chrysalis is suspended beneath a hanging pot of petunias.

I first noticed the caterpillar—they're easy to see with those bright-yellow stripes—hanging upside down from a tiny patch of silk that it had spun. Slowly it formed a pale-green chrysalis, studded with tiny golden dots. But now the chrysalis is turning transparent, and I can see the veined wings of the butterfly. Tomorrow or the next day the chrysalis will be empty, and the monarch will be gone, ready to join her sisters on the long flight to central Mexico.

I am too often in a hurry, and it does me good to watch a caterpillar slowly evolve into who she was meant to be. The process takes time, and it cannot be hurried. *Give yourself time to grow,* I tell myself. I believe that God is at work in my life, but transformation does not happen overnight.—Louis Lotz

You do not just wake up and become the butterfly. Growth is a process.
—Rupi Kaur

AUGUST 24

Movement in the Shadows

For at one time you were darkness, but now you are light in the Lord. Walk as children of light.

—EPHESIANS 5:8 (ESV)

DURING A RECENT unexpected hospital stay, I gazed out my bedside window at the woods beyond the parking lot. The midmorning sunlight cast long shadows behind the larger trees that extended into the understory. I found myself fixating on a dark spot that appeared to me to be moving ever so slightly. I began to wonder if it might be a bear.

Nurse Kiesha came into the room, and I motioned her to the window, pointing out the location of the dark spot I had been watching. She, too, thought she saw it moving. Needing a break from the confines of the hospital floor, she felt her curiosity kick in, and I saw her bravely walk to the edge of the parking lot. After staying there only a moment, she turned and came back.

She returned and reported her findings. It wasn't a bear or even an animal. What we both thought we saw moving was a stump. How could we have both gotten it wrong? The combination of the sunlight's fluid motion, mixed with the shadow as it panned across the stump, looked like movement. It wasn't all wasted time. Nurse Kiesha got to stretch her legs and breathe in some fresh air, and we both shared a smile.

Reflecting on the incident made me realize something about shadows. Things aren't always what they seem. Shadows can make me question what is real and what is imaginary. They play tricks on me, and many times I get it wrong. This allows distortion, fear, and doubt to creep into my mind. The truth that seems to be hiding in the shadows is easily revealed when one takes a closer look. My perfect Light clarifies and removes my fear and doubt. It casts out what I allow my imagination to see.—Ben Cooper

Lord, help me fixate on You today as I walk in a world filled with shadows. Don't let the movement in the shadows distract me. Amen.

AUGUST 25

Minding My Place

Rather, in humility value others above yourselves, not looking to your own interests but each of you to the interests of the others.

—PHILIPPIANS 2:3–4 (NIV)

WHEN A PAIR of robins nested under the eave of my front porch, I thought little of it. They'd been there before, so their return was not surprising. We'd coexisted happily for the last couple of years, and I felt sure we would get along again. I hadn't accounted for the changes in the calendar, theirs and mine.

Mine had shifted ahead as some unseasonably warm days caused me to arrange my porch furniture earlier than usual. Theirs shifted later, due to an unusually cool and blustery spring. My desire to enjoy warm afternoons on the porch now put me in conflict with a frustrated pair of robins intent on feeding their chirpy hatchlings. We were officially under one another's feet for the next week or so.

When Saturday came, I was determined to enjoy my comfy outdoor room no matter what. Well supplied with beverages and snacks, I settled into my porch glider to watch a ball game on TV—Blue Jays vs. Orioles, as it happens.

Mother Robin left in a noisy flourish the moment I arrived. After that, she dipped back under the porch roof every few minutes—and not to check the baseball score. Seeing me still encamped in what she undoubtedly saw as their space, she performed a turn-on-a-dime maneuver and swooped out again. It was terribly annoying.

Between innings, I chanced to look up to the nest. For the first time, I could see the cause of all this ruckus. Two yellow beaks, wide open, were just visible above the shelter of woven twigs. Muting the television, I could hear their cries for food. It seemed I, not the mother bird, was the intruder.—Lawrence W. Wilson

Lord, help me to remember You are first, others second, and I am third.

Why I'm a Hero

Let each of you look out not only for his own interests, but also for the interests of others.

—PHILIPPIANS 2:4 (NKJV)

MY COUSIN MICHELLE'S son and daughter were in elementary school when I became their hero. It happened at a family outdoor wedding. I saw the kids playing near a tree and wandered over to see what they were doing. Michelle's son, Ben, pointed to the dirt at the base of the tree and looked up at me with his big brown eyes. "Can you catch that frog for us?"

I looked at the eager children, then at the frog at my feet. I didn't have much experience with amphibians. It was smaller than the palm of my hand. I wasn't afraid of frogs, but I wasn't so fond of them that I wanted to pick one up. I knew it couldn't hurt me, but it might be squirmy and messy. I pictured myself nervously dropping the frog as soon as it started kicking its little webbed feet.

I couldn't resist the little faces in front of me. Ben and Bekah really wanted to hold that frog. I slowly knelt, cupped my hands, and moved as quietly and sneakily as I could to scoop it up. I smiled. It actually felt kind of cool to hold a frog. I carefully handed it over to Ben.

"Thank you." He and his sister marveled over their new friend.

Later, Michelle came up behind me. "Jeanette, you are a hero tonight."

I laughed. "I'm so glad," I said. "It was a bit out of my comfort zone." Holding the frog was surprisingly fun, and the smiles on Ben and Bekah's faces were worth every second of my nervousness.

Looking back, catching the frog wasn't all that heroic, but it meant a lot to those kids. It was a small-but-meaningful reminder that following Scripture's teaching to look out for the interests of others can be as simple as taking a step out of our comfort zone to make someone happy. In the process, we often experience joy as well.—Jeanette Hanscome

Heavenly Father, make me more willing to say yes when I could say no. Help me to prioritize others' needs over my own. Amen.

The Hawk's Flight

God is our refuge and strength, an ever-present help in trouble.

—PSALM 46:1 (NIV)

WHEN WE FIRST moved into our house, the previous owner told us that years ago a hawk family nested in one of the backyard trees. The hawks must still think of my yard as their territory, because several times throughout the year—especially during the summer—I will see them flying over my yard. I am awestruck by the wonder of their graceful flight and beauty. But I don't want them in my yard! I have a host of songbirds and squirrels that I would like to keep safe from these majestic yet fearsome creatures.

A few days ago, I was sitting on my back porch when I noticed a large bird fly into some trees beyond my yard. I immediately suspected it was a hawk, and on further investigation, I realized I was right. Concerned it might be hunting one of my songbirds, I hurried out into the yard, and as soon as the hawk saw me, it flew away.

This interaction reminded me how the natural world often parallels the spiritual. While I have little to no defense against the "hawks" in my own life, the Lord scatters them with just one step into the proverbial yard. I often find myself preoccupied in mind and heart—even in prayer!—with trying to work harder to rid my life of all that might prey upon my peace. But in reality, I'm accomplishing very little. Instead, I can take refuge in the One whose presence scatters my enemies, even when His plans look a little different from my own.—Ashley Clark

Father, help me by Your Holy Spirit to invite You into my day, for I know You soar high above everything and scatter my enemies simply with Your presence. Thank You for always standing beside me. Amen.

AUGUST 28

Tenacious

Not only so, but we also glory in our sufferings, because we know that suffering produces perseverance.

—ROMANS 5:3 (NIV)

I DIDN'T NOTICE THE spider's web in the backyard until it was too late. I paid no attention to it until I walked right into the sticky silk web. Within a matter of seconds, I destroyed what the spider had worked diligently to create. The next morning, I walked into a different web in the exact spot. It seems the spider had spun a new web overnight. Feeling bad for destroying the spider's web twice, I determined to pay attention and not make the same mistake again. Only, while I played with my dog the following day, I ran right into a newly spun web dangling from the same tree as the previous two webs.

Three times that unshakable spider spun a web. Three times I unintentionally destroyed it. Looking at a newly spun web on the fourth morning, I admired the spider's perseverance. I admired its tenacity and determination. The spider didn't give up on creating a web, despite having to rebuild it multiple times. It didn't quit because someone ruined its hard work. The spider did not allow disappointment and defeat to stop it. Instead, she went right back to work each time, spinning another masterpiece.

The next time I feel like giving up when I face one challenge after another, one delay after another, I need to remember a tenacious spider in my backyard who refused to give up. I need to remember what God showed me through a spider who didn't quit, regardless of the obstacles. No matter how frustrating things become, no matter how often my plans are interrupted or destroyed, I need to keep doing what I've been called to do in Christ.—Sandy Kirby Quandt

Father, forgive me for getting discouraged and giving up too easily. Help me be tenacious like the spider and refuse to allow disappointment and defeat to stop me. Amen.

AUGUST 29

Turkey Call

Blessed are those who listen to me, watching daily at my doors, waiting at my doorway.

—PROVERBS 8:34 (NIV)

WHILE DRIVING ON an Indiana country road, I encountered a quartet of wild turkeys. As much as I was startled by the colorful group, I had to smile at the young poults waddling along, just under the feet of their mother. Seeing those gobblers reminded me of the occasions I spent with my grandma in Missouri.

Grandma and I would meander into the woods around her farm, searching for the game birds. We'd perch on a log surrounded by crispy leaves, where the turkeys' reddish-orange feet had foraged for acorns or insects. Eventually Grandma performed one of her turkey calls. Not a "gobble, gobble," but a yelp, which was part screech and part fingernails on a blackboard. But to a rafter of curious birds, Grandma's vocalization would sound intriguing and entice them to discover what fascinating tom or hen was preening just beyond the trees.

The call might have worked too. However, Grandma preferred conversing with me the entire time, stirring up the leaves and then deciding, all in a rush, it was time to move on. In a brief and noisy amount of time, Grandma was telling the turkeys, "Come when I call you," but when they arrived, we weren't there.

In my prayer life, I have wondered if I've behaved like Grandma…or at other times like the turkeys? When I petition God, do I become impatient and give up? Will I fail to hear God's answer because I haven't searched or listened for it? On the other hand, when God calls, will I show up? Will I believe that He will provide an answer, even if the timing doesn't seem right to me? The signs that God is working in my life are all there. I just have to trust that He will wait for me, whether I come when called or not.—Glenda Ferguson

Dear Father, when I call out to You, I will be still and wait, listening and watching for Your answer. Amen.

AUGUST 30

A Perfect Little Bath

The birds of the sky nest by the waters; they sing among the branches. He waters the mountains from his upper chambers; the land is satisfied by the fruit of his work.

—PSALM 104:12–13 (NIV)

MY HIKING BUDDY, Pam, and I looked with disappointment at the dry granite wall where the waterfall usually provided a refreshing show. A thin stream of water trickled unseen between rocks and drizzled over a large boulder as it traveled downstream.

"Looks like the waterfall doesn't run this late in summer," said Pam.

"Yeah," I agreed. "We'll come back in spring after a good rain. Then there'll be something worth seeing."

Just then, a hummingbird flitted by and landed in the tiny pool of water from which the drizzle overflowed. With twinkling movements, it splashed water over itself, shivered the droplets off, took a drink, and buzzed away.

"Well, obviously there's still plenty of bathwater for a hummingbird!" I said with a laugh, feeling refreshed despite the lack of waterfall.

What a great and generous God we have! He provides for all the earth. The hummingbird couldn't bathe in a deep pool with a strong current. The conditions of its bath were perfect for such a tiny creature.

After watching the little hummer, I realized I need to work on a couple of things. One is identifying the many ways God takes care of me perfectly, surprisingly, *always*, even when it doesn't immediately seem that way to me. I also need to work on my gratitude. In light of God's generous provision, how often do I thank Him? It was humbling to see the hummingbird take its bath, and it changed my perception of what seemed to be an inadequate trickle. No matter the time of year, God does marvelous things for all the earth.—Marianne Campbell

Walk of Faith: *Just for today, note some of the ways God has given you exactly what you need. As you realize it is enough, be satisfied and thank Him.*

Petapalooza

In love he predestined us for adoption to sonship through Jesus Christ, in accordance with his pleasure and will.

—EPHESIANS 1:4–5 (NIV)

EVERY YEAR I set up a booth at Petapalooza, a pet adoption event, and sell my books about animals. The best thing about this is that some of the proceeds of my sales go toward pet rescue, a cause I feel strongly about. My own pets are adopted.

Last year, one of the local shelters set up pens of available dogs alongside my booth. "Oh, he's cute," I said, reaching over to pat a brown, shaggy dog in the pen closest to me. "What's his name?"

"Spunky," the rescue worker said. "He's been with us for eight months and has not yet found his forever home."

"Let's hope today is the day," I said. I found myself constantly looking over to keep track of Spunky's prospects. He was cute, but a little too laid back to be a strong contender. People visited my booth but passed him by. *Will he ever find a forever home?*

Then, late in the afternoon, a young woman stooped and reached over the pen. Spunky's ears perked. He ran to her, his whole body wagging. The woman laughed and picked him up. They looked so happy together. I was thrilled when, later, I heard she'd adopted him.

I like to think of Spunky when I think of my own adoption into the family of God. Similar to that shaggy little dog, we are given the undeserved gift of being accepted into the loving family of God. Spunky's new companion promised to care for him, train him, take him on walks, and love him forever. When God adopts us into His family, He cares for us, leads us, loves us, and gives us a forever home too.—Peggy Frezon

Walk of Faith: *Consider rescuing a homeless pet, remembering how our Father adopts us and blesses us with a forever home.*

September

SEPTEMBER 1

Collars of Love

Now I will break their yoke from your neck and tear your shackles away.

—NAHUM 1:13 (NIV)

HOLDING BACK TEARS, I stood in our new backyard, calling his name. Melchior, our big, gray tabby cat, had disappeared again, leaving his collar behind. I ran my fingers over his engraved name tag. "Come home, Mel-Mel," I whispered. "We love you."

A few weeks earlier, we'd moved two streets away. Melchior was stubborn. He not only refused to wear a collar, but he kept returning to our previous house. At more than twenty-five pounds, his neck and head were jumbo-sized. Yet somehow, he'd managed to slip out of several collars we'd bought.

I hopped into the car and drove to the old home, still calling for Mel. Once I spotted him, his ample girth made him slow and easy to catch. He was too large for a cat carrier, so I just set him on the passenger seat and headed home. All the way, I talked to him. "This is getting old, buddy. If I leave the collar off, would you stick around?" Mel said nothing, of course.

I toted him to the backyard. There was no way he'd be happy as an indoor-only cat, so I offered a compromise. "I'll leave off the collar if you'll stay here." Melchior gazed at me with his big green eyes.

I wonder if God ever shakes His head at my own penchant for independence. When I slip out of the constraints and rules of life to roam, God doesn't put extratight shackles on me to keep me in line. Instead, He showers me with love until I fall helplessly into His arms.

The next morning, I was astonished to see Melchior waiting for breakfast alongside our four other fur babies. At dinner, there he was again. In the days that followed, I didn't force the collar on him, and Melchior stayed in the yard. What a gift that I can look to Mel-Mel as a teacher for deepening my faith.—Linda S. Clare

Walk of Faith: *What places in life restrain you like a collar? How can you let the love of God unshackle those areas?*

Doing It His Way

And if you faithfully obey the voice of the LORD your God...the LORD your God will set you high above all the nations of the earth.

—DEUTERONOMY 28:1 (ESV)

LET'S GO, GALEN!" I hurried toward the parked van with my Leonberger puppy, cheering him on. Five feet from the van, he plunked down on the parking-lot blacktop and refused to budge.

Galen had started such protests at eight weeks old. He loved going to new places, meeting people and canine friends. But when the moment of departure came, Galen would throw himself to the ground rather than get in the vehicle. When he was little, I could end his protest by picking him up. He hit sixty pounds at less than four months old, and forcing him into the vehicle was no longer an option.

Ironically, he likes van and car rides. But Galen loves what I ask him to leave even more. He's had so much fun, whether at a pet store or day care, that he doesn't want to leave. It seems to me he wants a life where he can do only what makes him happy.

I can't blame him. I've gone out of my way to avoid situations that aren't fun, that might be difficult or challenging. When God leads me to a place I don't want to go, I put on the brakes. But because He is in charge, I must follow where He leads me, despite my protests.

Galen didn't realize I couldn't let him stay in that parking lot forever—it wouldn't be safe for him. I couldn't let him do what he wanted because I love him and know what's best for him. Sometimes, God doesn't let me do things my way because He loves me and knows what's best for me. And just as Galen can learn to look forward to what awaits him at home, I can keep my eyes on the home God is bringing me closer to every day.—Jerusha Agen

Walk of Faith: *Make a list of difficulties you're avoiding or areas where you are resisting what God wants you to do. Then pray and ask God to help you embrace all His plans for you.*

SEPTEMBER 3

On-Time Turtles

But about that day or hour no one knows, not even the angels in heaven, nor the Son, but only the Father. Be on guard! Be alert! You do not know when that time will come.

—MARK 13:32–33 (NIV)

THE WHIRRING SOUND startled me the first time I heard it. A neighbor, apparently an avid fisherman, had installed an automatic fish feeder on his lakefront property. As the mechanism cast food pellets in a wide arc over the lake, I had to laugh. Dozens of turtles bobbed in the water, waiting for the bonanza. They must have set some internal clock to the feeder's timer, because I see them there at the same time every day now, eager to beat the fish to a free dinner.

If someone set the table for me, I'd show up on the dot too. But although I do know when dinnertime is, I don't know when Jesus is coming back. Even Jesus didn't know, so I won't waste time trying to guess. What I will do is make sure I'm ready for His return. Praying and reading the Bible help me guard my heart against anything that would displease my Lord. Serving through church or Christian charities keeps me focused on esteeming others better than myself.

But maybe the best thing I can do is obey His command to share the gospel. Not everyone flocks to Jesus the way those turtles flocked to the fish feeder. Some simply don't know about Him. They can't stay alert and on guard if they don't know Jesus is coming back for those who have committed their hearts to Him unless someone tells them. I can be that someone.

Though Jesus's return is not on a timer, I have no doubt He will come back because He said He would. When He does, I want Him to find me faithful, not bobbing along watching for Him but actively working to feed His kingdom.—Tracy Crump

Lord, show me someone today who needs to hear about You. Amen.

SEPTEMBER 4

The Facade

And to be renewed in the spirit of your minds, and to put on the new self, created after the likeness of God in true righteousness and holiness.

—EPHESIANS 4:23–24 (ESV)

"WHAT A WEIRD-LOOKING mouse!" I said with a frown.

The little creature had just run in front of a street vendor and me in Madrid, where I was finishing up a mission trip. The rodent's back legs were extra long, and his snout looked like a worm had attached itself to its face.

I later discovered the animal was not a mouse but an elephant shrew—a species native to Northern Africa but also found in Spain.

The shrew looks like a mouse with a small body, large ears, and a skinny tail. However, what makes the appearance of this animal so special is its elephant-like snout. It does look like a miniature pachyderm to me.

I was reminded of my own identity. During this weeklong mission trip, I had been identifying myself as a Christian (a.k.a. little Christ). But did I look and act like Him? Did the title "Christian" truly represent my likeness?

Sadly, I had to admit it often did not. I had grumbled about the long hours and had felt frustrated over language barriers and disappointed if my food wasn't perfect.

Not exactly Christlike at times. Thankfully, God used me daily (despite my faults) to help point people to Jesus. But how much more effective could I have been had I been more like Him?

On the flight home, I reflected on the likenesses and differences between that elephant shrew and elephants and between Jesus and me. I desire to be like this animal, to better look like and model the characteristics of the One for whom I was named—my Lord and Savior, Christ.—Tez Brooks

To be like Jesus, to be like Jesus! My desire—to be like Him! All through life's journey, from earth to glory, my desire—to be like Him.

—traditional hymn

SEPTEMBER 5

Web Extraordinaire!

I have trusted in the LORD without wavering.

—PSALM 26:1 (NLT)

FIRST THING EACH day I walk in my neighborhood. One morning, everything was bathed in light fog. As I was passing a neighbor's house, I was startled by a spider's web glistening with moisture. It was the largest I've ever seen. It must have been five feet high and four feet wide. Its anchors stretched between a tree branch and the ground. I stopped to admire it and saw that the center was an intricate, perfect design.

"How lovely," I whispered in awe. It must have taken that spider a long time to create this masterpiece.

Looking closer, I saw that its perfection was unmarred. In spite of its size, the web had caught nothing for the spider's sustenance. *Little spider,* I thought, *you didn't gain anything with your overboard web. Don't you think a smaller web stretching between two twigs would have been sufficient to catch yourself a meal?* Despite my quip, I was sure my words were meant for me as well.

I recognize my own propensity to overdo and overthink. I often choose to spin in personal overdrive—planning, worrying, strategizing, overdoing—acting as if it is all up to me to take care of me. My efforts leave God's provision out of the equation.

How is it that I never overdo or overthink my trust in the Lord? The theme of trusting God is a continuous thread woven throughout Scripture. Our heavenly Father's message is consistent: *Don't rely on your own efforts for your sustenance and well-being. Trust Me!*

As I continued along on my walk, I was determined to reside in that august company of men and women in Scripture who have trusted the Lord without wavering. I will join them in saying, "Your provision, Lord, is what I rely upon and expect."—Darlene Kerr

Walk of Faith: *Is there anything you're anxious about or overthinking? Take a few minutes to turn the situation or task over to the Lord. Tell Him, "I give this to you," and repeat those words whenever you are tempted to pick it up again yourself.*

SEPTEMBER 6

Uptown Herons

Keep on loving one another as brothers and sisters. Do not forget to show hospitality to strangers, for by so doing some people have shown hospitality to angels without knowing it.

—HEBREWS 13:1–2 (NIV)

WHEN I WAS a little girl, the bayou that runs through our city was so polluted you had to get a gamma globulin shot if you fell into it. In the mid-1980s, concerned public and private groups realized that it was a significant natural resource and began to care for the area—cleaning it, tending the landscape, and creating parks for people and for dogs.

As the waterway became healthier, not only did more people begin to use it, but also the big waterbirds, once so common in our area, began returning. Now it's not uncommon to see a snowy egret fishing along the bayou's banks or a yellow-crowned night heron hunched over and foraging at dusk.

One rainy evening, I returned home, driving cautiously because the streets were slick. Turning onto my street, my headlights swept across my neighbor's lawn. I was startled to see a pair of great blue herons, apparently out for dinner. Like the lord and lady of the manor, they strode around the yard, expanding and contracting their long necks, and occasionally thrusting their bills into the grass when they found an insect or a frog to their liking.

As I watched them, it occurred to me that they were like angels among us, only present because we had prepared a place for them. By cleaning up the bayou, we had allowed these glorious creatures to return. This little yard, once ordinary, now seemed like hallowed ground. I lifted a prayer to heaven, asking that I remember to treat the environment as sacred, creating room for the divine to dwell.—Lucy H. Chambers

Let me seek, then, the gift of silence, and poverty, and solitude, where everything I touch is turned into prayer: where the sky is my prayer, the birds are my prayer, the wind in the trees is my prayer, for God is all in all.

—Thomas Merton

SEPTEMBER 7

Desert Hideaway

You are my hiding place.
—PSALM 32:7 (NKJV)

MY YOUNG GRANDCHILDREN love to find bugs and critters in my backyard. We'd moved to the high desert in central Oregon, so there are new creatures to be found—like tiny lizards scampering around the sagebrush, rocks, and wildflowers.

"I don't think you can catch a lizard," I told my grandchildren as they went on a lizard hunt, but they found it an adventure to try.

"There it is!" I heard several times, but they had no success in catching one. I watched the kiddos run and stoop, and there was a point when a tiny lizard stayed still long enough so we could get a glimpse of it. But the slightest move toward it made it flee. We couldn't believe how fast this creature could scurry across the ground—lickety-split!

"The lizard ran under a rock, Grandma," my grandson said, taking my hand to show me. "Can you lift the rock to see if the lizard is hiding?"

With my two hands, I lifted the rather heavy medium-sized rock, and there it was—but not for long. We all watched the lizard as it fled like lightning into the sagebrush. The kids were amused by how this little reptile knew where to hide by instinct, under a rock with a small cove for an entrance.

I couldn't help thinking about my own life, and how I run like I'm in a marathon with things to do, sometimes getting ahead of God. A simple afternoon with my little ones reminded me that I have a solid Rock where I can run and hide to find safety, security, guidance, and rest. That Rock is Christ, my hiding place, where He waits for me.—Kathleen R. Ruckman

He hideth my soul in the cleft of the rock that shadows a dry,
thirsty land. He hideth my life in the depths of His love,
and covers me there with His hand.
—Fanny Crosby

SEPTEMBER 8

Wild Thing

The Lord is not slow in keeping his promise, as some understand slowness. Instead, he is patient with you, not wanting anyone to perish, but everyone to come to repentance.

—2 PETER 3:9 (NIV)

BUN-BUN WAS A little wild. Six years ago, the stray, butterscotch-colored, lop-eared, domesticated rabbit hopped into our lives, but she wasn't tame. I wanted Bun-Bun to stay in her roomy cage, which was actually a large greenhouse fortified with sturdy fencing. My husband argued that she should be free to roam our fenced backyard. We settled on letting her roam in our fenced yard on good-weather days, while keeping her safe from predators in her enclosure at night.

Bun-Bun tolerated petting, but only on her terms. If I tried to pick her up, she bolted away as fast as she could. And whenever she roamed freely, getting her to go back inside her enclosure was like a bunny triathlon. We must have looked ridiculous, corralling her with brooms and sticks, and shouting at the top of our lungs, "Go home! Go home!" But Bun-Bun had a mind of her own—willful, wild, and independent.

I'm a lot like Bun-Bun. Sometimes, I run away from the compassion, mercy, and grace God freely offers. Like our silly bunny, I'm fiercely independent and often a little wild, preferring to go my own way. Yet the Lord is patient, allowing me to run around like a willful rabbit before gently corralling me back to safety as I race into His open arms.

Our lop-eared rabbit might never be fully tame. But that doesn't mean we'll stop loving and caring for her. Every evening when it's time to go back into the greenhouse, she still leads us on merry chases before finally dashing inside. Through Bun-Bun, God is teaching me that it's okay to be a little wild too.—Linda S. Clare

Lord, thank You for keeping us safe and for accepting a bit of wildness in each of us. Amen.

SEPTEMBER 9

The Joy of Obedience

I'll whistle and they'll all come running...They'll remember me in the faraway places.

—ZECHARIAH 10:8–9 (MSG)

A MAN WALKING HIS dog on the path behind my home stopped to talk. I scratched his Australian shepherd's ears while he told me how attentive this breed is to their owner and how eager to obey. The man said he has only two small problems with his Aussie. First, the dog's desire to herd was so instinctive that it wanted to herd his horse, sometimes while he was riding it! Second, the dog once tried to herd his family when they were picnicking. After a few minutes of chatting, the man gave a whistle, and he went on his way, his trusting dog by his side.

I researched the breed when I got home and found a video of shepherding dogs herding hundreds of sheep on a hillside. As a whistle blew, they changed direction to move to the right or to the left, stop, or drive the sheep in. I noticed that the dogs' response to the whistle was slightly delayed, then the camera lens pulled back and showed that the shepherd was directing his dogs from half a mile away! They began to move as soon as the sound traveled the distance and reached them across the meadow.

Shepherding dogs were created with specific skills, but they must hear and obey their master to accomplish their purpose—even when they cannot see him. God has also uniquely designed each of us to do good works. He trains us to do His will and guides us throughout each day. It's up to me to listen to His voice, which I hear through prayer and reading my Bible. When I show my trust in Him by obeying His Word, I experience the joy and satisfaction of a job well done...even if I don't get a belly rub.—Randy Benedetto

Trust and obey, for there's no other way to be happy in Jesus,
but to trust and obey.
—John H. Sammis

SEPTEMBER 10

The Sweet Smell of Success!

To those who are perishing, we are a dreadful smell of death and doom. But to those who are being saved, we are a life-giving perfume.

—2 CORINTHIANS 2:16 (NLT)

I WOKE UP TO the distinct odor of skunk. The smell wasn't that unpleasant at first. But as I investigated outside, near the bedroom window, the scent increased in dreadfulness. As I approached our underground cellar, the odor rose up from the wooden staircase that led down to the closed door.

I needed reinforcements. After a bit of pleading on my part, my husband, Tim, tiptoed down the unsteady steps. Sure enough, he found the animal trapped. The stuck skunk smelled freedom and dashed up the steps to safety. As I observed the freed animal scuttling across our yard, I admired its shiny, luxurious fur coat. I was tempted to follow...but didn't. That is the last I saw of its ebony and ivory–striped posterior with its tail dragging the ground. After the smell dissipated, I commended the skunk's effective rescue plan. After all, its distress signal was so successful that I sniffed the seriousness of the situation right away.

That episode was a warning to me about how neglecting one part of my Christian life may seem fine at first. I didn't mind the skunk smell at first, but after several large doses, I longed for fresh air. I might skip my Bible reading once...or twice. Or not attend a church service...or two. However, after a prolonged period, I am in distress and long for the support of other believers.

In 2 Corinthians 2:14–15 (NLT), Paul describes the Christian life of studying Scripture and spreading the Word as being a perfume to God, a wonderful "fragrance rising up." I'm thankful God provides the "life-giving perfume" of hope and freedom, a sweet smell indeed.—Glenda Ferguson

Dear Father, please use me to be an example to others so that I might produce a burst of Christlike fragrance to those who desire to be rescued. Amen.

SEPTEMBER 11

One Determined Beaver

And not only that, but we also glory in tribulations, knowing that tribulation produces perseverance.

—ROMANS 5:3 (NKJV)

ALTHOUGH THEY ARE primarily nocturnal, I often see beavers in the daylight crossing one of the roads near my home. On a gorgeous sunny afternoon, I watched intently as a hefty beaver waddled across the two-lane road ahead of me. Due to its slow pace, I had to stop the car and wait for it to cross.

Beavers spend most of their time eating, building, or sleeping. Fresh water is essential to their lives, and Ohio provides plenty of streams and rivers for them to choose as home. Dams create ponds, which beavers view as the ideal habitat.

The beaver crossing in front of me probably weighed fifty or sixty pounds. It disappeared into the woods on the other side of the road. Soon it would be swimming in its water habitat with closed ears and nostrils, which would allow it to work underwater for extended periods. I marvel that the beaver's eyelids are transparent so it can swim with its eyes closed and still see. I wish I'd had similar lids—I might have avoided running into the end of our pool last summer, which resulted in a concussion.

As I contemplated the beaver, God whispered a truth. My life will require similar focus and determination if I hope to meet my goal of starting a Bible study in my home. Weeks after the beaver encounter, this Holy Spirit moment steeled my commitment to the new Bible study. Though I gave out forty invitations to churchmates, friends, and social media contacts, only four people showed up the first night.

In the following weeks, God reminded me of the beaver's resolve to get across the road. I needed it often when doubts tried to creep in. Faithfulness pleases God, even when results fall short of human expectations.—David L. Winters

Do not boast about tomorrow, for you do not know what a day may bring.

—Proverbs 27:1 (NIV)

SEPTEMBER 12

Flying in Formation

But God has put the body together, giving greater honor to the parts that lacked it, so that there should be no division in the body, but that its parts should have equal concern for each other.

—1 CORINTHIANS 12:24–25 (NIV)

WHEN MY FRIEND visited from India, the Golden Gate Bridge topped the list of places to see in the Bay Area. Upon arriving at the iconic bridge one afternoon, my eyes widened as I took in the sight of this towering landmark. My friend and I walked halfway across the bridge and headed back. As we hiked the pedestrian pathway, I saw a variety of birds soar over and under the structure. A remarkable V-pattern of flying birds caught my eye.

Brown pelicans sometimes fly in formation because it reduces drag and helps the flock conserve their energy. By collaborating on their flying positions, they achieve an aerodynamic advantage that allows them to beat their wings less frequently. Nature taught us humans an important lesson in the power of collaboration.

I could see this lesson in action during my friend's visit. He wanted to visit the Bay Area to connect with the Indian diaspora. I used my network of contacts to arrange for him to attend a few gatherings with Indian Americans who could support his ministry back home in India. A few days upon returning to India, my friend introduced me to his mentor, who ran a publishing house in the UK. I began a series of communications with the publisher about a potential book project I had been working on.

Like a flock of birds flying in formation, my friend and I helped each other out, filling in the gaps in our skill sets and resources. As members of one body, each believer has an important role to play. God has created us with a unique set of talents and strengths so we can complement one another in kingdom-building work.—Mabel Ninan

Alone we can do so little; together we can do so much.
—Helen Keller

SEPTEMBER 13

Stay Near

With my whole heart have I sought thee: O let me not wander from thy commandments.

—PSALM 119:10 (KJV)

TRACY, COME LOOK at this!" my husband, Stan, called through the kitchen window.

The tiniest squirrel I'd ever seen clung to the massive oak tree beside our driveway. Its unsteady movements told me it was not yet ready to leave the nest. We looked around for parents but saw none. Knowing we could do more harm than good if we tried to intervene, I called a local wildlife rehabilitation center.

The rehabber confirmed that it was usually better to leave babies alone. "Just observe for now. The mama is probably close by. She'll come take him back to the nest. If it gets close to dark and she hasn't carried him home, put him in a box and call us."

By the time I got off the phone, our little squirrel baby had wobbled farther up the tree out of reach. Stan and I left on our evening walk, and when we returned home, the squirrel was gone. No doubt his mother had rescued him—and had probably given his ears a good boxing too.

Whenever I feel I'm not walking closely with God, when I can't hear His voice or feel His touch, I stop and realize it's not God who has wandered away. I have. Often the busyness of life has dragged me from His side. I think I'm doing kingdom work, but then I look up and realize I can't see the King. The realization alone sends me running back to the Cross in prayer and Bible study. I don't have far to go because God is looking for me, too, and we're both glad I'm back in His nest.

But I wouldn't blame Him a bit if He boxed my ears too.—Tracy Crump

Walk of Faith: *The next time you feel God is far away, stop and read James 4:8 and Hebrews 10:22. Then pray for the Holy Spirit to fill you with His presence.*

SEPTEMBER 14

My Diligent Defender

Be gracious to me, O God, be gracious and merciful to me, for my soul finds shelter and safety in You, and in the shadow of Your wings I will take refuge and be confidently secure Until destruction passes by.

—PSALM 57:1 (AMP)

DAVE AND SUSIE own a lovely ten acres of land in the center of the Land of Ten Thousand Lakes, the lovely state of Minnesota. After a period of drought, many of those lakes were quite low, and most of the swamplands in the area had dried up.

Standing on his back deck, Dave's eyes scanned his property. Realizing that he hadn't walked the perimeter of his land for some time, Dave set off on a prayer walk. After circling the acreage, he started to make his way back to the house, cutting through what used to be wet swampland. He stepped carefully, as there were still some damp spots that could trip him up.

Suddenly, a male sandhill crane rose up out of the weeds just twenty feet from him. At his full height, and with his wingspan fully extended, the crane loudly objected to Dave's presence so close to the nest he was protecting.

Dave cautiously inched his way out of the crane's domain. He noticed that as he angled away from the nest and out of the swamp, the crane shadowed his movements, keeping himself between his family and the human intruder.

The wild bird was acting according to the instincts that were embedded in his nature by the One who is equally watchful of all those in His care. Whenever I am surprised by danger or the unexpected, I know that my Protector is aware of everything. He is there to stand between me and any harm that may threaten my life.—Liz Kimmel

Thank You, Heavenly Father, that I can rest and grow underneath the shelter of Your covering. Help me to recognize what is a true danger and what may just be a new experience that You have placed in my path. Amen.

The Wasp on the Ceiling

Are not two sparrows sold for a penny? Yet not one of them will fall to the ground outside your Father's care.

—MATTHEW 10:29 (NIV)

WE WERE RESTING on the couch with our three-year-old grandson, when he said, "There's a bug on the ceiling." He was correct, except it wasn't a bug; it was a wasp, and the ceiling was not a normal one but a cathedral ceiling that was far out of our reach.

Our first concern was for the safety of our grandson. Wondering how I could kill the intruder, I pulled out my phone and turned to Google. The first instruction was, "Don't kill it," because that would make it release its danger scent, which would attract other wasps. I read that wasps don't like to fly in high winds and thought turning on the ceiling fan might keep it restricted to the highest part of the ceiling. That worked, and the wasp stayed at the ceiling's apex, giving us time to come up with a solution for capturing it and ushering it out. I thought maybe a swimming-pool net on a long pole would work. We didn't have such a net, but a quick trip to Lowe's remedied the situation.

So, I readied my net, turned off the fan, and tried to figure out how to control the long pole with my arms stretched above my head. Miraculously, as if directed by an unseen hand, the wasp flew to the lower kitchen ceiling only a few feet from the back door. I opened the door, and out it went.

As I thought about this situation, I realized how wrongheaded my response had been. The Lord had a way to keep us safe and to save the wasp. I needed to control my impulse to solve everything myself, have more faith, and wait for God's still small voice.—Harold Nichols

Give your burdens to the LORD, and he will take care of you.
—Psalm 55:22 (NLT)

Wild Kingdom in My Hand

In his hand is the life of every creature and the breath of all mankind.

—JOB 12:10 (NIV)

RECENTLY, I ACCOMPANIED my daughter and her family when they rented a vacation home in a California town to attend a big celebration. Summer was exhibiting its usual brutal self, and the temps were a sweltering 108 all week. I felt sad there was no wildlife around to entertain the children. No deer. Few birds. All the pets seemed locked in air-conditioned kennels. No animals to greet us. At least, until ten-year-old Nick, my grandgem, found me in the house on a chair under an air-conditioning vent and showed me a photo on his cell phone.

"Look, Gramsey. I thought it was a worm at first. But we looked it up. It's a sharp-tailed snake. See how the tail looks like an arrow? That's for balance." Only a few inches long, the creature posed like a shiny ribbon curled across Nick's pictured palm. His voice had an *aww* edge to it as he described the creature, as if it were a cuddly puppy. Then he showed me another couple of phone photos of a tiny frog cupped in his hand, saying it appeared on the edge of the swimming pool.

He went back out, but soon he came indoors and proclaimed, "Gramsey! Look…a ladybug." He grinned, twisting his arm around so he could watch it explore his elbow. Then he bounced back outside to hunt for more wildlife.

While I sat inside the cool house, Nick darted in and out, announcing his latest find. Not only did he see an orange dragonfly, but he spied a bright blue one too. Suddenly, the scorching weather turned bearable, and my heart turned thankful. No, there weren't deer, birds, or pets milling about, but through Nick's eyes, I saw tiny miracles everywhere. God's wild kingdom in miniature.—Cathy Elliott

All creatures of our God and king,
Lift up your voices and with us sing.
Alleluia!
—Saint Francis of Assisi

SEPTEMBER 17

Lost and Found

For this son of mine was dead and is alive again; he was lost and is found. So they began to celebrate.

—LUKE 15:24 (NIV)

MISS MAK-EH AND Mr. Kepo were in love. Turtle love, that is. The pair of yellow-bellied slider turtles had come all the way from Florida with my step-grandson, but he could no longer care for them.

The turtles lived in our backyard in a large, metal tank with a heat lamp for cold days and plenty of rocks for basking in the sunshine. The pair spent their days sunning themselves, eating veggies, and doing whatever else turtles do all day. But one morning, my son made a terrible discovery. Kepo was gone.

My husband and I prayed for Kepo's safe return and put "Lost Turtle" flyers on telephone poles. But after Kepo's disappearance, days turned to weeks. I don't know how to tell if a turtle is sad, but it seemed as if Miss Mak-eh was grieving—she was no longer doing the things she would do with Kepo. I took the loss hard too. I prayed God would help heal our broken hearts.

When the phone call came asking if we'd lost a turtle, we rushed over immediately. Miraculously, our yellow-bellied slider had survived. We took him home where he scrambled onto the rock next to Miss Mak-eh, as if they'd never been apart.

Turns out, Kepo had crawled into a stranger's yard where he was discovered. Although we rejoiced in his homecoming, I don't know if Miss Mak-eh scolded her partner in her own turtle way.

Whenever I've wandered off, away from God, I'm thankful He welcomes me home too. He doesn't scold me or turn away from me. He rejoices in our return, just like we did with Kepo.—Linda S. Clare

Life takes you unexpected places. Love brings you home.
—Melissa McClone

SEPTEMBER 18

Flashy Feathers

Every good gift and every perfect gift is from above.

—JAMES 1:17 (NKJV)

ON THE OUTSKIRTS of a central Oregon town, the Petersen Rock Garden attracts many visitors. Placed artistically throughout the park, rocks from all over the world have been used to design castles, bridges, towers, and even the Statue of Liberty. Stunned by the rock formations, I took my four-year-old granddaughter's hand as we walked among the rocks and noticed all their colors—orange, purple, aqua, gray, blue, yellow, and other unique hues.

"God made so many colors," I said, noticing the resident orange cat my granddaughter chased. And then, another blessing of color caught my attention, bright and beautiful in the sun.

Peacocks strutted through the rock garden fanning fancy feathers. These social and enchanting birds made themselves at home among the spectators. Iridescent blue and green designs around the eye-like spots on the males' long tail feathers, bright blue necks, and tufts atop their heads gave a fairy-tale feeling at this unusual place.

Part of the pheasant family, peacocks are one of the most beautiful creatures on earth. Their brilliant colors vary according to the angle in which we viewed them. The color is affected by the bird's pigments and the structure in the feathers that reflects light. Peacocks can flaunt up to two hundred feathers on their tail, and their fluorescent train is like a royal cape when it flies short distances and when it sweeps the ground.

My granddaughter picked up a peacock feather that lay on the ground just before we left the park, and you would have thought she had found gold! Walking among these exotic birds made me think more about the *gift of color* in nature—and the opportunity to teach my grandchild that God's "crayon box" has colored our world.—Kathleen R. Ruckman

Dear Creator, Author of Art, help me not to miss the blessing of colors all around me, for it is Your gift for us to enjoy.

SEPTEMBER 19

Protect Your Heart

Above all else, guard your heart, for everything you do flows from it.

—PROVERBS 4:23 (NIV)

SNOWY LET US know he wanted to go out by standing at the door to the backyard and staring at us, wagging his tail. It was almost 11 p.m., but my husband and I were awake watching a movie in our living room. Thinking he had to pee, we let him out. He charged toward the fence. When we heard him bark and growl, we knew something was amiss.

"Snowy, come back here!" I called. When he came inside the living room, we knew exactly what had happened. Holding my nose with one hand, I scooped the pooch with another and rushed to the bathroom. A noxious odor and yellow stains on his white fur indicated he'd been sprayed by a skunk. I spent the next hour scrubbing him with all sorts of homemade concoctions.

The bad odor lingered in our home for days. To prevent future encounters with skunks, my husband checked the fence for any holes. He closed up an opening in the gate to the side of our house. Before going to bed at night, I made sure the gates leading to our garden were locked. I also searched the internet for ways to train Snowy not to go near a skunk.

As I considered measures to protect our dog and property from skunk encounters, I asked myself if I was taking precautions to guard my heart and mind from harmful influences. I evaluated the impact of books, music, and podcasts I had been consuming on my mental state. I also made a commitment to continue meditating on the Bible and praying daily to help me fight fears and insecurities that could, like a bad odor, spread into different areas of my life and limit my faith.—Mabel Ninan

Dear Father, please help me make it a priority to cultivate a heart that loves You above all. Give me Your wisdom so I can evaluate my choices and keep worldly values from taking root in my heart. Amen.

Second-Chance Spider

I long to dwell in your tent forever and take refuge in the shelter of your wings.

—PSALM 61:4 (NIV)

ONE LATE SUMMER day, I balanced the tiny brown and yellow spider on a napkin and yanked open the sliding door. "This is your chance," I whispered, and gave the napkin a shake. "Have a happy life." But when I looked, there she was, still clinging to the napkin's edge. That little garden spider didn't budge.

I'm not frightened by most spiders, but I don't want them roaming the kitchen counters or sharing my bed either. My rule has always been to try to put any invading insects or arachnids back outside. But if they won't go, well, then it's squishville. Over the years, I've had to dispatch many interlopers who refused to return to the great outdoors.

Yet something about this garden spider felt different. Against the white napkin, she gracefully lifted first one leg and then another. She didn't run or seem afraid. I don't know what she saw with her compound eyes as I stared at her with curiosity and awe—one God-inspired being to another.

I imagined she was a lot like me—ignoring God's grace and crawling through life. Many times, I've failed to recognize when God has called me to a better place or a new adventure. I'd rather cling to the familiar, safe places instead of sailing out into new territory, even after God assures me He'll go with me.

"I don't normally do this," I whispered, and walked outside. "But I'm giving you a second chance." I held the napkin next to a flower bed. This time, Miss Orb Weaver skittered away. Now, when I face new challenges, I think of that little garden spider and send up a silent prayer to the God of second chances.—Linda S. Clare

Lord, thank You for gently helping me out of my comfort zone and offering me a second chance.

SEPTEMBER 21

Owl Blessings

So if you sinful people know how to give good gifts to your children, how much more will your heavenly Father give good gifts to those who ask him.

—MATTHEW 7:11 (NLT)

THREE-YEAR-OLD BENAIAH CUPPED the owl call in his hands and followed my husband, David. Before our visit with our grandson, we'd shared with him via FaceTime about the owl we heard one night. Convinced his granddaddy could produce the owl upon command, Benaiah bounced up and down as he handed the man-made device to David.

"The owl might be sleeping, Benaiah." I wanted to prepare my grandson for disappointment; still I whispered a prayer: *God, please let us hear the owl tonight.*

David blew into the handheld call and a perfect *WhoWho, WhoWhooooo* broke the silence of dusk. Benaiah stretched his dimpled, small hands for the call, then moved the device to his lips. *Whoooo. Whooo.*

"Good job, buddy," I replied.

David and I made eye contact. The call didn't sound very owl-like, but it was a stellar first try for a three-year-old.

WhoWho, WhoWhoooo. Benaiah tried again to mimic my husband.

We listened. And heard only silence. David moved us farther from the house and closer to the woods. "Try it again," he said.

Benaiah pressed the wooden surface against his lips: *WhoWho, WhoWhoooo.*

As quickly as the sound left the call, not one but two owls replied in a cacophony of hoots, bantering back and forth. We watched them fly close. One landed in the top of a pine tree, just above us. The other perched in the oak nearby.

"Right there, owl," Benaiah said, pointing to the beautiful birds.

"You did it, Benaiah!" I was so excited that I practically squealed.

On the way back to the house, I sent up a prayer to the One who really brought the owls for us to see.

Thank You, God. What a treat!—Julie Lavender

An owl sound wandered along the road with me.
I didn't hear it—I breathed it into my ears.
—William Stafford

SEPTEMBER 22

Storms Rage but God Remains

But as for me, the nearness of God is good for me;
I have made the Lord God my refuge.

—PSALM 73:28 (NASB)

IN CENTRAL SOUTH Carolina, pop-up thunderstorms and high temperatures stroll hand in hand through our summer. On this particular day, weather forecasters predicted triple-digit heat with a chance of an afternoon storm. I hoped they were right—about the storm. My crunchy grass and wilted zinnias desperately needed a drink.

When the promised rain swooped in, it arrived with a squalling wind that tossed the trees and my hanging plants, including the geranium that housed a nest full of Carolina wren babies. The tiny birds, only a week old, hunkered down as the storm rocked their little houseboat.

Fearing the geranium basket would blow off the plant hanger and potentially injure the babies, I scooped it off its hook and tucked it securely into a nearby corner of the porch. Minutes later, Mama bird appeared with a bug in her mouth. She flew to where the nest normally hung, then did a 360 in the air. A few more passes confirmed her suspicion that her home was gone. She landed on the porch railing and tilted her head this way and that, wondering where her babies were.

By then the storm had abated, so I gently returned the geranium basket to the hook. Soon I heard happy chirps as Mama flew in, counted heads (or beaks) I imagine, and went back to work feeding her hungry brood.

As I reflected on the events of the day, I empathized with Mama bird. I know what it feels like to have my life interrupted by an emotional, financial, or spiritual storm. I take great comfort in knowing my loving Father is nearby and in control. He orders the events of my life, even the ones I don't understand, and watches over me with loving care. And those times when I have no clue what's going on, like Mama bird, I can trust He's overseeing my circumstances and working out every detail for my ultimate good and His glory.—Lori Hatcher

If we cannot believe God when circumstances seem [to] be against us,
we do not believe Him at all.

—Charles Spurgeon

SEPTEMBER 23

A Sign of God's Presence

You have made known to me the paths of life; you will fill me with joy in your presence.

—ACTS 2:28 (NIV)

OFTEN MY SATURDAY mornings are relaxing affairs with a big breakfast and many cups of coffee. But one Saturday a month, I lead worship at a nursing home, and those Saturdays look a lot more like weekdays. I get up early and fix breakfast for my family, and my coffee is a to-go as I run out the door.

A few Saturdays ago, I was running late and had forgotten some things I needed at the church. I parked across the street, got out of the car, and looked up just in time to see a fox dart across the church lawn.

This fox was one of the prettiest animals I have ever seen. His fur was such a perfect shade of red with black at the feet like little boots. His ears were perked as he listened for danger, and his tail was a fluffy cloud as he crossed in front of me. That little guy took my breath away.

In that moment I stopped and remembered what I was doing. Every day is a day to praise God; every day is a day to pause in wonder; every day is a day to "be still and know." That fox stopped me in my tracks and brought me back to myself. I didn't need to run around hurriedly. I needed to slow down and take notice of signs of God's presence.

When I got to the nursing home that morning, I told everyone there about the little fox. The smiles on the residents' faces were priceless. *How often,* I wondered, *is God trying to get our attention, but we are too busy to notice?* As I led the worship service, I realized that I, too, can be a sign of God's presence when I bring calm and peace to my day. Instead of wandering hurriedly through life, I can slow down, notice God, and share Him with others.

That little fox encouraged me to slow down and see that God's presence is everywhere.—Heather Jepsen

Walk of Faith: *Keep your eyes open for signs of God's presence today, even in places you least expect it.*

SEPTEMBER 24

Riding a Blind Horse

I will lead the blind by ways they have not known... I will not forsake them.

—ISAIAH 42:16 (NIV)

WHEN I WAS fourteen, my uncle asked me to ride his horse several miles in the mountains of West Virginia, pick up a team of horses he had traded for, and lead them back. I had never ridden a horse alone. I was a city boy, and this was quite a trust my uncle had placed in me.

I didn't know one of the horses my uncle had traded for was blind, and neither did my uncle! That's what's called "buying a pig in a poke," but in this case it was a horse! The owner of the team failed to mention that in the trade negotiations.

Before mounting that blind horse, I tried to gain his trust by letting him smell my clothing while gently stroking and talking softly to him. I grew attached to this creature. He put his trust entirely in me, and I was committed to guiding him safely home. I spoke softly to him during the trip, patting his neck and encouraging him on. I gently guided him through the mountains and around each rock in the twisty road and talked to him encouragingly as we crossed a stream. I even sang tenderly to him, which must mean horses are tone deaf!

I've never forgotten that trusting blind horse and our ride together. Just as I guided that horse on a precarious journey, God has led me safely down uncertain paths and ridden with me through troubled waters. He has reined me in when necessary and given me free rein at other times. He has said, "giddyup" when I have been lazy and "whoa" when I needed a rest. I have placed my trust entirely in Him, and I know He will guide me safely home.—Randy Benedetto

True faith is not the intellectual ability to visualize unseen things to the satisfaction of our imperfect minds, it is rather the moral power to trust Christ.

—A. W. Tozer

SEPTEMBER 25

Funny Friends

A friend loves at all times, and a brother is born for adversity.

—PROVERBS 17:17 (NKJV)

EVERYONE NEEDS FRIENDS—people who have your back and lend a hand when you could use one. But friendship isn't limited to the human species; some in the animal kingdom also form beneficial partnerships.

In Africa, the hornbill and the mongoose have a mutually symbiotic relationship—an odd friendship that benefits both of them. Why should the hornbill, a tropical bird, work for his grub—sometimes literally—when he can follow behind the mongooses, who can't eat everything they find and leave behind juicy fruit, insects, and eggs? They don't seem to mind that the hornbill is sharing in their loot. In return, the hornbill has the mongooses' backs. He keeps watch and sounds an alarm when he sees a potential predator.

I am grateful for all the friends God has put in my life, and I feel very blessed by my church community. I love worshipping the Lord together as one, and these friends have come through to help my disabled husband and me when we have projects we can't do or a lawn that needs mowing. Sometimes I simply need to unburden myself from the stress of being a caretaker to my husband, and the Lord has provided amazing support in the form of my best friend. While we can rarely get together face to face due to our circumstances, we email back and forth nearly every day, sharing the highs and lows of our lives with each other.

Just as I am grateful for my friends, I also try to be a good friend, whether it's providing a shoulder to cry on or sharing something I learned in the Word with someone else.—Deb Kastner

Thank You, Lord, for special friends who have my back and offer me support when I need it. May I, in turn, lend them the support they need to get through tough days. Amen.

SEPTEMBER 26

Do You Hear the Mockingbird?

You will keep in perfect peace those whose minds are steadfast, because they trust in you.

—ISAIAH 26:3 (NIV)

ALL DAY LONG, nothing had gone my way. I couldn't stop worrying about what would happen if I didn't get my project done. I hurried home to let my black Lab, Ruby, out of her kennel. I would let her out for a little and then hop back on my computer to squeeze in more work before dinner.

"Ruby," I called, and I heard her thick tail wagging. She was glad to see me, nonjudgmental about my agitation. We went into the backyard, and I promised her when I finished the project, we'd go on a long walk.

She poked around the yard, and I ran over scenarios for the project. Lost in thought, I was startled when Ruby came and sat next to me. She leaned against my leg and looked intently up at the sky.

"What is it?" I asked. Ignoring me, she continued to look up. I followed her gaze. A mockingbird sat on the wire, singing its heart out. Ruby was mesmerized. She continued to watch it intently as it gave us a full-throated concert.

We sat there in solidarity, appreciating the varied songs of the mockingbird. I thanked Ruby. If she hadn't made me look up, I would have remained stuck in my cycle of worry. As I rubbed her head, I realized that the project would get done. It would be as good as it needed to be. But if I didn't take time to pay attention to the everyday wonders around me, I would never find peace. I took a deep breath and asked God to help me be more like Ruby, a faithful creature who focuses on what is before her, instead of wasting her time trying to do His job.—Lucy H. Chambers

When peace like a river attendeth my way, when sorrows like sea billows roll; whatever my lot, Thou hast taught me to say, "It is well, it is well with my soul."

—Horatio Gates Spafford

SEPTEMBER 27

Have You Heard the One About...

I will be your God throughout your lifetime—until your hair is white with age. I made you, and I will care for you. I will carry you along and save you.

—ISAIAH 46:4 (NLT)

IT WAS A beautiful morning in Texas. Birds were singing and flitting from tree to tree. Neighbors raised hands in a wave. Dogs were being walked and young children played.

As my husband and I waited on the driveway for our ride to the airport, an old car with its windows partially down slowly cruised through the neighborhood. Charlie, nearing eighty years old, had Amelia with him. Amelia is his fourteen-year-old dog, now too troubled with the ailments of old age to be properly walked. Charlie pulled into my father-in-law's drive and stopped to visit with us. I glanced in the car. Amelia, a midsize mixed breed, was standing on a blanket-covered backseat, her skinny legs atremble.

Charlie explained, "I'm taking Amelia out for a turn around the neighborhood since I can't walk her any longer." After a few minutes, Charlie backed out of the driveway. In a bit, we saw them pass again, Charlie with Amelia, making another slow circuit.

An aging man, an old dog, and a worn-out car. Sounds like the beginning of a good joke. On the surface, perhaps. Yet, I saw beauty and reassurance in it.

As I watched the scene unfold, I sensed that God was showing me how to gain peace in leaving my father-in-law. I was reminded that God showers gentle care upon His aging children. When they no longer have strength, He carries them in tender companionship. His unfailing love bolsters them in the midst of infirmity and frailty. He is their fortress when bodies are crumbling. The Lord upholds His children to the end of their days, just like Charlie cares for Amelia.

I embraced my nonagenarian father-in-law as we left for our eleven-hundred-mile journey home. I draw comfort as I personalize Psalm 68:19: I praise the Lord for each day He carries Dad in His arms.—Darlene Kerr

Oh no, You never let go through the calm and through the storm. Oh no, you never let go in every high and every low. Oh no, You never let go; Lord, You never let go of me.

—Matt Redman

SEPTEMBER 28

Having a Moment

For we know that the whole creation has been groaning together in the pains of childbirth until now. And not only the creation, but we ourselves, who have the firstfruits of the Spirit, groan inwardly as we wait eagerly for adoption as sons, the redemption of our bodies.

—ROMANS 8:22–23 (ESV)

HIKING ALONG THE dairy farms of northern Spain, I noticed a hedgehog scurrying in the tall grass. This little guy froze when I approached. His back, covered with white and brown spines, quivered. He rolled up into a ball in an effort to ward off whatever predator he thought I was.

I used my jacket to carefully pick up my new little friend. I couldn't take him with me—this was his home. But for a moment, I enjoyed a look at God's creation up close.

He relaxed, opened up, sniffed my jacket, and squinted at me. He and I (let's call him Henderson) had a moment together. I enjoyed gently touching his tiny, mouse-like paws and pink nose.

To diminish any stress Henderson might be experiencing, I released him into the grassy meadow so he could finish his journey. After one last sniff, he scurried away.

I squatted there on the trail, reveling in the encounter—a moment perhaps not unlike what Adam may have experienced each day in Eden. Henderson had turned my thoughts toward my blessed hope. I suddenly longed for that day when all creation would stop its moaning for freedom from this fallen world.

So often, I get wrapped up in the here and now that I forget to consider my amazing eternal future as a child of God. But there will be a day when my Creator and I will be face to face. No longer will I deal with the consequences of the Fall. I will be perfected. No longer will I poke others with my quills of self-defense. I'll be in the Lord's hands. Praise God!—Tez Brooks

Father, help me keep an eternal perspective in all I do. Remind me that I'm not home yet. Focus my thoughts and eyes on You—my future, my blessed hope. Amen.

SEPTEMBER 29

Queen Guinevere

I was young and now I am old, yet I have never seen the righteous forsaken or their children begging bread.

—PSALM 37:25 (NIV)

I CALL MY FRIEND Susy's house Critterville because of all the dogs, cats, and chickens, but especially because of the squirrels that scamper around her mountain property. Susy's daughter Teddy is a certified squirrel rehabber and keeps a barn full of sick and injured squirrels. Once healed, they often take up residence. During one visit, I noticed a gray squirrel that came to the back door every morning.

"That's one of the mama squirrels," said Susy. She explained the squirrel had been injured and released while pregnant, so they'd left nuts for her on the deck, even though that was usually discouraged. Once after tossing the chickens some granola, I saw her run over and snatch a piece. She'd gotten a bit spoiled, making her a regular visitor.

I decided the squirrel needed a name. I chose "Guinevere" and dubbed her the "Queen of Critterville."

Susy eventually had to stop providing nuts on the deck. But I appreciate that, for a while, she and Teddy made an exception for a pregnant squirrel while she readjusted. Guinevere still feels at home on their deck, nuts or no nuts, knowing Susy's family will never let her starve. Their kindness brought back memories of the friends God used to provide for me and my sons when I became a single mom. Some went beyond what was typically done to make sure we had what we needed. I didn't show up at their doors expecting handouts, but I knew who I could trust when I had a need. Guinevere now reflects my desire to pass the generosity I received on to others so they will feel safe, loved, and provided for.—Jeanette Hanscome

A generous person will prosper; whoever refreshes others will be refreshed.
—Proverbs 11:25 (NIV)

SEPTEMBER 30

Fearless Feat

God, the Lord, is my strength; he makes my feet like hinds' feet, he makes me tread upon my high places.

—Habakkuk 3:19 (RSV)

EAGER TO HIKE, we burst out of the gondola atop Untersberg mountain in Germany. Yellow arrows displaying place names we didn't recognize and couldn't pronounce pointed in all directions, so it seemed safe to take any path. Interpretive signs helped us notice and, with a little help from Google Translate, identify wildflowers. Our favorite was a blood-red orchid that smelled like chocolate.

Soon we were alone on a path, and the signs were nowhere to be found. A fit young hiker approached, explaining he was turning back because the trail was steep, but we pushed on, hoping to reach a mountaintop refuge where lunch might be served. Scat underfoot revealed that other creatures had enjoyed a meal nearby.

Gorgeous views and abundant wildflowers lured us on. We descended ladders into dripping rock caves and sidestepped along scree on goat trails. We began to question the wisdom of our focused pursuit of lunch.

As we rounded the corner of the cliffside, we saw a mountain goat grazing on a grassy outcrop below us, unconcerned by his precipitous perch. We spied a larger outcrop ahead; this one supported a small cabin, its deck crowded with hikers enjoying fried potatoes and bratwurst. Quickening our pace, we discovered a scene farther below—a tiny goat kid was playfully and fearlessly scampering about his mother. Satisfied with fresh food and secure on the mountainside with its mother, the energetic little guy seemed the image of joy.

Contentment, freedom from fear, beauty. These are certainly the elements of joy. We delighted in the adorable kid goat and his patient mother as we took in a delicious lunch and incredible views. Our joy was multiplied by wonder and gratitude.—Susie Colby

There are no obstacles which our Savior's love cannot overcome, and that to him, mountains of difficulty are as easy as an asphalt road!

—Hannah Hurnard

October

OCTOBER 1

Simple Little Moons

Let heaven and earth praise Him, the seas and everything that moves in them.

—PSALM 69:34 (NKJV)

WALKING ALONG THE Oregon coast after a storm, I saw moon jellies in countless numbers decorating the beach. Often referred to as "jellyfish," these gelatinous creatures are not fish. They are invertebrates, having no spine, and they are closely related to corals and sea anemones.

As I strolled along the shore, the moon jellies had the look of another world—like silvery-white, translucent full moons. I kneeled to take a closer look, then I gently touched one. It felt squishy like Jell-O, adding to the mystery of this unusual creature. I wondered how they survived the crashing waves.

Later, at an aquarium along the coast, I watched moon jellies swim in a large glass encasement. I stood mesmerized by the beauty, as they resembled flying saucers, and their short tentacles reminded me of fringes on a parasol cascading through the water.

Marine scientists term jellies as *simple beings*: they do not have brains, bones, or lungs, though they do have organized tissues and a nervous system. They are made up of 95 percent water but have a digestive and reproductive system. Green fluorescent protein makes jellies glow in the dark, and scientists have used this protein for important medical research.

My ability to observe this glory in simplicity was surely the Lord's doing. As I think about the creature that resembles a full moon, I am reminded of the evidence and purposes of our Creator everywhere I look—to the heavens, all around me, or in the sea.

The Lord is showing me in my encounter with the jellies that there is a glory to observe in simplicity. Shall I not also look at other creations that seem simple—to see the profound?

I smile as I think about the moon jellies on the shore. It was as though the heavens were turned upside down for me, multiplying the moon and glistening at my feet!—Kathleen R. Ruckman

There is no greatness where there is not simplicity, goodness, and truth.
—Leo Tolstoy

Eagles They're Not

But those who hope in the Lord *will renew their strength. They will soar on wings like eagles; they will run and not grow weary, they will walk and not be faint.*

—Isaiah 40:31 (NIV)

I NEARLY STEPPED ON the poor bird sleeping in the detritus of a fallen fir stand in eastern Oregon. But as I walked out of its way, the bird—a nightjar in several shades of brown—nestled back into the debris of wood chips and leaf litter, a perfect camouflage for the little guy. I thanked God I'd missed him.

Sometimes called nighthawk or poorwill, a nightjar is an unassuming bird. I wondered how it ended up with that name. At first, I thought of its shape—the nightjar I saw was a little bit pear-shaped, something my middle-aged body sympathized with. But a quick internet search showed me that in Europe's Middle Ages, these birds were called nightjars because their calls were literally jarring.

Other monikers were just as unflattering. Some superstitiously thought the birds sucked the milk from goats—goatsuckers. In America, Nebraskans knew that nightjars eat insects and called them Bug-eaters. But one word in the description of these birds is *meek*.

Unlike birds of prey such as eagles, nightjars catch insects with their short beaks, not their talons. In fact, as I watched the bird run from my inadvertent disturbance, I had to laugh. Its tiny feet made it look comical until long, sharp wings lifted it from the ground. Then it settled back into its hiding place, blending perfectly with its surroundings.

God promises that those who wait upon Him will rise up and soar like eagles, and I've had a few of those exhilarating moments. But mostly, day to day, I'm more like a nightjar, quietly receiving God's sustenance and grace and submitting to His Word.—Linda S. Clare

Walk of Faith: *Serve someone anonymously, and you just might feel as if you're soaring like an eagle.*

OCTOBER 3

The Company We Keep

Do not be misled: "Bad company corrupts good character."

—1 CORINTHIANS 15:33 (NIV)

MY SON WORKS late hours. One night he came home and let his German shepherd/husky mix, Ginger, out into the backyard. Then he took a shower. When he went to let Ginger in, she was nowhere to be found. She had jumped the fence, knocking over the extended barrier, and was gone. He searched frantically for her during the wee hours of the morning. Meanwhile, a young woman returning home from work spotted Ginger on the road with a couple of coyotes. She stopped her car, coaxed Ginger inside, and took her to the city holding pen. We were shocked when we learned of the company Ginger had been keeping and grateful she didn't get into worse trouble.

Sometimes we humans also need to be careful of the company we keep. Although I'm a Christian, I have hung out with the wrong crowd at times in my life because I wanted to "fit in." Thankfully, God protected me from my foolishness and made me uncomfortable enough to regret my decision. Over time, I learned there were people and places I was better off avoiding. One might argue that a person can be a Christian witness in those situations, but more often than not, ungodly people exert more influence on the Christian than the other way around. My witness is stronger by simply declining invitations to participate in unwholesome activities.

Ginger could have been injured or even killed by associating with wild animals. As Christians, we are not called to fit in with this world. The young woman who rescued Ginger realized a dog didn't belong with the coyotes. If people can't tell the difference between me and the rest of the world, I'm not standing out enough from the "coyotes" in my Christian walk.—Ellen Fannon

Be alert and of sober mind. Your enemy the devil prowls around like a roaring lion looking for someone to devour.

—1 Peter 5:8 (NIV)

OCTOBER 4

The Eyes of a Cougar

Stay alert! Watch out for your great enemy, the devil. He prowls around like a roaring lion, looking for someone to devour.

—1 PETER 5:8 (NLT)

ANYONE WHO KNOWS me knows I adore large cats. Not big kitty cats, but the really big ones—lions and tigers and cheetahs, oh my! And in my estimation, the grandest of all is the cougar.

Often known as the mountain lion or puma, this cat will fascinate me forever. I fell in love with them on a family vacation in the mountains of Pennsylvania. In a town we passed through, a man walked a cougar on a leash. We paused to get a better look, and sure enough, it was a cougar.

Each time we went through the town after that, I watched for the cougar, though I never again saw it. However, we heard about many unconfirmed sightings of cougars in the mountains. I waited for that time I'd see one slinking through a field or crouching on a tree branch. Even though I know this species is a dangerous predator, I've never felt as afraid as I undoubtedly should. Whenever I went to a zoo, I couldn't wait to see the cougar exhibit.

A few years back, we visited a unique animal park with only a few exotic animals, one of which was a cougar. It delighted me when this animal looked directly at me through the glass. Its eyes connected with mine, and neither of us blinked. The other patrons moved on, but I couldn't leave. His gold-green eyes seemed to stare right into my soul. And I felt no fear…with the safety glass between us.

When I walked away, his eyes followed me. No, I wasn't afraid, but the experience left me unsettled. Maybe it reminded me of how I'm warned in the Bible that the enemy watches me, waiting, ready to pounce. Yet I feel no fear. With Jesus as my safety glass between me and the predator, I feel protected.—Cathy Mayfield

So do not fear, for I am with you.
—Isaiah 41:10 (NIV)

OCTOBER 5

Changing Hours of Daylight

This is the message which we have heard from Him and declare to you, that God is light and in Him is no darkness at all.

—1 JOHN 1:5 (NKJV)

ANIMALS HAVE A keen sixth sense when it comes to weather and seasonal changes. For instance, the black bear increases her food intake when daylight hours shorten. Songbirds sing more as the daylight hours increase in the spring. My worker honeybees have shorter life spans as daylight increases and they work overtime to bring in pollen and nectar.

The scientific term for this is *photoperiodism*, which is the ability of plants and animals to measure environmental day lengths. God designed a way to react and anticipate changes in seasonal amounts of light. Animals were created with the ability to sense this recurring cycle, and it is most noticeable when they are compelled to begin migration or hibernation.

As I maneuver my way through my own seasonal changes as a Christian, I've noticed that the Bible gives me clues to what is coming next. I need to be just as reactive as the animals, but in a spiritual photoperiodism. The days of "Sonlight" on the earth are decreasing, triggering a reaction in me to get prepared for change. I am reminded of a time to come when there will be a great migration on the horizon and I will enjoy the best season of all. It will be the season of eternal daylight with my brothers and sisters in Christ where God Himself is the source of light. Oh, what a glorious change of the seasons that will be.—Ben Cooper

In a moment, in the twinkling of an eye, at the last trumpet. For the trumpet will sound, and the dead will be raised incorruptible, and we shall be changed.

—1 Corinthians 15:52 (NKJV)

OCTOBER 6

Making Friends

How good and pleasant it is when God's people live together in unity!

—PSALM 133:1 (NIV)

THE OTHER DAY on our cattle ranch, I found my husband, Craig, underneath a tractor and a buddy underneath the swather right next to him. The buddy wasn't a mechanic, though; it was one of a mule deer herd, a full-grown buck with an eight-point rack. As I approached, the buck backed out from under the piece of equipment and ran off. Craig said he had been working all afternoon on that swather, which cuts hay, and the whole time the buck just rested there in the shade, watching him.

That didn't surprise me much. Some herds have become so domesticated in our little mountain town in the Sierra Valley that they think the nearby cattle ranches, and sometimes homes in town, are their foraging places. Some even hop over our tall backyard fence to see what's for breakfast.

"I think he's used to me now," Craig said. "He seems curious about what I'm doing because he watches me constantly. Maybe he even thinks I'm one of the herd."

"But I'm not yet," I joked. "I guess he's got to get to know me."

Later I realized this is true for people I meet. We are strangers at first encounter—perhaps a bit distant. But as we hang out together and get to know one another, walls of caution, judgment, or fear slip away.

I have found this to be especially true when I work with others. During one season, a dozen or more couples, including Craig and me, took on a church renovation project. Together, we refinished pews and wood floors, painted walls, and replaced windows and wood trim. The project was exhausting but satisfying—not only for the work we accomplished but also for the bonded friendships we formed.

Perhaps that eight-point buck truly felt he was working with Craig. In any case, I know my husband appreciated the company.—Janet Holm McHenry

We share our mutual woes, our mutual burdens bear,
and often for each other flows the sympathizing tear.
—John Fawcett

OCTOBER 7

Going Batty

Just ask the animals, and have them teach you.

—JOB 12:7 (NASB)

I'VE LEARNED ENOUGH about bats to be both fascinated and impressed by these airborne mammals. Like flying felines, bats clean and groom themselves the way cats do. Some of these amazing creatures can hit air speeds of up to one hundred miles per hour. Bats eat their body weight in insects every single night, something I think we can all acknowledge as a good thing. And did you know that more than three hundred species of plants depend on bats to pollinate them?

What captures my imagination most, however, is bats' ability to find their way through the darkness by making sounds and listening to the way the sounds bounce back to them. This is called echolocation. Whales, dolphins, some birds, and even the dormouse also instinctively use this amazing navigation tool. But did you know that humans can learn this skill too?

In 2021, researchers at England's Durham University conducted studies to see whether people of various ages can be taught to echolocate, using twelve participants, both blind and sighted, over the course of twenty sessions in ten weeks. Using mouth clicks, the participants learned to navigate mazes and even discern the size and shape of objects and obstacles. Interestingly, echolocation taps into the parts of the brain cortex used for sight in order to map out and visualize spaces. When the study concluded, ten of the participants felt that the skill was useful to them.

God created animals to do things we humans can't do or can only do with help from inventions or technology: breathe underwater, defy gravity by flying, see colors in different light spectrums, shape-shift (like an octopus), regrow limbs, or even sniff out cancer. Echolocation seems to be that rare animal skill we can learn to do just using our brains. Makes me wonder what else we might learn if we emulate our friends in the animal kingdom.—Jon Woodhams

Lord, may I always be open to what Your creatures can teach me. Amen.

OCTOBER 8

Leopards Living in Peace

The wolf also shall dwell with the lamb, the leopard shall lie down with the young goat, the calf and the young lion and the fatling together; and a little child shall lead them.

—Isaiah 11:6 (NKJV)

THIS SCRIPTURE IS one of my favorites. I love to think about the day when the Bible says that even wild animals will be as gentle as doves. Believers will be able to cuddle and live with animals we once considered fearsome.

A majestic leopard sat stoically, staring at me through the glass at the Columbus (Ohio) zoo. Her massive body inspired awe, and those sizable teeth caused me to fight the urge to climb into the enclosure and try to snuggle with her.

I've always been fascinated by leopards because of their great strength and speed. The felines can run as fast as thirty-six miles per hour. The zoo leopard's fur looked so soft and thick, with patterns of spots and coloration associated with her subspecies. I thought about a plaque within the big cat enclosure. It pointed out that leopards are solitary creatures except for mating season and raising their young, preferring to wander alone for up to fifteen miles in a night prowling for prey.

Rudyard Kipling, through one of his Just So stories, is famous for memorializing the saying that a leopard cannot change his spots. Although poetic, this aspect of leopards reminds me of a major benefit of walking with Jesus.

As a Christian, I can indeed change my character for the better. It's central to the gospel message. By yielding to the power of the Holy Spirit, I become a new creature. God will transform my life through the washing power of His Word. Salvation through Jesus gives me endless opportunities to grow and become new. My life has changed remarkably since I first met Jesus as a teenager, but many opportunities for continued growth and newness of life remain.—David L. Winters

Then He who sat on the throne said, "Behold, I make all things new."
—Revelation 21:5 (NKJV)

OCTOBER 9

Bunny Delights

The young lions lack and suffer hunger; but those who seek the LORD shall not lack any good thing.

—PSALM 34:10 (NKJV)

I WALKED MINNIE THROUGH the field behind our home in the cool of the evening to observe the sunset. Minnie sniffed around as the sun dipped below the trees and cast gold and magenta hues across the sky. I turned to my right, and two bunnies caught my attention. One lay in the cool of the grass, and the other munched on greens.

Soon another bunny appeared. He stood in the shade of the avocado tree and nibbled on grass. I'd seen one and even two but never three rabbits by our home. What a delight for my heart. I thanked Jesus for the sweet sight.

With a deep exhale, I wondered, *What could be better?* Without pause, my heart declared, *Four. More. More bunnies would be better.*

I was struck by how easily I became dissatisfied with what had filled me with joy moments before. My desire for more leads to an unending pursuit. I've seen it in my work, my finances, and my achievements. Working to reach the next level, position, or acquisition leaves me feeling weary and empty, yet still wanting more.

Only in my desire for more of Jesus do I find peace. Studying and reading His Word. Seeking Him in prayer. Gathering with believers to worship Him. These things bring peace to my soul and fill my heart with a longing for heaven. In Christ alone, my heart is satisfied.

Jesus promises in Matthew 6:33, "But seek first the kingdom of God and His righteousness, and all these things shall be added to you" (NKJV). Things like bunny delights become a bonus when I see God as enough.—Crystal Storms

You say, "If I had a little more, I should be very satisfied." You make a mistake. If you are not content with what you have, you would not be satisfied if it were doubled.

—Charles Spurgeon

OCTOBER 10

Lord of All Comfort

The Lord is close to the brokenhearted and saves those who are crushed in spirit.

—Psalm 34:18 (NIV)

I COULDN'T HELP UGLY-CRYING the day we said goodbye to our eighteen-year-old Manx/Siamese, Paladine. For months we'd kept him alive with special food, medication, and under-skin fluids. We'd prayed for our kitty and for wisdom to know when to let him go. He'd lived a long, full life, but now he was gone. No more loud Siamese-meows or cranky stares. Sure, we still had our little gray Mamma Mia, another rescue kitty. But without Paladine, I had a giant, cat-shaped hole in my broken heart.

Friends tried to console me, telling me to picture Paladine frolicking with all our other deceased pets in a place where there was no more suffering. I tried, but for days, each time I walked into the bedroom, I expected to see him sprawled on my bed.

Then my husband hung a gallery of photos of Paladine on a living room wall next to a tall bookshelf. I studied each picture—there he was as a tiny white Siamese kitten without a tail; in another he leapt for the feather wand; in others he posed like the king he thought he was and slept upside down like a goof.

I broke down and begged God to take away my grief and pain. "I just need a hug," I wailed. Just then, I felt a soft tap on my shoulder. I turned. Perched on the bookcase, Mamma Mia extended a paw. She stroked my cheek softly, and I buried my face in her silky fur.

For several days, Mamma seemed to appear when I was feeling blue. I like to think that God's comfort and solace came to me with paws and whiskers as I healed. I'll always miss Paladine, but I'm grateful for God's love, no matter how it arrives.—Linda S. Clare

Lord, when I'm grieving, help me feel Your love everywhere I look. Amen.

OCTOBER 11

Take Care of God's Animals

The righteous care for the needs of their animals.

—PROVERBS 12:10 (NIV)

MY FAMILY TREASURES a particularly special academic legacy. My husband and I, all four of our children, and both sons-in-law graduated from the university in my hometown. Between the six of us, we have four master's degrees from Georgia Southern University, as well. In addition, my father-in-law taught math there, my mother-in-law worked for the extension service at the college, my dad took some classes there, and my maternal grandmother served college students at the dining hall after she was widowed.

One of my family's favorite traditions involves a rehabilitated bald eagle named Freedom. Freedom came to the wildlife center on campus as a bird with special needs. His beak is deformed, and he would never have survived in the wild. But Freedom quickly became a mascot for the university and flies at every football game.

The director at the wildlife center happens to be a high school friend of mine. Steve has rehabilitated and taken care of many of God's beautiful winged creations, as well as others.

Long before the wildlife center was established at my university, eagles were more plentiful in the wild. During a recent visit with our grandson, my husband and I took Benaiah to the wildlife center on campus, and our friend Steve just happened to be walking through the park with Freedom on his gloved hand.

Benaiah grinned with excitement at his up-close introduction to Freedom. His glee showed in the picture we snapped of him with the bald eagle. I'm so thankful there are people like Steve with a passion for animals, because I don't want my three-year-old to miss out on any of God's beautiful creations.—Julie Lavender

For every animal of the forest is mine, and the cattle on a thousand hills.
I know every bird in the mountains, and the insects in the fields are mine.
—Psalm 50:10–11 (NIV)

OCTOBER 12

Laugh, Kookaburra!

We played the flute for you, and you did not dance.

—MATTHEW 11:17 (ESV)

I GLANCED IN BOTH directions along the path by the kookaburra exhibit at the zoo where I volunteered. No visitors were nearby, so I sang the old Australian folk song that beckons the kookaburra to laugh.

The sturdy brown bird with shiny blue markings didn't move, though he appeared to watch me from his perch on a large branch. Undaunted, I gripped the clipboard I used to catalog my observations and belted out my best imitation of a kookaburra's "laugh."

The bird turned his head but didn't make a peep. I frowned. Other days, I'd heard the kookaburra sing his laughing song from a distance as I'd walked through this area of the zoo. Maybe those were happier days for the bird. But wouldn't he feel cheerier if he laughed? Despite my attempts at encouragement, the kookaburra sat still, looking morose.

I walked away, clutching my clipboard, disappointed I couldn't get a joyful noise out of the kookaburra. My mind turned to my own life circumstances, to the frustration, sadness, and depression I clutched as close as my clipboard.

Was I just like the kookaburra, resisting the attempts of my friends and family to encourage me? Sometimes, it seemed easier to hold on to dark feelings, using them as justification for complaints and self-pity.

But what if God was inviting me to laugh? I looked around as I continued up the path. A vibrant rainbow of flowers blossomed around me. The sky above formed a glorious painting of cotton-like clouds and tones of blue no human could blend. I would see my mom as soon as I left the zoo, and she was sure to smile, showering me with love.

I heard it then. God was singing a song of joy to me: "Laugh, my child. Laugh!"—Jerusha Agen

Joy is a choice. Joy is a matter of attitude that stems from one's confidence in God.
—Chuck Swindoll

OCTOBER 13

A Passion for Opossums

Better the poor whose walk is blameless than a fool whose lips are perverse.

—PROVERBS 19:1 (NIV)

I'VE ALWAYS HAD a dislike of opossums. I shudder when I see them scurrying across the road or crouching in the corner of the garage. I think they look like giant rats, with their grayish white fur, pointy nose, and sharp eyes. And what's with that snake-like tail? I've never held one, and frankly the mere thought gives me the willies.

But my sister Sandy—a trained animal rehabber—has tended injured opossums on numerous occasions. She's even fed the babies with a medicine dropper. Sandy thinks they are adorable and is quick to point out their many good qualities. Opossums seldom catch rabies as their body temperature is too low to carry the virus. They eat mice and insects—even cockroaches. Instead of being grossed out that they can grasp things with their tails, I should marvel. And as North America's only native marsupial, they carry their tiny pink babies in a pouch like kangaroos.

My sister chides me for my prejudice against the creatures, urging me to consider their finer qualities. I've given Sandy's advice some careful consideration, particularly as she's also good at focusing on the finer characteristics of unlikable people.

I need to revise my attitude about certain people, not just opossums. Sometimes I make hasty judgments about others, writing them off as too stubborn, too ignorant, or generally too difficult to deal with. I need to take the time to look for their virtues instead of focusing on their faults. Others have made erroneous assumptions about me, so I know how hurtful that can be. I don't yet have a passion for opossums, but I'm learning to appreciate them and their uniqueness. If nothing else, they've taught me the importance of looking past my shallow prejudices and seeing the good in others.—Shirley Raye Redmond

Walk of Faith: *Humbly confess the times you have misjudged someone, and ask for God's help in overcoming the tendency to do so again.*

OCTOBER 14

Traveling Froggie

The steadfast love of the Lord never ceases, his mercies never come to an end; they are new every morning; great is your faithfulness.

—Lamentations 3:22–23 (NRSVUE)

When my friend Tracy brings her plants inside each fall as the temperature drops, she takes a few of them to our church, where she works. In January, two months after she had placed the plants near her desk, something jumped out at her as she was watering them. It was a bright-green tree frog! She called a pet store and was told the frog had probably been in a state of hibernation but that he was fine staying in the plants in the church. She could release him once the weather warmed again.

Over the next few months, Froggie—his new name—became a mascot for the church staff. Tracy brought him mealworms, and everyone checked on him daily. Most days he was at the drainage saucer, the opening made for watering at the base of the pot. Sometimes he would be on the plant. Other times he couldn't be found.

When spring arrived, Tracy knew it was time to take the plant with Froggie back to her house. She placed the pot near the woods and cried as she left. After several days, she returned the plant to the stand on her deck. Later, when she went to get the watering can, something thumped inside. Froggie had returned! Her family had a couple more sightings but haven't seen him since. Now when they hear frog sounds at night, they know Froggie is part of the chorus.

I love how resilient Froggie was when his plant home was moved. And I love how God used Tracy to watch out for him until he could safely be released outside. God provided for a tree frog, and God is even more faithful to care for me. I'm grateful He always provides.—Missy Tippens

Lord, use us as we go about our day. Help us to shower Your love on every creature—human and animal—that we encounter today. Amen.

OCTOBER 15

Where the Buffalo Roam

The LORD is slow to anger but great in power.

—NAHUM 1:3 (NIV)

AS A CHILD, I watched Roy Rogers ride off into the sunset, singing about a home where the buffalo roam. A small herd of buffalo, more accurately called bison, lives near my home in Colorado.

Sometimes the buffalo venture close enough to the fence surrounding their pasture that I can marvel at their magnificence. I listen to the long bellow they use to communicate, which sounds much like a lion's rumbling roar. The little calves will eventually weigh as much as two thousand pounds and stand over six feet tall at their distinctive humped shoulders. Thick, shaggy fur that covers their enormous bodies makes them look even bigger and helps them withstand freezing temperatures and blowing snow.

I am careful to obey the posted signs that say, "Warning: Keep out! Buffalo are extremely dangerous!" They may look like their docile cow cousins, but these are wild beasts with unpredictable temperaments. Many oblivious hikers have learned this the hard way. A buffalo's horns may be short, but they are sharp!

I'm continually astounded that our wonderful Lord is so great in power yet slow to anger. God is not wild or unpredictable. He is patient and gentle, but He is almighty and all powerful too. I'd be foolish to ignore the warning signs about His judgment, but each warning comes with an invitation to come close and receive His forgiveness. God's incredible power is tempered by His unfailing love!—Randy Benedetto

Oh Lord, I am so thankful that You are a mighty God, yet You are so tender and patient and loving toward me. Amen.

OCTOBER 16

Guarding the Dog

The name of the L*ORD is a fortified tower; the righteous run to it and are safe.*

—PROVERBS 18:10 (NIV)

HAVING LIVED FOR about fifteen years near the foothills of the Rocky Mountains, I'm pretty sure you're supposed to make yourself appear as tall and as intimidating as you can when you encounter a mountain lion.

The tactics I'd learned came to mind one overcast early-fall Sunday afternoon, when Windsor and I set out on a walk around the neighborhood. As we turned the corner onto a new street, we were greeted by two large dogs. Easily twice Windsor's thirty-five-ish pounds, they were off leash and seemed to charge out toward us from their front yard, where their owners were taking groceries out of the car and ignoring the dogs entirely.

I'm not the boldest or most fearless person around, but as the dogs drew closer, my fight-or-flight mechanism kicked in in full force. I acted quickly and completely from instinct, pulling Windsor (who was on his leash) *behind* me to protect him against what I perceived as a threat. I am sure these neighbors must have questioned my sanity, because in addition to putting my body in front of Windsor, I tried to make myself as tall and intimidating as possible and made a great deal of noise, yell-growling at the dogs to leave us alone and go back home.

Later, after my adrenaline wore off, I realized it was probably unnecessary—I'm pretty sure neither Windsor (nor I) was ever in any real danger. In hindsight, Windsor didn't seem too worried. The dogs were probably just curious about us—they weren't growling or even barking. But I surprised myself with the fearsome (if somewhat unhinged) way I acted to protect my furry child.

I can't help thinking that if I, who has spent so much of my life learning to assert myself when needed, could move so easily and quickly into instinctive mama-bear mode to protect Windsor, then I certainly can rely on God to protect me when I need it.—Jon Woodhams

Dear God, thanks for the ways You protect me from threats, seen and unseen. Amen.

OCTOBER 17

A Profane Parrot

They sharpen their tongues like swords and aim cruel words like deadly arrows.

—Psalm 64:3 (NIV)

THE VETERINARY CLINIC where I used to work had a separate boarding facility. One day I had to check on one of our patients in the kennel. As I walked through the reception area, I spied a beautiful parrot sitting in his cage on the counter.

I stopped to admire the fine feathered friend. "Hello, pretty bird," I said in my sweetest voice.

The parrot looked me straight in the eye and responded with a vulgar obscenity that curled my hair. In my shock, my stunned brain failed to register that the profane parrot hadn't intentionally insulted me. It was merely repeating words it had heard without understanding their meaning. Still, I felt an irrational sense of personal offense and hurt feelings.

From the time I was a child, I was taught the old adage, "Sticks and stones may break my bones, but words will never hurt me." But it didn't take long for me to realize that simply wasn't true. Cruel or careless words often leave painful wounds that continue to sting long after they are spoken. Perhaps this is why there are so many admonitions in Scripture about keeping a tight rein on the tongue. How many times have I blurted out something unkind or insensitive without thinking? Even if I apologize, the damage is already done. I can't take back ugly or foolish words once they are spoken. Sometimes, even years later, I cringe when I remember hurtful things I have said.

Words have power—the power to lift people up or tear them down. I want to use my words to encourage, comfort, and bless others. I must stop and think before I speak. Imagine what a wonderful world it would be if everyone, including that birdbrained parrot, were taught to speak kindly.—Ellen Fannon

Do not let any unwholesome talk come out of your mouths, but only what is helpful for building others up according to their needs, that it may benefit those who listen.

—Ephesians 4:29 (NIV)

OCTOBER 18

A Contrasting Life

Do not conform to the pattern of this world, but be transformed by the renewing of your mind. Then you will be able to test and approve what God's will is—his good, pleasing and perfect will.

—ROMANS 12:2 (NIV)

IT WASN'T HARD to spot him.

"Look, there," my husband said as he pointed to the long rodent scurrying through the woods. If we had crossed paths with the ermine a week earlier, we would never have noticed him. He still would have had on his summer coat, obscuring him in a forest of pine. These weasels transform from brown to white as seasons shift and days grow shorter. Although he's already put on his white winter coat, the woods have not. Snow isn't falling, and the forest remains brown, so the ermine with its bright ivory fur contrasts with the thicket he runs through.

I imagine the ermine, sensing the molt of his summer coat, simultaneously wills snow's arrival. He wants to remain hidden from predators—to disappear into the underbrush. I'm familiar with the desire to blend in and go through life unnoticed. It feels safe and secure. And yet I see in the early molt of the ermine a reflection of my life as a believer. Perhaps I'm meant to exist and thrive in this contrast. Soon snow will blanket the landscape, and our ermine friend will skitter through the woods unannounced. But maybe I'm not meant to go through life in the same way. As a believer, I can find security not by fitting in but by reflecting my Creator's glory, even if it's drastically different from what I see around me.

As I learn to confidently uphold the Word of truth and stand for the values God has sown into my heart, He is my protection. I don't have to retreat into what feels safe. Instead, embracing my identity as a new creation in Christ, I find joy and peace in living the abundant and contrasting life God has for me.—Eryn Lynum

But in your hearts revere Christ as Lord. Always be prepared to give an answer to everyone who asks you to give the reason for the hope that you have. But do this with gentleness and respect.

—1 Peter 3:15 (NIV)

OCTOBER 19

Seagulls in Love

If I have the gift of prophecy and can fathom all mysteries and all knowledge, and if I have a faith that can move mountains, but do not have love, I am nothing.

—1 CORINTHIANS 13:2 (NIV)

WE PULLED INTO the parking lot of a deserted mall near Louisiana's Lake Pontchartrain to eat our fast-food lunch. It seemed like a peaceful break from our interstate driving, with the occupants of a truck nearby apparently doing the same thing. They finished their meal, and as they began to leave, they casually threw an uneaten piece of Texas toast out their window. The quietness was broken by the descent of a flock of seagulls. The birds noisily attacked the bread, pulling it apart and even stealing bits from another's mouth in midair. Loud, chaotic, and filled with fighting and squabbling, the scene made me think of the constant bickering that often fills social media.

Off to the side another scenario was playing out. Seagulls are monogamous and usually remain with the same mate for their entire twenty-year life span. A male seagull had nabbed a piece of the prized toast and was feeding it to his mate. The two of them nuzzled beaks while they shared their bread and then quietly flew off together. What a contrast to the chaos of the flock.

It reminded me of the way that love changes even the most chaotic situations and the way the love of my wife, my children, my grandchildren, and my friends changes me each day. And I hope that my love changes them in return in some small way. In the words of Andrew Lloyd Webber's song, "love changes everything." With enough love, I know I can change my own life and maybe even change the world around me.—Harold Nichols

To love another person is to see the face of God.
—Victor Hugo, *Les Misérables*

OCTOBER 20

Treading on Scorpions

Behold, I give you the authority to trample on serpents and scorpions, and over all the power of the enemy, and nothing shall by any means hurt you.

—LUKE 10:19 (NKJV)

THE MOVE TO Oklahoma represented a major life change. For career advancement, I uprooted my life and headed from Chicago to the Sooner State. Not only did I receive an immediate raise and a promise of career advancement, but also the cost of living would be much cheaper living as an Okie instead of a Chicagoan.

While I expected cowboy hats and an uptick in the number of pickup trucks, scorpions did not make the list of my immediate concerns. However, the first camping trip brought me face to pinchers with the primary indigenous species of scorpion in Oklahoma: the striped bark scorpion (*Centruroides vittatus*).

Having been raised with parents who like camping, I should have been better prepared for unusual outdoor visitors. We had run into bears in the Smoky Mountains and several angry raccoons at a local state park. None of my previous camping adventures prepared me for a scorpion climbing onto my sleeping bag. Screaming and hilarity ensued as I ran about the campsite yelling, "Get them off me! Get them off me."

As it turns out, the light-brown-and-tan-colored species endemic to Oklahoma can sting humans, injecting venom from their tail and causing redness, swelling, and itching. Unless one has a severe allergy, the bite is not dangerous—just annoying. I felt annoyed even without getting bitten.

During the sleepless night that ensued, my thoughts turned to Jesus's promise that His servants would step on scorpions (both physical and metaphorical) without being harmed. In His example, His followers headed out to share the gospel. Did that same promise apply to my camping trip? After much consideration, I decided that my authority in Christ should lead me to boldness in telling others the good news about Jesus. My new home state may include some unusual obstacles, but God is honored when I share the gospel.—David L. Winters

Father, grant me the boldness and faith to share the good news about Jesus. Amen.

OCTOBER 21

Protecting the Nest

Love does not delight in evil but rejoices with the truth. It always protects, always trusts, always hopes, always perseveres.

—1 CORINTHIANS 13:6–7 (NIV)

THE FLUTTER OF activity caught my attention. A large red-shouldered hawk sat on the wire nearby as three mockingbirds took turns attacking him. The mockingbirds squawked around the hawk's head. They flew into his tail. They pecked at his back. After one final attack, the hawk lifted from the wire and flew a short distance away. Apparently, the hawk didn't fly far enough. Immediately, two mockingbirds flew after him, forcing him to leave the area entirely.

At first, I felt sorry for the hawk. He was merely sitting there minding his own business. That's how it seemed to me anyway. But I was wrong. When I pointed out the perceived injustice to my husband, he explained why the mockingbirds attacked the hawk. They were attacking a predator to protect their nest.

When the adult birds noticed the threat to their young, they didn't wait for the hawk to leave on his own. They flew into action and fought the predator. Their relentless attack did not end until they were positive the hawk had moved on. The mockingbirds used everything in their power to protect what they held dear—their children.

Thinking about those mockingbirds, I am reminded that God wants me to do the same. I am to use everything in my power to protect the child I hold dear. That's what love does. It protects. It hopes. Love perseveres. A red-shouldered hawk may not be hovering near my child, but there is an enemy who, the Bible states, prowls like a lion looking for someone to devour (1 Peter 5). My weapon against this predator is not a sharp, pecking beak or screeching call. My weapon is prayer. It is the weapon I will continue to use, because I know even if the enemy moves on, he will return.—Sandy Kirby Quandt

Walk of Faith: *When those you love are under attack, protect them by getting on your knees to pray.*

OCTOBER 22

An Unexpected Benefit

You have hedged me behind and before, and laid Your hand upon me.

—PSALM 139:5 (NKJV)

FOR A SEASON my parrot, Lorito, lived with my mother and served as her companion. My Yorkie, Minnie, has treated Lorito as an intruder since he returned home. She's lunged at him a dozen times and barks every time he ruffles his feathers.

Her jealousy has a benefit I didn't expect. Minnie wants to be where Lorito is. She runs beside me on the stairs when I carry Lorito up to my office to keep me company while I work. Gone are the days when I need to call Minnie to come.

The other night as I read, Lorito stood outside his cage and said his name, indicating he wanted to be picked up. When I went to his cage and offered him my hand, he climbed on. I returned to the couch, placed the blue furry blanket over my lap, and held Lorito against my chest so I could massage his neck as I read.

Minnie hopped onto my lap for her share of attention. I was reading on my Kindle, so I didn't need my hands to read except when I tapped to turn the page. Rubbing Lorito's neck with one hand and Minnie's shoulders with the other, I felt surrounded by love.

In that moment I considered how David marveled at the closeness of God in Psalm 139:5. God stands before me and walks with me. Nothing is hidden from His eyes. He knows my struggles and my fears, surrounds me with His love, and leads me to His heart.

I love that my pets desire to be close to me. Surrounded by their love and God's love, my heart—and my lap—are full.—Crystal Storms

And the LORD, He is the One who goes before you. He will be with you,
He will not leave you nor forsake you; do not fear nor be dismayed.
—Deuteronomy 31:8 (NKJV)

OCTOBER 23

The Very Friendly Cow

The wolf will live with the lamb, the leopard will lie down with the goat, the calf and the lion and the yearling together; and a little child will lead them... They will neither harm nor destroy on all my holy mountain, for the earth will be filled with the knowledge of the LORD as the waters cover the sea.

—ISAIAH 11:6, 9 (NIV)

LAST FALL, MY family and I visited our favorite local pumpkin patch—complete with a visit to some farm animals within a petting-zoo area. A trip to the pumpkin patch is never complete without seeing some cute goats. Am I right? Well, imagine my surprise when I began feeding the goats some straw, only to look up and realize another animal had joined us—a cow! She clearly wanted some attention, so I petted her snout, and my surprise turned to shock when she offered a huge lick to my hand in return.

I rushed over to tell the rest of my family I'd just been kissed by a cow, and though they looked a bit skeptical at first, my mom assured them she'd seen the whole thing and that the cow was just as affectionate as I'd conveyed.

When we arrived back home that day, I sent a message to a friend of mine who frequents the farm and knows all the animals. She told me that particular cow is known for her huge personality and her friendly "cow kisses." It's hard to put into words, but when I looked at that cow and she offered such kindness in return, I felt a connection with her.

That sweet moment reminded me of what creation must have been like before humans sinned and what promise Isaiah prophesied when he referred to the age to come. God's plan is for His creation to dwell in peace and unity, and I believe animals offer a holy witness to God's heart for all His creation.—Ashley Clark

Father, what joy we can look forward to in the coming age,
when all Your creation lives peacefully as a witness to Your kindness.
When I spend time in Your creation, remind me of the hope I have
for what's to come. Amen.

OCTOBER 24

Ye Watchers and Ye Holy Ones

But the LORD said to Samuel, "Do not consider his appearance or his height, for I have rejected him. The LORD does not look at the things people look at. People look at the outward appearance, but the LORD looks at the heart."

—1 SAMUEL 16:7 (NIV)

LATE ONE AFTERNOON, I walked by the church courtyard. The sun had sunk below the roof of the church, and shadows striped the floor of the cloister. In front of me, I saw an armadillo. Our church book club had recently read a book that featured an armadillo, and I was intrigued that one should appear now, downtown. As I moved toward it, it walked confidently into the azaleas in the courtyard. I looked more closely.

It was not an armadillo. It was an opossum. While I had been excited about a literary armadillo walking around the courtyard, an opossum seemed ominous. I went and found one of the sextons, the wonderful men who take care of everything around the church.

"There's a big opossum in the courtyard," I announced. "We need to do something." I waited for him to react to this breaking news.

"Actually," he said, "there are four opossums. It's a whole family."

"Aren't you worried about them?" I asked. "It's broad daylight. They could have rabies. Shouldn't we trap them and move them somewhere else?"

He shook his head. "No. They're doing good work here. If the opossums left, we'd have rats and roaches. We've known about those opossums for a while."

Here I was trying to get this odd-looking creature out of the courtyard, and they were actually making life better for the other creatures. Not all animals are literary armadillos or cute or cuddly, but all of them have God-given roles in our shared life. Next time I go to judge someone, I told myself, I had better find out more about them and remember they, too, have a God-given purpose.—Lucy H. Chambers

No one is useless in this world who lightens the burdens of it for anyone else.
—Charles Dickens

OCTOBER 25

Facing Fears

So do not fear, for I am with you; do not be dismayed, for I am your God. I will strengthen you and help you; I will uphold you with my righteous right hand.

—ISAIAH 41:10 (NIV)

MY FRIEND AMBER worked in an office that was located in an old Victorian home. The staff was used to noises from small critters outside and sometimes even inside the office. But Amber told me about one night when she found herself alone, working late into the evening. Suddenly, a scratching kind of noise outside the window caught her attention. *What if there's an intruder trying to get in?* she asked herself nervously. She thought it was perhaps a large animal. She even contemplated calling the police for help.

Amber could not see outside the window since the blinds were down. Making up her mind to confront her fear, she tiptoed to the window, wiping her palms on her dress as she approached the shade. With one quick pull, she raised the blinds. A squirrel was hanging on the window screen. Alarmed by the sudden movement, it scampered away. Amber plopped into her chair with a sigh and started laughing. It was only a squirrel.

Amber told me that story as I was preparing to go to a bookseller convention. I had never before interacted with media professionals for book promotion, and I didn't know what to expect. I feared I would make a fool of myself. I was also afraid of rejection. But I turned to God for help. Prayer helped soothe my fears and redirected my attention toward Him. I knew I could count on His help and guidance.

At the convention, God opened doors for me to connect with the right people. I found plenty of opportunities to market my book. Of course, I had no reason to be fearful in the first place.—Mabel Ninan

Do the thing you fear to do and keep on doing it…that is the quickest and surest way ever yet discovered to conquer fear.
—Dale Carnegie

OCTOBER 26

Microscopic Changes

But many who are first will be last, and the last first.

—MARK 10:31 (ESV)

"PHYTOPLANKTON IS ANOTHER 'lung' on our earth like the rain forest," my son said.

We were walking around Woods Hole, Massachusetts, discussing all things environmental. Mingled among the quaint shingled cottages were the Woods Hole Oceanographic Institution (WHOI) and its research buildings. The team at the WHOI were studying phytoplankton and noted that the microscopic plankton are responsible for producing half the world's oxygen.

"Amazing," I said. I thought of how often God uses the smallest things to make large impacts: phytoplankton, a widow's mite, a mustard seed, and twelve uneducated men who became the Church. Even the "insignificant" poor carpenter and his fiancée were used as the earthly parents for the Savior of the world.

The scientists say phytoplankton affects much of the world's food chain and the balance of nutrients in the air. The individual phytoplankton may be microscopic, but together as an organism, they are significant to the planet.

Many times in life I feel like a phytoplankton: insignificant, invisible, and unimportant. I get down on myself for not making any noticeable impact in the world. The Bible's examples of God's economy of small, insignificant acts becoming large in His kingdom remind me that God wants me to perform small acts, like sharing what I have and praying for others. In turn, those acts might inspire and influence another to perform their own small godly acts. Like the microscopic phytoplankton, my individual actions combined with the individual actions of others can influence our world.

In learning how God created such a small creature to impact the world's balance, I got a glimpse of His economy. Those who may seem the least influential might actually be the most.—Virginia Ruth

Walk of Faith: *What small acts of kindness can you do today? For whom can you pray? To whom can you lend a hand?*

OCTOBER 27

A Forever Home

For we know that if the earthly tent we live in is destroyed, we have a building from God, an eternal house in heaven, not built by human hands.

—2 CORINTHIANS 5:1 (NIV)

MY FRIEND ALYSSA was on her way home from her kids' jujitsu classes when she saw a bird walking down the middle of the country road in the Sierra Valley. She immediately pulled over and watched as other cars whizzed by, blowing the bird in the breeze as it veered left or right, depending on the rushing traffic.

Thinking the bird was injured—or would be at any moment—Alyssa stopped the car in a safe place and raced over to retrieve the pigeon with a green and purple sheen. Her daughter Addie cradled it in her jacket and gently put it in her lap as they drove home. Though Addie dubbed the pigeon Drover, after a mutt in the Hank the Cowdog book series, Alyssa said most people think it's called Drover because it was almost "driven over."

Drover wasn't injured, but because of the band on Drover's leg, Alyssa knew the pigeon was a registered racing pigeon, used in competition. Pigeon racing involves releasing specially trained homing pigeons, which then return to their homes over a carefully measured distance. Some pigeons, she learned, race too much, become fatigued, and then cannot fly anymore. She also discovered that rehoming homing pigeons typically will not work, because they have an innate sense of where home is and usually return there.

Drover's home was about ninety miles away—about sixty miles as the crow or pigeon flies—the same community in which Alyssa herself was raised. However, the owner did not respond to Alyssa's inquiries, and Drover never tried to leave. He's now become part of Alyssa's family and growing menagerie. I guess you could say he found his forever home.

Just like Drover, I put one foot in front of the other each day as I try to do the next right thing in my charted path toward my heavenly home. I might veer to the right or to the left a little as I struggle to find my way. And winds sometimes set me off track a bit. But I know that God has me on a homeward course, and His watchful hands will scoop me up when it's time for me to go to my forever home.—Janet Holm McHenry

Dear Lord, thank You that my forever home is waiting for me in heaven. Help me to stay on course until it's time for me to arrive. Amen.

Dads, Daughters, and Furry Little Friends

Blessed are those who mourn, for they will be comforted.

—MATTHEW 5:4 (NIV)

THE FRONT YARD was for gymnastics and lemonade stands; the backyard was for growing vegetables, swinging, and tree climbing. But the side yard, a pebbly square planted with rosebushes, was for nothing much. We called it the "rock garden," and this is where Dad buried our pets. So, when my seven-year-old friend's hamster died, I invited her to bury it in our cemetery. It didn't occur to me to tell my parents.

At 7:30 the next morning there was a knock on our door. I opened it to find Dina holding a tiny white box, like a gift, before her. Her mom, undoubtedly noting the bewilderment of my parents behind me in the doorway, explained sheepishly that Dina was here to bury her hamster.

At the time it seemed to me most natural. Dressed for work in his suit and dress shoes, my dad led us around the house, grabbed a shovel from the garage, and began digging between red and pink rosebushes. Dina and I stood silently as the hole grew. Dad stood back as Dina carefully laid her box in the hole, then he covered her beloved pet and tamped down the dirt over the grave.

I don't remember if words were spoken or whether Dina shed a tear. What impresses me now is how my parents responded with compassion to an unexpected and inconvenient disruption. My parents honored the sacredness of life and love even in a cardboard box of fur and bones.

Five years later we would tamp down earth over my father's grave. I'm certain words were spoken and tears shed. But what I remember is a dad who was late to work one morning because his daughter tried to comfort her friend and honor a life lost, no matter how small.—Susie Colby

He will wipe every tear from their eyes. There will be no more death or mourning or crying or pain, for the old order of things has passed away.

—Revelation 21:4 (NIV)

OCTOBER 29

Making a Bear Out of a Toadstool...er, Toad!

Don't worry about anything; instead, pray about everything.

—PHILIPPIANS 4:6 (NLT)

TAKING OUR DOG, Kenai, outside to do his business in the dark usually falls to my husband, Kevin. Our motion-sensor light is persnickety, and I'm, shall we say, uncomfortable in the dark. This night, however, Kevin had gone to bed early, so it was up to me to either take Kenai out or hope he could hold his bladder until morning.

Choosing not to chance that, I tiptoed across the porch and into the yard, praying the light would work. Nope. The yard remained dark except for a tiny area lit by the porch light. I urged Kenai to hurry while I watched the edge of the lit area for dangers.

Suddenly, Kenai became rigid, ears perked up, nose aloft. I heard something near the house, like footsteps crinkling in the fall leaves. I peered into the dark, my imagination stirring. A deer? We see them often. Or it could be a cat or an opossum—both harmless critters. Maybe it was a rabid raccoon. And what if it was something bigger, like a coyote? Or even a bear?

Not waiting to find out, I urged Kenai, who emitted low growls at this point, back toward the porch. As we got to the steps, the porch light shone onto the culprit as it hopped into view from under the bushes—a plump toad!

Back inside, I giggled at my silliness and thought of how often I make mountains out of molehills or, in this case, bears out of toads. Maybe remembering the toad in the dark and the wisdom of God's Word would help me worry less and trust God more with my fears—be they bears or toads.—Cathy Mayfield

Before the toad becomes a bear, I'll drop to my knees in prayer.

—C.M.

OCTOBER 30

Budgie Whisperer

Show me your ways, Lord, teach me your paths.

—Psalm 25:4 (NIV)

MY HUSBAND, STAN, and I paid our zoo entry fee and purchased the deluxe treat set—souvenir cups full of dry food, romaine lettuce, and birdseed sticks. After feeding several farm animals, we headed to the budgie cage. A couple of years earlier, my daughter-in-law and I had taken my young grandson to the same exhibit. The budgies, also known as parakeets, had flocked all around us, landing on our sticks and greedily pecking at the seed.

I expected the same reception this time, but when I entered the crowded cage, the budgies kept their distance. They seemed disinterested in the food anyone had to offer—anyone, that is, except Stan. The little birds ignored the seed sticks he held out but landed all over him to make their way down to the cup of lettuce tucked under his arm. They took turns pecking the fresh leaves. At one point, I counted eleven parakeets of varying combinations of blue, white, black, yellow, and green attached to my husband.

I also noticed quite a few jealous looks directed Stan's way. One mom walked by and nodded. "Uh-huh. A budgie whisperer."

Oh, that I would draw close to God the way those budgies flocked to Stan. When I thought about it, the romaine lettuce was probably better for them than a constant diet of seed, even though they had to work harder for it. The little birds weren't just going for the good. They were going for the better. And what could be better for me than to walk humbly with God and do what He requires?

I enjoyed the lesson from the budgies that day, but I do need to have a talk with the little beauty who was nibbling Stan's neck.—Tracy Crump

Lord, draw me ever closer to You and show me the goodness
You alone reserve for me. Amen.

Knowing the Way

Thomas said to Him, "Lord, we do not know where You are going, and how can we know the way?" Jesus said to him, "I am the way, the truth, and the life. No one comes to the Father except through Me."

—JOHN 14:5–6 (NKJV)

AS THE AIR turns colder each October here in the Northeast, one of the sure signs that autumn has arrived is hearing and then seeing Canada geese heading south. From my vantage point, they fly east first, before they head south. It's common to see dozens of flocks flying in their trademark V formation. I always wonder how they know which direction to fly to get to their wintering grounds in the south.

Two of the major flyways for these migratory birds are the Mississippi River and the eastern coastal line. Geese read these visible waterways like GPS maps out our way on Waze, and the Potomac River is a directional feeder between these two main routes. Our church is a couple of miles from the Potomac, and most Sundays in October, I witness multiple flocks making their annual trek. It fascinates me every year that they know their way.

Thomas asked how he and the other disciples would know the way to where Jesus was going. Jesus replied with the well-known phrase, "I am the Way." After His death, the phrase "The Way" was the code name for the first-century followers of Christ. They used it to avoid being captured and put to death. I am glad I found this same "Way" in my own journey toward the Way Maker.—Ben Cooper

Lord, instill in me the desire to daily use Your Word as a compass to direct my migration to You. Thank You for being my Way and my Truth and my Life. Amen.

November

NOVEMBER 1

Skunk in the House

He will give a crown of beauty for ashes, a joyous blessing instead of mourning, festive praise instead of despair.

—Isaiah 61:3 (NLT)

MY FRIEND WAS devastated to return home from a shopping trip one day to discover that a skunk had somehow gained access to the recently renovated basement of the home she shared with her husband and three sons. One of the boys had already moved into the space after they had repainted the rooms, installed new carpet in the bedroom area, and upgraded some of the furniture.

Perhaps the skunk was simply snooping around in search of food. But for whatever reason, this particular polecat encountered something that triggered its defense mechanism. This resulted in every room in the basement suite being inundated with his distinctively noxious spray. Since no one was home at the time and the family had no pets, whatever caused the intruder to become so alarmed remains a mystery.

The damage was extensive, and their insurance agent was called in to assess the situation. My friend was quite distressed about the financial implications of this event. They had splurged and purchased furnishings that had stretched their household budget substantially. Typically, an insurance company will replace damaged goods with equally priced products. But when their agent submitted his report, the family was astounded to find that all the damaged goods were replaced with items that far exceeded the value of the original purchases.

Isn't that just like something Father God would do for us? He takes everything in my life that has been corrupted by the sin of this world and replaces it with treasures from His storehouse in heaven. He fills every area of my spirit with the sweet aroma of His presence.—Liz Kimmel

God can do anything, you know—far more than you could ever imagine or guess or request in your wildest dreams!

—Ephesians 3:20 (MSG)

NOVEMBER 2

Best Friend in Training

Don't let anyone look down on you because you are young, but set an example for the believers in speech, in conduct, in love, in faith and in purity.

—1 TIMOTHY 4:12 (NIV)

ROCKY, OUR LARGE and friendly German shepherd, curiously gazed at our infant grandbaby, who was lying on a blanket. Slowly, the dog nudged his bright orange-and-blue ball close to the baby, barked, and waited.

He wants to play catch. Poor Rocky. He doesn't understand that the baby is too young to play with him.

But perhaps Rocky understands more than I realize. Does he sense by the infant's bubbly coos and kicking feet that she's happy? Can he tell she's a wee human who will one day want to throw his ball and be his friend?

I don't think it matters to this canine that she can't currently play catch, scratch him behind his ears, or pet his tummy. He doesn't seem deterred but, rather, is persistent—picking up the ball, dropping it, and barking before nudging it over and over again.

Is it that Rocky is living up to his breed? A shepherd—yes, a teacher of sorts. Could it be he's already guiding this little one, demonstrating for her even before she truly understands what it is he wants her to do?

Indeed, perhaps our pup is much like the apostle Paul, who exhorted his spiritual son Timothy in the faith, telling him to not grow discouraged simply because he was young. Likewise, Rocky might exhort our granddaughter. His message—*I don't care that you're little. I want to teach you now about the love that's possible between a dog and a person.* After all, Rocky probably hopes our grandbaby will one day understand that dogs are among humans' best friends.

And maybe our gentle giant is shepherding me as well, teaching me more about the faithful love of my Father, so that I, too, can set an example for those who follow close behind. I want to teach them that our Good Shepherd is also my best friend.—Maureen Miller

Bless the beasts and the children…Keep them safe; keep them warm.

—Barry De Vorzon, Perry L. Botkin

Birdsong

Speaking to one another with psalms, hymns, and songs from the Spirit. Sing and make music from your heart to the Lord.

—EPHESIANS 5:19 (NIV)

I DON'T KNOW WHAT prompted me to buy a canary—a Gloster Fancy with dark hair-like feathers on the top of his head that reminded me of Friar Tuck in all the old Robin Hood movies. Naturally, I dubbed him Tuck. If he could sing as sweetly as the house finches that frequented our yard, I would be content. But Tuck didn't sing. When I consulted online sources to figure out why, I learned that male birds only sing under the right conditions. But what were those conditions? I moved his cage closer to a sunny window. I changed his birdseed to a more expensive brand. Sometimes I sang to Tuck hoping he'd join in. Nothing worked. I became disappointed, then frustrated. Tuck was not doing what he was supposed to do.

My annoyance led me to reflect upon the many passages in the Bible that encourage us to sing praises to the Lord—regardless of the situations we find ourselves in. When Jesus was greeted with enthusiastic song as He rode triumphantly into Jerusalem, the disgruntled Pharisees ordered Him to rebuke the crowd. Jesus responded by saying that if the people kept quiet, the rocks would sing out (Luke 19:37–40). We have been created to sing His praises. Colossians 1:16 reminds us that all creation was made for God's glory.

I wondered if the Lord might be aggravated with me sometimes—that perhaps I'm too much like Tuck, just waiting for the right conditions before I sing praises to my Lord. I'm changing that. Along with my quiet-time devotions, I'm singing to God. I keep an old hymnal next to my Bible. Tuck never did become a singing sensation, but he taught me a valuable lesson. For that I'm grateful.—Shirley Raye Redmond

Come, let us sing for joy to the LORD; let us shout aloud to the Rock of our salvation.
—Psalm 95:1 (NIV)

NOVEMBER 4

In Praise of the Foreigner

And you are to love those who are foreigners, for you yourselves were foreigners in Egypt.

—DEUTERONOMY 10:19 (NIV)

I DIDN'T GROW UP with squirrels—they seemed as exotic to me as zebras or kangaroos when we immigrated to Canada from California. Still today, the squirrels in our trees continue to be among my biggest delights. Eastern gray squirrels provide year-round entertainment in the hazelnut tree outside our kitchen window. They are thorough harvesters. By the time the ground below is littered with shells, the squirrels are resorting to brave and implausible feats to reach every last nut.

I love that I immigrated to a place that is home to squirrels. It turns out the squirrels are immigrants too. In 1909, eight pairs were brought to Vancouver's Stanley Park from New York City; every eastern gray squirrel in British Columbia is descended from those few forebearers. British Columbia also has three species of native squirrels: red, Douglas, and northern flying squirrels.

The squirrel situation reminds me what it is like to be an immigrant. When my family was new to Canada, we felt some suspicion directed toward us. Yet it's the wonderful people and merging of cultures that bring diversity to the place where we live. When we became citizens, the presiding judge gave an inspiring speech declaring that the richness of Canada is its diversity. My neighborhood is home to Chinese, Greek, Hungarian, Iranian, Polish, Taiwanese, and Trinidadian, as well as Californian, immigrants. We expect Syrians and Ukrainians later this year.

During the pandemic, the squirrels' hazelnut tree became a gathering point for neighbors too. Aware of our common vulnerability, we learned to look out for one another, celebrating a child's birthday, doing one another's chores, making deliveries, and sharing our gardens' produce.

My neighborhood is testimony to the beauty of an immigrant-enriched neighborhood. While I enjoy the immigrant-turned-resident squirrels, I'm more grateful that the community under the tree is as lively as the one in the tree.—Susie Colby

Walk of Faith: *Find out where your neighbors come from, whether across town or around the world, and share something with one or more of them—a story, a chore, a special food, or a cup of tea.*

NOVEMBER 5

Joy Dances

You will go out in joy and be led forth in peace; the mountains and hills will burst into song before you, and all the trees of the field will clap their hands.

—ISAIAH 55:12 (NIV)

GOD MUST HAVE created some of His creatures simply for the joy factor. Take Violet, for instance. She's a green-cheeked conure belonging to my granddaughter Faith. This bird loves to play and brings a nightly comedy routine to Faith's five siblings and parents.

Fifteen-year-old Faith diligently cleans Violet's cage, daily putting in fresh food and fresh drinking water, only to watch as Violet puts on a splashy show worthy of a SeaWorld routine. And when Faith and her sister and brothers are practicing their violins, Violet will dance and sing to the music—although her squawks aren't very melodic. As I watch and listen to the little bird, her antics remind me of folks whose enthusiastic karaoke renditions of their favorite tunes provide lots of laughs, despite the off-key tones.

Quite the bird-fact gatherer and afficionado, Faith picked Violet from another family's batch of ten conures. While the others shied away from Faith, Violet took interest in her immediately. And even though Faith was warned that Violet might initially bite her, the conure instead found Faith's shoulder the perfect place to perch and fall asleep on the drive home.

As someone who sends out the church prayer requests nearly daily, I find life can often weigh me down. Friends are seriously ill. Others need jobs with incomes to cover their basic needs. And many people simply seem lost. The weight of those needs often zaps my joy.

But then I remember that God also gives me abundant sources of joy. A silly bird like Violet splashing, dancing, and squawk-singing gives me something to feel joyful about. Joy can be found anywhere. Tree branches swaying in the wind. Hummingbirds sipping nectar from flowers. Kids telling jokes or jumping high on the trampoline. And those pauses remind me to keep looking for joy.—Janet Holm McHenry

Walk of Faith: *Make it a point today to look for and write down five simple joys. Thank God for creating joy in the simple aspects of life.*

NOVEMBER 6

My Loving Friend

For this reason we also thank God without ceasing, because when you received the word of God which you heard from us, you welcomed it not as the word of men, but as it is in truth, the word of God, which also effectively works in you who believe.

—1 THESSALONIANS 2:13 (NKJV)

WHEN I DECIDED to bring a golden retriever into my home, little did I realize the warm welcome she would give me each time I returned home.

As my car pulls in the driveway and I negotiate the gate to the back door, my faithful friend makes her way to the hallway. A key in the lock must build her anticipation. Regardless of the number of times per day I come and go, Snowy stands ready with wagging tail and humble eyes. There is no way to pass up that look of love without responding with some petting and hugs.

As I unload my pockets of wallet, keys, and phone, my pal follows along, ensuring my safety and affirming her companionship throughout the process. If a change of clothes is in order, she waits patiently on her dog bed. As soon as I'm again on the move, she tags along. After checking her food and water bowls, my next move is to get her a treat just because I love her.

God has taught me so many lessons through my hairy companion—love, patience, and companionship to name just a few. His love for me bubbles over as I spend time in prayer. He waits patiently for me as I read His Word. God's love welcomes me as I read the Bible and embrace the ageless teachings contained therein. Nothing pleases Him more than when I apply the principles and instructions transferred by His Spirit in these quiet times—and when I'm with Snowy.—David L. Winters

Thank You, Lord, for the clear road map of Your Word, the Bible. Help me to read and apply Your teachings to my life. Amen.

NOVEMBER 7

Honk! Honk!

There is a time for everything, and a season for every activity under the heavens.

—ECCLESIASTES 3:1 (NIV)

EVERY FALL, I listen for the *honk honk* of the giant Canada geese flying from Indiana where I live to their winter home. On many of my walks at the community park, I pause and gaze at the V-shaped flock overhead. The leader drops back while the others shift their positions. From my observations each year, I know they won't land at this park for food. They much prefer locations near a pond or lake with enough vegetation and water to sustain them on their lengthy journey to a warmer destination.

Most other walkers in the park don't pay attention to the honking from above. To some, the geese migration could be viewed as an ordinary event, not anything spectacular. However, for me, the predictability and pattern of their movement provides comfort. Each autumn, the fliers travel this very same flight plan south. And in the spring, I anticipate their boisterous announcement upon their arrival back in Indiana.

To others, my life of following Jesus may seem a little ordinary. Every Sunday and Wednesday you'll find me at church for prayer, fellowship, and spiritual development. For my lifelong journey, I need the Word of God to keep up my strength to face the difficulties along the way. That also means two days a week is not enough to sustain me. My journey requires the good news daily. When the world seems out of order, I am assured that God has orchestrated a time for everything. Jesus is my leader, and He is in control. Maybe I need a bumper sticker on my car: Honk Honk if you follow Jesus.—Glenda Ferguson

Dear God, thank You for the seasons of life. Guide me in Your ways so that I may stay the course on my flight to my heavenly home. Amen.

To Be Seen

You have searched me, LORD, and you know me. You know when I sit and when I rise; you perceive my thoughts from afar. You discern my going out and my lying down; you are familiar with all my ways.

—PSALM 139:1–3 (NIV)

IMMEDIATELY AFTER LYING back on my couch, I felt four little paws climbing on my chest toward my face. "Hello, Stella," I mumbled. I wasn't sure that this soon after foot surgery I wanted my cat friend sitting on me, but she soon put me to sleep with her purring. As the days went on, Stella continued to sense when I felt bad, forcing me to lie down by climbing on top of me and stretching out. As I began to feel better and grow stronger, she gave me more space by curling up next to my foot.

A week before I had surgery, I was on a motorized scooter at a big box store. I was surprised by the multiple times I was completely ignored, overlooked, and almost run into by people on their shopping mission. Averted eyes and verbalized frustration made me feel small and insignificant, despite the lumbering motorized vehicle I was driving down the aisle right next to them.

To be truly seen is a gift. For someone, or a cat, to look into my eyes and sense my needs fills my soul with acceptance. The contrast between Stella's behavior and that of humans, albeit strangers, was startling.

Like Stella, God knows me and sees me. I don't have to flag Him down to get His attention. He intuitively knows my needs, my desires, and my heart. Just like Stella, who wants to curl up next to me while I'm healing, I plan to stay close to the One who sees me as He cares for my body and soul.—Twila Bennett

Our deepest human need is not material at all.
Our deepest need is to be seen.
—Marianne Williamson

Sew Good!

For every house is built by someone, but the builder of all things is God.
—HEBREWS 3:4 (ESV)

I TOOK A SEWING class in eighth grade and made a few things. But I never had the inclination to learn the craft well. Now, I can handle a needle and thread enough to fix a seam, hem some pants, or sew on a button. That's about it. My sister, on the other hand, is quite skilled. She found a mini sewing machine that had been left behind when someone moved out of her building, and she gave it to me. I'm not sure I picture myself using it very regularly.

My disinterest and lack of ability cannot hold a candle to the skill of the tailorbird that lives in tropical Asia. This remarkable creature goes all out to provide a home for her chicks. The cradle is surrounded by large, thick leaves and lined with soft material, made up of plant fibers or spider webs. Then she uses her delicate beak like a needle to poke holes along the outer rim of the leaves. The holes are so small that they don't damage or discolor the leaves. She gently pulls up strands of the nest's lining, looping each through the holes, using a variety of techniques (including riveting and lacing) to make it secure. This provides excellent camouflage for her home. It typically takes her about four days to complete this safe haven for her clutch of eggs.

How do animals know how to do the things they do? This diminutive bird didn't attend a trade school to learn this skill. Rather, the knowledge is inherent in her DNA, placed there by an incredibly creative Designer. Just as God designed the tailorbird to do what it does, likewise He created me to do what I do. He has given me all I need to thrive in my corner of the world.—Liz Kimmel

You are amazing, God! Thank You for Your intentional purposes
and the beautiful design You wove into my life when
You envisioned who I would become. Amen.

NOVEMBER 10

Empowered

I will put My Spirit within you and cause you to walk in My statutes, and you will keep My judgments and do them.

—EZEKIEL 36:27 (NKJV)

I COULD SMELL THE aroma of baking fish. The food I had prepared for dinner was almost done. I called my Yorkie, Minnie, to come for her dinner. She stood at the top of the stairs outside my office door and grunted. I climbed a few steps toward her, and she turned back into the office. Minnie wants to climb down the stairs on her own, but she forgets she can and gets scared.

I returned to the base of the steps, and Minnie moved to the top when I said her name. I cheered her on. "Minnie, you can do this. You are strong and capable. Come on." After my pep talk, she ran down the half flight, rounded the corner, raced down the second half flight, and beat me to her food bowl.

I dished up Minnie's food and filled her water bowl. As I served dinner to my husband and me, God prompted my heart to realize that sometimes I forget my own abilities and get scared too. As His child, I'm strong, capable, and empowered by His Holy Spirit. But I can let fear and anxiety stop me from taking risks and doing things outside what feels familiar.

I have written verses on the last pages of my morning devotional that encourage my identity and confirm my calling. Reading through them the next morning, I realized that through His Word, God cheers me on just as I cheered for Minnie. It's okay if I'm forgetful or frightened. I can read my Bible to hear from my Lord, and through His Word, I know nothing can stop me.—Crystal Storms

Walk of Faith: *Write out verses that remind you that God created you, walks with you, and empowers you to love those around you through your unique gifting. Hang them in a spot where you can read them each day.*

NOVEMBER 11

Be Leaf Me

Then she called the name of the Lord *who spoke to her, You-Are-the-God-Who-Sees; for she said, "Have I also here seen Him who sees me?"*

—Genesis 16:13 (NKJV)

My ELEVEN-YEAR-OLD GRANDSON and I were headed out to the car one afternoon when he remarked, "Look, Granny. What a cool bug this is."

"What bug?" I asked, puzzled, as I surveyed the area to which he was pointing. All I saw were dead leaves.

"Right *there*," he insisted, pointing closer.

"That's just a leaf, honey."

Laughing, he poked the tiny leaf with his finger, and sure enough, to my utter surprise, it hopped up and flew away.

"How did you even see that?" I asked him, astonished.

"I was paying attention, Granny," he answered with a grin.

As we got in the car and drove away, I thought about Hagar in the Bible, who was Sarai's maid. Unable to bear a child, Sarai had the idea to give Hagar to her husband as a wife. Needless to say, that idea backfired. Hagar was sent packing.

She must have felt at the end of her rope, all alone and pregnant, yet God reached down to her and let her know He had seen her and was there for her and her unborn son.

Sometimes I feel insignificant like Hagar and that little leaf bug I missed, feeling as if no one sees me or my problems. That's when God's Word reminds me that He is the God-Who-Sees. He made me and cares for me, even when I feel as small and insignificant as a leaf bug.—Deb Kastner

Thank You, Lord, for being the God-Who-Sees. I can trust in You to be all-seeing and all-knowing. I'm grateful You'll never pass by me when I'm in need. Amen.

NOVEMBER 12

Following My Rescuer

Immediately he received his sight and followed Jesus, praising God. When all the people saw it, they also praised God.

—LUKE 18:43 (NIV)

FOR MORE THAN a week, my family followed updates on a great horned owl that one of our neighbors helped to rescue. An Uber driver had seen the baby owl in the middle of the street in front of our neighbor's house, and together they called a local wildlife rescue organization. After a thorough examination at the center, the owlet was found perfectly healthy and uninjured. He had just gotten separated from his mother somehow. After feeding and hydrating the baby, someone from the wildlife organization created a safe nesting place near where he had been found, left him there, and kept tabs on him, in hopes that the mother would return. She did. When we got the update, along with a picture of the mother and baby in a tree behind our neighbor's home, we celebrated and shared the exciting news on social media.

Later in the week, our neighbor sent pictures of the mother owl perched on a branch near their porch railing and another of the owlet just outside the patio. It was as if both owls wanted to be close to the people who had rescued the little one.

I thought of the blind man in the Bible who, after being healed, chose to stay close to Jesus. I reflected on some of my own experiences that I knew were "divine rescues." Each one deepened my connection to Jesus and my desire to be in His presence.

That mother and baby owl eventually flew away, but I pray that no matter what life brings, I will stay near my Rescuer.—Jeanette Hanscome

'Tis so sweet to walk with Jesus,
Step by step and day by day.
—Albert Benjamin Simpson

NOVEMBER 13

A Dog Named Mary

"Martha, Martha," the Lord answered, "you are worried and upset about many things, but few things are needed—or indeed only one. Mary has chosen what is better and it will not be taken away from her."

—LUKE 10:41–42 (NIV)

PIP IS A five-year-old Havanese, pure white with chestnut brown eyes. The playful pup weighs perhaps five pounds soaking wet, and he greets me at the door with a playful yip whenever I visit my friend's house. Pip absolutely bursts with energy for about ten minutes. After that, he seems to settle in.

First, he'll bring his squeaky toy and drop it at my feet, the universal sign for *Let's play fetch!* I oblige, tossing the toy into the next room. Pip scampers after it, then asks for a repeat performance. This goes on for several minutes.

When my arm tires, surprisingly early these days, I take a seat on the couch, and Pip hops into my lap. His fur is downy soft, and I stroke his ears and back. Once in a while he asks for a belly rub. That may last another two or three minutes. Then Pip is through. He hops off my lap, trots over to his doggie bed, and curls up like a cat.

"That's a Havanese for you," my friend said when I remarked on Pip's low battery. "They need very little exercise and are mostly content just to be near you. It's kind of nice."

On reflection, I realize I've been more like a Pekingese or a shih tzu, especially in my relationship with God. I always want to be busy, active, running, guarding God's house like a watchdog, or demanding His attention. And I suppose there's a time for that.

Yet, I like Pip's style. Like Mary, who sat at Jesus's feet while her sister, Martha, bustled around, Pip is content just being near the one he loves. That's kind of nice, isn't it? Simply being. Not demanding, not defending, just being nearby.—Lawrence W. Wilson

As the deer pants for streams of water, so my soul pants for you, my God.
—Psalm 42:1 (NIV)

The Horse That Bowed to Me

We love because he first loved us.

—1 JOHN 4:19 (NIV)

WHEN I WAS a preteen, my military dad was stationed in Guantanamo Bay, Cuba. Among the many activities provided for military families were riding stables. I took lessons as often as I could, but I also cleaned horses' hooves, fed them, mucked out stalls, and curried coats that needed attention.

One day as I exercised a horse on the trail, a sailor asked me to help with his horse. He and his friends were riding, but he'd gotten off to pick up something he dropped, and the horse wouldn't let him mount up again. The sailor kept trying to toss the reins over the horse's neck, but the horse threw up his head each time.

I slid off my mount and slowly walked over to greet the horse, a paint named Arapaho. I'd spent time grooming him recently and knew him. I stroked Arapaho's face with familiarity and whispered to him, telling him he was a "good boy."

After rescuing the reins from the ground, I led Arapaho away from the sailor, sweet-talking the steed all the time. Then the horse did something I didn't expect. As I held up the reins to try to toss them over his neck, he lowered his head to the ground so I could reach.

"Will you look at that horse?" the sailor said to his still-mounted friend. "He's bowing to that little girl."

I smiled, knowing we were already friends. Arapaho had no fear of me.

My favorite trait is kindness. From God. In anyone. To anyone. When I am kind to others, they respond the same way. And trust is built between us. Kindness—even to a horse—is long remembered.—Cathy Elliott

It's Your kindness that leads us to repentance, oh Lord. Knowing that You love us, no matter what we do, makes us want to love You too.

—Leslie Phillips

NOVEMBER 15

Ranch Manager

Not by way of eye-service, as people-pleasers, but as slaves of Christ, doing the will of God from the heart.

—EPHESIANS 6:6 (NASB)

OUR AUSTRALIAN RED heeler, Ruby, lived out her breeding as a cattle dog. She followed my husband on his beef-cattle ranch wherever he went. If there was room for Ruby on a piece of haying equipment, Craig would pat the floor, and she'd jump up. Even when there wasn't room, she would run behind him up and down the rows of cut or baled hay, putting miles and miles on her paws every day.

Ruby did more than just follow. As hay was being cut or baled, the equipment would cause mice to scamper out, and Ruby would pounce as a cat would on one, two, three at a time—just as adept as a pinball-machine player achieving a perfect score. And when Craig threw down bales from the haystack to feed the cattle at the long manger row, again Ruby would nab those mice that ran this way and that. Her highly developed herding and protective instincts made her function like the best possible ranch manager—one who responds to a need and simply takes care of it without being asked.

But she also liked to show she was boss. As the cattle lined up at the manger, Ruby would trot down the whole row, nipping at the cows' noses. She was dominant. She was in charge. Cows did not eat until she decided they could. Even Craig's huge bulls were afraid of Ruby and let her show them the way out of a pen or into one. Her work ethic was "Let's go!"

I've adopted a Ruby-like perspective. I know that strong leaders don't wait to be told what to do. If I'm entrusted with a position, I assess problems or needs, figure out what to do, delegate if appropriate, and follow through with decisiveness. Maybe I simply have a Ruby-like personality. While I don't need to be the boss or manager, I do like to see things get done. In any case, I know God has put me here on earth, and I often sense He is telling me, "Let's go, Janet. Let's go." —Janet Holm McHenry

A leader is one who knows the way, goes the way, and shows the way.
—John C. Maxwell

NOVEMBER 16

Risk vs. Rewards

The LORD is my light and my salvation—whom shall I fear? The LORD is the stronghold of my life—of whom shall I be afraid?

—PSALM 27:1 (NIV)

I ENJOYED SWIMMING IN the shallow waters of the beach, but I never ventured into deep waters. While my family was in Hawaii on a holiday, my son was keen to go on a boat tour to enjoy a snorkeling experience with sea turtles, so I reluctantly agreed. We boarded the vessel at a beach in Waikiki along with six or eight other passengers. As we sailed toward a popular snorkel spot called Turtle Canyon, I became afraid and regretted my decision.

When we reached the location, I helped my son put on his gear before putting mine on. My heart beat rapidly, but it was too late to turn back. Taking the steps behind the boat, I followed the other tourists into the ocean. Being in the water with others put me a little at ease. The guide motioned for us to look toward the sea floor. I hesitated at first, then took a deep breath before I submerged my face in the water, bringing my legs almost to the surface. Right there, in front of my eyes were two green sea turtles swimming lazily. I gazed at them in amazement. I resisted the urge to reach out and touch the turtle next to me, but I tried to stay as close to it as possible, observing its eyes, flippers, ridges, and shell. My breathing slowly steadied and my body relaxed as I started to enjoy the sights of the underwater paradise.

Sometimes when I take a leap of faith, the rewards can be greater than my fears or perceived risks. I had been praying about stepping up to a leadership position in my Bible study. With God's help, I can face my fears and prepare myself to experience the blessings of following His lead.—Mabel Ninan

Walk of Faith: *Is God calling you to take on a new role or greater responsibility at work or in church? Share your concerns and fears with a close friend and ask him or her to pray with you.*

NOVEMBER 17

Bovine Blockade

The LORD will fight for you; you need only to be still.

—EXODUS 14:14 (NIV)

IN SOME PLACES where I hike, the trail passes through public land shared with ranchers who graze cattle there. Sometimes the cows and I want to use the same path. Personally, I'm not afraid of cows. I find them homey animals with their big cow eyes and broad, moist noses. But when my head only reaches their shoulder, they can seem a bit intimidating and sometimes reluctant to move out of the way. Most of the time, though, just standing within their view motivates them to relocate. I guess they are no more eager to confront me than I am to confront them. I don't have to do a thing.

When I read the verse "The LORD will fight for you; you need only to be still," I was reminded of those cows. I'd been wrestling with something that had robbed me of my peace of mind. I was losing sleep over it. Like a large cow blocking my path, it was something I couldn't see around or remove, and despite my best efforts, I was discontented and unhappy.

God's Word tells me He will fight my fights for me. I need only to "be still." But sometimes it's hard for me to trust that God will act without my "help." Yet Scripture says otherwise.

Do I believe His promise to "fight" for me? *Yes!* Praying over this verse helped me put the obstacle into the proper Hands, and I was able to get to sleep, knowing all the "cows" in my life are taken care of. When I prayerfully approach God with my needs, He will often answer, *Be still.* In every case, I need only to stand by and watch the miracles, rescues, solutions, and blessings.—Marianne Campbell

The more you love and trust Him, the nearer you will feel to Him,
and the less you will depend on human power and wisdom.
His love and care never tire or change, can never be taken from you.
—Louisa May Alcott

NOVEMBER 18

The Big Switch

As for you, you meant evil against me, but God meant it for good.

—GENESIS 50:20 (ESV)

I HELD MY BREATH as I set the plate before my calico cat. Would she like the new canned food?

Switching the brand of a cat's food wouldn't usually be significant. For many felines, canned food is an optional treat. But for Videa, it was essential.

Videa had suffered years of severe health issues until I obtained a diagnosis. She would need daily doses of medication for the rest of her life. Thankfully, giving Videa her medicine wasn't difficult when I mixed the liquid formula into her canned food.

In addition to this latest health issue, she suffered from allergies and was a fussy eater, so there was only one food Videa could have that she'd usually eat. On days when she rejected it, I wondered what I would do if she stopped altogether or if the food became unavailable. That day came sooner than expected when her special food suddenly vanished from retailers. Thankfully, I had stocked up in advance. But without medicine, Videa's disease could kill her.

I searched for a different food that met her sensitivities and found one to try. That was the food on the plate I now held for Videa. She cautiously smelled it. Then her small tongue tasted it. She licked again. And again. I watched in awe as she cleaned the plate, faster than she had ever eaten her previous food.

What I thought was a disaster turned out to be a gift. God took away the other food so I would discover one that Videa would eat more consistently, making her healthier than ever. Now when I feed Videa her new food and medicine, I'm reminded of God's providence in every area of my life, redeeming even the bad and using it for good.—Jerusha Agen

Be obedient in the painful times, and trust that God is up to something more grand and wonderful than you can imagine.
—Susie Larson

NOVEMBER 19

Joy in the Backyard

So I commend the enjoyment of life, because nothing is better for a person under the sun than to eat and drink and be glad. Then joy will accompany them in their toil all the days of life God has given them under the sun.

—ECCLESIASTES 8:15 (NIV)

THE FLOCK OF birds in our tiny backyard is usually a joy. Every day we see wrens, cardinals, red-winged blackbirds, doves, and an occasional pigeon visiting our two feeders. We sometimes get to enjoy their romantic behavior as couples separate themselves from the feeding frenzy while the male feeds the female. And they fill the air with beautiful songs.

But on some days, my joy turns to grumpiness, as I realize the birds have messed up the patio table and chairs, which now need cleaning. Plus they have devoured half the food in their feeder, and I need to go buy more. The grumpiness gets worse when the store near our home is out of the food they prefer, and I have to drive thirty minutes across town to satisfy the birds' ravenous appetites.

Isn't it just a matter of attitude? If I follow the advice in Ecclesiastes and am glad, then joy accompanies me on my errands. But if I let the grumpiness take over, not only do I ruin my day, but I can also ruin the day for my family and friends. Changing my attitude is not easy, but it's worthwhile.

I remember a student advisee who was known for spreading joy. One day she came into my office and broke down. She said that it's very hard being the one who's expected to be positive and upbeat in every situation. I agreed that she was right and told her I understood. She thanked me for listening, put away her down attitude, and went out of the office spreading her usual joy. I try each day to emulate her positive approach to life and to spread joy like the birds in our backyard.—Harold Nichols

To conclude: you must all have the same attitude and the same feelings; love one another, and be kind and humble with one another.

—1 Peter 3:8 (GNT)

NOVEMBER 20

Whom Shall I Send?

Also I heard the voice of the Lord, saying: "Whom shall I send, and who will go for Us?" Then I said, "Here am I! Send me."

—ISAIAH 6:8 (NKJV)

I ARRIVED AT MY Toastmasters meeting to see one of the members with his German shorthaired pointer. "How come you brought your dog to our meeting?"

Our vice president of education pointed toward the large canine at his feet. "This is Jada. She's part of my speech."

"Sounds fun. I look forward to hearing about Jada."

Jada lay on the floor between Rick and his wife the entire evening, never making a sound.

As the prepared speeches part of the meeting opened, Rick led Jada to the lectern. He explained how he was training Jada to be a companion for his wife who has PTSD from her time in the military. Rick worked with Jada every night during their evening walks.

Jada's breed isn't traditionally used for service dogs, but she was their beloved family pet. Rick was working with a dog trainer to teach Jada how to become a service dog. At the end of his speech, he and Jada demonstrated "heel," "sit," and "stay." She obeyed every command, revealing hours of training and hard work.

On the drive home, I considered how God doesn't look for the person with the most qualifications. Just as Rick worked with their family dog, God seeks out the one who is available. The person who walks by His side. The one who is obedient to His Word. The one who, like the prophet Isaiah, hears God's call and responds, "Here I am! Send me."

My prayer as I laid my head on the pillow that night was for the Lord to give me a willing heart that follows His leading. Here I am! Send me.—Crystal Storms

God is looking for willing hearts… God has no favorites.
You do not have to be special, but you have to be available.
—Winkie Pratney

Strength in Stillness

For thus said the Lord GOD, the Holy One of Israel, "In returning and rest you shall be saved; in quietness and in trust shall be your strength."

—ISAIAH 30:15 (ESV)

I LIVE IN A college town, and according to my observation, we have a much higher percentage of squirrels than a noncollege town would have. The squirrels exist in highest density close to campus, where they hang out and fatten up on the good and plenteous treats left around by students. And in a rather symbiotic relationship, they help to keep the campus tidy.

My backyard, not overly far from campus, is often an ongoing riot of squirrel activity. There is a good deal of wild chasing up and down tree trunks, followed by acrobatic leaping from branch to branch. They are always happy to share their opinions about life, chattering and squawking at one another (and me). I had always thought there was never a dull moment with squirrels around.

Then, one afternoon I looked out the kitchen window to see a squirrel lying prone on one of the horizontal supports for our fence. It lay absolutely still in a block of sun, and I stared at it for several minutes until, with some concern, I went out to the yard to check on it. Of course, it bolted away as soon as I stepped into close range. And I breathed a sigh of relief!

Since that day, I have occasionally noticed my rambunctious friends, the squirrels, taking moments of deep rest, fully quieting themselves, stilling themselves to a shocking degree. I wouldn't have expected squirrels to be so intentional. When I look all around me in my own rambunctious world, I rarely see intentional rest or stillness there either. Yet, it is the example of the squirrel stopping to be quiet in the sun that my soul longs to follow. There I will be saved. There I will find strength.—Katy W. Sundararajan

Walk of Faith: *Intentionally take some time to allow your mind and body to become still. Rest in the Lord's presence. Offer a deep breath of gratitude.*

Baby Kitty/Snowball/Casper/Neo

But now thus says the Lord, he who created you, O Jacob, he who formed you, O Israel: "Fear not, for I have redeemed you; I have called you by name, you are mine."

—Isaiah 43:1 (ESV)

A PICTURE OF A snow-white cat with orange ears appeared one day on our neighborhood Facebook page. The post read, "Does this little sweetie belong to anyone? I opened my back door, and she strolled right in. Made herself comfortable on my sofa and let me rub her belly."

One neighbor commented, "She belongs to a lady on Goldleaf. Shows up at my house regularly and snacks on my cat's food. I call her Snowball."

Another chimed in, "Yep, she has a happy home, but likes to visit around. My kids named her Casper."

Finally, her owner put the question to rest. "That's Neo. She and her brother, Jack, belong to me. Thanks for looking out for her."

I met the playful kitten one day as I walked the neighborhood. She ran up to me, flopped down, and rolled over a few times, inviting me to stroke her soft fur. From then on, I called her Baby Kitty.

Like Baby Kitty/Snowball/Casper/Neo, I've been called a dozen names in my lifetime. Some have made me smile: Smart, Creative, Patient. Others have made me cry: Failure, Worthless, Hopeless. The only names that truly matter are the names God, my Father and Master, has given me: Precious (Psalm 116:15), Beloved (Romans 9:25), Redeemed (Romans 3:22–25), Treasured (Deuteronomy 7:6), Forgiven (Colossians 3:13), Masterfully Crafted (Ephesians 2:10), His Child (1 John 3:1).

When the world tries to give me a name that isn't my own, I remember God's names for me. With His voice resonating in my heart, I'm free to rest in confidence and love, no matter what anyone else calls me.—Lori Hatcher

The nations shall see your righteousness, and all the kings your glory, and you shall be called by a new name that the mouth of the Lord will give.

—Isaiah 62:2 (ESV)

I Love Lucy (and She Loves Me)

See what great love the Father has lavished on us, that we should be called children of God! And that is what we are! The reason the world does not know us is that it did not know him.

1 JOHN 3:1 (NIV)

THEY ASKED FOR volunteers. I had a free Saturday. I was searching for a way to be useful and thought this might be my opportunity. I showed up for the clothing giveaway and did my best. But after four (gentle) comments about how things should be done, I realized I was falling short. Rather than being useful, I was in the way. With a sad feeling I slunk toward the door and quietly left. As I drove home, I felt "less than," wounded, and inept.

Once I opened the door at home, my mood made a 180-degree turn. My dog, Lucy, greeted me as if I'd been gone for days. (It was an hour.) She spun around, tail wagging, and showered me with slobbery kisses like I was a five-star celebrity. She didn't care that I had just experienced rejection and felt like a failure. She only cared that I was back home safe and sound.

Lucy's behavior reminds me of how God accepts me, even when I've not lived up to others' expectations. He welcomes me back home to Him and never rejects me. I may be a disappointment to others, but to God I'm His child, and I'm never in the way. God always accepts me for who I am, who He made me to be. I may not be a five-star celebrity, but by God and Lucy I am loved unconditionally.—Linda Bartlett

A dog is the only thing on earth that loves you more than he loves himself.
—Josh Billings

NOVEMBER 24

The Shepherd's Voice

My sheep listen to my voice; I know them, and they follow me.

—JOHN 10:27 (NIV)

IS IT MY turn to hold them?" my son Jordan asked. He pointed to the pocket on his hoodie. "It's all ready for them."

Our family had just adopted two exotic pets called sugar gliders. Small marsupials originally from Australia, they look and behave like flying squirrels. The salesman told us that our sugar gliders, Max and Lucy, would bond with us by hanging out in our pockets. The more time they spent close to us, the more familiar they'd become with our scents and the sound of our voices and the more bonded to us they'd feel.

Naturally, each of my children wanted "pocket time" with our new pets. But when they left for school each morning, I donned my hoodie, and the pair spent all day in my pocket. I even began singing to them as I worked around the house. It built trust with Max and Lucy, and it kept me from obsessing about my father-in-law's declining health. His care was becoming more involved all the time, and I worried that it would become too much for us to do at home.

One day, Max escaped from someone's pocket and crawled inside our recliner. We turned the chair upside down and tried to grab him, but he was too fast. Max was "crabbing," the noise sugar gliders make when they're afraid.

I asked the kids to go upstairs, then I sat down next to the upside-down recliner and started singing. Within minutes, Max crawled out of the chair and into my pocket. He'd spent so much time listening to my voice that he now associated it with safety.

I realized that I'd allowed my worries to become louder than the Shepherd's voice. His voice assured me that both my father-in-law and I were among His beloved sheep. If we listened for His voice and followed Him, everything would work out the way it was supposed to.—Diane Stark

Lord, help me to listen for Your voice when I feel worried or scared. Amen.

His Unique Calling

The LORD came and stood there, calling as at the other times, "Samuel! Samuel!" Then Samuel said, "Speak, for your servant is listening."

—1 SAMUEL 3:10 (NIV)

I GREW UP ON a dairy farm, and our family never had a shortage of cats. They just showed up, especially around milking time. I can't remember naming any of the barn cats. When the milk lines were drained and the excess was placed in a pan, someone would call out, "Here kitty, kitty," and cats would appear. I guess they all responded to a generic name.

Fast-forward to today, when my family has one indoor and two outdoor cats. None of them would budge if I called, "Here kitty, kitty." These cats all know their names: Mouser, Roadie, and Cheeks. Of course, felines are fickle and obstinate—they won't always come when called. But my youngest daughter, Suzanna, discovered a useful cat call for Mouser, who lives indoors. It always compels her to come from any room in the house. Suzanna or I will whistle the national anthem annoyingly loud. Strangely, Mouser appears and often jumps in the lap of the person whistling. I am guessing she must be very patriotic.

God's calling on my life was just as unique. It wasn't annoyingly loud. I heard it in a quiet urging whisper at age twelve. There is something powerful about a whisper. It made me focus and listen to the message it contained: *Believe and follow Me!*

Like a cat, I can be fickle and obstinate at times when it comes to the "following Him" part. Still, He quietly whispers His unique calling, and I am compelled to listen and obey.—Ben Cooper

Father God, thank You for the unique way You have of getting me to respond to Your voice. Help me to run to You and willingly welcome Your whispers. Amen.

NOVEMBER 26

Tuff Love

First we were loved, now we love. He loved us first.

—1 JOHN 4:19 (MSG)

IF EVER THERE was a puppy sibling duo that was as different as night and day, it would be Tiny and Tuffy. These two little dogs (both a pug-dachshund mix) have been part of my daughter's family for several years. Tiny is bold, friendly, eager, exuberant, in-your-face, "I want to lick you everywhere!" Tuffy was born with a disability and was not considered adoptable until he met my daughter. He is timid, cautious, uncertain, afraid, "Don't come near me; you make me nervous!"

In the early days, the noise and commotion that accompanied my arrival at their home could not be quieted until one of his human housemates instructed Tuffy to be quiet. And even though the barking and snarling would diminish, he usually cowered in the corner until I left. Over the course of time, Tuffy learned to recognize me. He still barks but is willing to quiet his voice at my suggestion, once he has had a chance to sniff my hand and confirm my identity. The wagging tail is another clear indication of his acceptance.

He's gotten even more comfortable lately. Now he asks me for a tummy scratch in a very nonassertive way. He comes close and pauses tentatively in front of me. That is the first good sign. But before he will go any further, I need to reach out my hand to him. Only then will he flop down, roll over, and expose his tummy for some much-wanted attention. Someday the time may come when he voluntarily asks to be lifted into my lap for a hug.

Just as Tuffy came to understand that he is loved, I must do the same. I seem to need reminding of this fairly frequently. As I learn to let my guard down and am willing to be vulnerable, I become more aware of the tenderness of my Father. Thankfully, the Triune God always takes the first step.—Liz Kimmel

Thank You, Father, Son, and Holy Spirit, for modeling love for me,
that I might grow in trust and begin to reflect that love
to all I meet. Amen.

Speckles on My Spectacles

You hypocrite, first take the plank out of your own eye, and then you will see clearly to remove the speck from your brother's eye.

—MATTHEW 7:5 (NIV)

I WAS SEATED AT my home computer when my tortoiseshell cat, Speckles, leaped onto the desk. She commenced to demonstrate her attraction, not for me but for my glasses. She began sweeping her face along the corners of the frames. Then came the unladylike drooling across my lenses, which she smudged with specks. Speckles was making a spectacle of herself over my tortoiseshell spectacles. Her obsession coincided with my need to focus on my computer screen. I required privacy and clear vision but hesitated to push her away or speak harshly to her because she is my fond feline. However, despite her yowling protest, I picked her up and put her outside.

That incident reminded me that I was still distressed about a strained relationship. When a good friend suffered a loss, I consoled her and remained by her side. In other words, I insisted she not be left alone. After days of this routine, my friend finally spoke bluntly. She needed solitude so that she could grieve but hesitated to ask me to leave. However, she felt she had to let me know, even if her honesty hurt my feelings. Ashamedly, I left her with a bit of anger. Upon reflection, I wondered if I had prayed for my friend's needs or my own. Was I just getting in her way of healing? I resolved to take the first steps in reconciling with my friend.

The next time Speckles came around when I required clear vision, I stopped, hugged her, and thanked God for her companionship—and for the lesson I learned because of her. Then I tempted her away with some treats so that she would leave me and my speckled spectacles alone. —Glenda Ferguson

It's not what you look at that matters, it's what you see.
—Henry David Thoreau

NOVEMBER 28

A Safe Place to Land

Have mercy on me, my God, have mercy on me, for in you I take refuge. I will take refuge in the shadow of your wings until the disaster has passed.

—PSALM 57:1 (NIV)

WIND WHIPS AT the foothills of the Rocky Mountains, stirring up thick dust clouds. Tumbleweeds bounce and fly across the prairie as if thrown by giants. In the seven years I've lived here, I've never seen Colorado's wind so fierce. A flock of geese flies—or attempts to fly—overhead. I can nearly feel their angst. I wonder if they regret delaying the start of their migration until this late in the season. Had they left yesterday, they'd be well on their way. Instead, they press hard against wind gusts only to nudge an inch across the sky.

I feel like those geese more often than I like to admit. How often have I ignored an inner call, prompted by God's Spirit, to make a move? As I procrastinate, conditions shift, and it becomes all the more difficult to begin. I get in my own way and make an endeavor far more complicated than God ever meant it to be.

I watch the geese and know their weary wings won't last much longer—but they'll be okay. Birds have a strategy for these adverse scenarios. When a storm interrupts migration routes, birds practice a "fallout" and find a safe place to land—an early stopover to wait out the weather. God has graciously provided these shelters along my journey too. When I step outside the cadence of His timing or miss His direction completely, He does not leave me to my own wandering. Instead, He welcomes me into His haven and reminds me His yoke is easy and burden is light. He provides the refuge I need. In the wise words of friends, lyrics from a hymn, truth from His Word, and peace from His Spirit, I find the restoration and strength I need to continue.—Eryn Lynum

But let all who take refuge in you be glad; let them ever sing for joy.
Spread your protection over them, that those who love your
name may rejoice in you.
—Psalm 5:11 (NIV)

NOVEMBER 29

Only One Way?

Be anxious for nothing, but in everything by prayer and supplication, with thanksgiving, let your requests be made known to God.

—PHILIPPIANS 4:6 (NKJV)

MINNIE STANDS AT my side of the bed and looks up when she's ready to go to sleep. When my husband, Tim, offers to pick up our Yorkie and put her on his side of the bed, she runs to my side as if to get him to follow her. Sometimes Minnie hides behind me if he attempts to help her up. Once in bed she snuggles with Tim and plays with him before she cuddles next to me for some good sleep, but she wants to get up on the bed only by my side.

When we brought Minnie home from the breeder, we set up a makeshift kennel with old cardboard boxes on my side of the bed. This allowed her to use the potty pad as needed during the night, and I could rub Minnie's head as she fell asleep.

Minnie moved to our bed to sleep when she completed potty training. Her small size prevents her from jumping onto the bed, but she's convinced she can get up there only on my side.

I was pondering a relationship struggle I faced as I brushed my teeth. Just then Minnie ran behind my legs. Seeing Minnie in the midst of my thinking helped me realize that just as she thinks there is only one way to get on the bed, I could think of only one outcome that would be positive for everyone involved. I feared any alternative would bring more harm than good.

God prompted my heart through Minnie to know there's more than one way for this situation to play out. I can trust Him no matter how things end. And even if this struggle doesn't end in a positive way, God is still good.—Crystal Storms

I am no longer anxious about anything, as I realize the Lord is able to carry out His will, and His will is mine. It makes no matter where He places me, or how. That is rather for Him to consider than for me; for in the easiest positions He must give me His grace, and in the most difficult, His grace is sufficient.

—Hudson Taylor

NOVEMBER 30

Paws for Prayer

Give thanks to the Lord, for he is good; his love endures forever.

—1 CHRONICLES 16:34 (NIV)

OH, NO. IS Brother sick?" I asked my husband, Bill, one morning. Joining me to observe our cats' breakfast routine, Bill scratched his head. "Not sure, but you're right. He's not diving into his food like Sister."

And it's true, though over time, we've come to understand, even appreciate, this feline's unique feeding habit.

Unlike his sibling who, from the first day post-adoption, has attacked her food with vigor any time she hears the crack of a can, Brother pauses. Sauntering in at mealtime, he allows Sister to dig in while he sits back and waits, eyes glassy little half-moons.

After a moment, he'll jump upon the dresser where his bowl, filled to the brim, awaits. But before eating, he hesitates again, head low.

"Oh, I get it," I whispered to my husband on one such occasion, several weeks after their arrival. The space had a sacred aura, almost holy. "He's pausing to pray. To give thanks."

And whether or not this stealthy little creature, who loves to pounce and play like any other cat, knows it or not, Brother's continued mealtime ritual has set an example for our family—reminding us to slow down, to pause, to pray, and to appreciate. Mostly, he encourages us to give thanks to the One whose faithfulness endures and is evident all around.

God's love is embodied in a tiny cat named Brother—whose little gray paws stop short of the food bowl each day before breakfast. It's an exhortation to me, as well, to pause and thank the Giver of all good and precious gifts.—Maureen Miller

You created the world and all creatures, each wonderfully unique
and endowed with attributes that illuminate the poetries of
your mind, your power, your beauty, your sense of humor,
your playfulness, your delight.
—Douglas Kaine McKelvey

December

DECEMBER 1

Gandalf's Flock

I looked, and there before me was a white horse! Its rider held a bow, and he was given a crown, and he rode out as a conqueror bent on conquest.

—REVELATION 6:2 (NIV)

WE RAISE A variety of animals on Selah Farm, including a white Missouri Fox Trotter and a dozen sheep. I imagine the sheep look to the horse much like hobbits look to Gandalf, the wise wizard in *Lord of the Rings*. Though our horse's name is Mick, we affectionately call him Gandalf.

Gandalf's getting old. Our flock is, too, not to mention the two remaining Nigerian Dwarf goats, Abraham and Isaac, who keep to themselves after the passing of sisters Rachel and Leah. (Our goats and sheep don't get along, much like Tolkien's dwarves and elves.)

We're caring for mostly geriatric animals. Still, there's a lot of life in Gandalf, as long as he gets his daily dose of glucosamine and his anti-inflammatory tablet, which my daughter kindly tucks in an apple.

Sometimes, when the weather grows cold, she leads her steed into a stall, lays a blanket over his back, and offers him a peppermint, which he doesn't refuse. In the morning, she opens the barn doors, and he ambles up the pasture to find a dozen friends eating "second breakfast," another hobbit trait, just over the brink of the hill.

Since our animals resemble characters in a fantasy story, I wonder who I'd be. Unlike Tolkien's elves, I'm not immortal and am susceptible to old age. But like my animals and the hobbits, I want to enjoy each day, to be thankful for family, friends, food, and my faith. I want to make the most of the life I've been given by God.

Old Gandalf just might be around when God's Son returns. Perhaps the Lamb will point, then proclaim, "Look, a white horse!" After all, the very best story, the second coming of Christ, is no fantasy.—Maureen Miller

Well, here at last, dear friends… Go in peace!
—J. R. R. Tolkien

DECEMBER 2

A Big God

In the year that King Uzziah died, I saw the Lord, high and exalted, seated on a throne; and the train of his robe filled the temple.

—ISAIAH 6:1 (NIV)

MY SISTER AND her husband love Great Danes, one of the largest dog breeds in the world. They've raised several litters and can tell you all about the different color variations—blue and brindle, merle and harlequin—as well as the Danes' wonderful attributes. When my sister brought a puppy to visit one time, she playfully pulled up his floppy, bloodhound-loose skin as he sat on the floor and said, "Room to grow!" And grow they do.

I'll be honest—Great Danes intimidate me. They may be gentle giants, but when a dog can come up and look me straight in the eye while I sit on the couch, it gives me a jolt. They are just so…big.

Sometimes I think of God that way. When I visualize Isaiah's report of the Lord's robe filling the temple or imagine His voice thundering from heaven as described in the psalms, I'm more than a little frightened. He's just so…big.

Then I remember that God loves me. He sent Jesus to die for me and wants me to live forever with Him in heaven. Yes, I want to fear the One who is "high and exalted" by treating Him with reverential awe as the Creator of the universe, but I need not feel scared. I can trust God. He invites me to put my life in His hands and surrounds me with His faithfulness. As a redeemed child of the King, I have no reason to be afraid.

The Great Danes in my life have proved themselves to be gentle, consistent with their reputations. I don't mind so much now when they walk up and stare me in the eye. My only problem is when they turn around and try to sit in my lap.—Tracy Crump

In the council of the holy ones God is greatly feared; he is more awesome than all who surround him. Who is like you, LORD God Almighty? You, LORD, are mighty, and your faithfulness surrounds you.
—Psalm 89:7–8 (NIV)

DECEMBER 3

An Orchard Encounter

As the deer pants for streams of water, so my soul pants for you, my God.

—PSALM 42:1 (NIV)

IT WAS LATE afternoon, the gloaming hour, and I was far back in the woods, hurrying home—as much as one can hurry on snowshoes—trying to beat the storm. The wind was up, and the northern sky was the color of a bad bruise. A whopper of a snowstorm had been predicted, and soft, fluffy flakes were falling already.

I'd lost track of time out there in the woods, walking along, head down, ruminating on the troubles that had been coming at me lately. Financial setbacks, health issues, relationships that had gone off the rails. I remember thinking: *How am I going to deal with all this?*

Walking through an old orchard, I stopped and stared. It was a deer, a large doe standing on her hind legs, trying to reach a wrinkled, leftover apple that had forgotten to fall. The deer dropped to all fours and exhaled a tendril of steam. She stood there, as still as a tombstone, studying me. We gazed at each other for the better part of a minute. I see deer all the time where I live, but I'd never seen one this close. Finally, she bounded away.

Standing there in the snow, I felt a sense of peace. My orchard encounter seemed like a gift from God. My troubles did not magically go away, but they now seemed more manageable. I remembered what I never should have forgotten: that there is a God, that I live out my life in the palm of His hand, and that nothing is going to happen to me that I can't handle with His help. The apple was out of the doe's reach, but it was not out of mine. I tossed it on the ground. She'll find it there tomorrow.—Louis Lotz

Remind me, oh God, that anything under Your control is never out of control. When I am weak, be my strength. When I am frightened, be my courage. When I feel lost, show me the way. Amen.

DECEMBER 4

Way of the Donkey

One who has unreliable friends soon comes to ruin, but there is a friend who sticks closer than a brother.

—PROVERBS 18:24 (NIV)

MY SEVEN-YEAR-OLD GRANDSON, Amon, raced to a local farm's gate, where a couple of goats and a gray donkey stood waiting for treats. One goat knocked Amon's handful of cereal to the ground. The other goat quickly gobbled his portion, but the donkey hung back. We tried tempting the donkey with cereal, but the goats were always first to the goodies.

"Is that why they say donkeys are stubborn?" Amon asked.

"Maybe he wants to be sure he's not in danger before he'll be your friend and eat from your hand," I answered as Amon offered the donkey more treats. Still the animal, whose name was Zonker, just stood with his furry nose hanging over the fence.

Amon finally gave the last tidbits to the goats and frowned. "Donkeys *are* too stubborn. This one doesn't like me." He stuffed his hands in his jeans pockets and turned his back to the fence. "And I don't like him either." He looked ready to cry.

Just then Zonker nudged Amon's elbow with his nose. Amon's eyes lit up. Before long, he was petting the donkey and talking to him as if they were old friends. The goats had gone on to other visitors for more treats, but Zonker stayed and nuzzled Amon's side. Amon beamed as he petted his new pal, and the little gray donkey seemed content too. Looking at the unlikely pair, I couldn't help thinking how God wants me to be a friend to all—even those who seem stubborn at first.—Linda S. Clare

Walk of Faith: *Reach out to a person you don't know at church or in your community.*

DECEMBER 5

A Sensitive Sloth

Then God said, "Let Us make mankind in Our image, according to Our likeness."

—GENESIS 1:26 (NASB)

I RECENTLY READ A news report that gave me a new interpretation of the word *slothful*. Of course, the Bible has nothing good to say about slothfulness when applied to human laziness. But this story focused on the Central and South American tree dweller and the sensitivity of this sometimes-maligned creature. A Costa Rican animal-rescue team found an infant sloth on the tropical forest floor. They figured the whimpering cub had fallen from its mother's grasp in the top canopy of the trees. Although sloths are sturdy creatures, the team took it back to the center to be examined.

After a medical evaluation and a short rehabilitation period, the sloth was given a clean bill of health. The challenge was to find a way to reunite the cub with its mother. The team ingeniously devised a way to record the plaintive cry of the baby sloth. As they walked through the forest area where the baby sloth was found, the team aimed the recording toward the canopy of trees, hoping the cub's mother would recognize the sound. Their efforts were finally rewarded when they spotted one female sloth slowly, of course, descending a tree. The baby was placed in her arms when the mama sloth reached the lower part of the tree. The mother had recognized her baby's cries! She embraced her fallen cub to her stomach and began her glacial ascent.

The sloth is an example of how God meticulously fashions each of His creatures. The sloth's slowness contributes to its survival. Due to its lack of front incisor teeth, a sloth eats its diet of leaves and twigs by smacking its lips together, taking days to process the food. A low metabolic rate means sloths can survive on relatively little. So, for this being, slowness is a gift.

While the Bible does not condemn the sloth itself, it warns us against taking on similar habits, like laziness. When I'm feeling sluggish and unmotivated, I remember the sloth and God's message to be productive according to His will.—Terry Clifton

Lord, I give thanks that You will help me not to be slow or lazy but to act in determination and faith in following the path You have set before me. Amen.

DECEMBER 6

"Where We Used to See"

Seek the LORD while you can find him. Call upon him now while he is near.

—ISAIAH 55:6 (TLB)

I LOVE SPOTTING DEER while on family vacations in the mountains of Pennsylvania. At night, though, our spotlight catches many more animals than deer in its beam: raccoons, opossums, skunks, porcupines, and the occasional black bear. Our favorites range from the elusive bears to baby animals of all species.

One year, we spotted a tree filled with raccoon babies. Okay, there were just four of them, but in a small tree, baby raccoons playing peekaboo around its branches brought such delight that the number of coons seemed insignificant. We noted the location of said tree for the possibility of seeing them again on another night.

The following year, we were driving down the road of "the sighting" when my sister-in-law scared us by shouting, "There! That's the tree where we used to see the baby raccoons!" I couldn't help laughing at her phrase "where we used to see." We may have seen them only that one time, but because it was such a special treat, it filled our memories, even if not the tree itself. So, search for them we did, each year, in that same tree (if it was even the same tree).

When I compare looking for elusive baby animals or bears with looking for Jesus, it thrills me to know I will always find Jesus when I look for Him. And it needn't even be in a certain place "where we used to see" Him, such as in church, in my garden, or at a Christian concert. Jesus is everywhere, even in a tree playing peekaboo with fun-loving raccoons!—Cathy Mayfield

Jesus, I'm glad I can find You wherever I look, even without a spotlight. Thank You for always being near. Amen.

More Loves

And I pray that you, being rooted and established in love, may have power, together with all the Lord's holy people, to grasp how wide and long and high and deep is the love of Christ.

—EPHESIANS 3:17–18 (NIV)

ANNIE THE GOLDEN retriever greets patients with a doggie smile at her owner's physical therapy practice. Every Friday, I look forward to petting her and telling her what a good dog she is. But one day, Annie kept digging in the trash. Her human scowled and whisked away some garbage tidbit that Annie had pilfered from the waste bin. "Why is she trying to eat trash?" I asked, caressing Annie's snout in my hands. "After all, Annie's a very good dog."

My therapist said, "By the end of the week, Annie's tired. Tired of the patients taking all the attention away from her." She shook her head. "She's lonely and frustrated. She's trying to tell me I need to give her more loves."

As the therapist ran me through my exercises, I thought about how often I've eaten too much dessert or even shopped only because I was frustrated or lonely. Acting out in ways I knew could hurt me, I looked for relief, trying to fill that empty place inside. All the while, God whispered that if only I would look to Him, I'd find the kind of fulfillment I was searching for. As I did leg lifts, my therapist suddenly knelt on the dog bed and smothered Annie in kisses. "You need extra loves, huh, Annie?" The dog rolled over for a belly rub, indicating her approval. "Lotsa loves for Annie."

"More loves?" I got up and scratched Annie's ears. I felt God's smile assuring me that He loves me too.—Linda S. Clare

True love is knowing a person's faults and loving them even more for them.
—Anonymous

DECEMBER 8

The Kindness of Crows

The ravens brought him bread and meat in the morning and bread and meat in the evening, and he drank from the brook.

—1 KINGS 17:6 (NIV)

STUART DAHLQUIST OF Seattle reported on his Twitter feed that the crows he'd been feeding had left him gifts. He included a photo of the offerings: two small twigs from a pine tree, tucked into soda-can pop-top tabs. "This isn't only generous," Dahlquist said, "it's creative; it's art."

Another Seattleite, eight-year-old Gabi Mann, began finding gifts from the crows she had been feeding: buttons, beads, a Lego piece, and more, which she carefully recorded and wrapped for safekeeping.

A little farther south, San Francisco resident Melinda Green related that, after she'd begun feeding crows from her fire escape, they began leaving presents: a foil wrapper from a champagne bottle, gummy bears, and other objects. "The fact that it really is a gift makes it precious," she said.

It doesn't surprise me too much that God chose ravens to bring food to Elijah when he was hiding from Israel's notoriously evil King Ahab (1 Kings 17:6). Crows and ravens are part of the same genus, *Corvus*, and both raucous, big black birds are among the most intelligent creatures in the animal kingdom. Scientists have learned that crows remember faces—and they will hold grudges against those who mistreat them. Increasing evidence suggests that the birds remember kindnesses with the same zeal. Sort of like us humans.

I've never received gifts from crows, but I can learn something from them. As I get older, I am wondering what my legacy will be—how will people remember me? As I read about these amazing feathered friends, I thought about who in my life would remember me as kind and who would remember me—even hold a grudge against me—for being mean or hurtful. I know which one I want to be my legacy. I want to leave behind the gift of kindness.—Jon Woodhams

You cannot do a kindness too soon, for you never know how soon it will be too late.
—Ralph Waldo Emerson

DECEMBER 9

Tobias, the Jealous Goat

Let us behave decently, as in the daytime, not in carousing and drunkenness, not in sexual immorality and debauchery, not in dissension and jealousy.

—ROMANS 13:13 (NIV)

TUCK AND TOBIAS are old goat brothers, raised as orphans by a sweet woman who treated them like children and released them to our sanctuary when she became too ill to care for them. While social media shows photos of cute yoga goats and little kids dressed in pj's, these were Alpine goats weighing in at around a hundred pounds each. Definitely not pajama goats!

Appreciative of the homemade salads and fruit I gave them each night, they settled right in, and to be honest, I fell in love. They wound around my heart and would not let go until I brought home two little pygmy goat girls, Lizzie and Tink. They were the cute kind everyone loves, though loud like screaming children. Tuck and Tobias were not happy. They didn't care that the newcomers were cute. They didn't care they were girls. They only cared that Lizzie and Tink were getting attention from their farm mama. And that was not good.

One night Lizzie was in my lap. She is about the size of a miniature schnauzer with crystal-blue eyes. I was cooing to her and hugging her when all of a sudden, *WHAM!* Tobias tried to butt Lizzie from my lap but instead butted both of us right out of the chair into the yard. Lizzie ran off, and Tobias stood over me, nuzzling my face as if to say, "I just meant to get rid of her, not hurt you, Farm Mama!"

That's the way jealousy is. It overtakes us and can make us do things that hurt people we had no intention of hurting. We hit the target, yet collateral damage destroys love and life in its wake. Jealousy is never as controllable as we think, and before long it is controlling us. It pulls us into a black hole from which there is no satisfaction until we let it go. But like all sins, jealousy is a choice. And since it is a choice, we can choose to walk away from it with God's help. After all, there's enough room on His lap for everyone.—Devon O'Day

Walk of Faith: *Think of a time you've let jealousy overtake you. Envision yourself sitting on God's lap with that person, and let His love wash over you.*

DECEMBER 10

A Chorus of Joy

The morning stars sang together and all the angels shouted for joy.

—Job 38:7 (NLT)

TWELVE-YEAR-OLD BRECKEN LOVES to sing. She'll sing in the car, in the shower, in her room, definitely at church, and just about anywhere it's appropriate for her to do so. While visiting her grandmother's home one day, she couldn't keep the melodies in. At Grandma Carol's suggestion, Brecken went out onto the upper deck, which overlooks a wooded pond. As the exuberant song began to flow from her granddaughter's spirit, Carol noticed many of the birds in the neighborhood joined in. What started as one young girl opening her heart to the expanse of nature transformed into a beautiful symphony of trills, tweets, twitters, and whistles.

Because there were many kinds of birds in the nearby trees, you might think the sound was a cacophony of chaos. Instead, it was a masterpiece of creative expression. Carol noticed that when Brecken stopped singing, so did the bird chorus. But as soon as she picked up the melody again, her feathered friends joined in. Brecken and Carol tested this out several times to make sure they were hearing correctly. It proved to be the case every time.

Now, when Brecken visits, she asks her grandma, "Do you think I should go out and sing with the birds again?"

This is a lovely reminder of what happens when we join our voices together to honor God. When our anthems of praise are lifted in unity, all of creation joins in. What an awesome performance of joy, one I hope blesses the heart of the King.—Liz Kimmel

You are an awesome Lord! Thank You, God of all Creation,
for birthing in me a desire to praise and glorify Your name.
What a joy when, together, our praises are magnified and the
whole world is witness to the wonder. Amen.

DECEMBER 11

The Little Bully

Likewise, the tongue is a small part of the body, but it makes great boasts. Consider what a great forest is set on fire by a small spark.

—JAMES 3:5 (NIV)

MY DAUGHTER AND son-in-law adopted Arnold Schwarzenegger, a yellow tabby, as a companion for Michael B. Jordan, a brooding stray they'd invited home a couple of years before.

Michael had grown up on the streets and had little tolerance for a kitten's tomfoolery. Arnold would swat at the older cat's tail or otherwise pester him until Michael signaled *Enough!* with a swift kick. At that, Arnold would scamper back to his retreat under the couch. Michael was top cat, and he let Arnold know it.

After a year or so, Arnold Schwarzenegger, like his namesake, had bulked up considerably. No longer intimidated by his big brother, Arnold began to stake out a territory. He claimed first place at the feed bowl, the overstuffed couch cushion, and the coveted sunny spot atop the easy chair. Arnold defended his claim aggressively, so much so that it was now Michael who scurried away to avoid conflict. Arnold, once dominated, had become the dominator.

It wasn't the first time I'd seen a shrimp reinvent himself as the champ. As a younger man, I often felt like little Arnold, smaller and weaker than others. I found that a playful dash of sarcasm often helped level the field. It all was meant in fun, of course. Yet those lighthearted jabs grew into a steady stream of withering criticism. Without meaning to, I'd grown to become the intimidator, the verbal aggressor.

Cats are notoriously difficult to train, so I don't know what chance there is of reforming Arnold's domineering ways. As for me, I repented of the ill use of my tongue and vowed to use it only to build up, never to tear down.—Lawrence W. Wilson

O Living Word, You, above all others, understand the power of words. Help me to use my power for others' good and Your glory. Amen.

DECEMBER 12

Lionhearted

I have been crucified with Christ and I no longer live, but Christ lives in me. The life I now live in the body, I live by faith in the Son of God, who loved me and gave himself for me.

—GALATIANS 2:20 (NIV)

ATLAS WAS THE biggest dog I'd ever seen. A Rhodesian ridgeback, he could rest his paws on my friend Anna's shoulders and look her in the eye. He weighed as much as her middle-school son—ninety pounds.

But Atlas had a secret—one that didn't take us long to discover. Although he towered over other dogs and frightened every person he encountered, Atlas was a coward.

He had a fearsome size and ferocious bark, but Atlas responded to any real or perceived threat by ducking behind his owner's legs and trembling in fear. I suspect he hadn't read the AKC (American Kennel Club) entry that described how Rhodesian ridgebacks were once known as lion trackers in their native country.

Some days, I'm a lot like Atlas—minus the size. When a crisis threatens me or those I love, my first instinct is to run and hide. Financial challenges, spiritual attacks, or relational upheaval make me tremble in fear.

I forget that though I am weak, I am strong, because Christ lives within me. In Him, I have everything I need for life and godliness.

Courage? It's there. Love? In abundance. Wisdom? God promises I'll have it if I ask for it (James 1:5). Because of who I am on the inside—a child of God and a follower of Christ, I need not fear.

Sadly, Atlas never learned to conduct himself as a lion tracker. He remained cowardly and fearful. By God's grace, I'm learning to walk in faith and confidence. When I allow the Spirit of God to fill me and the Word of God to instruct me, I can be lionhearted and face anything that comes my way.—Lori Hatcher

Father, help me remember that because Jesus lives inside me, I can face life's challenges with the courage of a lion. Amen.

DECEMBER 13

A Lesson Learned from Surfing Turtles

The thief comes only to steal and kill and destroy; I have come that they may have life, and have it to the full.

—JOHN 10:10 (NIV)

WHEN MY HUSBAND and I planned our trip to Hawaii, we planned the dates we would travel. We planned where we would stay. We planned what we hoped to do while on Oahu. However, we didn't plan on my health creating physical limitations for me during our trip.

My husband is a surfer, so surfing was at the top of our list. One day, about midway through our trip, we were on a remote beach on the north shore. The only other people around were the man and his son staying in a nearby house. As my husband paddled out into the waves, I stayed behind on the beach. Several large shadows in the waves near the shore caught my attention. Once I realized the shadows belonged to turtles, not sharks as I first feared, I was relieved.

While I sat on the beach and watched the turtles, my relief turned into pure pleasure. The turtles looked like they were having so much fun. Over and over, they rode a wave to shore, flipped through the sea foam, paddled out a ways, then rode another wave into shore. They didn't just ride the waves once or twice—these turtles played in the water for over half an hour, all the while amusing me with their antics.

As I watched the turtles, it seemed to me that God created them to live life to the fullest. I wonder if they understood that the joy they would find in the water He created for them was His intention. It was His plan that they would ride the waves, not caring what went on around them.

During the remainder of our trip, whenever my physical limitations threatened to steal my joy, God reminded me of those surfing turtles who lived life to the fullest. And because of those turtles, I am reminded that He created me to live life to the fullest, regardless of what is going on around me.—Sandy Kirby Quandt

I love to think of nature as an unlimited broadcasting station, through which God speaks to us every hour, if we will only tune in.
—George Washington Carver

DECEMBER 14

Other Dog Games

Therefore, accept one another, just as Christ also accepted us.

—ROMANS 15:7 (NASB)

THUMP. THUMP. THUMP.

"What are you doing?" I asked my husband as I entered the living room to see him bouncing a small blue ball in front of our dog, Scuppers.

"Trying to get him to play ball with me," he said.

"Maybe you should just stick to tug-of-war," I suggested.

Our little rescue dog will not play ball. He might sniff at a ball, but he shows no desire to chase, catch, or retrieve one. I knew my husband was disappointed; all of our previous dogs had been avid ball players. Even though Scuppers wouldn't fetch, he has so many wonderful attributes; he is obedient, calm, and well mannered. He enjoys a good tug-of-war with one of his stuffed toys. He likes to play, just not a game of ball.

I thought about the many times I have been disappointed with friends who didn't meet my expectations because they did not prefer the same activities or hold similar opinions. However, these same friends might favor activities or have ideas that complement mine or encourage me to try something new. By accepting and embracing their differences, I am enriched.

Just as it is unfair for us to expect Scuppers to like everything our other dogs enjoyed, it is unfair of me to expect everyone whom I encounter to align with my opinions and favorite activities. The Bible tells me that Christ accepted me even when my activities or beliefs were not ones that He would espouse. Christ loved me first, and that is how I should see others—loving them despite our differences, for Christ also loves them.

How great is God to love all His creation, not just the ones who play ball but the ones who like to tug toys as well.—Virginia Ruth

Father, teach me to love people where they are and not expect or demand they change to my preferences. Amen.

DECEMBER 15

Blessings in a Poop Pile

The Lord replied, "I have forgiven them, as you asked."

—Numbers 14:20 (NIV)

STEVIE IS A fully grown steer who is over a thousand pounds of pure love and affection. He is also blind, which makes him dangerous in that he can't gauge how hard he is playing.

Stevie loves his feed bucket, whether it be donated peaches, apple slices, cabbage wedges, or his favorite—butternut squash. At our special-needs livestock sanctuary, we are often gifted surplus produce, so we stretch the expensive feedstore supplies with the gifts, and everyone is happy. Especially Stevie.

Having a steer on the farm also means he "fertilizes" the whole pasture. No matter where you go, you see evidence that Stevie has been there. And one day I realized there were butternut squash growing all over the pasture in all the poop piles. Stevie had unknowingly planted his favorite food everywhere.

God always sends me spiritual lessons in the lowliest of ways, and this epiphany was about forgiveness. I think of all the past unforgiveness patches that remain all over my life. When I return to those memories and leave resentment, hatred, and hopes of revenge in those places, nothing grows except those seeds. But when I ask God to plant forgiveness where I cannot, those beds of dark places end up as gardens where God can sow seeds of renewal and hope.

I've had a difficult time planting forgiveness seeds in beds of darkness. Asking God to grant forgiveness to people who had intentionally lied about me or wished me harm was like walking up to one of those pasture patties and expecting roses to grow. Yet, I did ask God. And when He receives a request to plant forgiveness, He does. Just like Stevie's favorite butternut squash, forgiveness grew all around my pasture from unintentional gardens.

Our most fertile ground sometimes starts in the yuckiest of places, but if we give it to Him, He will let beauty grow there.—Devon O'Day

God, please forgive those I cannot forgive, and let the good fruit grow until I feel it for myself. Amen.

DECEMBER 16

A Change of Plans

In their hearts humans plan their course, but the LORD establishes their steps.

—PROVERBS 16:9 (NIV)

NAOMA, THE SECOND guide-dog puppy I raised, was a beautiful black Goldadore (a purebred cross—half golden retriever, half Labrador). Although sweet-tempered and smart, Naoma had a few faults, one of which was her extreme food addiction. Every time I opened my refrigerator, her big black head shoved its way inside. But her most serious flaw—being distracted by other animals—ended up disqualifying her from becoming a guide dog.

Disappointed at first, I later learned Naoma had been "career changed" to become a therapy dog at Walter Reed Hospital. What a tremendous opportunity! Instead of spending her life helping one person, Naoma got to minister to multiple hurting people, all while receiving her coveted tummy rubs.

Sometimes, God changes our goals, as well. After my pilot husband retired from the air force, he felt called to use his aviation skills on the mission field. He began checking out Mission Aviation Fellowship in preparation for his new career. An aircraft accident, in which he ended up breaking his back, derailed those plans. He questioned why God allowed this accident to end his dream of serving Him in the capacity he loved best. But God had other plans for my husband. After spending six months flat on his back while his injuries healed, my husband started seminary. Thirteen years later, after many detours, he graduated with his master's degree in divinity. He served as the youth pastor at two churches before accepting the call as senior pastor at another church, where we have ministered for the past twelve years.

My husband never imagined serving God as a pastor rather than a pilot, and I certainly didn't plan to be a pastor's wife. But it is obvious God called us to where we are supposed to be. His plans are always perfect! —Ellen Fannon

Many are the plans in a person's heart,
but it is the LORD's purpose that prevails.
—Proverbs 19:21 (NIV)

Rocky's Cup Runneth Over

He said to me: "It is done. I am the Alpha and the Omega, the Beginning and the End. To the thirsty I will give water without cost from the spring of the water of life."

—REVELATION 21:6 (NIV)

I WONDERED WHY OUR feline Rocky spent so much time in the bathroom. He seemed delighted if someone entered and turned on a faucet or flushed a toilet. He didn't drink from the commode (too much dignity for that), but like a scientist perfecting an experiment, he was drawn to watch the water swirl. Maybe that's because it's difficult for cats to see water unless it's moving.

I worried about Rocky's ability to stay hydrated because he never seemed to visit his water bowl, so my son bought a little fountain. Rocky could watch the water bubble and drink all he wanted.

Rocky's quest for moving water made me think of how I can't see God but I can see how He moves. Like when I pray, and He answers my prayer. Or when I do acts of kindness spontaneously. But I especially see God in nature when seeds sprout, sparrows sing, the wind blows, and the sun sets.

If I look hard enough, I see God's movements every day in ordinary places. Sometimes they are unpredictable but delightful, nonetheless. Sometimes it is difficult to understand His movement in my life until I look at the situation with a different perspective.

Rocky is infatuated with running water no matter where he finds it, be it his fountain, a toilet, or the kitchen sink. And I have learned to look for God's movements in everyday places too.—Linda Bartlett

As the deer pants for streams of water, so my soul pants for you, my God. My soul thirsts for God, for the living God. When can I go and meet with God?

—Psalm 42:1–2 (NIV)

DECEMBER 18

Closer

Draw near to God, and he will draw near to you. Cleanse your hands, you sinners, and purify your hearts, you double-minded.

—JAMES 4:8 (ESV)

HE'S SO ATTACHED to you it's almost weird," I said to my wife, Christine.

"I know," she responded. "It's a little annoying. But I love it."

Winston, our medium-sized, mixed-breed dog, had been like this for years. Each night when it was TV time for our family, Winston would wait patiently for Christine to settle into her seat. Then, invited or not, he would jump onto her lap, tilt his head toward her face, and lick her chin. After two or three spins, he would then snuggle into the chair beside her and let out a long sigh of relief as if to say, *Finally, I can relax next to my favorite person.*

I watched with envy from across the room. *Chop me up and call me liver.*

Then it struck me how the Lord wants me to respond to Him like Winston responds to my wife—to long for that special time each day when I can crawl into His lap and relax in His presence with a sigh of relief. Since the Garden of Eden, God has desired to fellowship with mankind, to spend time in our presence daily. Surely, I should desire the same.

Yet I often go through my day scurrying about, dealing with problems and solving them on my own. I forget that I am most content and at ease when resting upon Him.

I had to smile as I observed Christine's calming effect on our pet. I was determined to be just as dependent and content with my Lord.—Tez Brooks

Let me come closer to Thee, Lord Jesus, oh, closer day by day.
Let me lean harder on Thee, Lord Jesus, yes, harder, all the way.

—John H. Lester

DECEMBER 19

Crying Out in Fear

Keep me as the apple of your eye; hide me in the shadow of your wings from the wicked who are out to destroy me, from my mortal enemies who surround me.

—PSALM 17:8–9 (NIV)

ONE OF THE many animals in my home is a sun conure parrot named Mango, a rescue bird from a local shelter. Mango was in four homes before mine, and it seemed like everyone who adopted him ended up bringing him back within a year.

I have often wondered just what it was about Mango that made him so hard to love. He is a bit grumpy, and he's certainly not the kind of bird to sit on your shoulder and coo, so it could be that. Mango can also bite, especially if you put your hand in the cage at the wrong time. But more than anything, Mango is loud—so loud that if you are too near his cage, you can feel pain in your ears. Simply put, Mango is a screamer.

One day when Mango was screaming, I looked out the window and saw vultures circling in the sky. *No wonder Mango cries so loud,* I thought. *Mango is afraid.* I had put Mango's cage near the window so he could see other birds outside at my bird feeders, but I never imagined he would see vultures flying high in the sky. Mango wasn't screaming to be annoying; Mango was screaming to warn me of impending danger. I know that neither Mango nor I was at risk from the vultures outside, but I struggled to convince Mango that we were safe.

Mango's cries got me wondering about how often I am afraid of things that won't hurt me. The psalmist wants God to hide him and keep him safe from enemies. Like Mango, the writer of the psalm feels threatened, so he cries out and turns to God for protection.

Personally, I struggle to always turn to God for protection in prayer. As my faith grows, I am learning to trust in Him more, so that when He tells me to not be afraid, I try to calm my anxious heart. Just as Mango needs to learn to trust me to keep him safe, I need to trust God.—Heather Jepsen

Walk of Faith: *List your fears on a sheet of paper. Offer them all to God in prayer, asking Him to continue to protect you no matter what the circumstance.*

DECEMBER 20

Terms of Endearment

The man gave names to all the livestock, and to the birds of the sky, and to every animal of the field.

—GENESIS 2:20 (NASB)

FOLLOWING IN ADAM'S footsteps, humankind has come up with myriad creative names for groups of animals. Some trip off the tongue without our having to think about it: a pack of wolves, a school of fish, a pride of lions. Others are obscure: a troop of kangaroos, a band of gorillas, a bevy of swans.

Some are downright whimsical or even poetic. Bird-group names alone bring a smile to my face. A cornucopia of fanciful words go far beyond *flock*: a gulp of cormorants, a charm of finches, a tiding of magpies. Then there's an ostentation of peafowl and an exaltation of larks. And let's not forget one of my favorites: a murmuration of starlings.

Among reptiles, we can enjoy such linguistic delights as a quiver of cobras (I'd be aquiver myself if I saw one!) and a maelstrom of salamanders. Frogs apparently form an army, while toads form a knot. Sharks gather in a shiver, while trout come together in a hover. Among the invertebrates, we can observe a grist, a hive, or a swarm of bees, as well as a bed of clams, a cloud of grasshoppers, a bloom of jellyfish, and the appropriately named intrusion of cockroaches.

Mammals and marsupials occupy such vivid-sounding groups as a shrewdness of apes, a parade of elephants, a tower of giraffes, a cackle of hyenas, a cauldron of bats, and a conspiracy of lemurs. A group of squirrels forms a scurry, porcupines a prickle, cats a clowder, and leopards a leap. (Doesn't alliteration add to the fun?)

All these amazing names remind me that God gives me names too—names that speak volumes about how He sees me: His beloved, His child, His friend, His handiwork, His treasured possession. And for that, there are no words adequate to express my gratitude.—Jon Woodhams

But now, this is what the LORD says…"Do not fear, for I have redeemed you; I have called you by name; you are Mine!"

—Isaiah 43:1 (NASB)

DECEMBER 21

In the Doghouse

But there is a [true, loving] friend who
[is reliable and] sticks closer than a brother.

—PROVERBS 18:24 (AMP)

MY SISTER GOT the surprise of her life when Butch appeared one Christmas morning with a red bow around his neck. Butchie, as she called him, was a friendly, white cocker spaniel with black spots. He was the perfect childhood companion at a time when she was learning about love and about life. Most ten-year-olds are trying to figure out where they fit in, and Sunny found her place with Butchie.

The two of them were together constantly, except during the school day. When the school bus doors opened, Butchie ran as fast as his legs would carry him to greet Sunny. Many times, I'd see them heading for the open fields, running and romping. Their relationship was marked by loyalty and unconditional love.

Dad made a spacious doghouse for Butchie with a shingle roof, but he added extra sheets of roofing so it would absorb the sound of rain. Butchie was an outside dog, but he wasn't fond of the hard summer rains of Ohio. Sunny sometimes crawled into the doghouse with Butchie, so she could comfort him while listening to the rain.

I know Butchie helped Sunny develop her ability to show others unconditional love and loyalty and opened her heart to the unconditional love and loyalty she received when she surrendered her life to the Lord.—Randy Benedetto

Lord, thank You for our loyal friendships,
especially the four-legged ones. Amen.

DECEMBER 22

Hooting Lessons

Teach me your ways, O Lord, that I may live according to Your truth! Grant me purity of heart, so that I may honor you.

—Psalm 86:11 (NLT)

FROM THE TIME he was an infant, I'd taught our grandson about the birds. I remember his dad laughing when I held him up to the window, showed him a cardinal, told him it said, "What cheer!" and urged him to say it.

By the age of four, we'd moved on to owls. The walnut trees in their backyard gave us the halved shells, which resembled owl faces. I'd stuff them in knots in the other trees, and we'd go on owl hunts, complete with toilet-paper-tube binoculars, calling out the owl sounds: "Whoo. Whoo. Whoo-hoo-hoo," for the great horned owl, and "Whoo. Whoo. Whoo-cooks-for-you," for the barred owl, which frequents our area of Pennsylvania.

That year, my grandson's mother enrolled him in a preschool, and one day a naturalist came to their classroom. He was still talking to the kids when she went to pick my grandson up at the end of the day. She listened in to see how her son was doing. The man had shared pictures and information about owls.

"What do owls say?" He asked the typical question anyone would ask and received the answer normal to a group of four-year-olds.

"Whoo! Whoo!"

"That's right! Owls say, 'Whoo! Whoo!'" The naturalist applauded their knowledge.

And then it happened. Our daughter wanted to hide, as our need-to-get-it-right grandson stood and called out, "Excuse me, sir. That's not right. Not all owls say, 'Whoo.' The barred owl says, 'Whoo. Whoo. Whoo cooks for you.' My grandmother taught me that. Now, you try it!"

Whether it's the sounds animals make or the words Jesus says, I pray to learn all God has for me in this wonderful world.—Cathy Mayfield

Father, from owls to grace, I'm grateful that You teach me about Your ways. Amen.

DECEMBER 23

The Digging-est Dog

Have I not commanded you? Be strong and courageous. Do not be afraid; do not be discouraged, for the LORD your God will be with you wherever you go.

—JOSHUA 1:9 (NIV)

WE ADOPTED OUR dog Honcho when he was six months old. During the first year, we watched him run around in our small fenced backyard, amazed at his speed. I often wished we could take him somewhere wide open to see just how fast he could run. I think Honcho also wished he could do that, as we learned too soon.

Honcho loves to dig and discovered he could dig out from under the fence. The first time it happened, he had been in the backyard playing. But when I went to check on him, he was nowhere to be found. I flew out the front door just in time to spot him running full speed across our cul-de-sac. And boy, could he run fast! Body stretched out, ears pinned back from the wind, he looked like a Thoroughbred racing for the finish line.

A teeny part of my heart gloried to see him having such joy. But because he refused to come when I called, my heart froze in fear that he could get lost or hit by a car. It took almost forty-five minutes to lure him home with treats and by throwing his Frisbees toward the front door. Finally, a Frisbee landed on the porch, and I thought his running days were over, but he darted off again. After an hour, thirst made him give up his freedom race. He was ready for a big drink of water.

We installed barriers around the fence, but Honcho still managed to get out a half-dozen times. Now that we have a second dog, he has plenty of entertainment and doesn't try to escape anymore. Throughout those scary times with Honcho, God taught me a lesson about running. Like Honcho, I might enjoy the freedom of running outside my own "backyard," trying to do things my own way. But my home—God—is what I want to run to. Just as Honcho realized, a home of love is all I need. —Missy Tippens

God, I thank You that You are the One in control. Thank You that we can depend on You to protect those we love. Amen.

DECEMBER 24

The Morning Blueberry

But blessed is the one who trusts in the LORD, whose confidence is in him.

—JEREMIAH 17:7 (NIV)

FROM THEIR CHUBBY cheeks to their noisy *wheeks,* I love guinea pigs. As a young girl, I raised one I got at the county fair and another that had been our fifth-grade class pet. I learned a lot about guinea pig care during that time.

This year, my childhood experiences far behind, I rescued two female guinea pigs. Memories of my fun, friendly pets came rushing back. But Petunia and Marigold were not cuddly and sweet. They ran from the sight of me. They squealed. They cringed inside their hideouts. Clearly, they were terrified.

"It's okay, I won't hurt you," I said as I reached into their cage to try to pick them up. I wanted to get them to trust me, but I knew it could be difficult—I, too, can struggle with trust. Then I got an idea—guinea pigs love food. I could use this to win them over. So the next morning when I walked into their room, I presented them each with a delicious blueberry. Petunia and Marigold came up to the side of the cage and cautiously took them from my hand. Over time they grew bolder in accepting the blueberries, and often they were waiting for me to arrive.

Starting their day off with a morning blueberry is important to our trust relationship, just as starting my day off with prayer and Scripture is important to my relationship with God. I depend on my quiet time to provide me with a vital connection to His Word. I do not run in fear when I know that the One who is feeding me is worthy of my love and trust.—Peggy Frezon

Walk of Faith: *Do you have trouble trusting that God is really on your side? Start your day by reading from your Bible or praying, then watch your trust strengthen and grow.*

DECEMBER 25

Party Animal

In humility value others above yourselves.

—PHILIPPIANS 2:3 (NIV)

IT WAS MY first Christmas since my wife, Sandra, had passed away, and I felt isolated.

I was pleased and a bit uneasy when I received an invitation to the McCarthys' Christmas gathering. The McCarthys resembled an Irish clan composed of four generations. Although we were close in my younger years, I had not seen any of them for more than three decades. *What if I don't have anything in common with anyone and can't find someone to talk to? Will the people at the party know about Sandra's death and want me to relive the entire story? Will I feel like the "old man" out?*

When I arrived at the boisterous gathering, a scampering shih tzu greeted me. He circled me several times, then moved on. *I feel like I am at a high school reunion,* I thought, *minus the name tags.* I scanned the room and thought I saw a few vaguely familiar faces. I grabbed a soda and headed toward a group that was chatting. I glanced down at the shih tzu walking beside me. They confirmed who they were and expressed condolences on my wife's passing. Our awkward conversation stalled. Self-conscious, I retreated to the empty living room. As I sat alone, the shih tzu was back at my feet. He ran back and forth across the carpet as if to say, *The party is in the other rooms. Let's go!*

Was the Lord, who spent His earthly life often misunderstood, using this little dog to jolt me out of my self-absorption? The only one keeping me isolated was me. I stood up from my chair in the empty living room and followed behind my four-legged messenger—back to the party to make some friends.—Terry Clifton

Let no one ever come to you without leaving better and happier.
Be the living expression of God's kindness: kindness in your face,
kindness in your eyes, kindness in your smile.

—Mother Teresa

DECEMBER 26

Live Like Our Loki

Always be joyful. Never stop praying. Be thankful in all circumstances, for this is God's will for you who belong to Christ Jesus.

—1 THESSALONIANS 5:16–18 (NLT)

OUR ADULT GRANDSON and his girlfriend have a new puppy, a Yorkshire terrier named Loki after the Marvel character and the Norse trickster god. Whenever we see him, Loki is happy, energetic, playful, and just wonderful to be around. It doesn't matter whether he's playing with our three-year-old grandson or with us (senior citizens), he creates happiness with his energy and his love. Like most dogs, Loki lives in the moment and, by doing so, seems joyful always, as the scripture verse bids us to be.

Loki is a great example of the type of spirit I wish I could share with others every day. But too often two things get in the way. First, I sometimes live in the past, worrying about those sins for which God has already forgiven me or dwelling on how I could have done something better. The past is the past, and I need to move on and not let it spoil the present moment. Or second, if I'm not looking backward, I'm contemplating the future, making lists of things I need to accomplish, worrying about how I'm going to get it all done, or planning how to avoid the pitfalls that could get in my way. Planning has its virtues, but it can definitely be overdone.

I need to spend many more days following Winnie the Pooh's philosophy: "What day is it?" asked Pooh. "It's today," squeaked Piglet. "My favorite day," said Pooh (A. A. Milne). If I could follow that philosophy and try to be more like Loki, I might fulfill Paul's exhortation to "Always be joyful."—Harold Nichols

Write it on your heart that every day is the best day in the year.
—Ralph Waldo Emerson

DECEMBER 27

Renewal Is Stirring

Why, my soul, are you downcast? Why so disturbed within me? Put your hope in God, for I will yet praise him, my Savior and my God.

—PSALM 42:5 (NIV)

IT'S LATE DECEMBER, and the earth is frozen solid. Trees are gaunt and skeletal. I look out my window and see a slate-gray sky and stalactite icicles hanging from the gutters. Everything looks dark. Everything looks dead.

But it's not. My honeybees are certainly alive. I tramp out to my hives, wading through the snow, and press my ear to the wooden boxes. I can hear them in there—*hummm*. Bees spend the winter awake and active, huddled together in a basketball-size cluster. To warm themselves, they vibrate their wing muscles, an action that burns calories and gives off considerable heat. Bees on the exterior surface of the cluster bear the brunt of the cold, but there is a gradual movement whereby bees on the inside migrate to the outside, while the outside bees move slowly to the inside. Every bee takes a turn on the outside where it is cold and spends time on the inside where it is warm. The hive box is half-buried in snow, and it looks cold and dead, but a December beehive is bursting with life and renewal.

Standing in the snow, my ear pressed against the hive, I'm suddenly overwhelmed with the thought that even when the world looks dark and hope seems cold and dead, renewal is stirring. Life is not as doomed as it appears. The solstice has come and gone, soon spring will arrive, and my honeybees will burst forth into the world. The daily news may be a torrent of sadness and sorrow, but creation has not spun out of the Father's control. God will yet have His way with wayward mankind, and someday soon my breakfast will include an English muffin dripping with fresh honey.—Louis Lotz

I have told you these things, so that in me you may have peace.
In this world you will have trouble. But take heart!
I have overcome the world.
—John 16:33 (NIV)

DECEMBER 28

Remembering the Birds

Do not withhold good from those to whom it is due, when it is in your power to act.

—PROVERBS 3:27 (NIV)

WHEN HE WAS in his midnineties, Dad lost much of his hearing. His eyesight was failing. He became feeble, unable to stand or walk without support. He could no longer do the things he'd loved doing in his younger years, like feeding the birds, growing vegetables in the garden, and caring for his roses and other shrubs. He became sad and restless. He'd often forget our names and frequently became confused about where he was. But surprisingly, he still remembered the names of birds that frequented his backyard. He'd peruse birding magazines, correctly identifying robins, mockingbirds, and hummingbirds. He remembered that his own father had referred to goldfinches as lettuce birds because they could always be found nibbling the lettuce in the garden.

One day, Dad cut out some bird photos from a travel magazine. When he asked for a three-ring binder so he could start a scrapbook, we happily complied. We also offered notebook paper and tape, which he eagerly accepted. The family scrambled to find magazines, old birding guides, and even an outdated animal encyclopedia with bird photographs and illustrations for his use. Dad spent many happy hours cutting and taping photos of birds. We were delighted he'd found something to do that interested him. We were also amazed that he could correctly keep naming the birds—the woodpeckers, blue jays, and cardinals.

Before he died, just a few weeks shy of his ninety-ninth birthday, Dad had filled numerous binders. Aging had meant many losses for Dad. But God—in His infinite mercy—had blessed him with sufficient memory to recall the birds he'd so loved in his younger days. It reminded me that all good and perfect gifts, including happy memories, come from God.—Shirley Raye Redmond

Walk of Faith: *Consider keeping a scrapbook of something meaningful in your life.*

The Backup Bowl

And my God will meet all your needs according to the riches of his glory in Christ Jesus.

—PHILIPPIANS 4:19 (NIV)

I HEARD THE CLANGING of our dogs' metal bowl hitting the baseboard, startling me. I'd been sitting at the table, looking over our bank statement, which was full of debits to doctors' offices because of my husband's recent medical issues. Piper, our Pomeranian/poodle mix, pushed the dish into the wall with her paw and then looked at me hopefully. *It's empty, Mom,* she seemed to say. I shook my head and got up to fill it, despite the futility of doing so.

Filling the bowl was futile because neither Piper nor our terrier mix, Peyton, would eat out of that dish. Instead, they shared the smaller dog bowl, politely waiting their turn to eat, even when both bowls were full.

Even though they wouldn't use the second bowl, Piper always let us know when it was empty. If no one came immediately, she would nudge it around the floor with her paw or her nose until someone filled it. But the moment we did, she lost interest and wanted nothing to do with the food it contained.

Our family called it the backup bowl, joking that Piper just felt better knowing that the extra food was there. Like there was a tiny part of her that didn't trust us to keep the first dish full and needed a backup plan.

As I added up last month's medical bills, I wished for a backup bowl of money to help cover the extra expenses. *Lord, I'm trying to trust You with this, but we don't have extra cash.* I hated to admit it, but there was a tiny part of me that struggled to trust God to take care of our family's finances.

Needing a break, I took the dogs for a walk and picked up our mail. In it was a check we hadn't been expecting, and the amount would make a sizable dent in the medical bills. Trusting God to provide for our needs is always the right decision. No backup bowl needed.—Diane Stark

Thank You, Lord, for proving over and over that You will meet our needs. Amen.

DECEMBER 30

Traveling Light

Cast your burden on the LORD, and he will sustain you.

—PSALM 55:22 (ESV)

IS THAT A drone?" I asked my husband as we walked along a marsh path.

"No," he replied. "I think it's a bird."

I could see the bird silhouette but did not recognize the dirigible-looking object in its talons. I then realized it was an osprey carrying a fish. I had heard that they carry all objects parallel to their body. That position creates less wind resistance when they fly so that while the burden of carrying the fish doesn't disappear, it does make carrying the burden easier.

That osprey with its catch made me think of different burdens I've had to carry: caregiving for family, financial responsibilities, health-care decisions, housing, work and career choices. While some days I wished the heaviness of the burdens would disappear, I knew it was not a realistic or natural goal. But much like the osprey that holds its burden parallel to its body to make life easier, I have found that when I pray for God to sustain me through the difficult times, my burden is lighter. I remember one particularly stressful day of tending to the demands of little children when I received an encouraging email. Or the time our family budget was extremely tight and we were worried about paying the bills—until an unexpected check came in the mail. In essence, the troubles and burdens I face can be made lighter with His help. Jesus tells us that the best way to carry burdens is to turn them over to Him and allow His yoke to ease the load (Matthew 11:28–30).

When God created the osprey and the parallel-baggage-handling method, He engineered the most efficient way for it to fly with an extra load. Likewise, God has engineered a way for us to navigate through life by casting our cares upon Him.—Virginia Ruth

Cast your care on Jesus;
He will share it, He will bear it—
There is none like Jesus.
—Robert Lowry

DECEMBER 31

Daisy, NO!

I call on you, my God, for you will answer me;
turn your ear to me and hear my prayer.

—PSALM 17:6 (NIV)

A LITTLE BORDER COLLIE–BEAGLE mix puppy named Daisy came to live with us at the farm. Her energy was boundless. She tested all our patience. She heard "NO" so many times, I'm sure she thought that was her name!

It wasn't long before Daisy discovered a hole in the backyard fence we didn't even know existed, turning a quick visit outside for a quick run into an escape from the sanctuary. She would run out to the road, back again, and into the driveway behind cars. She wouldn't come to us when we called because the chase was far more exciting than the end, when she would have to go back inside. Daisy ran headlong into danger because she didn't even know what danger was. She was so young and felt so invincible that she knew no fear whatsoever.

One day as she ran to the street with me chasing behind her, a big truck blared its horn just as she was about to enter its path. Daisy stopped in her tracks, shaking in terror as I reached her with her harness and got her to safety. Although she started listening more after that incident, she still has moments of temporary "amnesia" and tries to take off.

Daisy's "amnesia" makes me think of all the times God has told me no to things I wasn't supposed to do. Like Daisy, my name could actually be "no" too. A relationship was toxic and God said no, but I jumped in anyway. A job sapped my energy, but I stayed, until God said no. Every "no" God has given me through the years has gently put me on the path to where He wanted me to be, ultimately allowing me to be safer and happier on the journey.

Just as I've trained Daisy to realize that "no" isn't bad, God is training me to realize that sometimes His best work is done when He says no.—Devon O'Day

God, help me hear Your gentle no before I run headlong into danger
I don't see coming. Amen.

About the Authors

As a teacher and student of God's Word, **JERUSHA AGEN** is awed by the letters of love the Father writes into every moment of our lives, including through the animals we encounter. Jerusha is the daughter of two veterinarians and has always shared her life with a menagerie of pets, which she now uses as models for the animals featured in her suspense novels. You'll often find Jerusha sharing adorable photos of her two big dogs and two little cats in her e-newsletter. Get a free suspense story from Jerusha, and find more of her writing at jerushaagen.com.

As a former teacher, **LINDA BARTLETT** is excited to watch her grandchild step into his first classroom this fall. As a former flight attendant, she is excited to travel the world again, with a trip to Sri Lanka planned for fall. Linda continues to write for fun and says it is an honor to immortalize some of her favorite four-footed friends in *All God's Creatures.*

RANDY BENEDETTO has been fascinated with God's creation in nature and God's relationship with people since childhood. He's passionate about studying God's Word and is involved in various Bible studies. An award-winning artist, he's noted that some of his favorite works are of the animals he admires and the people he loves. He has carved intricate dioramas of prospectors with their mules and hikers with their gear.

With his lovely wife, Randy lives in a mountain town in Colorado. They are blessed to regularly spot their children and grandchildren who live nearby, as well as the bears, bobcats, elk, and various critters that are neighbors.

TWILA BENNETT is a contributing writer to *The Cat on My Lap, The Dog at My Feet,* and *Guideposts One-Minute Daily Devotional* and a regular contributor to *All God's Creatures*. Twila is the communications manager for Camp Roger and Camp Scottie. She is also the founder of Monarch Lane Consulting (monarchlaneconsulting.com), helping writers create proposals and providing branding consultation.

For twenty years, Twila was a branding and marketing executive for Revell Books. She loves camping, boating, and sunsets. Twila lives with her husband, Dan, in Rockford, Michigan. Connect with Twila on Facebook and Instagram.

TEZ BROOKS enjoys discovering biblical truths by observing animals. With his knack for befriending creatures, he's been called Dr. Doolittle. Whether he's hiking with his dog, rescuing injured wildlife, or writing about nature, his passion for hearing God's voice is evident. As a multiple-award-winning author and speaker, Brooks writes primarily on family issues, and his work has appeared in Clubhouse, Focus on the Family, and CBN.com. His editorials are featured regularly on jesusfilm.org and seen by more than thirty thousand readers each month.

Tez is a full-time missionary journalist and filmmaker and lives in Colorado Springs with his family. He loves time-travel movies. You can learn more at tezbrooks.com

Homemaker **MARIANNE CAMPBELL** lives in Sonoma County, California, where she was born, raised, and educated. She developed her love of animals during her childhood on her family's Gravenstein apple farm. Her spirit of adventure led her to visit Japan, Thailand, Nepal, Israel, and Egypt in the early 1980s.

From 1984 to 1990, she served in the United States Navy, where she met her husband, Scott. They have two married daughters and a granddaughter. When not writing, Marianne enjoys reading, studying history, baking, gardening, hiking local trails, and playing World of Warcraft. She serves as church musician on Sundays, playing woodwinds or electric bass.

LUCY CHAMBERS serves Christ Church Cathedral and the downtown Houston community as manager of the historic Cathedral Bookstore. A firm believer in the power of sharing stories to deepen connection and improve lives, she has worked with books for over thirty-five years as an editor, publisher, teacher, and writer.

In addition to reading and writing, she makes miniature gardens and volunteers for the altar guild and literary and green organizations. She and her husband, Sam, have two grown daughters, two very soft rabbits, and one energetic puppy.

LINDA S. CLARE is the award-winning author of eight books, including *Thank God for Cats!* (June 2023), *Prayers for Parents of Prodigals* (Harvest House, 2020), and the novel *The Fence My Father Built* (Abingdon, 2009). A frequent contributor to Chicken Soup for the Soul and Guideposts, Linda is a writing coach and mentor.

No matter how chaotic life becomes, God and her fur babies carry her through it. She lives with her family in Oregon. Connect with her on Twitter (@Lindasclare), Facebook, or her website, lindasclare.com.

ASHLEY CLARK (ashleyclarkbooks.com) writes devotions for Guideposts and southern fiction for Bethany House. With a master's degree in creative writing, Ashley teaches literature and writing courses at the University of West Florida and also homeschools her son. She lives with her husband, son, and a rescued cocker spaniel off Florida's Gulf Coast. When she's not writing, she's dreaming of Charleston and drinking all the English breakfast tea she can get her hands on.

TERRY CLIFTON has a background in the performing arts, having performed around the country with musical dinner theatre productions. He also worked as an associate producer for a popular Los Angeles morning TV talk show. He met his wife, Sandra, in LA when he booked her on the talk show. Terry has spent the last twenty years doing freelance book design, writing, and editing.

Terry and Sandra, who went home to be with the Lord in the fall of 2021, taught adult Sunday school and volunteered in community feeding programs for those in need. Terry is currently finishing up work on projects he and Sandra were cowriting before she passed.

SUSIE COLBY is a proud mom to three adult kids: Caleb, Phoebe, and Lily; she is the bereft widow of the funniest, funnest guy ever, Steve Colby; and she is a reluctant but devoted servant of an extremely extroverted cat, Tango. Susie has worked in student ministry for over thirty years, and if that doesn't qualify her as an animal lover, nothing would! If she hadn't been hanging out with students all these years, she might have joined Team Otter at the aquarium.

BEN COOPER is a husband, father, author, speaker, educator, and beekeeper. He grew up on a family farm in western Pennsylvania and went on to get an Agricultural Science degree from Penn State University. Ben retired after working as an Agricultural Specialist for the State of Maryland. He teaches beekeeping courses at Allegany College of Maryland and mentors new beekeepers.

Ben and his wife live in southern Pennsylvania where they homeschooled and raised their five children. He is the author of *All Nature Sings: A Devotional Guide to Animals in the Bible,* and children's picture book series that include *Created Critters with Wings* and *Created Critters with Fur.* Ben speaks at churches, youth groups, and camping ministries about God's wonderful creation and can be reached at cooperville@breezeline.net.

TRACY CRUMP dispenses hope in her multi-award-winning book, *Health, Healing, and Wholeness: Devotions of Hope in the Midst of Illness,* based on her experiences as an ICU nurse. Her articles and devotions have appeared in diverse publications, including *Focus on the Family, Mature Living, Ideals, The Upper Room, Woman's World,* and several Guideposts books. But she is best known for contributing twenty-two stories to Chicken Soup for the Soul books.

Tracy and her husband love observing wildlife near their country home and doting on five completely unspoiled grandchildren. Find encouragement from Tracy's blog for caregivers at tracycrump.com.

CATHY ELLIOTT is a full-time writer in northern California, whose cozy mysteries reflect her personal interests, from quilting and antique collecting to playing her fiddle with friends. She also leads music at church and cherishes time with her grandchildren. Cathy's cozy plot-twisters include *A Vase of Mistaken Identity, Medals in the Attic,* and *A Stitch in Crime.* In her early author days, she wrote ten children's books for an educational publisher and is delighted they are still in print, fifteen years later.

Cathy is also a contributing author to Guideposts' devotional books *Every Day with Jesus* and *All God's Creatures* (2019–2023). Last year, she joined the Someone Cares Cards team at Guideposts, a box she longed to check because sending sweet, meaningful cards to her friends and family is the best kind of reward.

Award-winning author **ELLEN FANNON** is a veterinarian, former missionary, and church pianist/organist. She and her pastor husband fostered more than forty children and are the adoptive parents of two sons. She has published five novels: *Other People's Children, Save the Date, Don't Bite the Doctor,* and *Honor Thy Father, episodes 1 and 2.* Her articles and stories have appeared in *One Christian Voice, Divine Moments—Remembering Christmas,* and Chicken Soup for the Soul; and her devotions have been published in *Open Windows, The Secret Place,* and Guideposts. She also has stories published in *Go, You & Me,* and *Sasee* magazines. Follow her blog at ellenfannonauthor.com.

GLENDA FERGUSON has contributed to *All God's Creatures, Angels on Earth,* Chicken Soup for the Soul books, *Mules & More, Reminisce,* and *Sasee.* The Indiana Arts Commission has included her poem "The Buffalo Trace Trail: Then and Now" in the INverse Poetry Archive. Her writing encouragement comes from the Writers Forum of Burton Kimble Farms Education Center and the ladies' prayer circle at her church.

Glenda and her husband, Tim, live in Paoli, Indiana, where they have an acre of land that they share with Speckles the cat and a variety of wildlife visitors.

PEGGY FREZON is a contributing editor of *Guideposts* magazine and author of books about the human-animal bond, including *Mini Horse, Mighty Hope* (with Debbie Garcia-Bengochea, Revell, 2021). Peggy and her husband, Mike, recently moved from the city to a country cottage. "It's a treat to see a heron across the street, hear coyotes howling at night, and even witness raccoons raiding the bird feeder," she says. BrooksHaven, as they call their new home, is a "retirement home" for senior golden retrievers. They live with their goldens, Ernest, Petey, and Sophie, and two rescue guinea pigs, Petunia and Marigold. Connect with Peggy at peggyfrezon.com.

Though she doesn't have any creatures in her home, **JEANETTE HANSCOME** savors every opportunity to play with other people's pets. She is the author of six books, including *Suddenly Single Mom: 52 Messages of Hope, Grace, and Promise* and the Christmas novella *Gifts,* as well as a speaker, writing coach, and proud mom of two adult sons. Jeanette's newest passion is writing novels for Annie's Fiction and one of Guideposts' upcoming cozy mystery series.

Jeanette spends her free time enjoying her many creative pursuits, including singing, knitting and crocheting, art, and playing ukulele. She lives in the San Francisco Bay Area. Learn more about Jeanette at jeanettehanscome.com.

LORI HATCHER has loved animals since she received her first pets (two tiny turtles named Speedy and Pokey) at age six. She and her pastor-husband, David, have had the pleasure of cohabitating with more fish than they can count, a pair of hermit crabs, four birds, and two amazing dogs. They're currently petless due to a delightful influx of tiny humans into their family.

Lori is the author of *Refresh Your Faith, Uncommon Devotions from Every Book of the Bible; Refresh Your Prayers, Uncommon Devotions to Release Power and Praise;* and *Hungry for God...Starving for Time*. She's written for several other Guideposts projects including *Evenings with Jesus* and *Guideposts One-Minute Daily Devotional*. Connect with Lori on her blog at lorihatcher.com.

REV. HEATHER JEPSEN is the pastor at First Presbyterian Church in Warrensburg, Missouri. She has been serving small churches for over seventeen years. She and her husband, Lars, have two kids, Olivia and Henry, as well as a wide variety of pets. When she is not pastoring or writing, Heather likes to garden, quilt, and play the harp. Heather also writes for Guideposts' *Inspiration from the Garden* devotional. Read more at pastorheatherjepsen.com.

As a *Publishers Weekly* award-winning author of over fifty novels and with two million books in print, **DEB KASTNER** writes contemporary inspirational and sweet western stories set in small communities, often including animals as major secondary characters.

Deb lives in beautiful Colorado with her husband, her puppers Gabby and Sadie, and two mischievous bonded brothers, black tuxedo cats Hype and Dab. She recently went through what she terms her midlife crisis and adopted her very first ever real live horse, whose name is sweet Moscato.

She is blessed with three adult daughters and two grandchildren, with a third on the way. Her favorite hobby is spoiling her grandchildren, but she also enjoys reading, watching movies, listening to music (The Texas Tenors and The High Kings are her faves), singing in the church choir, and exploring the Rocky Mountains on horseback.

DARLENE KERR lives in Ohio with her naturalist husband, Jeff, who is most often found traipsing through forests and meadows. Sometimes his wife joins him, especially if old-growth forests are involved. Darlene is a former English teacher, scientific research librarian, and coordinator of a national advocacy organization against child labor. In addition to writing devotionals, she is writing children's picture books and daydreams about new stories introducing children to a life of faith.

Darlene loves hiking, traveling, reading picture books, watching classic movies and sci-fi, volunteering in children's ministry and conservation organizations, and exploring small, off-beat museums.

LIZ KIMMEL has self-published two books of Christian prose/poetry and a grammar workbook for middle-school students. She enjoys writing for several Guideposts projects and for the Short and Sweet series through Grace Publishing.

Married to Cary for forty-four years and living in St. Paul, Minnesota, she has two children and four grandchildren.

Liz provides administrative support for four nonprofits: Dare to Believe Ministries, Great Commission Media Ministries, MN HOP, and Minnesota Christian Writers Guild. She retired last year from her front-office position at her church and is excited to see what projects the Lord will bring to her in the coming season.

Having lived her whole life in the same house until she married, **JULIE LAVENDER** was excited to see more of God's beautiful world when her high school and college sweetheart, David, joined the navy. Reluctant to move at first, Julie ended up loving living in Florida, North Carolina, Virginia, California, and Washington before returning to Georgia.

A former elementary school teacher, Julie homeschooled their four children, while David served first as a navy medical entomologist and later as a wildlife biologist for an army installation. Julie is the author of *Children's Bible Stories for Bedtime* and *365 Ways to Love Your Child: Turning Little Moments into Lasting Memories* and would love to connect with you on social media and at julielavenderwrites.com.

ERYN LYNUM is a certified Master Naturalist, national speaker, and author of the books *936 Pennies: Discovering the Joy of Intentional Parenting* and *Rooted in Wonder: Nurturing Your Family's Faith Through God's Creation*. She lives in northern Colorado with her husband, Grayson, their four children, and their German shorthaired pointer, Boreal.

They spend their days hiking, camping, and adventuring through the Rocky Mountains.

Eryn has been featured on Focus on the Family, FamilyLife, Proverbs31 Ministries, MOPS International, Bible Gateway, Her View from Home, and For Every Mom. Every opportunity she gets, she is out exploring God's creation with her family and sharing the adventures at erynlynum.com.

REV. LOUIS LOTZ is an ordained minister in the Reformed Church in America and has served as president of the Reformed Church General Synod. His writing for the *Church Herald* and *RCA Today* magazines have won multiple awards from the Evangelical Press Association. He is a frequent contributor to *Words of Hope* devotional magazine.

Lou and his wife, Mary Jean, live in rural Michigan. Caring for their land, being stewards of God's creation, is important to them. Lou enjoys gardening, beekeeping, long walks with his bride of forty-nine years, and tending his fruit trees—apple, peach, and cherry. He enjoys fishing but concedes that there is a difference between fishing and catching. The Lotzes have two grown children and two grandchildren.

CATHY MAYFIELD draws much inspiration for her devotions from the animals God's blessed her and her husband with on their partly wooded property in the mountains of central Pennsylvania. Their German shepherd mix, Kenai, adds his own crazy antics to pull from. As their youngest daughter says, "He's part kangaroo, part mountain goat!" And if there is ever a need for grandparenting devotions, Cathy's storing plenty of ideas from their five grandchildren (ages one to nine at the time of this writing in 2022). "They keep me feeling young...at least when I'm with them!" Cathy delights in being part of the Guideposts family of writers.

JANET HOLM McHENRY is the author of twenty-five books. She often takes a prayer walk through her Sierra Valley town, where she encounters all kinds of God's creatures. Janet and her husband, Craig, have raised four children and a variety of pets. A journalism graduate of UC Berkeley, Janet worked as a reporter and English teacher and is the creator of a course called Prayer School and host of the Sierra Valley Writers Retreat. Through her business, Looking Up!, she encourages others to pursue a praying life.

Janet loves traveling, kayaking, and spending time with their grandchildren. Connect with her at janetmchenry.com.

MAUREEN MILLER, wife, mother of three, and "Mosie" to two, lives on Selah Farm, a hobby homestead nestled in the mountains of western North Carolina. With a passion for God's Word, she's an award-winning author and photographer, contributing to several online devotion sites and anthologies, as well as writing for her local newspaper. Praying to have eyes and ears open that she might experience God in the miracles of His created world, she blogs at penningpansies.com.

HAROLD "NICK" NICHOLS is a retired university professor and administrator living in Lafayette, Louisiana, with his amazing wife of thirty years and best friend, Anna Marie. Nichols earned his PhD in Theatre History at Indiana University and taught at Kansas State University for twenty years before turning to administration. He served as a Dean at the University of Nebraska at Kearney and at Georgia Southwestern State University before finishing his career as Dean of the Mississippi State University Meridian Campus. Nick and Anna Marie have five children and thirteen grandchildren.

MABEL NINAN is the author of *Far from Home: Discovering Your Identity as Foreigners on Earth* and host of the YouTube podcast *Immigrant Faith Stories.* Her mission is to inspire believers to embrace their pilgrim journey on earth and boldly pursue their heavenly calling. Her articles and devotions have been published in *The Upper Room*, CBN.com, *Leading Hearts Magazine,* and (in)courage.me.

Mabel is currently pursuing a master's degree in Theological Studies from the Southern Baptist Theological Seminary. She enjoys reading and traveling but finds her greatest satisfaction and joy in studying the Bible and having conversations about her faith. Mabel lives in Northern California with her husband, son, and Maltese pup. Connect with her at mabelninan.com or through social media @mabel_ninan.

DEVON O'DAY is an award-winning career radio broadcaster with songwriting credits by George Strait, Dolly Parton, Hank Williams Jr., and more. As an author, she has written several books for Thomas Nelson and United Methodist Publishing House and has narrated over a hundred audio books for HarperCollins, Thomas Nelson, and Zondervan. She has been a contributor to *All God's Creatures* since the inception of the franchise when devotions from her book, *Paws To Reflect,* were included.

Currently Devon works for Main Street Media of Tennessee, where she hosts three lifestyle streaming shows. She lives on a rescue sanctuary therapy farm outside Nashville called Angel Horse Farm, where senior equines and special-needs livestock offer an infinite well from which to draw stories about animals and their gifts and lessons connecting us to God. Look for Angel Horse Farm on Instagram to see pictures of the animal family that inspires her devotions.

SANDY KIRBY QUANDT is a former elementary school educator and full-time writer with a passion for God, history, and travel, passions that often weave their way into her stories and articles. She has written numerous articles, devotions, and stories for adult and children's publications including *Today's Christian Woman, Power for Living, The Lookout, Mature Years, Standard,* and *Alive!* Her devotions appear in *So God Made a Dog, Let the Earth Rejoice,* and several Guideposts devotional books. She has won multiple awards for writing in young adult, middle grade, and children's categories.

Are you looking for words of encouragement or gluten-free recipes? Check out Sandy's blog at sandykirbyquandt.com, where she posts twice a week. Sandy and her husband live in southeast Texas.

SHIRLEY RAYE REDMOND has written many articles for *Focus on the Family Magazine, Home Life,* and *The Christian Standard.* Her devotions have appeared in multiple volumes of Guideposts' *All God's Creatures* and *Daily Guideposts.* Her book, *Courageous World Changers: 50 True Stories of Daring Women of God* (Harvest House) won the 2021 *Christianity Today* Book Award in the children's book category.

Shirley Raye has been married for forty-eight years to her college sweetheart. They are blessed with two adult children and their spouses, plus five precious grandchildren. They live in Los Alamos, New Mexico.

KATHLEEN RUCKMAN enjoys various forms of writing and has published devotions, articles, short stories, poetry, and children's books. Her desire as an author is to inspire readers to draw close to the heart of God and to His Word. She has also taught women's Bible studies for several years.

Kathleen is the mother of four adult children and nine young grandchildren, the love of her life and her inspiration. Kathleen and her husband, Tom, live in central Oregon.

VIRGINIA RUTH brings to her writing her experiences as a registered nurse, certified health and wellness coach, and wellness program director. Her mission is to encourage and inspire others to live well.

Her work has appeared in various devotionals and anthologies, and she has contributed to numerous Guideposts publications since 2020. While she loves to write about all things inspirational, writing about animals brings her much enjoyment. She, her husband, and their rescue dog, Scuppers, live in Rhode Island. Learn more about Virginia at wellofencouragement.com.

DIANE STARK is a wife and mother of five human kids and two canine ones. When she's not busy writing, Diane is usually trying to persuade her husband to adopt another furry friend. Diane loves to write about the important things in life—her family and her faith.

CRYSTAL STORMS is an author, artist, and host of *The Heart Rest Podcast*. Her passion is to see people break free from striving to prove their worth so they can rest secure in who they are in Christ. Crystal has been married to her husband, Tim, since 1995. They live in Florida with their sweet Yorkie, Minnie, and snuggly parrot, Lorito.

Visit crystalstorms.me for encouragement to anchor your heart close to His heart as Christ's beloved, so you can weather life's storms.

KATY W. SUNDARARAJAN is an ordained minister in the Reformed Church in America and has served as a youth pastor, college chaplain, missionary, and international student advisor. It has been her joy to learn and grow with God's people in these diverse settings, relishing the beauty and creativity of God, and celebrating the vastness of God's love. Katy resides in west Michigan with her husband, two children, and an adoring goldendoodle named Honey.

MISSY TIPPENS is a pastor's wife, mother of three, and an author from near Atlanta, Georgia. She loves being involved in their church by singing in the choir and playing hand bells. Missy has loved many fur children through the years. Her family now has two rescue dogs, and she also enjoys pet sitting for her grand-dogs.

After more than ten years of pursuing her dream of publication, Missy sold her first novel to Love Inspired in 2007. She has been writing devotionals for Guideposts since 2018. Visit Missy at missytippens.com.

LAWRENCE WILSON believes that God is love, life is good, and we can all be a bit better than we are now. He writes to remind people of simple truths so they will be inspired to live a better story. He got his start as a writer by penning and producing a play for his fourth-grade class. It closed after one-half a performance. Since then he has written five books and countless articles, lessons, scripts, sermons, podcasts, and news articles.

Larry lives in an Indiana small town, just like John Mellencamp—but not the same one.

DAVID L. WINTERS is an author and speaker living in Huber Heights, Ohio. David is a regular contributor to Guideposts, including five previous editions of *All God's Creatures*. His nonfiction books include *Exercise Your Faith, Taking God to Work, The Accidental Missionary (A Gringo's Love Affair with Peru)*, and *Sabbatical of the Mind (The Journey from Anxiety to Peace)*. David's fiction titles include *A Baby's Right to Choose, Driver Confessional,* and *Stock Car Inferno.*

A 1981 graduate of Ohio State University with a BA in journalism, David also earned an MBA from Regent University in Virginia in 2003.

JON WOODHAMS enjoyed ten great years as a Guideposts book editor, including serving as the editor of *All God's Creatures* for several years. While with Guideposts, he had the privilege of editing several Guideposts fiction series (including Miracles of Marble Cove, Mysteries of Silver Peak, and Tearoom Mysteries) and nonfiction titles *Divine Interventions* and *Angels All around Us*. He now freelances as a writer and in editorial capacities for several publishers, including Guideposts.

In addition, Jon is an artist and photographer, shooting both digital and film. You can see his work at jonwoodhams.com. Originally a Michigander, he currently lives and works in Memphis, Tennessee.

Scripture Reference Index

Acts
2:28, 276
17:27, 54

1 Chronicles
16:27, 215
16:34, 346
29:11, 91, 164

Colossians
1:16, 236, 319
3:13, 144, 338
3:23–24, 129

1 Corinthians
3:10–11, 242
4:7, 230
12:4, 194
12:7, 74
12:24–25, 265
12:27, 64, 190
13:1, 47
13:2, 303
13:4, 73
13:5–7, 73
13:6–7, 305
15:33, 287
15:52, 289
15:58, 152

2 Corinthians
2:14–15, 263
2:16, 263
3:18, 208
5:1, 311
6:2, 171
13:12, 41

Deuteronomy
6:7, 177
7:6, 338
10:19, 320
28:1, 255
31:8, 50, 306
32:11, 199
33:27, 168

Ecclesiastes
1:3, 48
2:13, 30
3:1, 107, 323
4:9, 55, 113
4:10, 183
4:12, 119
8:15, 335

Ephesians
1:4–5, 252
1:18–19, 81
2:10, 338
3:17–18, 354
3:18, 17
3:20, 317
3:20–21, 10, 34
4:4–6, 6
4:23–24, 257
4:29, 176, 301
4:32, 117
5:8, 245
5:15, 172
5:19, 186, 319
5:25, 98
6:6, 331
6:12, 110

Exodus
14:14, 333
15, 205
18:20, 130
33:14, 157
34:21, 134

Ezekiel
12:1–2, 161
36:27, 326

Galatians
2:20, 359
5, 26
6:7–8, 174

Genesis
1:20, 101
1:21, 68
1:25, 22
1:26, 352
1:27, 43
2:15, 184
2:20, 367

16, 145
16:13, 327
22, 79
22:18, 79
50:20, 334

Habakkuk
3:19, 283

Hebrews
3:4, 325
3:13, 241
10:22, 266
10:24, 104
10:25, 131
10:35–36, 32
11:1, 36, 238
13:1–2, 259
13:5, 231

Isaiah
6:1, 349
6:3, 53, 58
6:8, 336
9:2, 123
9:6, 9
11:6, 34, 292, 3079
26:3, 152, 279
30:15, 337
37:16, 229
40:11, 216
40:28, 112
40:29, 21
40:31, 217, 286
41:10, 288, 309
42:16, 277
43:1, 20, 338, 367
43:19, 100, 135
43:21, 147
46:4, 280
52:7, 84
53:3, 9
54:17, 213
55:6, 353
55:12, 321
60:22, 67
61:3, 317
62:2, 338

James
1:4, 89
1:5, 359
1:17, 235, 271
3:5, 358
4:8, 266, 365
5:16, 28, 210

Jeremiah
1:5, 43
17:7, 139, 371
17:14, 125
29:11, 93, 150

Job
2:13, 24
12:7, 103, 291
12:10, 269
37:6–7, 39
38:7, 357

John
1:3, 143
1:4, 85
3:8, 83
4, 59
4:48, 128
7:38, 59
8:12, 44, 106
8:36, 38, 42
10, iv
10:10, 197, 233, 360
10:27, 340
12:36, 44
12:46, 106
13:34–35, 178
14, 109
14:5–6, 315
14:27, 137
15:4, 122
15:16, 165
16:13, 12
16:33, 374

1 John
1:5, 289
3:1, 338, 339
4:1, 163
4:7, 51
4:18, 225
4:19, 330, 342

3 John
2, 46

Joshua
1:9, 66, 99, 370
9:14, 185
17:3–6, 81
24:15, 232

1 Kings
17:6, 355
19:12, 179

Lamentations
3:22–23, 298

Luke
1:37, 111
3:22, 9
6:29, 13
10:19, 304
10:39–42, 57
10:41–42, 329

11:9–10, 219
13:34, 151
14, 109
15:24, 173, 270
18:1–8, 219
18:43, 328
19:37–40, 319

Mark
1:13, 52
6:31, 231
10:31, 310
11:24, 159
13:32–33, 256
15:34, 231

Matthew
2:12, 96
5:4, 312
5:16, 200
5:30, 15
6, 37
6:8, 61
6:20, 37
6:21, 49
6:25, 62
6:33, 293
7:5, 343
7:7–8, 141
7:11, 274
7:15, 114
7:24–25, 242
7:26, 96
9:36, 94
10:8, 230
10:29, 226, 268
10:30, 43
11:17, 296
11:28–30, 377
13:3, 848
13:3–9, 84
15:11, 26
16:27, 32
20:16, 203
22:9, 109
23:37, 23
25:40, 35
26:34, 168
28:20, 198

Nahum
1:3, 299
1:13, 254

Numbers
14:20, 362
27:1–11, 81
27:7, 81

1 Peter
2:9, 123, 178
2:17, 169
3:4, 22
3:8, 136, 335
3:15, 302
5, 305
5:7, 159
5:8, 287, 288

2 Peter
3:9, 261
3:13, 16
3:17, 191

Philippians
1:6, 108
2:3, 372
2:3–4, 246
2:4, 87, 247
3:1–2, 239
3:2, 114
3:8, 49
3:13–14, 117
4, 26
4:5, 107
4:6, 313, 345
4:8, 4
4:19, 65, 376

Proverbs
1:33, 132
3:5–6, 7
3:27, 218, 375
4:23, 272
8:34, 250
11:25, 282
12:10, 295
13:20, 102
14:15, 60
15:1, 222
15:11, 227
15:14, 45
15:30, 97
16:9, 212, 363
16:28, 224
17:17, 3, 278
17:22, 209
18:10, 300
18:24, 351, 368
19:1, 297
19:21, 363
20:12, 228
22:3, 60, 96, 149
22:6, 166, 180, 211
27:1, 264
27:23, 72
29:9, 206
29:25, 240
30:27, 121
30:30, 237

Psalms
1:1, 102
4:8, 142, 201, 207

5:11, 77, 344
16:8, 76
16:11, 86, 146
17:6, 378
17:8–9, 366
18:30, 199
18:32–33, iv
19:1–2, 133
23, 14, 99
23:1–3, 234
23:2, 14
23:6, 198
24:1, 153
25:4, 314
26:1, 258
27:1, 332
27:14, 244
30:2, 11
30:5, 99
32:7, 260
34:4, 132
34:7, 175
34:10, 293
34:18, 294
36:6, 19
37:4, 140
37:25, 282
39:5, 145
40, 193
40:2, 193
40:10, 170
42:1, 329, 350
42:1–2, 364
42:5, 374
46:1, 248
46:10, 196
50:10, 62
50:10–11, 295
51:10, 27
55:6, 9
55:17, 88
55:18, 5
55:22, 226, 268, 377
57:1, 267, 344
61:4, 273
62:1, 90
64:3, 301
68:3, 80
68:13, 9
68:19, 280
69:34, 285
73:28, 275
74:17, 243
86:11, 369
86:17, 8
89:7–8, 349
91:2, 142
91:3, 175
91:4, 23, 69
91:11, 92
91:14–15, 69
94:18, 141
94:19, 31, 223
95:1, 319
96:1–3, 205
98:4, 116
102: 6–7, 70
104:12–13, 251
104:20, 71
107:14, 42
116:15, 338
119:10, 266
119:18, 82
119:32, 182
119:105, 167
121:3, 71
121:5, 115
121:5–8, 212
133:1, 290
139:1–3, 145, 324
139:5, 306
139:14, 43
139:14–15, 143
139:23–24, 227
143:7, 154
143:8, 148
145:5, 124
145:9, 162
150, 188
150:3, 1886
150:6, 116

Revelation
2:2, 75
5:5–6, iv
6:2, 348
21:4, 312
21:5, 292
21:6, 364
22:17, 187

Romans
3:22–25, 338
5:3, 249, 264
8:17, 81
8:22–23, 281
8:28, 29, 156
9:25, 338
11:17, 2
12:2, 163, 181, 302
12:6–8, 43
12:12, 118
12:18, 206
13:10, 160
13:13, 356
15:7, 361
15:13, 105, 202

1 Samuel
3:10, 341
16:7, 308
17:32, 25

2 Samuel
6:14–15, 78
22:29, 127

Song of Songs
2:12, 204

1 Thessalonians
2:13, 322
4:16, 192
5:16–18, 373
5:24, 195

1 Timothy
4:12, 318
6:6, 56
6:17, 124

2 Timothy
1:5, 120
1:7, 170, 234
2:13, 240
4:3, 114
4:18, 40

Titus
2:3–4, 18
2:7, 155

Zechariah
4:10, 138
10:8–9, 262

Zephaniah
3:17, 214, 220

A Note from the Editors

We hope you enjoyed *All God's Creatures 2024,* published by Guideposts. For over 75 years, Guideposts, a nonprofit organization, has been driven by a vision of a world filled with hope. We aspire to be the voice of a trusted friend, a friend who makes you feel more hopeful and connected.

By making a purchase from Guideposts, you join our community in touching millions of lives, inspiring them to believe that all things are possible through faith, hope, and prayer. Your continued support allows us to provide uplifting resources to those in need. Whether through our communities, websites, apps, or publications, we inspire our audiences, bring them together, and comfort, uplift, entertain, and guide them. Visit us at guideposts.org to learn more.

We would love to hear from you. Write us at Guideposts, P.O. Box 5815, Harlan, Iowa 51593 or call us at (800) 932-2145. Did you love *All God's Creatures 2024?* Leave a review for this product on guideposts.org/shop. Your feedback helps others in our community find relevant products.